THE OUTLINE
OF SANITY

A Biography of
G. K. Chesterton

BY ALZINA STONE DALE

AN AUTHORS GUILD BACKINPRINT.COM EDITION

The Outline of Sanity
A Biography of G. K. Chesterton

Grateful acknowledgement is given to A.P. Watt Ltd. on behalf of the
Royal Literary Fund for non-exclusive permission, free of charge, to include
Extracts from the published writings of G.K.Chesterton in a new edition of
The Outline of Sanity.

AN AUTHORS GUILD BACKINPRINT.COM EDITION

Published by iUniverse, Inc.

For information address:
iUniverse, Inc.
2021 Pine Lake Road, Suite 100
Lincoln, NE 68512
www.iuniverse.com

Originally published by W B Eerdmans

ISBN: 0-595-34076-8

Printed in the United States of America

When corruption and chaos are disturbing ordinary minds, and many good men are only worried and serious, it has often happened that a great man could apparently be frivolous; and appear in history almost as a great buffoon. One of the sonnets of Mr. Maurice Baring has a haunting line about the souls of lovers blown upon a wind: "to rest for ever on the unresting air." In a very different connexion, it can be said that these rare and sane spirits did rest on the unresting air of a revolutionary epoch or a dissolving civilization. And there is always something about them puzzling to those who see their frivolity from the outside and not their faith from the inside. It is not realized that their faith is not a stagnation but an equilibrium.

G.K. Chesterton, *Chaucer*

To two men who reminded me of
G. K. Chesterton
My father, Professor Raleigh Webster Stone
and
My uncle, the Reverend Paul Stevens Kramer
in loving thanks for what they taught me

Grateful acknowledgement is given to A.P. Watt Ltd. on behalf of the Royal Literary Fund for non-exclusive permission, free of charge, to include extracts from the published writings of G.K.Chesterton in a new edition of The Outline of Sanity

ACKNOWLEDGMENTS

IN each and every book written about Gilbert K. Chesterton, one acknowledgment is always found, and it must come first in this book, too. It is heartfelt praise and thanksgiving for his literary executor, Dorothy Collins. She wants the world to know Chesterton, and anyone working toward that goal she believes in *freely* helping in any way. Her agents at A.P. Watt, Michael Horniman and Sarah Barkeley-Smith, worked tirelessly on my behalf, and there is no way to thank them enough.

I owe a second great debt to Chesterton's bibliographer, John Sullivan, who not only answered letters and looked over typescripts, but whose work made it possible to deal with the immense Chestertonian corpus. Thanks to his careful chronology of Chesterton's writings, I have been able to correct some prevailing myths about Chesterton's career, particularly the one that he burst upon Fleet Street, fully formed, in 1900, and never changed.

When I decided that the major thrust of this book should be to re-establish Chesterton's importance in his own period as a way of showing his relevance for our own, I enlisted the aid and comfort of a group of experts who have read draft after draft: Margaret Canovan, Mary McDermott Shideler, Laurence Lafore, and Aidan Mackey. (To those readers well versed in British history, I apologize for including so much background, but previous books about Chesterton have either assumed such knowledge or ignored it, making him a creature of eternity, a strange fate for one proud to be a journalist.) In addition to my primary readers, others like Lawrence Clipper, William Furlong, Ian Boyd, and John McCarthy have contributed important insights from their books and through our correspondence, as have also Garry Wills, Lynette Hunter, Samuel Hynes, Stephen Koss, Alfred Havighurst, Peter Rowland, and Norman and Jeanne MacKenzie, and I thank them all. Perhaps one of the most delightful pleasures has been the excuse the book gave me to correspond with such illustrious members of the Detection Club as its president, Julian Symons, and writers Gladys Mitchell and Ngaio Marsh.

Chesterton and I have gone through three editors at Eerdmans: Jon Pott, Sandy Nowlin, and, finally, Mary Hietbrink, to whom has fallen all responsibility for those details Chesterton habitually ignored. But if the end notes and the text do not correlate, it is the author's fault, for I chose to use a great many of them to make accessible to my readers the sources of my ideas about Chesterton as well as the many quotations from him who is one of the most quoted men about.

I want to thank Marjorie Mead and Barbara Hendershott of the Wade Collection at Wheaton College for their continual support, as well as Anton Masin, curator of Special Collections at the University of Notre Dame. My friends of the midwest Chesterton Society, led by Frank Petta, have argued Chestertonian ideas with me, while my own immediate family has grown reconciled to my finding a Chestertonian reference in any topic of the day. In rediscovering Chesterton, I also found my own father, a classical economist of the nineteenth-century Liberal school, as well as my uncle, an orthodox Christian with an engaging, absent-minded personality. But it was the uncritical, steadfast companionship of my small dog Lucifer that really helped me complete the book. Chesterton himself knew that "there is something deeper in the matter . . . only the hour is late, and both the dog and I are too drowsy to interpret it."

ALZINA STONE DALE
Epiphany 1982

CONTENTS

Contents

Prologue

THE INVISIBLE MAN

The Art of Biography
Is different from Geography.
Geography is about Maps,
But Biography is about Chaps.

E.C. Bentley, *Biography for Beginners*,
with 40 diagrams by G.K. Chesterton[1]

THE first biography of Gilbert Keith Chesterton appeared anonymously in 1908, when he was only thirty-four. It was called *G.K. Chesterton: A Criticism*, and its author not only set the scene for all who followed him, but also drew the familiar cartoon of the absent-minded reactionary "born out of his time. ... [His] huge form and great flapping hat and romantic cloak, his walk and his laugh are familiar to everyone who knows the world of Fleet Street."[2] The biographer was Gilbert's younger brother Cecil, himself a twenty-nine-year-old aspiring journalist, who had recently lost his bid for re-election to the governing board of the Fabian Society. In contrast to Gilbert, Cecil Chesterton was short and stout, with a mane of wavy chestnut hair and a brash smile that appealed to the ladies. Although he labeled his brother a child, Cecil himself remained a perpetual adolescent.

In his biography, which appeared just after Gilbert's highly successful second novel, *The Man Who Was Thursday*, and just before Gilbert's own "slovenly autobiography" called *Orthodoxy*, Cecil Chesterton aired his political arguments with Gilbert and characteristically tried to have the last word. His book abounds in the dramatized episodes that have become the accepted legends about Chesterton — his hiring a cab to take him two hundred yards from a Fleet Street pub to his newspaper office, or writing copy standing stock-still in the middle of traffic. But Cecil's book also shows that he lacked his brother's characteristic humor.

He insists that Gilbert must not be "praised as a buffoon" nor the world allowed "to dispose of him by calling him paradoxical," for "he may be right or he may be wrong. ... If he is right, let us do all we can to strengthen his hands, and let us welcome his humour and fascination not merely because they amuse us, but also because they are weapons to be used in the fight against the evil of our world. If he be wrong, let him be denounced, let him be burned as a heretic."[3] Cecil the Fabian Socialist then proceeds to attack his brother for being old-fashioned and far too whimsical, even though he sees Gilbert as "primarily a propagandist, a preacher of a definite message to his time [who] stands for Anti-Imperialism, and Catholicism with its back to the wall, for the hunger of a perplexed age for the more lucid life of the Ages of Faith, for the revolt against Modernity, in a word, for what may legitimately be called 'reaction.' "[4]

To make his portrait more dramatic and to prove his own points, Cecil also telescoped events in his brother's life, insisting, for example, that Gilbert had been an overnight success, and stating categorically that he never changed his opinions after 1900 — both untrue statements. Like a good debater, Cecil also twisted his brother's ideas to make them match positions that he wanted to refute. The resulting picture is distorted, like the reflection in a fun-house mirror.

Characteristically, Cecil explained that if anyone thought he should apologize for attacking his brother anonymously, he must realize that if Cecil "waited until Mr. Chesterton were dead, I, too, might quite probably be dead myself." He added that whatever circumstances had put him in possession of the facts about Mr. Chesterton, he had used them without scruple, "[because] to good taste, the modern name for snobbery, I hope I am indifferent. Some people will blame me for this; but one person will not, that person is Gilbert Chesterton."[5] In making this sweeping claim, Cecil was perfectly correct, for nothing he ever said or did was publicly criticized by his adoring brother.

Succeeding biographers of Chesterton have assumed that Cecil knew what he was talking about, forgetting, among other things, that Cecil was engaged in presenting one side of an ongoing debate. They have uncritically adopted his chronology, ignoring its quite obvious inaccuracies.[6] Ironically, the worst offender in this respect was Chesterton himself, who clearly made use of Cecil's book when he wrote his *Autobiography*, treating events as symbols and recording them heedless of accurate dates, a slapdash pattern he was guilty of following in his other biographies as well.[7]

But it was Cecil's anonymous study that led to the first myth of Gilbert Chesterton as nothing more than a jolly, childlike giant filled with gusto and uncritical Christianity, the drinking companion of more famous men like G. B. Shaw. More recently his critics have reacted against this cartoon by suggesting that Chesterton was a stunted Peter Pan, full of dark sexual inhibitions, reactionary and rational to the point of madness. Both approaches ignore Chesterton's fundamental feel for common sense, his unfailing sanity and balance in an unbalanced age. He displayed both in a cheerful observation in his review of J. M. Barrie's *Peter Pan*: "The only objection about living in a nursery where the dog is the nurse or the father lives in a dog-kennel is that there seems no necessity to go to the Never-Never Land."[8]

It is also thanks to Cecil that the one sure touchstone for understanding Chesterton as an adult — his intellectual commitment to Christianity as expressed in its historic creeds — is used to make him seem remote from our contemporary concerns. But the "modern world" began about 1880, when Gilbert was an impressionable adolescent, and he was a product of it. His own life is more understandable if, like his King Alfred in *The Ballad of the White Horse*, he is seen not as one determined to keep old traditions free from weeds, but as a fighter struggling to preserve the Western world against the pagans of post-Christianity. Although some of his contemporaries dismissed him by saying he was a romantic born out of his time, Chesterton never thought he was writing for "the ages." He proudly claimed to be the most ephemeral of writers, a journalist, and it is this title which fits him best.

Chesterton's description of himself seems to have come true: within this generation he has become historically invisible. Textbooks twenty-five years ago still featured him as "one of the most brilliant and prolific modern writers"; today, the same editors cut him dead, despite the fact that he is still quoted everywhere.[9] Part of his problem is that he has always been hard to classify as a writer because he did not work seriously in the "right" forms, but like most journalists practiced his profession on whatever came to hand, becoming a master without a masterpiece.[10] This master, who wrote about an "invisible man" able to commit a crime because he was so much a part of the social scenery that no one noticed him, has himself been cut out of the background of his own time. What is left today is a large blank space shaped like a portly gentleman dressed in a flowing cape and slouch hat and carrying a sword stick. As a consequence, his many friends and opponents are left to debate with themselves, which gives their era an oddly one-dimensional look.

The most recent studies of Chesterton do not redraw the old "Toby Jug" portrait of Old King Cole, merrily fiddling while civilization goes up in smoke, but they do try to categorize him: he is a metaphysical jester-philosopher involved with eternity, or a Populist out of the mainstream of political thought, or an artist who carefully kept his convictions out of his work.[11] Often he is still only a plaster saint for Roman Catholics to love, particularly those who do not admire Vatican II. These portraits do not make a case for reading him today.

To do that, one needs to rebuild the story of his life, using — ironically — the prosaic tools of dates and facts which he tended to ignore. He himself believed that it was more difficult, finally, to speak about a writer's life than about his work, because his work "has the mystery which belongs to the complex; his life the much greater mystery which belongs to the simple."[12] His biographer should take this more difficult approach, putting himself in the position of "the ordinary modern outsider," trying to use what is under-stood to explain what is not, so that he can help his reader see "the consistency of a complete character." He must also study his subject in his own period, because "it is useless to urge the isolated individuality of the artist, apart from his attitude towards his age. His attitude to his age is his individuality, men are never individual when alone."[13]

It is high time for Gilbert Chesterton to become visible again, for many of his judgments about his own time have once again become historically valid. Chesterton himself understood this kind of process very well, and explained it in *The Napoleon of Notting Hill*, which he wrote in 1904 but set in 1984:

> The human race, to which so many of my readers belong, has been playing at children's games from the beginning, and will probably do it until the end, which is a nuisance for the few people who grow up. And one of the games to which it is most attached is called, "Keep to-morrow dark," and which is also called "Cheat the Prophet." The players all listen very carefully and respectfully to all that the clever men have to say about what is to happen in the next generation. The players then wait until all the clever men are dead, and bury them nicely. They then go and do something else. That is all. For a race of simple tastes, however, it is great fun.[14]

Part One

THE COLOURED LANDS
1874-1894

I found myself standing in a very different sort of place; and opposite me was my old friend the Wizard, whose face and long rolling beard were all one sort of colourless colour like ivory, but his eyes were of a colourless blinding brilliancy like diamonds.

"Well," he said, "you don't seem very easy to please. If you can't put up with any of these countries, or any of these colours, you shall jolly well make a country of your own."

G.K. Chesterton, *The Coloured Lands*
(posthumously published)

1

Chapter One

HE WAS BORN AN ENGLISHMAN
1874-1879

There were . . . these two first feelings, indefensible and indisputable. The world was a shock, but it was not merely shocking; existence was a surprise, but it was a pleasant surprise. . . . [But] the vision always hangs upon a veto. . . . In the fairy tale an incomprehensible happiness rests upon an incomprehensible condition . . . and it cannot be coincidence that glass is so common a substance in folk-lore. . . . For this thin glitter of glass everywhere is the expression of the fact that the happiness is bright but brittle . . . and this fairy-tale sentiment also sank into me and became my sentiment towards the whole world. I felt and feel that life itself is as bright as the diamond, but as brittle as the windowpane; and when the heavens were compared to the terrible crystal I can remember a shudder. I was afraid that God would drop the cosmos with a crash.

G.K. Chesterton, *Orthodoxy* [1]

. . . the coming . . . was like the birth of a child in a dark house, lifting its doom; a child that grows up unconscious of the tragedy and triumphs over it by his innocence. In him it is necessarily not only innocence but ignorance. It is the essence of the story that he should pluck at the green grass without knowing it grows over a murdered man or climb the apple-tree without knowing it was the gibbet of a suicide.

G.K. Chesterton, *St. Francis of Assisi* [2]

GILBERT'S childhood has been called the "happiest in literature," but this is not completely true. This idea was created by Cecil, who had shared part of that childhood, but who had not yet been born when the Chesterton's middle-class Eden was shattered almost beyond repair, teaching

3

Gilbert the truths about existence he associated with fairy tales. To correct Cecil's version, it is necessary to begin at the very beginning.

When Gilbert was born on May 29, 1874, the Chestertons had been Londoners for four generations, sharing in the wealth of the city as it became the greatest metropolis in the world. England herself was the thriving center of an ocean empire, a world leader in manufacturing, shipping, and finance. Her prosperity was founded upon the Industrial Revolution of the eighteenth century, which had changed her from an agricultural country into one made up of manufacturing cities linked by railroads; one of the results was a new and growing urban middle class. Their manners and morals were influenced by the heroic and humanitarian ideals of the French Revolution, the growth of population, and the reduction of legal restrictions for those who were Dissenters. Gradually, they had changed traditional English institutions like Parliament, the courts, the established church, and the old universities, giving new meaning to old terms but preserving a sense of continuity with the English past. Liberal Utilitarian politics and economics linked the industrial worker and the middle class, who preferred laissez-faire to protectionism and shared a distrust of government control.

During the 1870's the Chestertons still thought that with hard work, common sense, and education, they could create worldwide peace and prosperity for all. For Liberals the ideal was a world of nation-states, held together by ethnic or racial identity, with a broadly elected government to promote the freedom of the individual and the country's own freedom from foreign rule. Free trade and economic growth, built by science and technology, the tools they had developed in the recent past, would make everyone so rich and secure that the causes of war would disappear. This utopia was just around the corner, making all earlier times seem "dark" by comparison.[3]

In fact, however, the year 1875 was to mark a turning point in history, when the old balance of power disintegrated under the pressure of Bismarck's newly created German Empire. Adding to this pressure were the rumbles and periodic revolutions in the Balkans, where deprived minorities dreamed of becoming nation-states and the Russians coveted a warm-water port. Although Karl Marx had issued his *Communist Manifesto* in 1848, England had seen nothing but improving social and economic conditions; and, by the 1860's, when Gladstone and Disraeli alternated as prime minister, both political parties had a broad, vertical base of Englishmen who felt that they had a real stake in the country. Reforms in the "public" schools, where the upper classes were educated along with a broader, middle-class base of students, had begun to educate the bureaucrats needed to rule an empire and to give the middle classes a new sense of identity with the older ruling elite. At the same time, beneath its veneer of prosperity Gilbert's world was suffering from "a period of increasing strain. It was the very reverse of solid respectability; because its ethics and theology were wearing thin."[4]

Gilbert's own family was a perfect example of this new, prosperous middle class when, as he explains, "it really was a class and it really was in the middle ... separated from the class above it and the class below it ... an educated class unduly suspicious of the influence of servants." He noted wryly that it was a world that placed great importance on proper speech, ". . . [where] nobody was any more likely to drop an h than to pick up a title," which he had proved at age three when he screamed for his hat: "If you don't give it me, I'll say 'at!'"[5] Customarily, however, the Chestertons were unwilling to "ape the aristocracy" whom they only knew "in the way of business," although they clearly separated themselves from the upwardly mobile lower-middle classes of servants and small shopkeepers with "bad" accents — classes that produced so many twentieth-century reformers.

Gilbert's great-grandfather had begun their family real-estate business (later known as Chesterton and Sons and run by his father and uncles) as a land agent for the Phillimore family, who owned a large estate in the suburb of Kensington. Soon the family had taken advantage of the expanding housing market to go into business for themselves, buying and selling land. Like Galsworthy's Forsyte family, the young Chestertons of the next generation were given a good secondary education, then articled to the family business or some other profession like law. But Gilbert's father, Edward Chesterton, who was passionately interested in the arts and literature, gave a curious twist to this stable family pattern. He went into the business but managed, by pleading ill health at quite a young age, to enjoy its income yet extricate himself from its day-to-day concerns. He then led an urban variety of leisured upper-middle class life, occupying his time with his family and his many artistic and literary hobbies in a manner which his son declared to be very English.

Edward Chesterton, known as Mr. Ed, was also much interested in and well informed about social and political affairs; he was a Liberal by birth, and, typically, it was the future, not the past, that intrigued him. As a family, therefore, the Chestertons cared very little about ancestors, although they told tales about a dashing friend of Charles Dickens named George Laval Chesterton who fought as a soldier of fortune, but then came home and worked for prison reform, which he wrote about. To them he was a true Dickensian hero, with the humor of Mr. Pickwick and the conscience of a Nonconformist.

Gilbert could just remember his Grandfather Chesterton, a patriarch with a white beard and old-fashioned, rather Dickensian manners, who liked to play the host at family dinner parties, where he offered toasts and led the singing of old patriotic songs. Gilbert recalled with amusement the walks he used to take as a small boy with the patriarch and another old gentleman, who never went to church but carried a small prayer book as an example to others.[6] Mary Louise, Gilbert's mother, once characterized her in-laws as "very dear but rather worthy," demonstrating the sharp tongue that prompted Cecil to call her "the wittiest woman in London."

Mrs. Chesterton's family had come from Switzerland and had the French surname of Grosjean, although they were completely Anglicized. The Grosjean relatives "ran smaller in stature, often darker in colouring, [and were] tough and tenacious, prejudiced in a humorous fashion and full of the fighting spirit" in a manner not wholly English, a comment which at once reminds one of Gilbert's description of Cecil, a child "born a fighter . . . [who] argued from his very cradle."[7]

Gilbert's maternal grandfather, whom he never met, was not only a Nonconformist and a Methodist lay preacher, but also a teetotaler with strong convictions about God and his creation. Gilbert was told that once during a family argument about the Prayer Book's General Thanksgiving, the old man solemnly declared that he should thank God for his creation if he knew that he was a lost soul. Instinctively, Gilbert identified with that praise of life, which he echoed in his first book of poems in "By the Babe Unborn."

His parents, especially his father, were acquainted with the current philosophy of Huxley and Darwin as well as Herbert Spencer, but their real creed was liberalism. As Cecil put it, "they were undogmatic," and assumed that the truths they still accepted were self-evident, "like the Fatherhood of God, the Brotherhood of Man, and the final salvation of all souls."[8] Gilbert agreed with his brother's assessment, adding that his father's generation was the first "that ever asked its children to worship the hearth without the altar . . . whether they went to church at eleven o'clock . . . or were reverently . . . latitudinarian, as was much of my own circle."[9] But there was a special reason why the Chesterton boys, somewhat like their future friend Belloc, were "moulded by the Unitarian world" of ethical rather than theological concerns.[10]

When Gilbert was born his family was living on Sheffield Terrace in Kensington, just below the great brick waterworks on Campden Hill, which captured his imagination so strongly that he thought the tall tower "took hold upon the stars." The hill itself appears in his first novel, *The Napoleon of Notting Hill*, as the symbol of his Chestertonian birthright of local patriotism, with its sense of neighborhood loyalty. As a small child he imagined that the tower itself might be a colossal water serpent, but he later denied that "it needed the whole water-power of West London to turn him into a Christian."[11]

Like all proper English babies, Gilbert was baptized according to the rites of the established Church of England in the little church of St. George, across from the waterworks on Campden Hill. His father's cousin Tom Gilbert was his godfather, and gave him his first name, while according to a custom of his mother's family, he was given the middle name of Keith from her Scottish mother. Thus Gilbert always associated his love of Scottish legends with his Keith grandmother, a love that led him to devour the novels of Sir Walter Scott and Robert Louis Stevenson.

When he was born Gilbert had an older sister named Beatrice, who was five and the "idol of the household." She seems to have accepted the new baby with love and delight, and they soon became such inseparable playmates that they were nicknamed "Birdie" and "Diddie," presumably Gilbert's own earliest efforts at speech. Gilbert himself clearly recalled a daily ritual of this period: he and Birdie would come out of their house, accompanied by their starched nursemaid, that "solemn and star-appointed priestess of democracy and tradition," and stand on the hill of houses which rose above Holland Park. There they saw terraces of new red houses looking across a vast hollow toward the Thames River, and far, far away they could see the sparkle of the Crystal Palace, which had been built in 1851 to exhibit the wonders of the Industrial Revolution. The whole scene had the shine and glitter of a fairy world, with the prince's palace in the distance. Years later Chesterton remarked that this sparkling memory was a "memory of a sort of white light on everything ... [with] a sort of wonder in it, as if the world were as new as myself; but not that the world was anything but a real world. ... At this time, of course, I did not even know that this morning light could be lost; still less about any controversies as to whether it could be recovered."[12]

In fact, this paradise was lost when Gilbert was only three, still a toddler wearing long dresses, his hair in ringlets. Beatrice Chesterton died when she was eight, and little Gilbert was so inconsolable that he, too, became dreadfully ill. The rest of his life he said he remembered vividly that "children feel with exactitude, without a word of explanation, the emotional tone or tint of a house of mourning." The emotional situation within the immediate family was greatly complicated by Edward Chesterton's behavior, for, in a travesty of grief, he turned his daughter's picture to the wall, got rid of all her possessions, and refused to allow Gilbert or his wife to mention Beatrice's name again. But his incredible effort at suppression failed: Gilbert's mother kept pictures of Beatrice which she finally showed to Cecil's wife, Ada, after her husband had died, and Gilbert never forgot Beatrice, although he knew that his memories were "more and more ... the memory of the thing rather than the thing remembered." As he said years later, "I had a little sister who died when I was a child. I have little to go on; for she was the only subject about which my father did not talk. It was the one dreadful sorrow of his abnormally happy and even merry existence; and it is strange to think that I never spoke to him about it to the day of his death."[13]

The lingering result of this effort at repression was that Gilbert's memories of his childhood became confused, so that he did not remember Beatrice dying, but remembered her falling off a rocking-horse and felt that it was a tragedy. He also associated happiness with his nursery, which was "filled with the light that never was on sea or land" as he watched a white

7

hobbyhorse being painted. Thus part of his lifelong love of the symbol of the "white horse" is clearly related to his earliest memories of his sister.

Two years later, in November 1879, joy returned to the Chesterton home and to Gilbert personally, just the way it did in the fairy tales he was brought up on — a new baby was coming. When his parents told him the news, they may have put it into fairy-tale terms, explaining that if he ate his porridge or took his tonic, God, or the fairies, would bring him this pearl beyond price, a replacement for the lost Beatrice. They all must have been hoping for a baby sister, too, which helps to explain Gilbert's somewhat ambiguous remark when he was told that he had a new baby brother: "That's all right; now I shall always have an audience." Later he would whimsically correct his idea, saying that Cecil was not at all disposed toward being only an audience, but adding, "I will say that the man who has got used to arguing with Cecil Chesterton has never had any reason to fear an argument with anybody."[14]

Though he made many such humorous observations about Cecil, Gilbert was threatened by a lifelong dread that Cecil, like Beatrice, might disappear. Having had an older sibling, he grew up exhibiting the qualities of the middle child, a loving, caring boy who didn't expect to be the family pet. In fact, he assumed toward Cecil the role that Beatrice had assumed toward him: that of the protector-playmate who drives off the bullies little brother has willfully teased.

Because of his position, Cecil grew up assuming the existence of an unbroken dream world in which sun, moon, stars, parents, and big brother — especially big brother — bowed down before him. His family's uncritical support, combined with his inheritance of his mother's argumentative personality, gave Cecil Chesterton the foolhardiness that his older brother lovingly called a "courage [which] was heroic, positive, and equal. . . . He never in his life checked an action or a word from a consideration of personal caution."[15] While Gilbert became world-famous for his friendships, it was this relationship to Cecil that defined the boundaries of his career. Cecil's perpetual alarums and excursions, his susceptibility to conversion, his rebellions — all came from his unclouded Victorian childhood. Gilbert, on the other hand, had learned very young the lessons of loss and recovery.

Gilbert remained even-tempered, always trying to strike a balance by bringing up the opposite side of the teeter-totter to keep Cecil from falling off — or to keep God from dropping the world. Unlike Cecil, Gilbert saw his brother humorously; he even portrayed their relationship fictionally with his own special brand of humor, satiric but kindly, in books like *The Club of Queer Trades*. The common denominator in this early group of detective stories is the detective, a benign man who sits peacefully in his study and produces the correct solutions to mysteries with his understanding of human nature. Meanwhile, his young brother — silly, romantic, flamboyant — rushes about London seeking visible clues and misinterpreting them.

Perhaps the best commentary on their relationship as Gilbert perceived it is the final scene in *The Napoleon of Notting Hill*. Set in the very streets of their childhood, this scene shows the humorless and heroic Adam Wayne admitting to the irrepressibly humorous king, Auberon Quin, how similar they really are:

> "You and I . . . have both of us throughout our lives been again and again called mad. And we are mad. We are mad, because we are not two men but one man . . . , we are two lobes of the same brain. . . . It is not merely that you, the humorist, have been in these dark days stripped of the joy of gravity. It is not merely that I, the fanatic, have had to grope without humor. It is that though we seem to be opposites in everything, we have been opposites like man and woman, aiming at the same moment at the same practical thing."
>
> And the king, Auberon Quin, hesitated for a moment. Then he made the formal salute with his halbard, and they went away together into the unknown world.[16]

Chapter Two

THE ETHICS OF ELFLAND

1879-1880

Growing up . . . nothing could harm us — nothing. This was the solid, well-found conviction at the back of the British national mind in the days of my boyhood. . . . We were [not only] the richest people in the world . . . [but] the security of the island was absolute. No one could possibly get at us, and everyone of us knew it and felt it.

E.C. Bentley, *Those Days* [1]

VERY shortly after Cecil's birth in 1879, Mr. Chesterton moved his family to a different house in an entirely new part of Kensington. Their new home was Number 11, Warwick Gardens, which stood on a quiet square south of Kensington High Street, where Mr. and Mrs. Chesterton lived for the rest of their lives. Cecil's wife Ada described it many years later:

> It stood out from its neighbours . . . [with] flowers in dark green window boxes and the sheen of paint the colour of West Country bricks, that seemed to hold the sunshine. The setting of the house never altered. The walls of the dining-room renewed their original shade of bronze green year after year. The mantel-piece was perennially wine colour, and the tiles of the hearth [were] Edward Chesterton's own design. . . . Books lined as much of the wall space as was feasible and the shelves reached from floor to ceiling. . . . The furniture was graceful . . . [but] there were deep chairs. . . .
>
> On party nights wide folding doors stood open and through the vista of a warm yet delicate rose-coloured drawing room, you saw a long and lovely garden [with] walls and tall trees . . . where on special occasions Edward Chesterton . . . would hang up fairy lamps among the flowers and trees. [2]

Below these welcoming rooms, which all of Gilbert's and Cecil's friends came to know well, was the dark basement that housed the kitchen and servants' quarters, symbolic of the class divisions Gilbert later deplored. The family bedrooms were on the upper floors, together with a nursery where

10

on rainy days the boys could race about playing cowboys and Indians or attacking each other with wooden sword and buckler. Like their father, each boy had his own small "den" in which he could play to his heart's content with messy things like paints and clay. (Cecil chose to raise cockroaches for pets until his mother secretly eliminated them.) Both boys "wrote" stories which they also illustrated — childhood memorabilia that their father kept among his own possessions until he died. At the top of the house was Gilbert's bedroom, complete with a bookshelf that covered an entire wall. As he grew older it became packed with his notebooks; his friends also got used to finding his books and manuscripts scattered about the sitting rooms, in the hall or conservatory, or under the big tree in the garden.[3]

The family had just moved into the house when Gilbert and his father, walking in the square, were approached by an itinerant Italian painter, who begged to paint the portrait of the beautiful little boy. Inevitably, Edward Chesterton agreed; the finished picture was hung in the dining room, where it remained until Gilbert's mother died. In the portrait, Gilbert looks exactly like a real-life little Lord Fauntleroy in a sailor suit. His wavy chestnut hair curls on his shoulders, and he has a dreamy, reflective look in his eyes, though that may have been more a result of increasing nearsightedness than a tendency to daydream.

At this time "properly brought up" middle-class children were relegated to the top floors of their homes with their nurses and governesses; they joined their parents only for daily visits or special occasions, and were shipped off to boarding schools at the tender age of six or seven. But Gilbert and Cecil were brought up far differently; they clearly were the center of their parents' lives. Gilbert's closest childhood friend, Edmund Bentley, remarked that he "had never met with parental devotion or conjugal sympathy more strong than they were in the exceptional woman who was his mother [or] his father . . . whose feeling for literature and all beautiful things worked so much upon his sons in childhood."[4] Mr. and Mrs. Chesterton not only adored their sons and rarely punished them, but also had the very unusual habit of respecting their sons' opinions. They allowed the boys — even when they were very young — to take part in family discussions instead of insisting upon the old-fashioned rule of children "being seen and not heard," which was customary in most households. As a consequence, by the time they were young men, the brothers had a reputation for actually breaking up their mother's parties by falling into prolonged discussions that destroyed the social atmosphere.

Most people felt that Gilbert was his father's son, while Cecil was unmistakably his mother's, but in his biography of Gilbert, Cecil insisted that "anyone who wishes to know from whence G. K. C. gets his wit need only listen for a few minutes to her conversation." Gilbert, on the other hand, remembered his father as most amusing, with an ironic (or paradoxical)

11

touch that reminded him of Mr. Bennet in *Pride and Prejudice*, though he quickly added that his mother was nothing like the silly Mrs. Bennet. Between them the Chestertons raised their sons to argue passionately about ideas, but to do so without interrupting one another or raising their voices.

In such a home it was natural that Gilbert never understood the snobbish upper-class attitude that domesticity was narrow. His home was always a place of delight, shadowed only by the memory of his sister. This memory continued to make him highly sensitive to certain situations: if Cecil "gave the slightest sign of choking at dinner Gilbert would throw down his spoon and rush from the room." In fact, Gilbert's sensitivity figured in the family's move, and made Mr. Chesterton hustle the boys away from the window if a funeral procession was passing by.

With their two young sons the Chestertons began to go to Bedford Chapel to listen to the preaching of the Reverend Stopford Brooke, whose "whole system of religious thought is . . . now called The New Theology." The Reverend Mr. Brooke had been a royal chaplain in the Church of England, but in 1880 (when Gilbert was just six), he had left the established church to become a Unitarian (and a Socialist). Although Cecil presumably was baptized as Gilbert had been in the local parish church, from this point on Mr. Brooke's sermons were the only "religious" education they had. Years later Gilbert wrote to Father Ronald Knox that his father "was the very best man he ever knew of a generation that lived almost perfectly by the sort of religion men had when rationalism was rational. . . . He was always subconsciously prepared for the next generation having less theology than he [had]; and [was] rather puzzled at its having more."[5]

Mr. Ed was the most important person in Gilbert's childhood; he became his small sons' habitual companion, able to spend much of his time at home since his weak heart had allowed him to retire. (A contemporary, Leonard Woolf, saw very little of his father, a barrister, during the week, and only once remembered the glory of going to hear his father plead a case.) Edward Chesterton was quiet, but his manner masked what Gilbert called a "great fertility of notions": he remembered hearing his father tell some ladies that a wild flower they were admiring was "merely a sprig of wild bigamy, probably Bishop's bigamy." When the family had company, however, he liked to retire into his den.

Gilbert said his father might have reminded people of Mr. Pickwick (though he was bearded and wore spectacles) because he had a Pickwickian evenness of temper, good sense tinged with dreaminess, and a tranquil loyalty in his relationships with other people — a description that fit Gilbert as well. But in Gilbert's opinion it was Mr. Ed's hobbies that made him so supremely English, a man who was "by temperament something of a craftsman and something of a philosopher." He liked to conduct scientific experiments, and his den was piled high with layers of creative projects, most of which reflected the fact that he had wanted to become a professional artist, but instead had been articled to the family business because it was "safer" — a good bourgeois attitude. Despite his lifelong love of drawing, Gilbert felt that he was too unhandy to be his father's equal as an amateur, someone who proves, in Gilbert's wry description, that "if a thing is worth doing, it's worth doing badly."

The most important role Mr. Ed played in Gilbert's life, however, was that of the Man with the Golden Key, the magician who delighted in making surprises for the boys. Gilbert's very first memory of happiness was the sight of "a young man walking across a bridge":

> He had a curly moustache and an attitude of confidence verging on swagger. He carried in his hand . . . a large key of a shining yellow metal and wore a large golden crown. The bridge he was crossing sprang on the one side from the edge of a highly perilous mountain chasm . . . and at the other it joined the upper part of the tower . . . of a castle. In the castle tower there was one window, out of which a young lady was looking.[6]

What Gilbert was remembering was one of his father's favorite hobbies: a toy theatre. Its charm for Gilbert lay in the fact that "in that little pasteboard play . . . [there was] the positive outline of everything, the hard favor of the heroine, the clumps of vegetation, the clouds rolling up stiff as bolsters, . . . definite outlines and defiant attitudes." He added that he always loved such "frames and limits" because they "remind us of the main principle of art, that . . . it consists of limitations. . . . By reducing the scale of events [the toy theatre] can introduce much larger events . . . falling cities or falling stars. . . . When we have understood this fact we shall have understood . . . why the world has always been first inspired by small nations."[7]

In his biography Cecil suggested that Gilbert's fondness for toy theatres (as a grown man he built one of his own to entertain his friends) was a romantic escape from reality. But when he looked back at this hobby at the end of his life, Gilbert quietly contradicted Cecil's interpretation. He saw that his father, the craftsman-magician who built the toy theatre, had also "built" his image of God the creator. Gilbert therefore first called Mr. Ed what he later called God: "Pontifex," the Builder of Bridges, and "Claviger," the Key Bearer. He testified further that his childhood was not dreamy, but sharp and clear and real, shared with a father whom he admired for his ability to observe life about him with a broad and humorous philosophy. Gilbert agreed that he associated toy theatres with happiness, but he added that such an explanation did not tell why he was so happy. Some memory of his lost sister, as well as the company of his father, played a part in his joy.

Gilbert's mother, Mary Louise, was a far more forceful personality than Mr. Ed — clever, opinionated, and tart. She was well known for telling others what they liked to eat as well as providing magnificent feasts for both her family and their friends. (In later years she liked to "feed" Gilbert, who

13

clearly did not need it.) Though she was never demonstrative in public, she adored both boys, especially Cecil, to whom her mere presence meant "home." She had a romantic theory that if the boys never handled money, it would make them less worldly, with the result that they both grew up irresponsibly dependent upon other people, learning neither to keep track of expenditures nor to save. Gilbert's financial history makes this obvious: first his father, then his wife, and finally his secretary Dorothy Collins had to manage his business affairs, together with his literary agent, but their combined efforts still did not solve the problem altogether. Shaw even wrote to Gilbert's wife at one point to say that she ought to divorce him for a stupid contract he had signed for a play because he had "failed to look after her old age." Cecil adopted the casual, borrow-and-lend manners of the Fleet Street crowd; he also went on asking his mother for money, borrowed from Gilbert, and lived at home until he was married in 1916 at the age of thirty-seven.

To Gilbert his mother represented the strong dichotomy he saw between men and women, whom he called the only realists, the true rulers of the home "whose whole object in life is to pit their realism against the extravagant, excessive and occasionally drunken idealism of men . . . [while] real selfishness, which is the simplest thing in the world to a boy or a man, is practically left out of their calculation."[8] It was again his mother he was thinking about when he made his famous statement that it could not be a narrow vocation to teach your own children about the sun and the moon and the stars.

The fact that Mr. Ed loved to read aloud to his family may explain why Gilbert, who had played with books from babyhood — pulling them off the shelves, chewing or scribbling in them, so that all his life a book looked "well read" if he had read it — was slow to read well to himself. What Gilbert wanted to do was draw, and he did, everywhere, littering the house with sketches and maps of fabulous countries peopled with ogres and dragons. His father carefully preserved these productions, which were often sewed into booklets made of old insurance forms or pasted in scrapbooks. He kept, for example, one of Gilbert's earliest sketches drawn at about age seven, a crude but lively drawing of Christ crucified, surrounded by large ministering angels and wrapped in a long, trailing cloth on which is printed, "Gord is my sord and my shell and bliker." This phrase, although badly spelled, is certainly imaginative, and it shows Gilbert's precocious facility with the sound and sense of words. But the drawing should not be taken as a proof-text of infant piety.[9]

Among the very first books that Gilbert heard and later reread for himself were fairy tales, many of which his father also dramatized in the toy theatre. From them Gilbert learned the lesson that the ordinary world is a wild and exciting place where the price of enjoying it is often to obey strange commands; a world bound together by mysterious bonds of trust, so that "even green dragons keep their promises"; a world where "all doors fly open to courage and hope [and] nothing is wasted. . . . A jewel thrown into the sea, a kindness to a stricken bird . . . have some . . . terrible value and are bound up with the destiny of man."[10] He vividly remembered another book which taught him that in ordinary houses like his own there could be "goblins hiding in the cellar and a fairy grandmother in the attic." This book, of course, is George MacDonald's *The Princess and the Goblin*.

In homes like his, fairy tales and myths and legends had taken the place of a more orthodox Christianity, which had become one story among many. Gilbert later made the statement that "fairy stories are spiritual explorations and hence the most life-like since they reveal human life as seen, or felt, or divined from the inside." It is interesting to note that Dr. Bruno Bettelheim, who works with emotionally disturbed children, quoted Gilbert's statement in his writing. He also made it clear that his own clinical work has shown that these stories do have curative powers, because they introduce the child to the existential mysteries of life, the anxiety of loneliness, the need for comradeship, the quest, the struggle against odds, victory, and death itself. They tell him that nature is not innately good, that life is harsh before it can be happy, reassuring the child about his own fears and sense of self.[11] With his father's help Gilbert got all these things from fairy tales; the fact that he liked them all his life is probably an indication of his balance, not proof that he remained a child like Peter Pan.

Gilbert's parents also read him the story of Saint Francis, which established other important images for the small boy. He felt that there was "something of harmony between the hearth and the firelight [so that] even the fantastic shadows thrown by that fire make a sort of shadowy pantomime that belongs to the nursery . . . connecting my boyhood with my conversion to many other things."[12] Gilbert was also strongly affected by the very English tradition of Christmas in its Dickensian sense, when surprise was paramount and children "should not touch or see or know or speak of something before the actual coming of Christmas Day [when] children were never given their presents until the actual coming of the appointed hour. . . ."[13] As a result, Gilbert "believed in the spirit of Christmas before I believed in Christ . . . and from my earliest years I had an affection for the Blessed Virgin and the Holy Family, [for] Bethlehem and the story of Nazareth." Gilbert was not the first person to discover that he could recapture his childhood emotion in adulthood by accepting the story as real, but he made an interesting connection by according the same truth-telling to fairy tales, saying in *Orthodoxy* that "the whole spirit of its law I learned before I could speak and shall retain when I cannot write . . . a certain way of looking at life, which was created in me by fairy tales, but has since been meekly ratified by the mere facts."[14]

Gilbert's perspective was also developed by his father's love for the English language, its literature and its history. Mr. Ed raised his son to see that Kensington was "laid out like a chart . . . to illustrate Macaulay's *Essays* [with] all the great names of the Whig aristocrats who had made the Glorious Revolution." Although Gilbert himself came to share his generation's mistrust of many of Macaulay's ideas about history, he still felt that he had the "music of history in him just as Walter Scott had it." He said that Macaulay was "passionately traditional" because "he was fond of proper names even though he slandered his opponents by using the scientific method, which avoids the dangers of describing great men by the bright and simple solution of not describing men at all [but] looking down on all movements of men as if they were ants."[15]

In the 1870's Kensington was a hub of late-Victorian arts and letters, as well as the symbol of prosperous and respectable middle-class virtue. Queen Victoria herself had been raised there and always loved Kensington; in her will she even granted the neighborhood its own coat of arms. It was the place that taught Gilbert to love "boundaries, sharp lines, and small nations better than empires where the sun never sets." This sense of community was a natural result of the influence of his family's real-estate business on him, a business in which, as he humorously remarked, it was considered a great experiment to open an office outside Kensington.

But, like the world, Kensington was in transition. In his writing, however, Gilbert often harked back to its earlier stage, just as H. G. Wells tended to use the eighteenth-century manor house where his mother was a servant as a model for an ideal future. They were like most utopians, for whom a better world was often the one that lay in their own immediate past, while visions of ultimate horror came from overdramatizing their present circumstances.[16]

When he was a child Gilbert was familiar with the many small specialty shops along Kensington High Street, such as the "oil and colour" shop where they sold gold paint inside shells; the dairy where he always ritualistically consumed a glass of milk; the confectioner's "where the chocolates were all wrapped in those red and gold and green metallic colours which are almost better than chocolate itself; and the huge white wedding cake in the window was somehow at once remote and satisfying, just as if the whole North Pole were good to eat."[17] And there was the familiar grocery store with "its cargoes from the sunrise and the sunset . . . India at your elbow . . . China before you . . . America over your head."[18] Northward toward Notting Hill there was even a flourishing old-fashioned flea market along the Portobello Road, with stalls and hawkers and shills and pickpockets and a Punch-and-Judy show.

Besides offering young Gilbert the variety of the wide world in miniature, Kensington was also a flourishing hodgepodge of Victorian architectural romance. As land agents, the Chestertons took a professional interest in its development, not just in the terraces of new red-brick townhouses, but also in curiosities like the Leighton mansion, whose owner, Lord Leighton, was president of the Royal Academy of Art. His Arabic Hall was decorated with inlaid tiles and graced with silver columns and splashing fountains — lavish features very like the Oriental splendors of Lord Ivywood's ancestral castle in Gilbert's novel *The Flying Inn*. Also noteworthy was the parish church of St. Mary Abbots, where Gilbert was to be married and Cecil confirmed, which was rebuilt during their childhood by the man who designed the "Gothic" Albert Memorial. When they took walks farther south the Chesterton children could see the rich atmosphere of Italian baroque in the Roman Catholic Brompton Oratory and in Westminster Cathedral, then being built. Many years later in Jerusalem, asked if he were not horrified by the weird assortment of churches and shrines decorating the Holy Land, Chesterton only laughed and said that a Turk might ask him the same thing about the Albert Memorial.

When they were older, Gilbert always recognized instinctively the Victorian values of Kensington as his own, while Cecil tried to identify their family with those from which "the Socialists of the 'eighties [were] drawn, . . . exclusively . . . middle class [and] very fond of denouncing the middle class . . . for its stupidity, narrowness, and inaccessibility to ideas . . . when as a matter of fact all the ideas fermenting the minds of men came from the middle classes."[19] Ultimately, however, Cecil in a sense returned to the family fold, agreeing with his brother, who had said all along that they had been raised and remained Liberals, whose philosophy came from the "burst of optimism born of the American and French Revolutions which set up against the governing class . . . and the government, the citizen . . . whose influence on the state depended on his independence of the state."[20] Or, as Gilbert had put it in 1908 in *Orthodoxy*, the "things which are common to all men are more important than the things peculiar to any man and ordinary things are more valuable than extraordinary things. . . . In short, the democratic faith is this: that the most terribly important things must be left to ordinary men themselves — the mating of the sexes, the rearing of the young, the laws of the state."[21]

Finally, whimsically, Gilbert defended his comfortable, nurturing home with this humorous apology:

> I am sorry if the landscape or the people appear disappointingly respectable and even reasonable, and deficient in all those unpleasant qualities that make a biography really popular. I regret that I have no gloomy and savage father to offer . . . as the true cause of all my tragic heritage; no pale-faced and partially poisoned mother whose suicidal instincts have cursed me with the temptations of the artistic temperament . . . and that I cannot do my duty as a true modern, by cursing everybody who made me whatever I am.[22]

Chapter Three

THE MYSTICAL CITY OF FRIENDS
1881-1892

*The change from childhood to boyhood, and the mysterious
transformation that produces that monster the schoolboy . . . is
a most complex and incomprehensible thing. . . . There grows all
over what was once the child a sort of prickly protection like
hair; a callousness, a carelessness, a curious combination of random and quite objectless energy with a readiness to accept conventions. And . . . by some primordial law they all tend to . . .
going about in threes.*

G.K. Chesterton, *Autobiography*[1]

UNLIKE most middle-class boys, Gilbert was not sent off to boarding
school at seven or eight, but he still remembered acutely a sharp line
that divided his childhood from his boyhood, a time when he began to
brood consciously upon "doubts and dirt and daydreams." His instinct was
sound, for there is a pictorial record of the dramatic change formal schooling
made in his life, a change that must have made him feel as if he had been
transformed from a prince into a pauper. In the oil portrait that hung in
the dining room, he was a golden child with flowing locks; but within the
next year a studio photograph of the two brothers shows him with hair
clipped short, wearing regulation short pants and long black stockings, and
peering at the camera as he anxiously hugs baby Cecil, who is still dressed
in a long white gown with a lacy collar. From this point on his education
was divided into two parts quite unrelated to one another: school and home.

It was the January of 1880 when he was not quite six that Gilbert was
sent off to be "prepared" to enter St. Paul's, a famous London "public
school." All the Chesterton cousins of his generation were sent to prepa-
ratory school and on to St. Paul's — an interesting progression, because such
an education represented a social step up from their parents' generation and
a part of the typically English pattern of movement toward the upper classes
of which Gilbert later disapproved. Although they were known at school
as either "Books" or "Games" Chestertons, none of these boys performed

18

brilliantly as scholars or scholarship winners. Predictably, Gilbert was labeled one of the "Books" Chestertons.

Like all English "public" schools, St. Paul's was actually a private school open to any boy who could pass its entrance examinations and pay its fees. It had begun as a choir school in the churchyard of St. Paul's Cathedral, but during the Renaissance had been reorganized as a "middle-class" institution by the great Greek scholar Dean Colet. About 1875 the High Master, Frederick Walker, had moved St. Paul's out of the city to the suburbs, so that the new school building was only a five-minute walk westward along Hammersmith Road from Gilbert's home. Moreover, it was a day school (the High Master actually thought a home's influence was beneficial), and thus it was different from the more typical public boarding schools like Eton, where masters and peers took the place of the boy's family. St. Paul's, however, also had the aura of the Establishment, of a place where the old-boy network of friendships and career opportunities was cemented; its students won more and more classical scholarships each year to both Oxford and Cambridge, which attracted poor, intellectual boys like young Leonard Woolf. At the same time it also had a more urban, modern curriculum offering English literature, history, math, and science.[2]

Across Hammersmith Road from the new red-brick St. Paul's was a small elementary school called Colet Court, run by a master called Bewsher, and it was here that Gilbert was first sent. He later wrote his fiancée that he was sent off to school "when he had drawn pictures on all the blinds and tablecloths and towels and walls and windowpanes because he obviously needed a larger sphere."[3] But his real feelings were that this sphere was smaller and less interesting than home. He was not only a messy, absent-minded little boy with a high voice and a loud laugh, a child growing so fast that he towered over the other boys his age and moved awkwardly; he was also a boy with a head full of ideas that were more interesting than what went on in the schoolroom. In addition, he did not learn to read well until he was nearly nine, so that schoolwork must have been not only boring, but terrifying, and his masters concluded that he was a dunce. At one point his parents took him to a brain specialist, presumably to try to make sense of the puzzle that Gilbert was as bright as a button yet brought home poor school reports — only to be told that he had a large and very sensitive brain, and it was an even chance whether he would grow up a genius or an imbecile.

By his own account it is clear that there was a drastic difference in style between 11 Warwick Gardens, where his father had built a magically creative world, and Colet Court, where everything was dull and rote. Gilbert illustrated the difference vividly:

> The ancient capital letters of the Greek alphabet ... still have quite an
> unaccountable charm and mystery, as if they were the characters traced in

wide welcome over the Eden of the dawn. The ordinary small Greek letters
... seem to me quite nasty little things, like a swarm of gnats .... I learnt
the large Greek letters at home ... merely for fun, while the others I learnt
during the period ... called education, when I was being instructed by
somebody I did not know, about something I did not want to know.[4]

As a result, Gilbert simply did not take the routine of school seriously. He
covered his schoolbooks with drawings and ignored ordinary schoolwork
and athletics. His textbooks became so tattered and torn that his masters
assumed he could not do his lessons, but his personality was such that they
all believed him when he said he had forgotten to do his homework — or
when he wandered about the playground during class, saying he thought
it was Saturday. No one bullied him, but they did play tricks on him (like
filling his pockets with snow), and one irritated master exclaimed that if he
opened Gilbert's skull, he would find a lump of white fat. But Gilbert's
classmates soon realized that if he felt like it, he could prepare his lessons
perfectly well; in fact, he was often just being lazy or avoiding behavior that
would make him seem like a "swot."

One thing that is not clear is how soon his parents and masters realized
that Gilbert had become very nearsighted. He did not wear spectacles in
photographs until he was a teenager; as a boy he was said to peer with a
"brooding expression" which changed magically to a beaming smile when
he recognized a friend. The clear, sharp edges of his childhood world were
blurring, something that would not be as apparent to him at home, where
everything was familiar, and where the pages of a book, held closer to his
nose, were still available for company. As a result, a part of his early school
behavior can be blamed on the normal behavior of a nearsighted child who
finds the outer world withdrawing from him but does not know what he
is missing until he is given glasses. At this age he was not fat, and he loved
to walk for miles, so his ineptness at games also may be blamed on poor
vision rather than physical ineptitude.

While he was playing the dunce at school, however, Gilbert's other
education was proceeding rapidly at home, where he still spent more than
half his time. When he finally began to read, he made up for lost time by
reading everything he could lay his hands on, and remembering much of
it verbatim: encyclopedias, novels by Scott, Dickens, Thackeray, Austen, and
Dumas, Shakespeare and all the English poets from Pope to Swinburne and
Robert Browning, Macaulay and Carlyle — and even the Bible itself. Cecil
claims they were never made to read the Bible, and the results are apparent:
Gilbert devoured it, and developed a writing style clearly influenced by the
major Old Testament prophets and the Book of Job, whose themes are
humorously twisted in his novel *The Man Who Was Thursday*. In boyhood and
thereafter, Gilbert had a happy, eclectic taste in literature, reading the best,
but also enjoying boys' adventure stories, pulp magazines, and penny dread-

fuls, the cheap detective stories sold in railway stations. He refused — on principle — to be a highbrow.

But perhaps the most important part of his home education between 1880 and 1887 was the lessons he learned about the time which Cecil sarcastically called the "Saint Martin's Summer of Liberalism." This was the period when Gladstone once again became prime minister, a leadership lasting until his party broke apart over the perennial problem of Ireland. Some of Gilbert's earliest cartoons are heads of Gladstone, whose strong features and righteous Anglican bent were a continual topic in the Chesterton household. Characteristically, Cecil early decided that he detested the sound of Gladstone's name, while Gilbert, consciously or not, took Gladstone as the leader who was the closest to his ideal of the public man.

Gladstone took government seriously but not patronizingly. He represented the middle-class Liberal ideal that wanted all men to become their own masters, that saw the country's enemies as the vested interests — like the hereditary monopolies in land, government, and the religious Establishment. He was consistent, not rigid, with a tendency toward extravagant language and sentiment typical of the Victorians, but he was no state planner "doing good" to people he saw as less able to run their own lives. He was also a devout High Churchman, the forerunner of those concerned Christians who founded the politically oriented Christian Social Union, which itself was a descendant of the Christian Socialist Movement founded in 1848. Like its members, Gladstone stood as much for the adoration of God as for the ethical thrust toward the establishment of a New Jerusalem, which in Gilbert's own lifetime led to both the "new" theology and the welfare state.[5]

Gladstone had come back to power on a platform of protest against the arbitrary English takeover of the small South African country of the Transvaal. Diamonds had been discovered there in the 1870's, making the fortune of empire-builder Cecil Rhodes. When the English were defeated by the Transvaal Boers at Majuto in 1881, Gladstone was able to redeem his campaign promise and give the Transvaal its freedom, but shortly thereafter, having decided on moral grounds that he must support the idea of Irish Home Rule, his party came apart over the issue. While he had the full support of the radical Little Englanders like Gilbert's parents, he now lost the support of the old-line Whigs who were the big landowners, as well as that of younger political stars like Joseph Chamberlain, a rich businessman from Birmingham, who was developing an "imperialistic" instinct and saw Ireland as a "piece" of England.

Thus Gilbert at an impressionable age saw Gladstone destroy himself and his party for principle. But it was only Cecil who concluded that Gladstone's attitude was irrelevant to "modern times and attitudes"; Gilbert responded positively, developing an emotional loyalty to ethical liberalism, which remained his parents' true religion without their realizing its Christian roots. Their liberalism was very "Distributist" in its acceptance of the value of virtues like independence, industry, and restraint.[6] Businessmen like his father and uncles instinctively felt it right to mind their own businesses "instead of trying to ruin or absorb everybody else's," a belief in the kind of liberalism founded upon the self-supporting individual voter whose economic and political interests would not be helped by either collectivism or a dictatorial party structure. But by the 1890's, although Gilbert was not aware of it, many family businesses had gone public or collapsed, and the average industrial worker had begun to need economic help to counter the worldwide conditions which were destroying England's Victorian prosperity.[7] For Gilbert, however, the firm of Chesterton and Sons (which still exists today) remained a prototype of the urban yeoman's right to "life, liberty and property," a business run as ethically as Gladstone ran the country.

In January 1883, when he was about eight-and-a-half, Gilbert made the big move across Hammersmith Road to St. Paul's School. Still behind for his age, he was placed in the second form with a group of boys who were two years younger than he was. He sat in the back, taller than ever, paying no attention to what was going on. He had graduated to a suit and tie, though his nails were usually dirty and chewed, and his clothes were as messy as ever. But he was quickly recognized as a good-humored boy who laughed at jokes played on him and defended smaller boys against bullies.

At this time St. Paul's School had a very good reputation and won many scholarships. According to Leonard Woolf, who was in the same form as Cecil, the brighter boys were put in a form on the classical side, while the others were on the side emphasizing science and history and the army. The best classical scholars were tutored specially by the High Master's son. Gilbert was never on the classical side, and Cecil, who began there in 1894, was transferred to the modern side within the year. (He had done far better in school than his older brother; he may have been transferred because he was not planning to go on to a university but to enter the family business.)

Unlike Woolf, who early on regarded himself as an "intellectual," Gilbert went along with the prevailing anti-intellectual atmosphere among the boys. He could remember running to school in sheer excitement, repeating lines from *Marmion*, then going into class and saying them "in the lifeless manner of a hurdy-gurdy, hoping there was nothing to indicate that I distinguished between one word and another."[8] Although Gilbert later poked fun at the snobbery and philistinism of the old universities in essays like "Oxford from Without," he never shared the passionate rebellion of the Woolfs, who resented the fact that "to work, to use the mind . . . was to become an untouchable." Young Woolf only solved his dilemma when he got to Cambridge and found himself like-minded friends with whom he founded the prevailing counter-culture organization of his day — the Bloomsbury group.[9]

Gilbert found his connecting link between home and school — "brains and brawn" — earlier. On the St. Paul's playground one day he came across the boy who was to become his best friend: Edmund Clerihew Bentley. Bentley was a neat, poised, well-coordinated boy with a grave expression and a quickness of movement which, as Gilbert later explained, made it "a poetic pleasure to see him walk, a little pompously, down the street and suddenly scale a lamppost like a monkey . . . then drop down and resume his walk."[10] He was two years younger than Gilbert, who by this time was nearly fourteen. Although they were in the same form, they had never noticed one another; on this day, for some reason, they began to fight. The next day they met and fought again, and this combat went on until, during a pause in their punching, one of them quoted a line from a Macaulay poem and the other capped it. This instant rapport ended their fighting forever and made them "comrades in arms." They were united by a love of literature and a sense of humor, which in both of them hid a strong commitment to improving the world.

From that day forward the two were almost inseparable, in school and out of it. They spent many an afternoon at each other's house, particularly at Gilbert's, where Bentley later commented he might find Gilbert's idle books lying about all over — in the sitting room, the hall, the conservatory, or under the big tree in the garden. They worked together happily on a large project, too: an adventure story in which they wrote alternate chapters, with characters who were masters they liked at St. Paul's. In this story two masters marched about carrying the third, who turned out to be a robot whom they wound up from time to time. (Bentley noted that from boyhood on Gilbert hated to have someone read anything he had written while he was around — and having it read aloud was torture.) While bored one day in chemistry class, Bentley himself actually invented a new verse form, which he called a "Clerihew" after his middle name. What he had scribbled down was "Sir Humphrey Davies detested gravy./He lived in the odium of discovering sodium." He and Gilbert went on to write hundreds more "Clerihews," many of which were published much later in *Biography for Beginners*, with Gilbert's cartoons for illustrations.[11]

But the most revealing summary of their friendship is Bentley's dedication of his detective story, *Trent's Last Case*, to Gilbert. In the book, which was published in 1913 when they were both grown men, Bentley wrote:

> Dear Gilbert,
> . . . I have been thinking again today of those astonishing times when neither of us ever looked at a newspaper; when we were purely happy in the boundless consumption of paper, pencils, tea, and our elders' patience; when we embraced the most severe literature and ourselves produced such light reading as was necessary . . . in short, when we were extremely young.[12]

Bentley said later that his friendship with Gilbert was the most important thing in his life then because Gilbert had the power — which he never lost — to inspire trust and affection, but did so unconsciously, without design. He recognized in Gilbert a strong "moral influence," probably in contrast to the smutty language and habits of the typical schoolboy, whose precocious interest in sex was matched by the adults' total refusal to discuss it. Gilbert matured very late, so his innocence of manner was partly physical, but it was also true that he never lost that refreshing mental attitude which combined idealism with fun and common sense. Bentley also felt that Gilbert "needed" him less than he needed Gilbert, because Gilbert could live happily in his own thoughts. But in letters to his fiancée Gilbert made it plain that he, too, adored the comradeship of like minds to which Bentley's friendship introduced him, which had the happy effect of relating his two worlds of home and school.

Some critics say that Chesterton's friendship with Bentley was excessively emotional; they see latent homosexual tendencies in both Gilbert and his close friends. But this assumption fails to take into account that the boys' imaginations had been formed by romantic literature, in which the Arthurian quest is matched with the sentiments of Dickens. True, overt homosexuality was a plague of the public schools that boarded their pupils, but Gilbert lived at home; he also categorically denied any impulse to "the sin of Oscar Wilde." To make his strong attraction to Bentley more than the obvious teenage "crush" seems futile, especially since there was a prevailing tendency in English society for strong same-sex friendships.

Though he was no doubt happier at school after he met Bentley, Gilbert's academic performance didn't improve. As far as St. Paul's was concerned, Gilbert continued to be a dunce. His school reports said things like "he has the knack of forgetting, is always in trouble, though his work is well done when he remembers to do it," and "he is a great blunderer with much intelligence," and "he belongs in a studio, not a school." But he did make another friend. Late in the fall of 1890, when Gilbert was sixteen, he and Bentley enlarged their charmed circle to include the third musketeer, who possibly had just arrived at St. Paul's.

He was Lucian Oldershaw, a thin, dark youth who was more sophisticated than the other two, as befitted the son of an actor who had traveled abroad and attended other schools. He had unusual hobbies; one was dabbling in magic and conjuring tricks, a diversion to which he introduced Bentley first. He was not only more daring than the other two, but also a born promoter. Once all three became acquainted, he vied with Bentley to be Gilbert's "best friend," but he felt that Bentley won. On the other hand, Oldershaw eventually became Gilbert's brother-in-law.

It was Oldershaw's appearance on the scene that led to the creation of a private "club" of the type being created by bright, literary-minded teenagers all over England. He thought they should form their own debating society, which they could call the "Junior Debating Club" to distinguish it from the School Union Society. This was the special preserve of the seniors, who did other "awful and appalling things, such as dining with the High Master." Oldershaw proposed that they should also publish their own magazine and have it printed by a real printer. Gilbert had already been horrified by Oldershaw's suggestion that they contribute essays to the *St. Paul's School Magazine*, an idea he felt on a par with offering to write articles for the *Encyclopaedia Britannica*. Now he was dumbfounded to have Oldershaw explain that he also had a scheme in mind to set up a cooperative effort between all the public school papers! Clearly, the new musketeer was a lad of large ideas, and however much he was impressed by Gilbert, Gilbert was equally impressed by him.

The J.D.C. was duly formed by the three early in 1891 (using initials was also a very common habit then, as shown by J.R.R. Tolkien's group setting up the T.C.B.S. in Birmingham, and Dorothy Sayers establishing the M.A.S. at Oxford). The club's initial purpose was to discuss Shakespeare; one of the first papers read to the membership was by the chairman, G.K. Chesterton, explaining how Shakespeare opens his plays. But the boys soon decided that Shakespeare was too limited a topic, and broadened their range of subjects, though they did not include politics — perhaps to discourage Cecil, who talked of nothing else. The three founding members, however, indulged themselves by writing an ongoing "political" correspondence, each playing a fictitious character, using his own initials as a cue for the invented name. Gilbert was Guy Crawford, a Liberal artist.[13]

The J.D.C. met in its members' houses, first after school and later on Saturdays. The host's mother was expected to provide huge amounts of tea and cake while they assembled around the dining-room table to eat and talk. The original group was added to as time went on, joined by some friends Cecil's age as well as some members' younger brothers. Some remembered that Gilbert was chosen chairman because he was two years older than everyone else, being behind for his age in school; others felt that he was elected because the group admired him the most, especially for the serious poetry he wrote. Clearly he was a budding intellectual among intellectuals. As Leonard Woolf later pointed out, the majority of boys in this group were Jewish, which meant that they, like the other members, were considered misfits in mainstream English society, with its emphasis on sports and playing the game.[14] Gilbert once addressed two Jewish brothers as "the children of Israel" in a letter, but jokingly, much the same way he later called Shaw a "heretical Irishman" to his face.

Tagging along from the beginning, at first still wearing short pants and attending Colet Court, was Cecil, whom his brother called "the Innocent Child." An early photograph of the club shows him curled up right in the center of this group of serious teenagers, whom he called *his* friends, despite the fact that Bentley, for one, actively disliked him. It was Cecil's idea that the formation of the J.D.C. was "the most important event in [Gilbert's] school career so far as its influence on his own future was concerned." In strictly chronological terms, however, Gilbert's earlier friendship with Bentley and then their mutual friendship with Oldershaw were equally important to him, since it was those two boys with whom he shared his adolescent anxieties and with whom he worked out the basic solutions to his problems. But the larger group did provide him with his first real audience outside of his own family circle, and taught him the pleasure that comes from being well received.

It seems likely that it was Oldershaw who was the prime mover in getting Gilbert to submit some of his poems to a "real" magazine, and who thus should be credited with this breakthrough: that by December 1891 the Club Secretary (Oldershaw) recorded in the minutes that he proposed a vote of congratulation to the chairman for having a poem accepted by the *Speaker*. The poem was a very serious, high-minded one called "The Song of Labour," and marked Gilbert's first appearance in print.

In his biography of his brother, Cecil created the impression that the Gilbert who wrote this poem was a serious, bookish youth who after a shy and secret adolescence suddenly burst upon the London literary scene, a jovial giant bubbling with Rabelaisian mirth.[15] And Cecil is not alone in this opinion; Maisie Ward adopted it, too. But while it is true that Gilbert helped to fill the pages of the club magazine with essays on heroes of the French Revolution, he also contributed others such as "Half Hour in Hades, An Elementary Handbook on Demonology," written in 1891. In this essay he describes the "Common or Garden Serpent" and mentions a Mr. J. Milton, who "has discussed at some length the leading characteristics of a fine species of which he was primarily the discoverer."[16] It is the picture of this "learned" author that comes closer to matching Bentley's description of Gilbert — that he was "by nature the happiest boy and man I have ever known; even in the adolescent phase of morbid misery that so many of us go through . . . laughter was never far away."[17] Since Bentley was the person most deeply involved in Gilbert's adolescent "misery," his remark seems more trustworthy, and the record also shows that laughter and fooling were a regular feature of many meetings of the J.D.C.

As chairman, Gilbert tried to keep order, but the boys were often rowdy, tossing buns at each other or trying to shout down Cecil, who was constantly arguing. Gilbert tried fining the disturbers of the peace a penny, but then one bright lad named Edward Fordham, who figured he owed the club over ten shillings, decided to "strike a blow for freedom," and refused to pay up. Fordham was often a ringleader in mischief: it was recorded that one day the chairman had to speak seriously to Mr. F. Though they had fun, the J.D.C. also read papers and discussed quite mature topics. Once they got into an argument over the meaning of "good," and Gilbert said, "The word 'good' has many meanings. For example, if a man were to shoot his grandmother at a range of 500 yards I should call him a good shot, but not necessarily a good man."[18] This is not a remark from which all humor is missing.

Thanks to Oldershaw's pushing, in that March of 1891 the first issue of the club's magazine, the *Debater*, appeared. It featured an article by Gilbert called 'Dragons," which provided the J.D.C. with their secret password, his delicious comment that "the dragon is the most cosmopolitan of impossibilities." (Their official motto, however, was "Hence Loathed Melancholy.")[19] Their first issue of 100 copies was run off on a duplicating machine at home, but Oldershaw was so successful at selling the magazines to their families and friends and schoolmates at St. Paul's that they were able to have the next issues produced by a regular printer, starting what Gilbert called his lifelong martyrdom to misprints.

Besides the original three, the J.D.C. had nine members (not including Cecil), but the membership fluctuated as some of the boys left London for the universities. Most of the original members went on to Oxford or Cambridge University, where four of them were elected president of the most prestigious political club: the debating society or union. Borrowing a phrase from Walt Whitman, one of Gilbert's adolescent enthusiasms, Cecil called the J.D.C. a "mystical city of friends," and, all in all, they were a remarkably able bunch. Several of them — including Gilbert, Cecil, and Bentley — became journalists as well as authors, two became university professors, three worked in government, and several passed the Bar to practice law. Surprisingly, only one, Robert Vernede, was killed in the First World War.

The greatest moment of the J.D.C. undoubtedly occurred when someone put a copy of the little beige magazine on the desk of Frederick Walker, the High Master of St. Paul's. All of Walker's students describe him in much the same way: he was a loud, terrifying, and unpredictable giant of a man, both "curious and alarming . . . with a deep and raucous voice of immense volume. His vision of the school was narrow and fanatical. . . . He seemed interested only in the clever boys."[20] By Walker's standards, Gilbert Chesterton was of no use whatsoever to St. Paul's, an attitude that Gilbert reciprocated, finding St. Paul's of very little use to himself. But when Walker read the *Debater*, he found it highly amusing. He was particularly impressed by Gilbert's writing, the work of the school dunce, and therefore did something he was famous for doing to the unwary: he caught Gilbert walking along Kensington High Street and bellowed at him that he had literary abilities if he could manage "to solidify" them.

Gilbert was horrified: he had been officially "discovered," and his comfortable spot at the bottom of the form was lost to him forever. Not only that, but all the boys' parents were startled to have the High Master mention the *Debater* at Prize-Giving Day, saying that it was an unauthorized publication whose writers might yet reflect honor on their ancient school. Everyone had barely recovered from this publicity when the J.D.C. — principally, no doubt, Oldershaw — managed to get Gilbert to enter a poem for the school's Milton prize (Milton had attended St. Paul's), and Gilbert's poem won. It was the first time the honor had been bestowed on a boy who was not in the top form.

The assigned subject was Saint Francis Xavier, the Jesuit missionary to India. In his poem Gilbert waxed eloquent about the saint's apparent failure in life, exclaiming that his work was "a waning flame." Nevertheless, he ended the poem triumphantly:

> Since he had bravely looked on death and pain
> For what he chose to worship and adore
> Cast boldly down his life for loss or gain
> In the eternal lottery not to be in vain.[21]

In Gilbert's eyes, Francis Xavier was a success, and he turned the missionary into a romantic hero, almost a cross between Stevenson's David Balfour and Kipling's Gunga Din. Convinced by this effort that he was a poet, Gilbert tried to fill this role for a number of years, until he realized that writing poetry was only one of his many talents. But during this particular period (though he continued writing light verse with Bentley), poetry represented to him the clearest voice for public causes, the proper form for a battle cry.

It is interesting to note the recorded reactions of Gilbert's friends to his success. Bentley said that he never forgot the sight of his tall, gawky, untidy friend as he read his masterpiece aloud to the assembly of schoolmates, teachers, and parents at the end-of-the-year ceremonies. Gilbert was so nervous that he kept wiping the sweat from his forehead — and so unnerved that he forgot the prize itself, and had to return to the stage to collect it. Cecil may not have been present at the ceremony; years later he remarked that he could not remember what the poem was about, "if I ever knew." The *Debater* took full credit for the event; as its editor, Oldershaw had a habit of congratulating himself for Gilbert's successes. In Number 15, issued July 1892, he triumphantly proclaimed that "as we go to press we hear the pleasant news that our Chairman, Mr. Chesterton, has gained the Milton Prize for English verse at St. Paul's School, the subject for treatment being St. Francis Xavier, the apostle of the Indies. . . . A vote of congratulations [was duly] awarded to Mr. Chesterton."[22]

That same June, shortly after winning the Milton prize, Gilbert was frozen with astonishment to read the following item posted on the school bulletin board: "G.K. Chesterton to rank with the Eighth. F. W. Walker, High Master." Thus, for what little remained of his school career, Gilbert, who at eighteen was the right age for the eighth form but had never made it there, was allowed to enjoy the privileges of the seniors and outrank his friends back in the sixth form. He remembered the shock of this honor all his life, but he had little time to enjoy it.

Chapter Four

THE PICTURE OF DORIAN GRAY
1892-1895

A cloud was on the mind of men, and wailing went the
*   weather,*
Yea, a sick cloud upon the soul when we were boys
*   together . . . .*
This is the tale of those old fears, even of those emptied hells,
And none but you shall understand the true thing that it
*   tells —*
The doubts that drove us through the night as we two talked
*   amain*
And day had broken on the streets e'er it broke on the brain.

G.K. Chesterton in his dedication to

E.C. Bentley in *The Man Who Was Thursday*[1]

It is through Art, and through Art only, that we can
realize our perfection. . . . There is no such thing as a
moral or immoral book. Books are well written, or badly written.
That is all.

Oscar Wilde, *The Picture of Dorian Gray*[2]

Nothing sublimely artistic has ever arisen out of mere art. . . .
There must always be a rich moral soil for any great aesthetic
growth.

G.K. Chesterton, "A Defence of Nonsense"[3]

DURING that summer of 1892 after Gilbert had won the Milton prize, his father took him for the first time across the Channel to France. The trip was unlike the usual Chesterton family vacations at some seaside resort, where they stayed in hotels and spent their days on the beach or hiking on country roads, armed against bad weather with books and pen and paper. It was a "graduation" present, because Gilbert was not going to go back to St. Paul's that fall. He and his father went by train from Rouen

29

along the coast and down to Paris and back, adding to Gilbert's affection for his father's way of life, which taught him to be a "traveler, not a tripper," a mere tourist. Gilbert already had a romantic attachment to the liberal ideals of the French Revolution, but now he discovered that although England and France were neighbors, they were very unalike. In the words of W.S. Gilbert, he, "in spite of all temptation to belong to other nations, remained an Englishman!" He wrote to Bentley about seeing "solemn old abbes in their black robes [and] . . . fiery bronzed little French soldiers," then added, "The people talk too much."[4] He does not reveal much of his adult affection for the quaintly different look of the small French coastal towns which appear so often in his novels.

This was one of many brief excursions abroad Gilbert was to make, for the young men and women of his generation and class often went to Italy, as he did in 1894, or to Germany, or to Paris to enjoy the arts. But, unlike the upper classes, who visited one another on private estates, Gilbert and his friends did not think of themselves as cosmopolitan Europeans, but as Englishmen, citizens of the best and most prosperous country in the world.

Unhappily, what Gilbert now "graduated to" was a period of intense depression; the memory of it remained for him another of those sharp lines drawn across his life, making him acutely aware of "before" and "after." There are as many suggestions about what triggered this fairly typical late adolescent state of mind as there are studies of Gilbert, suggestions that range from sudden sexual maturation to abstract philosophical despair, based upon the assumption that in his teens Gilbert was a brilliantly rational thinker (in fact, *French*). Another group of critics ignores this period, assuming Gilbert was a "happy giant writ small" who never suffered doubt; yet another group tries to prove that he experienced a religious conversion.

In his early study, Cecil again muddied the waters, both because he telescoped time and because he wanted, for polemical reasons, to make Gilbert out to be not only a romantic "born too late" but also a crypto-Catholic. Just as typically, Gilbert tells the story in vivid word pictures and relates the whole problem to the atmosphere he found at his next school. He had mixed-up feelings of intense egotism, feelings not natural to him, which most probably were produced by the fact that he was supposedly following a career he wanted, when in fact he was not. The only way to try to show what happened is to follow strict chronology, because Gilbert, too, telescoped his problems and solutions, so that what was a somewhat drawn-out process of growing up sounds like a clap of thunder on a Damascus Road.

By the fall of 1892, Gilbert had begun to attend art school. He first went to a small school in St. John's Wood, which was northeast of Kensington near Regent's Park, but quite soon afterward, possibly by January of 1893, he went on to the Slade School of Art, which was a part of the University of London. Almost from the beginning of this training, Gilbert found himself suffering from what our period would call an identity crisis. Unlike Cecil, who seems to have had no problem abandoning the career his parents chose for him, Gilbert was "not convinced of his own powers and his parents were mistrustful of writing as a means of livelihood. They were therefore behind his quite fruitless enterprise of study at the Slade."[5] The situation was complicated by the fact that Mr. Ed had wished to study art but instead had been put in the family business, and by his assumption that Gilbert would be happy at the Slade because he would be doing there what he had always enjoyed — drawing pictures.

Inevitably, Gilbert found it hard to quit art school and equally hard to make himself work at something that he found he really did not want to do professionally. Since quitting would have hurt his beloved father, Gilbert did not quit, but neither did he apply himself as his professors would have liked, so, as Bentley put it, "he was never able to see that Gilbert learnt anything there." The head of the Slade is on record as suggesting tactfully that they could not teach him anything without spoiling his originality, while Gilbert cheerfully explained that "there is nothing harder to learn than painting and nothing which most people take less trouble about learning. An art school is a place where about three people work with feverish energy and everybody else idles. . . . Those who work . . . do not want to be discursive and philosophical."[6] Gilbert did.

When he had completed the Slade's requirements three years later in 1895, the masters, like those at St. Paul's, suggested that he take up any career *except* art. But both his drawing and his writing suggest that the Slade did teach him several things. Bentley's son Nicholas, for example, was a comic illustrator, and he felt that Gilbert's real artistic ability lay in being a cartoonist, because he had the sardonic eye and hand of a Daumier. And when Gilbert wrote he employed the perception of an artist: in his adult work he wrote in vivid scenes. He was particularly fascinated all his life by light itself, and loved to describe sunrise and sunset, mists, streets, and dappled country lanes, "setting the scene" by means of a very Impressionist imagination. Gilbert also learned the artistic value of inversion: he wrote that "it is really a fact that any scene can sometimes be seen more clearly and freshly . . . if it is seen upside down. . . . That inverted vision is much more bright and quaint and arresting. . . ."[7] Finally, his study at the Slade had one practical result: because of his training he was asked several years later to do his first regular writing assignments — reviews of art books.

Before discussing the philosophical influence of the Slade and Gilbert's psychological state of mind, it is necessary to sort out the chronology of this part of his life. By casually borrowing the telescoped dates from Cecil's book (an unscholarly habit for which Gilbert was reproached in other works all his professional life), Gilbert himself reinforced the impression that he had been left friendless in London.[8] In his *Autobiography* he said that he began to "be a lunatic, troubled by problems and concerns it had been the sustained and successful effort of my school life to keep to myself . . . [when] I said farewell to my friends when they went up to Oxford and Cambridge while I . . . went to an Art School and brought my boyhood to an end."⁹

Cut off from daily contact with his friends at school, he undoubtedly felt lonesome, but he was not left entirely on his own with only Cecil and his friends for company, because the fact is that Oldershaw, Bentley, and the other original J.D.C. members did not leave London for the university until two years *after* Gilbert started at the Slade. Not only was Gilbert two years older than they, but when he left St. Paul's they were only in the sixth form, with two years of school to complete; they could not have matriculated before the fall of 1894.¹⁰ The fact that Gilbert was particularly depressed that year is thus quite natural: he was alone and facing the dilemma of what to do next, like any college senior without a crystal-clear goal.

But even while they were away at the university, his friends came home for an occasional weekend and attended the Saturday gathering of the J.D.C.¹¹ By the time they had reassembled in London in 1898, Gilbert had left the Slade, worked for two publishers, and fallen in love with his future wife, who was — in Gilbert's opinion — the person primarily responsible for teaching him about orthodox Christianity.

This mythical telescoping of time in Gilbert's adolescence is contradicted by other concrete evidence. In his long dedication to Bentley in *The Man Who Was Thursday*, for example, Gilbert makes it clear that he was not alone in his adolescent broodings about sex and death. "That period of doing nothing . . . in which I could not settle down to any regular work" was shared by his two closest friends, Bentley and Oldershaw, the latter being the one who introduced him to both Whitman and magic. The same sort of legend about his appearance can be easily exploded. Contrary to Cecil's statement, Gilbert did not suddenly appear on Fleet Street as the "Laughing Cavalier" as early as 1895; in 1895 he was the tall, lanky, wild-haired youth he caricatured at the Slade, and he did not "appear" on Fleet Street until 1899 at the earliest. To match Cecil's statements with the dates would make Gilbert's adolescence last from 1892 to 1900, when he was twenty-six.

One of the confusing sources for this period of his life is his "Note-books," which is a title that has been used to lump together a miscellaneous collection of exercise books, most of which are undated.¹² The one which is clearly the last (and referred to by Mrs. Ward as *the* Notebook) is one that can be dated roughly from the period between 1892 and 1896. It is written in his "Slade School" Gothic handwriting, unlike his earlier school-boy scrawl, and contains a number of finished "pieces," including thoughts about his J.D.C. friends and his gratitude for being, many cartoons of Gladstone, biblical "bits," pages of drawings of daggers and long rabbit ears, and, finally, poems to Frances Blogg, his future wife.¹³

32

This Notebook has been used to "prove" that Gilbert was becoming a Christian, a homosexual, and a child; and clearly it has scraps from all his moods of this intense and unhappy time. But what it seems to echo are Gilbert's later comments about adolescence, which he saw as a period when it is very common for the young to feel "omnipotent" — that is, to suffer from the intellectual pride which is like "playing God." He described it later in a novel in which he said,

> A very large number of young men nearly go mad. But nearly all only nearly do it. . . . You might say it is normal to have an abnormal period. The inside gets too big for the outside. . . . In one way his own mind and self seem to be colossal and cosmic. . . . In another . . . way the world is much too big for him. . . . Now . . . there's a dreadfully dangerous moment; when the first connexion is made . . . between the brain and real things.[14]

What he means is that this moment of truth can make a sensitive young man mad. He illustrates the condition by having his hero, who is convinced he is in control of the universe, learn otherwise: he gets tied to a tree, and though he struggles as hard as he can, this would-be god cannot get free. In another story, his heroine is "saved" from mental anguish simply by learning that others share the same nightmare that she has. The fact seems to be that it was Gilbert's "mystical city of friends" who were the source of his own discovery that whatever morbid thoughts and fantasies he was being plagued with were ones that they, too, had experienced.

Apparently Gilbert and his friends also shared the other, related form of brooding so very typical of bright, sensitive adolescents with no clear sense of vocation: the temptation to commit suicide. Gilbert clearly was tempted by the idea. Several of his earliest poems are about suicide, including one using Bentley's initials and another called "Thou Shalt Not Kill," which says,

> I had grown weary of him. . . .
> I did not hate him: but I wished him dead. . . .
> That man I sought to slay was I. . . .[15]

But his own ethical background still called suicide wrong — and in strictly religious terms, this was the point at which Gilbert began to believe in ". . . the objective solidity of Sin . . . when he made the acquaintance of the Devil . . . which taught him that men who say Evil is only relative, Sin is only negative, there is no positive badness . . . are talking shallow balderdash only because . . . they are more innocent and more normal and more near to God [than I]."[16]

Many years later, Gilbert kidded himself and his youthful terrors by writing the smooth and sassy poem "A Ballade of Suicide," in which he jokes,

The world will have another washing day;
The decadents decay; the pedants pall
And H.G. Wells has found that children play,
And Bernard Shaw discovered that they squall;
Rationalists are growing rational. . . .
I think I will not hang myself today.[17]

But like most adolescents he had to live through the painful period of the "enlarged" self, a time when the very line "I think I will not hang myself to-day" was too scary, too close to the bone to be used as a joke about himself or the human race.

There has been another misconception fostered, perhaps unintentionally, by Cecil and other biographers. This is the theory that Gilbert was already becoming a "Catholic" — that is, an orthodox Christian — by this time. This idea is suggested despite his own very clear statement that he "was a pagan at twelve and a complete agnostic by the age of sixteen [who] retained a cloudy reverence for a cosmic deity and a great historical interest in the Founder of Christianity."[18] Cecil quotes an early poem from the *Debater* called "Ave Maria," but in it Gilbert addresses the Virgin Mary in terms that are closer to the Edwardian version of courtly love: the woman is on a pedestal "to warn, to comfort and command" until she condescends to accept the transforming role of wife and mother. Cecil also cites another poem about Saint Francis, who Gilbert said was a fairy-tale figure common in the nursery of his youth. Looking back, Gilbert did see the hand of God in his troubled adolescence, but that is not the same as a conversion experience. Raised not in a strict Evangelical family but in a broad-mindedly agnostic atmosphere, Gilbert had no reason to spend his adolescence rebelling against piety nor converting its dogmas into secular creeds like Fabianism; his conversion was not primarily a result of adolescent trauma but the consequence of a slow, thoughtful process of intellectually weighing the "heretics" against the "orthodox."[19]

During that first year away from St. Paul's, Gilbert not only shared long walks and conversations with Bentley; he also had two other experiences with Oldershaw that made a deep emotional impression on him. First of all, Oldershaw introduced Gilbert to his preoccupation with magic; he was interested in conjuring tricks as well as fortune-telling with a ouija board. At this time, when serious scientists and psychologists had banded together with famous men of letters to found the Society for Psychical Research in Cambridge, Oldershaw's hobby was very fashionable.[20] Gilbert's broad-minded and curious father good-humoredly decided that the ouija board was a pure fraud, but Gilbert himself was very suggestible, and he developed terrific headaches from these sessions, along with what he described as a "bad smell in the mind."[21] The showman's tricks of conjuring also made a strong impression on him, as his writing proves. In several of his Father

Brown mysteries there is a practicing magician, and his intellectual and emotional conviction that playing with psychic phenomena was not only dangerous but wicked — a kind of playing God — was dramatized convincingly in *Magic*, a play he wrote in 1913. In it he plainly stated that calling up powers, thrones, and dominations was an ancient and perilous sin.

He also shared a happier and more productive "spiritual" experience with Oldershaw one long afternoon, when the two of them holed up together in his bedroom and read aloud Whitman's *Leaves of Grass*. At this point in his crisis, Gilbert, always deeply influenced by literature, maintained the courage "to be" through Whitman's and Robert Louis Stevenson's sharp and brightly colored view of life as a grand fight against odds. Whitman was fully aware of his soul and his body; he was talking personally, privately, yet concerned with all men; he celebrated life — and he awed Gilbert:

> [He] seemed to me something like a crowd turned to a giant, or like Adam, the first man. . . . I did not care about whether his unmetrical poetry were a wise form or no, any more than whether the true Gospel of Jesus was scrawled on parchment or stone. . . . What I saluted was a new equality, which was not a dull leveling, but an enthusiastic lifting. . . . Real men were greater than unreal gods; and each remained as mystic and majestic as a god, while he became as frank and comforting as a comrade. . . . A glory was to cling about men . . . the least and lowest of men. . . . A hump-backed negro half-wit, with one eye and homicidal mania, must not be painted without his nimbus of gold-coloured light.[22]

At that time, in that place, Whitman was for Gilbert the perfect extension of the creed of his youth, the belief that the movement (of Rousseau and the French Revolutionists) was the beginning of bigger and better things. But Whitman was more than an idealist: he "was brotherhood in broad daylight," a man who truly wanted his dreams for mankind to come true. In Whitman Gilbert found a child's view of the world, simple and accepting, and a child's questions — like "What is grass?" — that have a thousand answers. Whitman also helped Gilbert see himself as a part of humanity, not an isolated fragment of it. Not surprisingly, grass became a symbol that appears and reappears in his poetry, his essays, and his stories from then on. For him it stood for the ordinary, everyday life shared by everyone, which was more important and more real than the emotional uncertainties of the individual imagination. This saving grace Gilbert called the "mystical minimum of gratitude." Again, it is stretching a point to insist that because Whitman is known to have been a homosexual, Gilbert must have been one, too.

All during this period — when Gilbert was working out the bare beginnings of his salvation in conversations with Bentley and Oldershaw and in his writing, particularly his poetry — he was going to classes at the Slade. His daily walks through a different "London" than he had grown up in were perhaps the best part of the day, since he loved the city and had the capacity to see in it the kind of romance that characterized the stories of Sherlock Holmes as well as *New Arabian Nights*, the story collection by Robert Louis Stevenson. He best expressed his affection for the atmosphere of London in all its many neighborhoods when he wrote,

> Men lived among mighty mountains and eternal forests for ages before they realized that they were poetical; it may reasonably be inferred that some of our descendants may see the chimney-pots as rich purple as the mountain-peaks, and find the lampposts as old and natural as the trees. . . . For while Nature is a chaos of unconscious forces, a city is a chaos of conscious ones. . . . There is no stone in the street and no brick in the wall that is not actually a deliberate symbol. . . .[23]

His path to the Slade took him east and north to Bayswater Road, a symbol of middle-class respectability; next into the upper-class district of Mayfair bordering the edge of the royal parks; then along the length of fashionable Oxford Street in the West End until he reached the older neighborhood of Bloomsbury. There, eighteenth-century townhouses had been converted to boarding houses and flats for students, struggling writers and artists, and the lower middle-class world of law clerks and tradesmen. The post-World War Bloomsbury group, who took their name from this area, were all schoolchildren living conventional upper middle-class lives at home and at school, but the neighborhood was already the center of intellectual and Liberal London.

At the heart of Bloomsbury, between Bedford and Russell Squares, was the British Museum, which housed important manuscripts and antiquities like the Elgin marbles, as well as a copy of every book published in England. Poor scholars and writers from Karl Marx to G.B. Shaw had used its circular reading room as their private study, enjoying its warmth and its free pens and paper. Just a block north began the various buildings of the University of London, of which the Slade School was a part.

This university was a product of the Industrial Revolution. When it was founded in 1828, the universities of Oxford and Cambridge excluded anyone who was not a member of the established Church of England. Since so many of the new, urban middle class were Nonconformists, the university was founded so their children could study not only the classics, but also modern subjects like science and mathematics and even English literature. Both students and curriculum were dedicated to the "godless" principles of utilitarian liberalism, which stressed that all human affairs could be experimented with and improved upon. (For this reason Gilbert found it highly appropriate that the embalmed body of utilitarianism's founding father, Jeremy Bentham, actually sat in a glass case in one of the halls.) It was the first English university to establish a student union and, in modern times, to allow its students some voice in university affairs. Many students, like

Robert Browning and, later, Gilbert himself, lived comfortably at home and "commuted" to class.

The University of London was also the first university to admit women, which it did in 1869 as a part of the women's rights movement for education, the vote, and careers. Gilbert had been outspokenly in favor of women's rights in the *Debater*, as became a good Liberal — but he probably had not met any zealous feminists until he began attending the Slade. There is a suggestion in one of his stories that they did not appeal to him a great deal. The story is about a "blue land in which there are living blue-stockings who are always reading books . . . all wearing blue caps and gowns and all the wives of Bluebeard."[24] But in his novels the heroines are all intelligent, likable women.

The university was popular with the new middle class, and grew impressively. Already by 1836 a separate undergraduate school called University College was organized in buildings a block north, with the parent University of London acting only as the examining body and degree granter. The Slade School of Art was opened later, in 1871. It was named after Felix Slade, a wealthy London art collector who had left his paintings to the British Museum and his money to the university to establish art professorships. Begun in an addition to the north wing of the main building, the school grew so rapidly that by 1881 it had to build another addition. Its students could take classes in the other parts of the university as well.

From the beginning the Slade School promoted a "modern" philosophy of art that echoed experimental science. Students were allowed to use any treatment they thought effective, just as science students were encouraged to conduct experiments with a free hand, the goal being to increase human knowledge. The Slade not only permitted women to share the men's classes a generation before Oxford or Cambridge did, but also allowed its students to draw by studying live models instead of plaster casts of the human form. Gilbert later remarked, "Art may be long, but schools of art are short . . . and there have been five or six since I attended an art school. Mine was the time of Impressionism. . . . The very latest thing was to keep abreast of Whistler and take him by the white forelock. . . . There was a spiritual significance in Impressionism in connection with this age of scepticism."[25]

Gilbert soon found that he had a temperamental disagreement with Impressionism as a "school," a response that he translated, in typical fashion, into a concern about truth and the nature of reality. Its doctrine was that if all an artist could see of a cow was a white line and a purple shadow, then that was what he drew. Like all nearsighted people, Gilbert was well aware that with his naked eye he could see no more than the white line and purple shadow, but the minute he put on his spectacles, there was the real cow. Consequently, he never was convinced that "seeing is believing."

The early 1890's were the height of a period that was aesthetically lush and decadent, with the kind of depression that resulted from "the sense that man's two great inspirations had failed him . . . the Christian religion . . . and the republican enthusiasm." As a result, the times "were like one long afternoon in a rich house on a rainy day. . . . Everybody believed that anything happening was even duller than nothing happening."[26] This feeling gave rise to an artistic attitude that Gilbert disliked:

> A nocturne by Whistler of mist on the Thames is either a masterpiece or it is nothing; it is either a nocturne or a nightmare of childish nonsense. . . . The decadents, in short, may fairly boast of being subtle; but they must not mind if they are called narrow. This is the spirit of Wilde's work . . . an attitude in the flat, not the round; not a statue, but the cardboard kind in a toy-theatre, which can only be looked at from the front.[27]

This description is fascinating, because in his own writing Gilbert was to produce his effects framed in a "toy theatre" of sharp outlines and bright colors, without the extensive, realistically detailed descriptions common to the writing of his Edwardian contemporaries like Arnold Bennett. Gilbert himself was a fugitive from the fin de siècle who borrowed from it almost all of his equipment as a writer, but took none of its ideas.[28]

Gilbert was particularly intrigued by Oscar Wilde. His "playing the sedulous ape" to Wilde in technique is evident in a short story taken from his Notebooks, as a comparison easily shows. Wilde ends *The Fisherman and His Soul* this way: "Yet never again in the corner of Fuller's Field grew flowers of any kind, but the field remained barren as before. Nor came the Sea-Folk into the bar as they had been wont to do, for they went to another part of the sea."[29] In his story about a search for the wild goose, Gilbert echoes Wilde's sound and style, but writes with a different spirit: "And I have not said whether he ever found the wild goose and the story ends abruptly. And must not all stories of brave lives and long endeavours and weary watching for the ideal end so, until all be ended? I cannot tell you whether he found what he sought. I have told you that he sought it."[30] The emphasis here shows that even in 1892 Gilbert was clinging to the positive idea that the search itself was significant, not a tale told by an idiot.

As he spent his time arguing with other "fledgling philosophers" around the University of London, as well as corresponding with the J.D.C., who were being exposed to the current *zeitgeist* at the universities, Gilbert began to grow more optimistic again. In debates he took "the other side" and found to his delight that there was a case for it, an attitude reflected in the Slade-period Notebook, in which he gradually moves from somewhat sententious explorations and comments like "I cannot worship Humanity: I have loved men," to comments about pleasure in little, everyday things like a stone "stained with yellow lichen." Finally, sometime in 1895, he is being positively cheerful and more like his adult self, making remarks like "a moderate is a man who wants children to be moderately clean, houses to be moderately sanitary, and their inhabitants to be moderately sober."[31]

During the fall of 1894 Gilbert's friends left for Oxford. Bentley had won a history scholarship to Merton College, and Oldershaw a scholarship to Christ Church, where he would continue his clever promoter's ways. It may have been about this time that Gilbert, in his last year at the Slade, began going to lectures on English literature at University College. (English literature was not even a part of the curriculum at other universities, and the professors giving lectures on his favorite subject were also "men of letters" who wrote for a living.) On one daunting occasion Gilbert found himself alone at a lecture by the Chaucer expert W.P. Ker, who, after giving "as thorough and thoughtful a lecture as I have ever heard . . . in a slightly more colloquial style," quizzed Gilbert about his reading and remarked with satisfaction, "Ah, I see you have been well brought up."[32] It was at these lectures that he met a man who was to become a lifelong friend: Ernest Hodder Williams, whose family was in publishing. He was captivated and impressed by Gilbert's personality and insights, and — even more important for Gilbert's future — convinced without any evidence that Gilbert could write.

Later Gilbert was to characterize the period's prevailing intellectual outlook as summed up by FitzGerald's translation of Omar Khayyam. His verses, "elegant and gloomy," either sapped or swept away "many of the other fledgling philosophers"; they were "songs without words . . . a thing like opium . . . never a food for us who are driven by an inner command not only to think but to live, but to grow, and not only to grow, but to build."[33] Gilbert himself had discovered again that "at the back of our brains . . . there was a forgotten blaze or burst of astonishment at our own existence . . . [a] submerged sunrise of wonder."[34] A considerable amount of this glory must be attributed to the young lady he met in 1896, of whom he soon wrote, "God made you very carefully/ He set a star apart for it."[35]

This connection between love and delight in being alive is dramatized in his novel *Manalive* (the title tells all). Although it wasn't published until 1912, Gilbert actually began writing it about 1895-6, when he was working in publishing. The novel's hero, Innocent Smith, was originally meant to be the hero of a detective story, a nihilistic aesthete who conquers his philosophical doubt and learns to appreciate and enjoy life. In the course of the final story, this Dostoyevskian "fool for Christ" is literally blown about the world, demonstrating how to be happy: his secret is never to act like a bored decadent.

Gilbert really seems to have found himself "cured" almost before he knew it, much as he later realized that he had become a Christian almost unawares. He said he accidentally discovered that he had become an optimist again while arguing with a fellow student, a discussion he later described in realistic detail as taking place on the wide flight of steps of the neo-classic university building "on a black wintry evening":

Visible below us in the blackness was a burning and blowing fire . . . and from time to time the red sparks went whirling past us like a swarm of scarlet insects in the dark. Above us also it was gloom, but . . . one became conscious of the colossal facade of the Doric building, phantasmal, yet filling the sky, as if Heaven were still filled with the gigantic ghost of Paganism. . . .

There Gilbert stood and argued with a fellow student who also liked Gothic architecture and Milton's poetry, but "for hours of the night he would go where I [had] no wish to follow him . . . a man with a long, ironical face . . . and red hair." The student abruptly asked Gilbert why he was becoming orthodox, a question that prompted Gilbert's realization that he had changed:

Until he said it, I really had not known that I was; but the moment he said it I knew it to be literally true. And the process had been so long and full that I answered him at once, out of existing stores of explanation.

"I am becoming orthodox because I have come, rightly or wrongly, after stretching my brain til it bursts, to the old belief that heresy is worse even than sin. . . . I hate modern doubt because it is dangerous."

"You mean dangerous to morality," he said in a voice of wonderful gentleness. "I expect you are right. But why do you care about morality?"

I glanced at his face quickly. He had thrust out his neck as he had a trick of doing . . . and . . . brought his face abruptly into the light of the bonfire . . . lit up infernally from underneath. . . . I had an unmeaning sense of being tempted in a wilderness, and even as I paused a burst of red sparks broke past.

"Aren't those sparks splendid?" I said.

"Yes," he replied.

"That is all I ask you to admit . . . and I will deduce Christian morality. Once I thought . . . one's pleasure in a flying spark was a thing that could come and go with that spark . . . that the delight was as free as the fire. But now I know that the red star is only on the apex of an invisible pyramid of virtues. That red fire is only the flower on a stalk of living habits, which you cannot see. . . . Shed blood, and that spark will be less red. . . ."

A common, harmless atheist would have denied that religion produced humility or joy . . . but he admitted both. He only said, "But shall I not find in evil a life of its own. . . . What you call evil I call good."[36]

The wasting thistle whitens on my crest,
The barren grasses blow upon my spear,
A green, pale pennon: blazon of wild faith
And love of fruitless things: yea, of my love . . . .
The love of God:

I hear the crumbling creeds
Like cliffs washed down by water, change and pass;
I hear a noise of words, age after age,
A new cold wind that blows across the plains,
And all the shrines stand empty; and to me
All these are nothing: priests and schools may doubt
Who never have believed; but I have loved . . . .
Think you to teach me? Know I not His ways?
Strange-visaged blunders, mystic cruelties . . . .

So, with the wan waste grasses on my spear,
I ride forever, seeking after God,
My hair grows whiter than my thistle plume
And all my limbs are loose; but in my eyes
The star of an unconquerable praise;
For in my soul one hope for ever sings,
That at the next white corner of a road
My eyes may look on Him . . . .

G.K. Chesterton, *The Wild Knight*, 1900

Chapter Five

THE TAMING OF THE NIGHTMARE
1895-1900

*Little Jack Horner sat in the corner . . . listening to the . . .
night-wind. Then there came a violent rattling at the window.
. . . "You're wanted," said the creature who appeared. . . . "What
for, Sir," gasped Jack. . . . "To find the Mare's Nest. . . . Her
. . . youngest . . . is called the Nightmare. Her you must catch
and tame and saddle and bridle, and she is the only steed you
shall ever ride."*

G.K. Chesterton, "The Taming of the Nightmare"[1]

IT was during Gilbert's last year at the Slade in 1895 that the crucial break occurred — when his J.D.C. friends, having finished at St. Paul's School, went up to Oxford. Left in London, Gilbert wrote them long letters, joyfully greeted them when they came home on vacation, and faithfully escorted them back to the train at vacation's end. At this point he had to decide how he was going to earn a living while he tried to become a writer. The Chestertons never pushed their sons out of the nest, but they did have a properly middle-class view that able-bodied young men should work once their education was over. The family income, however, was clearly sufficient to provide food, clothing, and shelter indefinitely, and neither son showed any sign of wanting to set up his own establishment until he got married.

Inevitably, Gilbert was lonely, although he enjoyed the company of newer friends like Hodder Williams, as well as that of Cecil and the friends his age now added to the J.D.C. Even though he missed his old friends, he did learn a great deal from their university educations. He indirectly absorbed most of what they learned, particularly from that part of college life that was most influential: the endless extracurricular debating over political and economic ways and means, which had as its culmination the Oxford Union, a debating society that launched its members into the real world of Parliament. He heard about his friends' amusements and their love life, but he also gained a pretty good idea of the unconscious social elitism that their education taught them.

Bentley, for example, avoided the "acutely self-conscious believers in Art who called themselves the Decadents," and the "Bloods," the noisy drinking and gambling aristocrats who for fun one night broke every lamp in his college. But he discovered the university sport of rowing and proceeded to work harder to make the team than he did to excel in his studies. He not only became captain of his eight, but won his Oxford "blue," or letter. Watching from the distance of London, which gave him a perspective that the others did not have, Gilbert found Bentley's field of concentration very strange. He probably expected Bentley to go more the way of Leonard Woolf, who found Cambridge "very heaven. . . . Suddenly to my astonishment there were a number of people . . . about me with whom I could enjoy the . . . profound happiness of friendship . . . unconcealably and unashamedly [belonging] to that class of human beings which is regarded with deep suspicion in Britain . . . the intellectual." Woolf even became a member of the Apostles, a "secret" discussion group in existence for over 200 years, whose members still form the most elite old-boy network in England today.[2]

All of his life Gilbert was to learn not only from his own experiences but also from those of his intimate friends. From these particular experiences, which were relayed to him at home, Gilbert developed a quizzical idea of university life. His opinion, formed then and never changed, was that the majority of the students did not work hard at anything:

> The plain and present fact is that . . . the lads at Cambridge and Oxford are only larking because England . . . wishes them to lark. All of this would be very human and pardonable . . . and harmless if there were no such things in the world as danger and honour and intellectual responsibility. But if aristocracy is a vision . . . it is not a working way of managing education to be entirely content with the mere fact that you have . . . given the luckiest boys the jolliest time.[3]

During this period the chance to lark was being shared by more boys of Gilbert's own class, as well as a few very bright boys from the lower classes, but Gilbert was not greatly impressed by this fact. In his instinctive protest against joining the upper classes, he was defending the classic Radical-Liberal position, which was in favor of enlarging the membership of the middle class — especially in the ownership of land — while removing the monopoly of privilege.

Meanwhile, both Bentley and Oldershaw, whose opinions mattered the most to Gilbert, had abandoned the staunch conservatism that they had been raised to believe in. They became "new" Liberals, identifying with those who felt that there must be more "social" legislation. At the same time they also joined the Oxford Fabian Society; it promoted middle-class values and emphasized scientific studies and its program of "permeating" the main political parties in order to reform England by Parliamentary act. The two friends saw no contradictions in their allegiances; at this time, as

Gilbert pointed out, it was hard *not* to call oneself a Socialist when socialism seemed to offer the chief camp in which people really worried about the worsening economic position of the working classes. Bentley and Oldershaw were not the only ones to change. Sixteen-year-old Cecil read the best-selling booklet *Merrie England* by the Socialist editor Robert Blatchford of the *Clarion*. He totally adopted its message, which "stated in simple, warm, good-humored language, with lively and effective examples, the conviction that society as constituted was unjust."[4]

Gilbert recorded most of his intellectual probings in his Notebooks, where he tried to reconcile his Liberal upbringing with the new ideas of society based on the philosophies of Kant and Hegel, who had "invaded" Oxford in the 1870's. There the general impulse toward a legislative restructuring of society came from Professor T. H. Green, who taught that government existed to help man to full self-realization, but that man as an individual was nothing. Green's point of view had also been adopted by Herbert Spencer, who was looking for an answer to the individualistic Huxley-Darwinian competition of the "survival of the fittest." Spencer, in turn, was a great influence on the brightest Fabian of them all, Beatrice Webb, herself very upper middle-class and Victorian, and inclined to be a scientific lady bountiful. Her strong sense of mission suited the other Fabians, many of whom came from lower-class Evangelical backgrounds, but it bothered Gilbert: to him it seemed a humorless sense of duty strongly colored by patronage.

Gilbert labeled this Hegelian philosophy "Prussianism"; in the 1890's it was leading to the development of an imperialistic philosophy at the expense of the "isolationist" Little England position. For many bright young men, the conviction that the empire was "good for mankind" was also replacing religion. Educated to rule, they called it, using Rudyard Kipling's phrase "the white man's burden" without catching the irony that Kipling intended. They absorbed the prevailing theory that Parliamentary government had been created in the Teutonic forests, with its corollary that "pure-blooded" nations were superior and destined to rule mankind. All of these fashionable ideas Gilbert took with his usual grain of salt; later he was to play devil's advocate against them in an effort to restore a little balance to current thought, to make people see that the root of Western civilization was not Bismarckian Germany.

In one youthful poem, "An Alliance," Gilbert wrote, "the sea be a Saxon river/That runs through Saxon lands." This poem gave first Cecil and then Gilbert's other biographers the idea that at one time he, too, had been strongly imperialist and racist. The problem with this assumption is that it makes it necessary to convert Gilbert almost overnight to a non-imperialist stand, and it runs counter to the arguments he was writing in his Notebooks, in which he clearly recognized his sympathy with the old Liberal idea that it was the individual who was the vital unit of society. He commented that no Socialists seemed to be able to explain how they would improve human nature to reach Utopia, but they all assumed it was a "change of heart" they were seeking. Gilbert had begun to work out for himself the fact that orthodox Christianity supported the classic Liberal position best, and also provided a method for accomplishing its goals — but again, too much has been read into his Notebooks as well as his early poems and letters. In them he used "God" and Christian symbols like the cross as a way of opposing scientific humanism without these terms or images meaning anything to him emotionally.[5]

While Gilbert was getting his university education by correspondence, his friends at Oxford had met a former president of the Oxford Union, Hilaire Belloc. Bentley had seen Belloc before, one memorable morning during the previous January, when he had come up to Balliol to try to win the Blakenbury history scholarship for the glory of St. Paul's. Bentley had found himself sitting at a long table across from a stern-looking, sturdy young man with a thin face and a husky voice "who fell upon each paper and tore it limb from limb with . . . startling rapidity."[6] Bentley told himself that this was the scholarship winner, and he was right. Belloc was half-French and Roman Catholic, but descended on his mother's side from a long line of English Radicals; now he became a great influence on fledgling Liberals like Bentley and Oldershaw. While he continued to support the Radical position that imperialism, protectionism, and collectivism were all motivated by hopes of private gain for the few, his French background made him fiercely "Republican," and as president of the union he had debated with the young Conservative F. E. Smith.[7] Belloc won first-class honors in history in June of 1895, but he was not given the fellowship that he wanted at All Souls College (he was passed over, he decided, because he was Roman Catholic); consequently, he had to support himself by writing and tutoring. Since he stayed on at Oxford for several years, his friendship with Bentley and Oldershaw had time to ripen. Eventually, in 1906, Bentley signed Belloc's citizenship papers so that he could run for Parliament.

By the spring of 1895, when his old friends were thoroughly at home at Oxford, Gilbert was finishing his art studies. He was also openly admitting that he was going to try to become what he had always wanted to be: a writer. Like many young writers, he thought of himself as a poet, and he spent much of his spare time working on the poems which ultimately were published with his long verse drama, *The Wild Knight*. On April 20, 1895, a poem of his called "Easter Sunday" appeared in Blatchford's *Clarion*. Bentley called it his first professional appearance as a writer, but Gilbert himself always dated the beginning of his career from the glorious day just before his twenty-first birthday — May 29, 1895 — when he was asked by Mr. Cotton of the *Academy*, an art magazine, to write a review of *A Ruskin Reader*. Gilbert wrote a happy description of the event to Bentley:

Mr. Cotton is a little briskly bohemian man, as fidgety as a kitten, who runs about the table as he talks to you. . . . He read my review and [said] This is very good: you've got something to say. . . . So I am to serve Laban . . . and my joy in having begun my life is very great. I am tired, I said to Mr. Brodribb [Cotton], of writing only what I like. Oh, well, he said heartily, you'll have no reason to make that complaint in journalism.[8]

Gilbert's article, unsigned, appeared in the *Academy* in June of 1895.

That summer of 1895, Gilbert also began his first full-time job, which was not in journalism but in publishing; it offered fewer risks — but less money — than free-lance writing. Gilbert went to work for a small publisher called Redway, located in a dusty little office across the street from the British Museum. The firm's main publications were books on the occult and spiritualism, and both their authors and their customers were often very odd. One lady insisted she was in touch with one of their deceased authors, while another assured Gilbert he got good tips on betting from a medium.

Most of his time Gilbert was working very hard as a Man Friday — or, as he explained it, "I have half a hundred things to attend to. . . . Redway says we've got too many MSS, read through them . . . and send back those that are too bad at once. I go slap through a room full . . . [and] post back . . . MSS to addresses, which I imagine must be private asylums. . . ." He was also given charge of the press department, which meant he had to keep track of review copies, sending them out to every magazine that existed. After a "nine hours' romp at Redways," Gilbert went home and settled down to what he considered his real work: writing, about which he wrote, "I have been scribbling . . . the whole evening. . . . This sounds like mere amusement, but I solemnly pledge myself to the opinion that there is no work so tiring as writing. . . . [It] leaves me inclined to lie down and read Dickens." Gilbert was industriously putting in about a fourteen-hour day.[9]

By midsummer of 1895 Gilbert had changed jobs to work for a more important publishing company called Fisher-Unwin. It was located on Paternoster Row near St. Paul's Cathedral, in the ancient district dedicated to publishing and printing since the Middle Ages. It had narrow winding streets with names like "Ave Maria" and "Amen." Gilbert daily went past Bloomsbury to Cheapside, past the law courts and north of his goal: Fleet Street, home of the newspaper world. He was in Dickens' London, near the sound of Bow Bells, close to the Cheshire Cheese Pub, where his hero, Dr. Johnson, had been a part of the mythical "Grub Street." But he had not gotten himself any more free-lance assignments.

In spite of the legend that he only stayed in publishing for a short time before he rocketed to fame on Fleet Street, Gilbert worked for Fisher-Unwin for six years, from 1895 until 1901. It is not clear why he began working in publishing instead of trying to get a job as a cub reporter on one of the Fleet Street papers; he may have thought that publishing would leave him enough free time and energy to write his own stuff, like poetry. Just as his definition of himself as a journalist never quite fitted his unique situation, so his choice of breaking in as a writer is somewhat inexplicable — unless it was influenced by his parents' natural wish that he be stably employed in a respectable part of the writing world. Fleet Street itself was considered quite "bohemian," and it was a very hard place to make a good living unless one got a permanent job on an economically sound paper.

But Fisher-Unwin was a step up for Gilbert, because there he began to do real editing work. He was given charge of a book on Rome: he was to edit the copy, choose the illustrations, and write the introduction and notes, "all because I am the only person who knows a little Latin. . . . If I hadn't been there they would have given it to the office boy." He quickly decided that if he knew next to nothing about the publishing world, "the vast mass of literary people know less."[10]

Gilbert was also ghostwriting the memoirs of a tiny man with a waxed moustache who had survived a shipwreck that had left him living with cannibals; in addition, he was choosing pictures for a history of China, and writing publicity releases for the firm. These he had to print himself on a duplicator, and he usually covered himself with ink in the process. He was beginning to gain weight, and had grown a moustache; he also took to flourishing a sword stick, poking it about "looking for adventure." Occasionally he dropped it, and it would clatter behind him as he raced down the iron steps in the office. He was clearly waiting for a chance to use his enthusiasm, wit, and energy to fight for the world, ". . . to make it beautiful again by beholding it as a battlefield [and himself as the knight ready to fight the dragon for his lady]. When we have defined the evil thing, the colours come back into everything else. When evil things become evil, good things, in a blazing apocalypse, become good."[11]

In reality, he had no time to wait. Although Queen Victoria's Diamond Jubilee of 1897 was staged when English pride was at its strongest, by the 1890's there had already begun what Winston Churchill was to call "these violent times of our own century." In following Gilbert's adult career, therefore, it is extremely important to understand what he meant when he said of himself in 1913, "I also was born a Victorian; and sympathize not a little with the serious Victorian spirit."[12] As a young man he saw things very wrong with some of the Victorian assumptions, but he did not support the breakup of that world in favor of "totally new forces."

Three events of 1895 prefigured the increasing uncertainty of the future, and significantly affected Gilbert's own career because he took the "unpopular" or "unsuccessful" view of them. First, Oscar Wilde had sued the Marquis of Queensbury for calling him a homosexual, a charge based on the fact that Lord Alfred Douglas, Queensbury's son, had been Wilde's lover. (While not discussed publicly, homosexuality was not uncommon among the upper classes.) Wilde had thought his literary reputation would save him from legal prosecution. Instead, on July 22, 1895, he lost the case, his career was subsequently ruined, and he eventually died in exile — all because he had broken the unwritten law that one might do anything so long as it did not become public. In another sense, Wilde was a victim of the old-boy network, which closed ranks to protect its own, a kind of social hypocrisy which Gilbert hated all his life.

Secondly, that same year the concept of "the glory of the empire" was undergoing a trial run, planned to save England from the unpleasant fact that economically she was falling behind both Germany and America. Gold had been discovered in the Rand, a part of the Transvaal that Gladstone had liberated in 1881. Cecil Rhodes, his fortune already made in African diamonds, obtained a charter for his British South Africa Company which gave him an excuse to send "pioneers" into Rhodesia. In 1889 the gold-mining company Wernher-Beit was formed by friends of his from the diamond rush, two Jewish, naturalized Englishmen called the "Gold Bugs." By 1895, when he was forty-two, Rhodes was High Commissioner at Cape Town and had gotten his "Big Idea" of painting Africa "red" (or English).[13] The Colonial Secretary in the Conservative government was Joseph Chamberlain, a renegade Liberal who had once been destined to succeed Gladstone. Instead, Joe Chamberlain had destroyed Gladstone's party by refusing to support Irish Home Rule, and now, as a Tory, he was all for imperial unity. He and Rhodes conspired to create an incident that would make it easy for England to take over the Transvaal, to control Africa from Rhodesia to the Cape. These facts did not come out in the open for years, but they were suspected, despite Chamberlain's bland assurances that "there exists nothing which affects Mr. Rhodes' position as a man of honour."

It was precisely this kind of betrayal of the public trust that Gilbert always found appalling, a response which his detractors belittle, suggesting that he was either paranoid about politics or had a dream of a golden age when men were giants. The truth of the matter is that Gilbert at a young age saw Chamberlain destroy his hero, Gladstone, and keep the Liberal Party out of office from 1887 to 1906. This is not paranoia or fantasy; this is history.

Rhodes' and Chamberlain's plot was based on the hope that the Uitlanders, the pioneers mining the gold, would rise up against the Boers, who cannily refused them citizenship. Rhodes urged Dr. Starr Jameson, his company's agent in Bechuanaland, to ride on Pretoria with five hundred mounted police. Jameson did so on December 29, 1895, only to be ignominiously captured by Kruger, president of the Transvaal. World opinion was solidly against powerful England, in her "splendid isolation," jumping a tiny nation, but Jameson became a hero instead of a laughingstock when the Queen's imperialistic grandson, Kaiser Wilhelm II, sent Kruger a telegram of congratulations. (It is clear that the person Gilbert saw as the hero was wily old Kruger, defending his hearth.) When Rhodes was discredited, Chamberlain next sent out to the Cape Alfred Milner, another member of the old-boy network who believed passionately in the dream of "consolidating" the empire so the English could become the master race.

The final event of 1895 which meant much to England's future was the Fabian Society's founding of the London School of Economics, which became a part of the University of London. A member had left them money to help publish the serious scientific pamphlets that had grown out of their educational meetings. But Sidney Webb, the society's leading light, decided instead to use it to teach the bright young lower-class intellectuals like himself that reforming society "is no light matter and must be undertaken by experts specially trained for the purpose. ... Reform would not be brought about by shouting. What is needed is *hard thinking.*" Webb was supported in his decision by the other principal "brain" of the group, G.B. Shaw, who was just beginning to be popular as a playwright. In general the Fabians were against marching, waving red flags, and "organizing"; their aim was to "permeate" the regular parties and subtly influence their legislation. In forming this group they changed significantly: they were no longer simply one of many debating clubs, but virtually a lobby group with a permanent London base. Although Gilbert did most of his public sparring with the Fabians, there is no conclusive evidence that he was ever a member of the group.[14]

At the same time that Gilbert watched public affairs from his vantage point in London, Hilaire Belloc was at Oxford, where he was becoming an increasing influence on Gilbert's friends Bentley and Oldershaw. These two had by now decided that they were Liberals, not Socialists, and had made friends with a group of young Liberal writers who in 1896 published *Essays in Liberalism.* Belloc, who had graduated but was supporting himself as a tutor, wrote the introduction. The book restated the basic beliefs of liberalism, stressing the importance of treating the individual, not the state, as the important political unit, of broadening the middle class, of destroying the monopoly of the great landowners to restore the prosperity of the ordinary farm worker, and — one dear to Belloc's heart — of disestablishing the Church of England. Belloc also wanted Members of Parliament to be paid so that they would be independent of the party power structure.[15]

Born in France and raised a Roman Catholic, he was very anti-German; at Oxford he was almost alone in refusing to believe automatically in the innocence of the Jewish officer Dreyfus. By 1897 he had contributed his classic put-down of Oxonian intellectual postures to the *J.C.R.*, a magazine that Oldershaw had started and which Gilbert undoubtedly read. Using as his mouthpiece a fuzzy-minded, German-loving professor named Lambkin, Belloc not only attacked German philosophy and racist theories, but went after the jingoism of the popular yellow press. Although it was three or four years before they met, Gilbert was certainly aware of this clever and original man, as brave as they came, particularly since his hopes of securing a university position had been destroyed.[16]

Around 1896, when Gilbert was just getting started in publishing, the J.D.C. began increasing their social life. When they were home for weekends or vacations, they took Gilbert in tow and began going to many of the clubs and societies (like the Fabian) which flourished in London to provide entertainment and education for middle-class young adults. These groups were not all serious; they put on plays and played charades and went on picnics and held restaurant dinners, too. They were thought of as "modern" because they included both men and women.

Many of these gatherings were simply enjoyable larks. On one occasion spent with a family named MacGregor, it had been announced that Professor Pumperdinkel would speak on heathen mythology. As Mr. MacGregor, dressed for the part, began an imitation of a long, boring German lecture, there was a flash of fire, and Lucian Oldershaw appeared as the Devil to call up the gods to avenge themselves. In came Gilbert dressed as Bacchus and another young man dressed as Thor, carrying a large hammer, and they proceeded to beat up the "professor." Another time at the Moderns, "a society which debated everything in heaven and on earth at irregular intervals," Gilbert himself was supposed to speak, but he turned up late, insisting that the blame belonged to the custom of giving roads and streets irrelevant names. This house was on Church Street, but not a church could he see. He therefore began discussing "the disadvantages of nomenclature":

> If I go out of my father's house in Warwick Gardens . . . and turn to the left, I find myself in what is called High Street, Kensington. It is not high, it is quite flat, and it is a long way from Kensington. . . . It has . . . a distinguishing peculiarity. There are seven tobacconists. . . . If High Street Kensington were called the Street of Seven Sorrowful Tobacconists these deserving tradesmen would grow prosperous, their shops become landmarks. . . .

No sooner had Gilbert stopped than Cecil got the floor. He looked up at Gilbert, his head a little to one side, his eyes dancing with combative glee, and quipped, "When my brother goes out of our father's house . . . if he turns left he will not find himself in High Street. . . . That lies to the right. . . . As for the tobacconists, there are only five." Gilbert just smiled serenely at the attack.[17]

In this dramatized account, written much later by Cecil's wife Ada, there is a clear delineation of the relationship between the brothers, whether or not the quotations are exact. Both loved to play devil's advocate for the fun of arguing; both used debater's tricks. On the night of this particular match about fifty people were there, including Bentley and two others who were to be close friends of Gilbert's, Conrad Noel and Charles Masterman. All of them were young, and none of them was rich or famous — yet.

One evening in 1896 Oldershaw took Gilbert to a debating society called the I.D.K. (When asked what the name meant, the members replied mysteriously, "I Don't Know.") This group met in Bedford Park. During his hikes about London, rambling past St. Paul's School toward Kew Gardens, Gilbert had once climbed a railway bridge and spied on the far horizon "the queer artificial village of Bedford Park like a ragged red cloud of sunset."[18] He did not investigate it that day, but he remembered it later when he came visiting. He also wrote about it in *The Man Who Was Thursday*, where it is thinly disguised as Saffron Park:

> [It] lay on the sunset side of London . . . built of a bright brick throughout; its sky-line was fantastic, and even its ground plan was wild. . . . It was described with some justice as an artistic colony, though it never in any definable way produced any art. But although its pretentions to be an intellectual centre were a little vague, its pretensions to be a pleasant place were quite indisputable.[19]

Bedford Park was a "garden suburb" that bankrupted its builder, but it produced some artists, principally the poet Yeats, who was known there as "Willie" and went about in a floppy velvet bow tie, professing to believe in fairies. Gilbert remarked that it was amusing to know the "nest," or family, from which a poet like Yeats had come. He found Yeats very sound when he came out against Victorian materialism, but wrongheaded when he based his imagination upon the faddish fascination with mysticism and the occult, what Gilbert called "Asia and Evolution and the English lady."

On this particular evening, Gilbert met the family of his future wife. Lucian Oldershaw took him to Number 6, Bath Road, where a family named Blogg lived, whose younger members were officers of the I.D.K. The Bloggs were originally Huguenots whose last name had been De Blogue. Their father, a diamond merchant, had died, leaving the family poor enough so that the three girls had to work — not because they were ardent suffragettes, but because their younger brother, Knollys, was unable to support them and their mother adequately. Ethel, in whom Oldershaw was interested, was the secretary of a group of women doctors who had taken over the Royal Free Hospital, the first hospital to be staffed by women; Gertrude was Rudyard Kipling's secretary; and the oldest, Frances, was the secretary of the P.N.E.U., or Parents National Educational Union, a very advanced organization that Gilbert nicknamed the "Parents National, Highly Rational, Education Union." The three sisters all commuted by train to their jobs further east in metropolitan London. Although they were well-read and interested in the events of the day, they seem to have typified Gilbert's witty wisecrack about the women's rights movement — that "fifty million young women declared they would not be dictated to, then went out and became stenographers."

About this first visit to the Bloggs, Gilbert said, "There was no one there," meaning that he met Frances' mother, her sisters, and some other visitors, but not Frances. The next visit, however, he found himself sitting next to Frances (who was several years older than he). Looking like a small, poised, Pre-Raphaelite madonna in a somewhat typically "arty" Bedford Park gown, she calmly and coolly disagreed with everything Gilbert said. She and her sisters were all good-looking, but Frances' special appeal lay in her attitude, "which was . . . one of the paradoxes of the place. Most of the women were of the kind vaguely called emancipated, and professed some protest against male supremacy. Yet these new women would always pay to a man the extravagant compliment which no ordinary woman ever pays him, that of listening while he is talking."[20] Like the heroine of *The Man Who Was Thursday*, who represents the hero's link with everyday reality, Frances "laughed [at Gilbert] with a mixture of admiration and disapproval." Interestingly, she took him up on every whimsy, very much the way Cecil liked to do, but with a subtle difference, a result of both her sex and her firm convictions.

As secretary of the I.D.K., she refused to participate in the debates, not really liking to argue. But she was very vocal with Gilbert: she told him that she thought the moon looked like an idiot, and that she really did not like wild natural phenomena like high winds and roaring tides, which served no particular purpose. She also disclosed that she loved gardening — she would have been happy to practice farming. Oddest of all, she practiced Christianity, a behavior that "was something utterly unaccountable both to me and to the whole fussy culture in which she lived." Here in Bedford Park, where everyone liked to think of himself as a rugged individualist, Gilbert quickly saw that Frances Blogg truly was one. She had gone to an Anglo-Catholic (High-Church) convent school, and she not only continued to go to church on Sundays and feast days, but also said her prayers and read her Bible.

At their very first meeting she gave Gilbert the kind of jolt of recognition that Dante had upon seeing Beatrice: she changed his world. He tried to explain this feeling by saying that she gave him the impression that "if I had anything to do with this girl she would never deceive me: if I depended on her she would never deny me: if I loved her she would never play with me: if I trusted her she would never go back on me: if I remembered her she would never forget me."[21] Frances was such an intensely private person all her life that her reactions were not left for posterity to read. But the person she met that day was a twenty-two-year-old with "a striking figure . . . upright and with a gallant carriage. His magnificent head had a thick mane of wavy chestnut hair, inevitably rumpled. His hands were beautifully shaped, with long, slender fingers, but . . . his feet were very small . . . and never seemed to afford a stable base."[22] Here was the "Laughing Cavalier" of Fleet Street, as described by Cecil's wife and others who knew him.

53

Impressive as Gilbert was, it is equally likely that his coat was askew, his tie undone, his cuff links off, and his shoes untied — the perfect picture of someone who needed the constant attention of a good woman. This is what Frances became for him, in a way replacing his mother, who was well known for her casual "policing" of her sons. In fact, the one place where strong criticism of Gilbert breaks into the general affection that nearly everyone showed him is in regard to the "job" he gave Frances of looking after him. Not surprisingly, almost all of Gilbert's fictional heroines are patterned after Frances: they are attractive, intelligent, and "motherly" in the best sense of the word.

Gilbert's mother greatly disliked what she called the artsy-craftsy manner and costumes of Bedford Park; she also disliked its "bohemianism," an opinion in which Cecil vehemently supported her. In his chosen role as a lower-class intellectual (which contrasted oddly with his actual upbringing), Cecil stood for "reality against sham," which he translated into the duty to "call a spade a spade." In this case it seems possible that his dislike of Bedford Park stemmed from the fact that it produced the person who took Gilbert away from him. His descriptions of Frances make it clear that he did not like her very well. In his book on his brother, for example, Cecil described Frances as a great (reactionary) influence on his brother, a "lady of a type [of] which a generation of advanced culture is producing a plentiful crop — the conservative rebel against the conventions of the unconventional. Living amidst the aesthetic anarchism of Bedford Park, she was in a state of seething revolt against it."[23]

Cecil's opinion needs some correction. Certainly it was a period of great social tension. At this time both Victorian sexual manners and mores were being verbally attacked and to some extent ignored by many of the educated young, particularly the rich and well-born. But the group of Anglo-Catholics with whom Frances identified were not part of this rebellion; in fact, the evidence suggests that Cecil was probably more "unconventional," or bohemian, than Frances.

Fortunately for Gilbert, the fact that Cecil and Frances did not like each other did not stop him from spending all the time he could in Bedford Park. His continual visits did not pass unnoticed by either family, of course — and neither family was pleased by the romance. Gilbert was only making twenty-five shillings a week slaving in a publisher's office, and in their social class a woman did not work after she married; instead, she waited until her husband could support them both. Mrs. Chesterton also felt that Gilbert ought to marry a strong, hearty, games-playing girl, but he wanted a queen, not a buddy. In any case, both families had justice on their side: Gilbert, foolish about money to begin with, earned a precarious living for years, and Frances was frequently ill. But she gave Gilbert the gift which he always regarded as the most important thing in his life — Christianity. There is no reason to doubt his own testimony that it was her influence that gradually convinced him of the intellectual "rightness" of orthodoxy, as he proclaimed publicly in *The Ballad of the White Horse*, which he dedicated to her, "who brought the cross to me."[24]

While his old J.D.C. friends were finishing up their university careers with a flourish (Bentley in 1898 was president of the Oxford Union), Gilbert was already working hard at his job, wooing Frances, and writing. Most of what he wrote were serious poems, and he managed to get a few of them published, such as "The Earth's Shame" in the *Speaker* in 1897 and "To Them That Mourn" in 1898. Those with a Christian theme probably owe something to the influence of Frances and her friends, but she was very anxious that Gilbert write a novel, too, so it was now that he began what eventually became *Manalive*.[25] He was also writing a long narrative verse poem called *The Wild Knight*, which echoed the themes of both *Manalive* and *The Man Who Was Thursday*.

Early in their relationship Frances asked Gilbert to leave her out of his writing. Although his heroines all have a lot of Frances in them, he did, in his way, respect her wishes, never talking chattily about "my wife says" or describing their personal relationship in a biographical way. Publicly he showed her a kind of romantic respect that had something in common with the intellectual, somewhat formal love letters of Beatrice and Sidney Webb, as well as the delightful but perfectly proper relationship of E.C. Bentley's hero and heroine in *Trent's Last Case*.[26] The "permissive society" had been born as early as 1880, and Edward VII, who became king in 1901, represented the high-society view that one should show propriety without while enjoying promiscuity within. But for every proponent of the new morality, there were hundreds of couples like the Bentleys and the Chestertons, or the young Winston Churchills, who had relationships in which a bright, shy, handsome woman devoted all her energies to the career of her husband, who remained devoted to her.

During their long courtship and engagement, Gilbert and Frances usually saw one another in the company of other people, going in groups to debates and club meetings, to the theatre and dances on the lawn. Their real courtship was carried on in letters, most of which Frances later destroyed because she felt they were too private for anyone else ever to read. Love also made Gilbert act in a mock heroic style, one night balancing wildly on a bicycle until he fell off, another evening rescuing Frances' umbrella from a railway station by crawling up the embankment, going out on the line, and clambering up on the platform itself, all the while observed by the benign eye of the moon, "the patroness of lunatics."[27]

It was not long after this heroic effort that Gilbert hiked from the City to meet Frances during her lunch hour. They were standing on the bridge over the pond in St. James' Park when he suddenly proposed to her, afterward saying that "the bridge of St. James' Park can frighten you a good deal." He obviously drew on this experience when, in his essay on Louisa

May Alcott, he wrote, "The account of the quite sudden and quite blundering proposal, acceptance, and engagement between Jo and the German professor under the umbrella, with parcels falling off them, so to speak, every minute, is one of the really human things in literature. . . ."[28] Frances did accept him, although they both knew that neither family approved and that it would be a long time before they could afford to marry. The little bridge became symbolic, because now Gilbert had played the role of the jaunty prince in his father's toy theatre, rescuing the princess in the tower. He went home that night and wrote Frances that he had been "appointed to the post of Emperor of Creation." Although being her accepted lover had a lot to do with Gilbert's total recovery from his mental depression, it did not solve the problem of his future.

When Gilbert paid his first visit to the Bloggs after he and Frances were engaged, everyone was embarrassed. Attempting a diversion, Mrs. Blogg, a "worn but fiery little lady in a grey dress who didn't approve of catastrophic solutions to social problems," asked Gilbert how he liked her new wallpaper. Gilbert politely got up to look, then took a piece of chalk out of his pocket and drew a picture of Frances on the wall. Mrs. Blogg managed not to say a word, but had the paper cleaned before he came again. But Gilbert was not as dazed as he seemed, for he wrote Frances that "your mother would certainly have worried if you had been engaged to the Archangel Michael (who is bearing his disappointment very well). . . . How much more when you are engaged to an aimless, tactless, reckless, unbrushed, strange-hatted, opinionated scarecrow who has suddenly walked into the vacant place?"[29]

Mrs. Blogg wanted to keep the engagement a secret, which Gilbert didn't mind, since he feared his mother's blunt opinion. But since every day on his way to work he climbed the steps to Frances' office and left a poem or a note for her, she soon leaked the news to her friends. Mrs. Blogg next told poor Lucian Oldershaw, a suitor for her daughter Ethel, to try to make Gilbert more tidy. Much embarrassed, he took Gilbert away for the weekend to lecture him, whereupon Gilbert blithely assured him that since Frances had accepted him the way he was, he shouldn't change. Frances herself took on the job with more success, for there is a running joke in their letters about his looks; in one, Gilbert joked, "My boots are placed, after the fastidious London fashion, on my feet; the laces are done up; the watch is going, the hair is brushed . . . for of such is the Kingdom of Heaven."[30]

As Gilbert kept putting off making the announcement to his family, Frances became embarrassed. But Gilbert finally succeeded: he sat down one night, and as his mother made him some cocoa, he wrote her a letter. In it he said he "imagined you do not think I go down to Bedford Park every Sunday for the sake of the scenery. . . . I will not say you are sure to like Frances, for all young men say that to their mothers. . . . I should like you to find out for yourself. . . . Here you give me a cup of cocoa.

Thank you."[31] What Mrs. Chesterton said is not recorded, but it was accepted that he and Frances were officially engaged.

Gilbert and Frances were surrounded by friends their age waiting out long engagements. Bentley, for example, was engaged to the daughter of an Indian Army general; soon he began to work days at one job and moonlight at another to shorten his wait for solvency — and marriage. At that time Gilbert's own possibilities were dubious. His salary was about enough to buy his lunch and snacks and to pay for his transportation, but little else, and the future in publishing was not bright. Even his senior editor, Edward Garnett, moonlighted to make ends meet.

In the spring of 1899, when Gilbert was working days and writing nights, a tragedy struck the Blogg family: Frances' favorite sister, Gertrude, was struck and killed by a bus. Frances subsequently fell into a deep depression that threatened her religious faith. Gilbert and the others tried to pull her out of it; Gilbert finally decided that she needed a new, strong focus for her energy — him. So he bravely told his disapproving mother they must marry as soon as possible, then went to his father for advice on how to maximize his income. Unlike a wealthy upper-class father, Mr. Ed did not at once offer to provide Gilbert with a regular income, although it is possible he could have afforded to do so. Instead, he began negotiations with Gilbert's employer for a larger salary. Fisher-Unwin then wanted Gilbert to do more work, which would cut down on his free writing time, a situation he did not want and Frances disliked, for she was convinced he was meant to be a novelist.

At the same time Mr. Ed decided it would help Gilbert to have a book published, so Gilbert illustrated a silly story in verse that he had made up for one of Frances' cousins — a story about a crew of pirates who hauled a fish on deck because it was getting wet, only to throw it back when it insulted the captain. But it took over a year before a publisher was found for *Greybeards at Play* (dedicated to E. C. Bentley), and then it was close to vanity publishing, because it was put out by Gertrude's former fiancé, Brimley Johnson. It didn't do very well: the book was reviewed a little, but hardly sold at all.

This same month of October 1899, the J.D.C., now all returned to seek their fortunes in the big city, threw a formal J.D.C. dinner party (stag) in a Soho restaurant called Pinoli's; the organizer, naturally, was Lucian Oldershaw, now engaged to Ethel Blogg. All the original club members came except Bentley, who was in Paris. Gilbert sent Frances a long letter describing the event in detail, from the illustrated menus to his toast to Queen Victoria. (He said there was nothing that could be alleged against her, except that she was not a member of the J.D.C.) Fordham, the bun thrower, talked about food, education, and sex (he was married), and Langdon-Davies embarrassed Gilbert by telling how much his influence had meant when they were boys. The evening ended like a university party, with loud, happy singing and drinking.

More important to Gilbert's career than these joyful festivities was the fact that both Oldershaw and Bentley wanted to get into journalism themselves — and they were close friends of the group of young Oxford graduates who had just bought the *Speaker* to use as a political platform for liberalism. The new editor was J. L. Hammond, with whom Oldershaw was rooming at the Temple. Bentley, who was reading law, began writing articles for him at night; Belloc's friend Eccles became the new literary editor. To help Gilbert make more money so that he could get married, his friends proposed that he, too, write for the *Speaker*. Gilbert was perfectly willing to do so, but nothing he wrote was published in that paper until a full year after the suggestion was made — not until December 1900. Although Cecil's scenario links the birth of the new *Speaker* with Gilbert's brilliant debut on Fleet Street, the initials "G.K.C." did not become familiar in London until 1902. Moreover, while his friends' interest and aid were useful, Gilbert's wish to be married seems to have been the chief factor that motivated him to increase his income.

That fall of 1899 was marked by the outbreak of the Boer War, an event that did affect Gilbert's writing career, although not so quickly and dramatically as Cecil intimated in his biography.[32] Milner and Chamberlain, working hand in glove and supported by the wealth and influence of the "Gold Bugs" of the Rand, had finally provoked their "Small War." All that summer Milner had been working the old-boy network to get a favorable press for England's taking over the Boer republics. His most jingoist supporters were the Conservatives' *Times* and Harmsworth's *Morning Post*. Many young intellectuals of all parties, including Cecil Chesterton, saw the establishment of English rule across Africa as their responsibility, or the natural route of progress. Shaw and the Webbs, for example, felt that nation-states were too small to be efficient and that a world ruled by Britannia would be more systematic. After some tricky, bad-faith negotiations, Milner manipulated the Boers into issuing an ultimatum that the English used as the excuse for an attack. The war began on October 11, 1899, less than a week after the J.D.C. banquet, and the day after the first issue of the "new" *Speaker* came out — which probably explains why Cecil telescoped this time element in his brother's career by saying that the two events happened simultaneously.

The Boers knew that they were fighting for their lives and their freedom; the English gleefully expected the war to be over by Christmas. But the first battles were all won by the Boers, who took advantage of the fact that the English had not fought a big war since the Crimea, and had not yet mobilized their army. These battles read like a replay of colonial skirmishes, like the time General Braddock and young Captain Washington had their men marching in neat red columns at Fort Pitt while the Indians wisely hid among the trees. From December 7 to December 15, 1899, there were a series of disasters that the newspapers called "Black Week." By December 18 the general in charge was replaced by a Kiplingesque hero from India, Lord Roberts, who was known as "Little Bobs"; his own son soon died there in battle.

Egged on by the popular press and the telegraph, which made this a war whose every blow was written up in the daily paper, most of the English people became violently patriotic. World opinion was against the English, yet no one gave the Boers much help. Volunteers from all the empire's scattered colonies rushed to enlist. The Germans became very unpopular in England, and used the war as an excuse to double their navy, threatening England's image still more. Ultimately the war led to the reorientation of English foreign policy toward France, triggered the reorganization of the army and navy, and destroyed the whole idea of "splendid isolation."

Despite the loud cries of Harmsworth's yellow press for death and glory, a small part of the Liberal Party, maintaining the Little England position, refused to adopt the slogan "my country, right or wrong." The young men of the *Speaker* were among them. A young Liberal politician named David Lloyd George, speaking of the crime of attacking a couple of countries the size of some Welsh counties, was booed, and was labeled a "pro-Boer." It was these "pro-Boers" who were to revitalize the Liberal Party under Gladstonian principles combined with social welfare policies like those of the Fabians.[33]

It was in the midst of this public hysteria that Gilbert published his first articles as a journalist, but the articles are not about the Boer War. They are his articles about art criticism, written for his Slade friend Hodder Williams and printed in the *Bookman* — hardly material to make a man famous overnight.

Chapter Six

THE JOLLY JOURNALIST

1900-1903

> ... it was not the superficial or silly or jolly part of me that made me a journalist. On the contrary, it is such part as I have in what is serious or even solemn.
>
> G.K.C., *Autobiography*[1]

> The truth was that he insisted all his life that he was a journalist. What he meant by being a journalist was being engaged in direct democratic appeal to the reading public. ... He made his living by writing for the Press; for what he earned by that means was the backbone of his income.
>
> E.C. Bentley in his introduction to *The Selected Essays of G.K. Chesterton*[2]

THE dawn of Chesterton's writing career did coincide with the "dawn" of a new millennium, when, just because it was 1900, most of his generation felt that a new day must be coming. This hope was related to their Pro-Boer crusade, which itself helped to revitalize the Liberal Party and led to its political victory in 1906. By the time the term "Edwardian" became appropriate — on January 18, 1901, when Queen Victoria died — Chesterton was on his way to becoming a working journalist. His brother Cecil described the beginning of Chesterton's career in this way: "In the spring of 1900 everyone was asking everyone else: Who is G.K.C.? Before the year was out his name and his writing were better known than those of men who had made reputations while he was still an infant." But this observation simply isn't accurate: Chesterton was neither regularly published nor well known as a writer in London before 1902.[3]

Chesterton went at becoming a· financial success as a journalist in the hardest possible way, unlike his friend Bentley. Bentley chose to continue working as a law clerk, having passed the bar, but he also moonlighted every evening on the *Daily News*. After a day's work he would leave the Temple and walk north to Bouverie Street, where he stayed until midnight, when the paper was "put to bed"; then he walked all the way home. At

60

the *Daily News* he gained a great deal of experience because he did reporting, rewriting, headlines, and fillers. He also got a regular salary, and in a fairly short time he was able to drop law in favor of full-time newspaper work. By contrast, Chesterton was working full-time at his publishing job, and in his spare time tried to write poems, worked on at least one novel, and tried to sell articles to papers like the *Speaker*. The Arts section, however, was being edited by one of Belloc's Oxford Republicans named Eccles, who decided that Chesterton's handwriting looked Jewish and so refused to read anything he wrote. Bentley has described that same, very unusual handwriting as having a certain "grotesque shapeliness."

Chesterton worked hard: a typical day might include "reading an MS called 'The Lepers' (light comedy) . . . coming home . . . writing the Novel til 11, then writing [Frances] and going to bed." What kept him going was Frances herself. As he wrote her,

> Last of all comes the real life. . . . For half-an-hour he writes words upon a scrap of paper . . . that are not picked and chosen . . . but words in which the soul's blood pours out . . . his passion and longing, all his queer religion, his dark and dreadful gratitude to God. . . . And he knows that if he sticks it down and puts a stamp on it and drops it into the mouth of a little red goblin at the corner of the street . . . all this soliloquy will be poured into the soul of one wise and beautiful lady.[4]

Cecil Chesterton, meanwhile, had left St. Paul's School in 1898 and, having qualified as a surveyor, entered the family real-estate business. He worked in it for a year or so, but by 1900 he had quit to try his luck as a reporter, too. He had already tagged along after Chesterton to many odd clubs and debatings halls, where he quickly insisted on being an active participant. The two became involved with the Pharos Club; they also attended meetings of the Moderns, where Cecil first met Ada Jones, a very emancipated woman reporter fifteen years his senior who wrote under the masculine pen name of John Keith Prothero. She first acted as a kind of comrade and mother confessor to Cecil, but eventually she married him.

Frances and her friends like Charles Masterman and Conrad Noel, both members of the Christian Social Union, were introducing Gilbert to Christianity, but by 1900 Cecil had left him far behind to plunge headlong into Anglo-Catholicism. Its appeal for Cecil seems to have been a combination of its intellectual "certainty" and its "Socialist" activism, manifested primarily in the Christian Social Union. Started in 1889, the Christian Social Union was made up of members of the Church of England, both clergy and laymen, who were Anglo-Catholic. They shared a High-Church interest in the historic, apostolic orders, the sacraments, and the ritual observances that had come from the Oxford Movement of the mid-nineteenth century. By now they were beginning to attract non-church members and to call themselves "liberal Catholics." The union was established to reconcile traditional Christianity with Socialist proposals concerning poverty, universal education, and the inequities of the class structure, but it was never Marxist. Its most famous leader was Bishop Charles Gore; other well-known men were Canon Scott Holland and Percy Dearmer, in whose church Cecil was confirmed.

Both Cecil and Gilbert Chesterton probably first met Conrad Noel at a meeting of the Fabian Society, where Cecil had been going regularly. There he came under the influence of one of its founders, Hubert Bland, the Roman Catholic journalist married to E. Nesbit, who wrote children's books. The Blands ran a perpetual salon at their home to which anyone could go; there Bland was surrounded by his young female admirers, and his wife was the focus of attentive young men. By 1901, when he was just twenty-two, Cecil Chesterton had formally joined both the Fabian Society and the Christian Social Union; but there is no real evidence that his brother paid much attention to the Fabians or was ever confirmed in the Church of England.[5]

More important for Chesterton's own religious development was the fact that both he and Frances liked Conrad Noel. Noel was one of several curates at St. Mary Magdalene, Paddington Green. The grandson of a peer, he had a striking face and dark curly hair; in his novel *Manalive* Chesterton used him as the model for his radical young minister, who wears "his hair like a pianist and behaves like an intoxicated person." Noel was famous for his weird costumes, which were a peculiar mixture of the dress of High-Church cleric, bohemian, and guttersnipe. Even when he was dressed appropriately he liked to wear a furry cap that Chesterton said made him look like a rat catcher. His long-suffering wife was used to finding that she had strange guests at all hours. But Noel was not merely odd; in debate both Chestertons had noticed that it was Noel who "got up and applied to the wandering discussion at least some sort of test of some sort of truth." Noel alone showed all the advantages of having been tolerably trained in "some sort of system of thinking."[6] These young men also ran into one another in strange places, such as the Theosophic Society, where they heard preached as "new" the same Unitarian-Socialist ideals that Stopford Brooke had preached in Bloomsbury in the 1880's. When someone said that the world needed love, Noel answered that "love" needed doctrinal definition, which he proceeded to give in orthodox Christian terms.

During that same summer of 1900, Hilaire Belloc had moved to London with his Irish-American wife, Elodie. They already had a number of small children, and Belloc had found it impossible to support them adequately doing tutoring and free-lance writing in Oxford. He therefore came to the hub of the journalistic and literary world, taking a house in Chelsea near the Thames. Although their mutual friends Bentley and Oldershaw had undoubtedly talked about them to one another, Belloc and Chesterton probably did not meet before the end of 1900. This can be assumed partly because all the accounts of their first meeting include Belloc saying, "You wr-rite ver-ry well, Chester-ton." Since Chesterton did not sell any articles on a regular basis to the *Speaker* (or other papers) before December 1900, Belloc could hardly have made this comment before then.

The tide of the Boer War was turning in England's favor as the lessons of Black Week were learned, and a bigger and more modern army was assembled. In October 1900 the Conservatives took advantage of the victories won by Lord Roberts, which made it look as if the war were nearly over, and called an election, known as the Khaki Election for that reason. The election was close, despite the fact that public excitement had risen as Ladysmith and Mafeking were relieved, and Pretoria was captured and the old Boer president Kruger sent into exile. The Pro-Boers' protests, whether political or evangelical, reflected a popular concern that was reminiscent of liberalism under Gladstone in his prime.[7] There was dissatisfaction with the prime minister's about-face: he had begun the war insisting, "We want no gold, we want no territory," only to annex the Transvaal and allow the Rand mines to reopen to finance the rest of the war.[8] There was concern, too, because so many soldiers pulled off the city streets in industrial areas were physically unfit for service, a concern that was aggravated by the hostility Europe had shown.

Lucian Oldershaw got Chesterton personally involved in the Khaki Election by taking him along to help a Liberal candidate put out an election newspaper. Chesterton had so many good ideas that their paper came out the day after the election, which their candidate fortunately won; he had a marvelous time canvassing and going to drink at the local pub to bait the Tories. That October the *Speaker*, which editorially supported the classic Liberal position that both war and empire were immoral, also published a poem by Chesterton called "An Election Echo." In it he prophetically suggested that the last laugh about the election results would be had by the Liberal Party, out of power for nearly a generation. His instincts were sound, for during 1901 the Boers turned to guerrilla warfare and made the war drag on for two more long, miserable years; one major reason the Boers finally did sue for peace was the secret suggestion that the Liberals might win the next election and grant them their independence.

Mr. Ed, meanwhile, had decided to pay for the publication of Chesterton's second book, a poetic drama called *The Wild Knight*. He felt that having another book published would help build his son's literary reputation. *The Wild Knight* duly appeared in November 1900, only a month after his first book, *Greybeards at Play*. Bentley remarked that he used to wonder what the bookish world that got hold of both books made of the fact that they were written by the same person. He added that a "part of the reading public never did understand that Chesterton's work was written by someone who was passionately in earnest about his ideas, but also had an enormous, original sense of humor."[9] Many critics still are bemused by this seeming paradox, just as Cecil was when he protested against his brother "playing the buffoon."

Commentary made about these two books typifies all later criticism of Chesterton's work. *Greybeards at Play*, an early example of his satiric verse for which he is much admired today, was scarcely noticed. *The Wild Knight* attracted considerable attention, but sold badly; critical comment then (and now) is divided between those who think it to be one of his most carefully crafted creations and those who dismiss it as unreadable.[10] The book contains several poems that were to be forever identified with Chesterton, particularly "The Donkey," which haunted him all his life and still turns up in anthologies; and "By the Babe Unborn," with its plaintive line: "They should not hear a word from me/Of selfishness or scorn/If only I could find the door/If only I were born."[11] Most of these poems clearly reflected the influence of the poets Chesterton had admired as a teenager, especially Swinburne, Browning, and Whitman. In a kind note to Brimley Johnson, who had sent him a copy of the book, Rudyard Kipling said that Chesterton showed promise, but then suggested he needed to be careful of "using other poets' special words — in this case, of borrowing Swinburne's "aureoles."[12] Although both books sold badly, *The Wild Knight* and *Greybeards at Play* helped to put Chesterton's name before the editors who could give him work.

It is interesting to look at *The Wild Knight* as the prototype of all of Chesterton's serious writing. It not only has a strong structural resemblance and thematic relationship to his later prose play, *Magic*, as well as to his novel *The Man Who Was Thursday*; it is also related to *Heretics* and *Orthodoxy*. It is melodrama, like the toy-theatre productions, with cardboard characters and stage scenery, but it is also an example of what has been called Chesterton's religious imagination, which "seeks to interpret the many signs of a sacramental universe through which God speaks to man," as well as a "connected system of surprises in the nature of reality — the inner division and unity of things."[13] In simpler terms, this long narrative poem-play states for the first time Chesterton's basic affirmation of existence as he saw it *before* he called himself a Christian. Its villain is very like his fellow student at the Slade, and the hero is a ramshackle knight urged on by the strong-minded heroine. Cecil was to declare that this play was his brother's first attack on the Establishment, which he then defended when he wrote *Heretics*. This is an involved way of saying that as Chesterton became more convinced of the rational truth of Christian doctrine, he found in it increasing support for his instinctive need for balance. In one sense, he attacked the Establishment all his life, but he learned to see it in more places and under different disguises, among friends as well as so-called enemies. Chesterton was always playing ombudsman to the world more than he was lobbying for a single cause.

Sales of *The Wild Knight* had not been good, despite Mr. Ed's suggestions to the publisher. Finally, realizing that his gifted son simply could not be trusted to remember elementary details or to handle his own contracts, let alone act to sell his wares, Mr. Ed arranged for his literary affairs to be handled by one of London's first literary agents, A. P. Watt, whose firm still handles Chesterton's literary estate today.

At this time Chesterton was meeting more and more people involved in the literary world of London, but most of them were other struggling young writers and reporters like himself. W. R. Titterton was one of the people who began to pop in and out of his life, meeting him first at the Pharos Club, and developing what amounted to a lifelong crush on Chesterton, whom he characterized as a "wise child."[14] Titterton himself might have been called a rather aggressive child, but he did understand one fact very well: to make Chesterton happy, all he had to do was praise Cecil and Frances.

Late in 1900 Chesterton got his first assignments from the *Speaker* in his own domain: art and literature. This was an era when editors and journalists were known to their reading public by their initials — Robert Louis Stevenson was called "R.L.S.," for example. It was on articles about Saint Francis of Assisi and William Morris that "G.K.C." first appeared in print. (These essays were later published in book form in *Twelve Types*.) The articles were written in Chesterton's adult style, distinguished by his humor and the upside-down look at the world that he called "paradox"; he comes across as genial and appreciative, a cross between a prophet and a clown who willingly plays the fool to make his point. It is this stylistic technique that has led to his being called "a metaphysical jester," but it was not his style alone. It owes less in both form and content to Oscar Wilde than it does to Shaw, whose characters all talk in this fashion.[15]

In the article on Saint Francis, whose asceticism seemed so wrong to the twentieth century, Chesterton turned the tables by saying that what seems like fun in one historical period often seems gloomy and wrong to another. He suggested that future historians will write,

> in the dark days of Queen Victoria young men at Oxford and Cambridge were subjected to a horrible sort of religious torture. They were forbidden ... to indulge in wine or tobacco during certain arbitrarily fixed periods, before certain brutal fights and festivals. Bigots insisted on their rising at unearthly hours and running violently around fields.[16]

In the article on William Morris (whom he has been accused of imitating), Chesterton struck the note that became his trademark: a hope for the present that was *not* a wish to return to the past of a pre-industrial world. He appreciated Morris's love of beauty in ordinary objects, but saw that Morris "made no account of the unexplored and explosive possibilities of human nature"; he "sought to reform modern life, but hated it." To Morris, "Modern London is a beast. ... But unless the poet can love this fabulous monster as he is ... he cannot change the beast into the fairy prince." For this reason, Chesterton said, Morris "was not honestly a child of the 19th Century."[17]

Also demonstrating Chesterton's original charm and common sense is his first group of essays, published in book form by Brimley Johnson in 1901 with the title *The Defendant*. In them he daringly defends all kinds of popular culture against the highbrows, as well as attacks the philosophic mood of "grey-green pessimism," which he hopes is not "the greyness of death but the greyness of dawn," appropriate to a new century. He defends slang, babies, nonsense, rash vows, and detective stories, and makes this observation:

> The cause which is blocking all progress today is the subtle scepticism which whispers in a million ears that things are not good enough to be worth improving. If the world is good we are revolutionaries, if the world is evil we must be conservative. These essays ... seek to remind men that things must be loved first and improved afterwards. ... A Defendant is chiefly required when worldlings despise the world....[18]

This statement not only represents a true picture of his subsequent career, but also explains why all his life Chesterton saw himself called to be a defendant — at one moment a revolutionary; at another, a reactionary. Both positions for him were different sides of one coin, which was a sense of obligation for the gift of the world.

Chesterton's first meeting with Hilaire Belloc became a legend, one that Chesterton himself helped along. The original creator of the legend was Cecil, who wrote that, after they met, Belloc overwhelmed Chesterton and added him to his disciples, teaching him all he ever knew about history, politics, and Roman Catholicism. This statement is really truer about Belloc's effect on Cecil Chesterton; it is too simple and inaccurate a picture of the relationship of Gilbert and Belloc. Bentley, Oldershaw, and Eccles all claimed they made the introduction and possibly, since all three were working for the *Speaker*, they all *were* there. But it seems most likely that it was Oldershaw who brought Chesterton along to a small restaurant in Soho that had become "a haunt for three or four of us who held strong but unfashionable views about the South African War. ... Most of us were writing on the *Speaker*."[19]

Belloc was near a newspaper stand, where he was stuffing his pockets with his favorite reading: French Nationalist and atheist newspapers. He was wearing his "public costume" of formal dark suit and hard straw hat, his shoulders held high and his long chin thrust out belligerently like Napoleon's. (Chesterton had always liked to draw cartoons of Gladstone's famous profile; now he also became well known for drawing heads of Napoleon on everything around him.) Belloc told Chesterton that he wrote very well, another interesting comment in view of the fact that he later admitted he had read very little that Chesterton wrote; then they all went inside the Mont Blanc and ordered a bottle of Moulin a Vent burgundy and began to talk. Or rather, Belloc talked and Chesterton listened; Chesterton was never the sort of person to take charge of the conversation and carry on a monologue.

At this time Belloc was about thirty and Chesterton only twenty-six, but it was not age that gave Belloc an advantage — it was his personality. He was an intense, brooding, brilliant, and opinionated talker. Raised both a Radical and a Roman Catholic, he felt an underdog's urge to fight, and he seemed "foreign" in many ways. He was still a French citizen; the fact that his close university friends had almost all been impeccably upper middle-class probably emphasized his feelings of being a second-class citizen. Chesterton, on the other hand, never developed this "sour grapes" attitude, perhaps because his university friends had been both his friends and his admirers before they left for school. Besides, from all accounts of him, Chesterton was never that self-conscious about what others thought of him.

Chesterton was a good listener, and Belloc liked that, so he talked at length about some of his favorite topics, such as whether King John had been the best English king, finally working his way to the subject of the Boer War, which he saw as a typical example of international Jewish financiers manipulating nations to do their will. There was some truth in his opinion, but it is unlikely that this particular concern "converted" Chesterton, since, as a convinced Little Englander, he was already against the idea of imperialism.[20] His Gladstonian liberalism, which stood for nationhood and local patriotism, was something he whimsically claimed he had learned from Kensington (or Notting Hill). The person whom Belloc did ultimately convince was Cecil Chesterton, who now was a fire-breathing Fabian Imperialist like Shaw, supporting the war with great enthusiasm as a part of his own fight against his family background with its "Gladstonian ghosts." Chesterton and Belloc, however, found that they did agree on being Pro-Boers, and liked one another for it.

Most of the tendency to lump Chesterton and Belloc into one animal — humorously nicknamed "the Chesterbelloc" by Shaw — comes from assuming that they met and spent the following thirty-five years standing together in one place. What is said or thought about one is said or thought about the other as a matter of course, as if they did not have separate identities which affected how they viewed both the world and their fellowmen.[21] Biographers of Chesterton have assumed that he was the disciple, and biographers of Belloc, that he had the whip hand.[22] But, although they came to be seen as "twin" Roman Catholic apologists, it was not Belloc who converted Chesterton; in fact, he publicly stated his belief that Chesterton would never make a good Catholic, and tried to stop him from becoming one. Recently, however, their "togetherness" has begun to be examined more closely, and the popular misconception shown up, as it is in the introduction to *Mr. Chesterton Comes to Tea:*

Many of his contemporaries dismissed Chesterton as a boy who never grew up, contrasting him with the worldly, knowledgeable and much-traveled Belloc. This estimate now seems utterly mistaken. More than forty years after Chesterton's death we can with the benefit of distance see clearly that Belloc, the "man of the world" with his strange feuds and dogmatic propaganda, was the immature if lovable schoolboy, while his friend who apparently had his head in the clouds was blessed with the kind of instinctive wisdom which enabled him to discern the nature of reality. Not that Chesterton would have minded being compared to a child.[23]

A part of the reason why Chesterton is assumed to be the child and Belloc the leader is that, as Chesterton often pointed out, pessimism is usually considered more "adult" than hopefulness. What the two shared was a fondness for discussion and argument, parties, writing satiric verse, and — ultimately — for Western civilization, which they both labeled "Christendom."[24]

During the winter of 1900 Chesterton found that he and Belloc were "brothers in arms" because they both belonged to a "minority of a minority" who were Pro-Boer but hated most of the other Pro-Boers because they were pacifists. Unlike them, Chesterton identified with the Boers themselves, who were taking to horses and rifle, followed in the field by their wives and children in the covered wagons of pioneers, determined to fight for their own small country the way he knew he would fight for "one small block of little lighted shops" in Kensington. With this unorthodox approach, Chesterton was trying to take the picture the English had of the Boers and turn it upside-down, to make them see themselves in a similar light and stop being glamorized by jingoist calls for "empire."

When the old queen died in January 1901, she was mourned by almost everyone, including Chesterton, who admired her "housewifely qualities, her stamina, and her common sense." He shared the nervous anticipation of his contemporaries about the dawn of a new century and a new reign, because, unlike their parent's generation, these new "Edwardians" sensed they would have to live in a scientific universe supported by industrialism, without being sure any longer that all change was progress. Their "mood was sombre," a mixture of nostalgia for what was past and of apprehension for what was to come.[25] Some historians now argue that the reign of Victoria's son Edward VII was a continuation of hers, and the drastic break in politics and the arts which mark the "modern" world came in 1910. Still others insist on 1914 as the great divide between Victorian and modern times. But people like Chesterton living during that era were able to perceive both the breaks and the continuity, both of which seemed more momentous at the time than they do in retrospect.

As a literary period, this short "Edwardian" interval had a character all its own; it is during this era that Chesterton became famous, and within whose boundaries his career is best understood. Its writers were concerned with the state of society, but not interested in "literary" revolutions. With a kind of religious enthusiasm they saw their work as a part of the public scene, not an exploration of private worlds in a universe without street lamps. As a writer Chesterton must be drawn against this particular land-scape, with its inescapable similarities to our own; his work reflects its moral conviction that literature is not so much an agent of change as a reflection of it, influenced by its spirit. He and his contemporaries were all building utopias which were meant to deal with the present but which reflected their own immediate but idealized pasts.[26] In Chesterton's case this was not the old medieval days and ways he is so often accused of loving, but the Dickensian mid-Victorian world of the Radical-Liberal. The Edwardian writer's typical role as activist in public affairs also helps to define Chesterton's own concept of himself as an artist.

His posture was very common on Fleet Street, for this was a time when the press reached the height of its influence on public affairs, and every editor and every paper stood clearly for a particular social and political outlook.[27] The highly successful ones were Harmsworth of the *Daily Mail* and later of the *Times*, Garvin of the *Observer*, and A. G. Gardiner of the *Daily News*. The era later was called the "Golden Age" of newspapers, when the editors acted as "the consciences, the partners, and the antagonists of the politicians," and they were so well known to their public they needed only to use their initials. This period ended before the First World War and the postwar growth of syndicates and mass marketing.[28]

Very shortly after the death of the queen, Chesterton had begun to write book reviews for the *Daily News* on a regular basis. This paper's first editor had been Charles Dickens himself, a fact no successor was allowed to forget, and during the latter half of Victoria's reign it was a strongly Radical-Liberal paper that supported the anti-slave trade cause, the North in the U.S. Civil War, Italian unification, and the campaign against privilege and monopoly in land. It even lectured Gladstone when he was not following the correct Liberal line. But by 1900 it was being edited by a Liberal Imperialist who had helped to widen the division in the Liberal Party by making a hero of Joseph Chamberlain and agreeing that the Boer War was necessary to make the world safe for the British empire. Although many old-time Whig landlords had followed Chamberlain out of the party over Irish Home Rule (which threatened their land monopoly), there were still many rich, Liberal industrialists with strongly Evangelical views, pacifists or Pro-Boers. Since the *Daily News* was in financial trouble, some of them decided to buy it.[29]

This takeover of the *Daily News* was engineered early in 1900 by a young Welsh M. P. named David Lloyd George. One member of the new board was a birthright Quaker, George Cadbury, whose family fortune came from making chocolate. This "new" *Daily News* now gave daily death tolls for the

Boer civilians shut up by the English in concentration camps. Until 1901 its editor was R. C. Lehman, who hired, among others, Belloc, Bentley, and Chesterton as staff writers. Chesterton chiefly wrote book reviews, and this steady work, combined with his articles for the *Speaker*, promised enough income for him to quit his publishing job and get married — a goal he had been working toward for two full years.

In the *Speaker* of May 26, 1901, Chesterton wrote his most famous attack on imperialism in the article called "A Defence of Patriotism," which was clearly a reflection of the growing horror of the Boer civilian deaths and other atrocities; it also decried the fact that the "little war" was lasting forever and killing many Englishmen. In the article Chesterton made this now well-known observation:

> My country, right or wrong, is a thing no patriot would think of saying, except in a desperate case. It is like saying 'my mother, drunk or sober.' No doubt if a decent man's mother took to drink he would share her troubles to the last; but to talk as if he would be in a state of gay indifference as to whether his mother took to drink or not is certainly not the language of men. ... What have we done and where have we wandered, we that have produced poets who would walk with Dante, that we should talk as if we have never done anything more intelligent than found colonies and kick niggers?[30]

Cecil claimed that this was the article that made his brother famous, but if it really did so, it was probably later that year, when the article appeared in *The Defendant*. Its real importance lay in the fact that it was read by a young provincial editor named A. G. Gardiner. When he became the editor of the *Daily News* in 1902, he gave Chesterton his regular weekly column or "Saturday pulpit," which made him a household word in London.[31] In the meantime, since Chesterton was making about 120 pounds a year, he and Frances were married on June 28, 1901, by their friend Conrad Noel at St. Mary Abbots, the Kensington parish church.

From first to last their wedding day was a comedy of errors, much laughed about and recounted by their friends and families, which has given rise to numerous psychological innuendos about their sexual relationship. The basic charge, which can be neither proved nor disproved — since Frances herself ordered the destruction of most of their letters and the love poems Chesterton wrote her, and neither of them was the type to kiss and tell — is that he was physically immature and a totally inadequate lover for his frigid wife.[32] So far as can be determined now, the charge originally came from some things that Cecil told his wife, Ada, who repeated them with embellishments in her book about the brothers.[33] These represent one version of the details of their wedding night, with the inferences drawn from them; the tales also seize on the fact that Chesterton did mature slowly, and was called "a child" by his contemporaries. The issue is clouded in the same way as the issue of Chesterton's alleged homosexuality. Who is to decide when "latent" characteristics can be used to label someone; how much are these efforts at reading back into events and actions a connotation completely unrelated to the time in which they actually occurred? There is no solid information about the Chesterton's sex life except that they remained happily married for over twenty-five years, and that Frances did have an operation specifically to make it possible for her to get pregnant, an operation which failed to produce the desired results.[34]

What remains verifiable are the family stories about the silly things that happened that day. As best man Lucian Oldershaw managed to get Gilbert to the church on time, though he was wearing no tie and still had the price tag on his new shoes. Guests noticed that the brothers were unnaturally peaceful during the reception, not arguing at all, which probably meant they were both greatly moved. Next poor Oldershaw, as the man in charge, took the luggage and put it on the train bound for Ipswich that Gilbert and Frances were to catch, but it went without the honeymooners.

Chesterton had stopped twice on the way to the station, once to buy a gun and some cartridges to "protect his wife from the pirates doubtless infesting the Norfolk Broads"; and the second time to buy Frances a glass of milk at the dairy bar "under the sign of the white cow," where his mother had always taken him. (He saw this cow as a close and friendly relative of his beloved symbol of the white horse.) Very much later they caught a slow train to Ipswich and were driven to the White Horse Inn, whose very image Chesterton saw as a "fitting ceremonial to unite the two great relations of a man's life . . . at the beginning of my new journey and . . . at the end."[35] Once they had arrived at the inn, Chesterton realized that Frances was exhausted, as well she might be, and persuaded her to have a glass of wine and lie down to rest. He then went for a walk and got lost, a typically Chestertonian end to the day.

Whatever the Freudians wish to make of Chesterton's completely characteristic absent-mindedness, as well as the straws in the wind which pointed to a "revolution" in sexual morality among the Establishment, by birth and education both Gilbert and Frances clearly belonged to the circumspect, bourgeois middle class, as did most of their friends. Sex was a private affair, and they did not approve of the "double standard." Women before marriage were princesses on pedestals, and after marriage became the matriarchal rulers of their homes; Englishmen from boyhood had a tendency to get away from feminine domination by getting together at school, the university, clubs, and Parliament. This idea of society is faithfully preserved in the popular literature of the day and is reflected in Chesterton's own novels, in which the heroines are more adult than their boyish lovers, witty, practical, loyal, and chaste. They inspire love and admiration, and very often they are acknowledged to have excellent brains, but they never try to be "as good as a man" or in the thick of the action. Often, however, they precipitate the action of the novel by providing the concern that becomes the crusade. In contemporary terms, then, Chesterton was very decidedly sexist: he knew the two sexes were different, and he insisted that the superior sex was the female one.

His ideas about women were formed by his own home life, first with his mother, and then with his wife. He was also influenced by literature, and apart from the work of Shaw and Ibsen, both of whose world views he disagreed with, there were not many examples of "new women." His wife had worked before their marriage at a hard, drudging, boring occupation, purely to earn money. Chesterton could not see that such a role had suited her more than being his wife; it was when one was too poor that one could not afford the pleasure of "being domestic." Frances basically shared his opinion: she always considered Gilbert "her job," although she also helped out with illnesses and crises in her family and his, invited nieces and nephews to their home for extended visits, and wrote poetry published in a number of periodicals. Although Hrances is not a role model for feminists, she was also Chesterton's chief critic and a real partner in his work, as well as the person who "ordered the beer and sausages [or] . . . built the studio . . . in a meadow at Beaconsfield."[36] Some observers felt that Chesterton took terrible advantage of her, while others thought that she manipulated him; in fact, there was a sense in which it was possible to divide their acquaintances in two camps: those for Frances and those against her. To a certain extent, then, her job was a thankless one; her husband was probably loved and admired for the very qualities she had to keep under control.

A very similar marriage of the same period is detailed in Soames' recent portrait of Winston and Clementine Churchill.[37] The more "modern" kind of marriage was being developed by couples like Beatrice and Sidney Webb and Leonard and Virginia Woolf. In these relationships the women depended on their husbands to devote much of their own career time to supporting or enhancing their brilliant but unstable personalities.[38]

About this time Chesterton happily and proudly called himself a "journalist," although Bentley wryly commented that he was only a journalist "if you made the scope of the term far wider than normal, for . . . [he] chose his own subjects and dealt with them in his own way under his own signature, writing them at home or wherever else he chose; often he dealt with them in a manner that was extremely distasteful to large numbers of his paper's public." Bentley added that Chesterton was in love with the idea of Fleet Street reborn as "Grub Street," where a group of "erratic, brilliant, and untidy men who were always hard up and never sorry for themselves made the world go round."[39] Bentley himself was on his way to becoming one of the most respected editors on Fleet Street, so his comments point up Chesterton's unique position as a writer far better than Chesterton's own impish remark that his success came from taking the advice to study a particular paper and to slant materials toward it, and then doing the exact opposite.

By 1901 Chesterton was a familiar sight on Fleet Street, especially after his wife conceived the brilliant idea of covering up his untidyness with a voluminous cloak and a slouch hat, so that he looked like "Falstaff in a brigand's costume" and was a cartoonist's delight. The suggestion that he (and Frances) deliberately devised this outfit to publicize him ignores the fact that, apart from young Charles Masterman, no one on Fleet Street matched Chesterton for sheer messiness, unless it was Cecil. It was also a commonplace among writers to wear this kind of trademark costume: Shaw had his red beard and jaeger suits; Yeats, his floppy velvet bows; and Bland, his monocle and spats.[40]

Chesterton was often seen sitting in a bar, a glass of wine at his elbow, writing and laughing to himself. When he was finished writing he might hail a cab to drive him 200 yards to the *Daily News*; or he might stand, oblivious of traffic, in the middle of the street, thinking. At any time he was delighted to catch sight of a friend, though when he had a long piece of writing to do he sought out a place that was peaceful and quiet, like the British Museum's reading room.

At first Gilbert and Frances lived right around the corner from his parents in a small Georgian house they rented from a friend of the Bloggs, with a garden wall on which Chesterton helpfully drew a crayon mural of knights and ladies to delight the owner when he came home. (When he was asked what kind of wallpaper he wanted, Chesterton had replied brown paper, so he could draw on it.) Chesterton often wandered home to engage Cecil in a friendly argument, and once a week the young couple paid a formal visit, during which Chesterton had to look at the scrapbook of his clippings that Mr. Ed was keeping. Bored by this role, Chesterton doodled all over them. All his life he was to upset family and friends by his refusal to take his work seriously. If someone offered to read his poetry aloud, he was known to seize the book and sit on it; he refused to recite a line of it, and actually hated to have friends read his writing in his presence. Asked to autograph a copy of *Orthodoxy*, he solemnly inscribed it "Bosh, by G.K. Chesterton."[41]

Cecil's newest Fleet Street comrade was Ada Jones, who at thirty-six was the epitome of the emancipated female.[42] Since the age of sixteen she had been supporting herself, and various members of her family, by working as a free-lance reporter and pulp novelist. She was one of very few women working as a journalist at the time, and her favorite role, although she was very feminine in looks and dress, was to be one of the boys; Chesterton teasingly called her "the queen of Fleet Street." In her own way she was as single-minded and obstinate as Cecil, and they both enjoyed the news-paper world's atmosphere of dormitory larks and parties.

They also soon discovered that they shared an enthusiasm for the cutthroat struggle to scoop other reporters, the feeling that every man's hand was against them; but Chesterton had early confessed to Frances that he hated that part of his chosen trade. Fortunately for him, his innate originality as a writer was soon recognized, giving him the scope to develop his talents and demonstrate his versatility without concentrating on competition. If this hadn't happened, Chesterton, like Bentley, might have spent his life in an office getting out a paper, much as he had spent six years in a publisher's office getting other people's books published. Rather than being asked to follow precisely the editorial party line, Chesterton was left free to develop into one of the outstanding "Edwardian Evangelists," preaching a gospel in the costume of a "capering humorist ... who will defend or attack anything," but underneath the dazzling manner remaining a very serious-minded commentator on the scene.

Chesterton very much enjoyed having his own hearth and home and entertaining friends. Some of the Christian Socialists, like Conrad Noel and Charles Masterman, the young, brilliant, untidy journalist who was about to blossom into a politician, helped Gilbert realize that there was no real freedom in being "free" from creeds of the past. He recognized that idealistic theists and pragmatic atheists had much in common: both were bleating sheep looking for a shepherd. In addition, through the actions of his beloved younger brother and the daily example of his wife, both practicing Christianity in a formal, traditional way, he saw acted out before him the kind of personal parable to which he was always acutely sensitive. But there were other influences at work, for, as he later explained, his opinions were more influenced by the "heretics" than by the "orthodox."

Perhaps the most literary "heretic" Chesterton debated was George Bernard Shaw. Like his friendship with Belloc, his friendship with Shaw has been confused by myths. Both Chesterton and Shaw agreed that by 1901 they had heard about each other, but they were not instant friends, as Cecil's story suggests; their actual friendship grew slowly over the next five years or so.[43] It is true that Chesterton published an article on "The Position of Sir Walter Scott" in the *Daily News* on August 10, 1901, an article that Shaw read and wrote about to Chesterton, asking him who he was. But Shaw also recalled that he never heard from Chesterton, who was either "too shy or too lazy to answer." He added, confusingly, that "the next thing I remember is his lunching with us ... accompanied by Belloc."[44] There is no way of dating this intimate lunch, but other evidence suggests that it happened much later, perhaps in 1906 or 1907. In the meantime, the Chesterton whom Shaw got to know well was Cecil.

By 1901 both Cecil and Conrad Noel had formally joined the Fabian Society, a ceremony that Bertrand Russell declared to be much like initiation into some esoteric religion. For Cecil, part of the society's charm lay in the fact that its leaders were rebelling against their parents' ideals, convinced that individualism was wasteful and that society must be run "collectively" by superior civil servants. Shaw and the others also had broken with the Radical Liberals to support the Boer War, because of what Shaw called "the inefficiency of leaving stray little States lying about in the way of great powers," while Beatrice Webb disliked "Gladstonian sentimental Christianity." Having begun in the 1880's with the mission of civilizing darkest England, the Fabians now proposed to civilize darkest Africa — once again offering a kind of secular salvation to the world's poor.[45] Although there is no official record that Gilbert Chesterton ever joined the society, it is very likely that Cecil often talked about it to his brother, using Fabian arguments in debate.[46]

By the winter of 1901 the young Chestertons had moved to Overstrand Mansions, an apartment block in Battersea on the south bank of the Thames. Battersea was a popular, inexpensive area for young professionals who needed to be near the center of London. As a way — doubtless futile — of reminding Gilbert of their engagements and his assignments, Frances put up a huge bulletin board in the living room with the heading "Lest We Forget." Belloc, who lived north across the Thames on Cheyne Walk, contributed a poem to it, which ran, "Frances and Gilbert have a little flat/At eighty pounds a year, and cheap at that."

Chesterton was obviously happy as a married man. In one of his essays in *The Defendant*, he defended the "rash vow" of marriage by saying that "it is the nature of love to bind itself and the institution of marriage merely paid the average man the compliment of taking him at his word."[47] He argued in another that Shaw's hero in *Candida* is a fool because he hates to have his lady love peel potatoes, instead of seeing that those potatoes are the very stuff of romance.

The Chestertons became friendly with other young couples in the same building, chiefly the Rann Kennedys and the Saxon Mills; Mills was a Liberal imperialist with whom Chesterton would cheerfully argue for hours. They also became better acquainted with the Belloc children, who loved to have Chesterton come and do puppet shows for them. Elodie Belloc, like Frances, seems not to have cared much for her husband's taste for masculine parties, and even found his aristocratic English friends snobbish by her Irish-American standards, but the Chestertons and the Bellocs got along well.

It was through the Bellocs that Chesterton and his wife met Maurice Baring, who became a lasting friend of theirs. (He is the third person in the portrait by Sir James Gunn in the National Portrait Gallery.) Baring was the younger son of a lord whose family fortune was made in banking. His uncle was a member of Queen Victoria's official household, and he had grown up in upper-class luxury — taught by governesses and sent to Eton and Cambridge, where his father decided to make him a diplomat because he won prizes in French. (Baring had already met Bentley, Oldershaw, and Belloc at Oxford, where he had been tutored in math in order to pass the diplomatic examination.) His family was multi-lingual, well-read, and very eccentric in an English way; Baring himself acted all his life like an overgrown child, throwing parties where pats of butter were tossed at the ceiling, or entertaining his company by balancing a wineglass on his head.

Predictably, Baring was a very casual young attaché; he often sent the wrong telegrams to embassies. By 1901 he was out of the corps and back in London, living in an apartment on Lord North Street in Westminster with an underground passage to Parliament. He was starting a new career as a journalist, and was soon off to cover the Russo-Japanese War; his dispatches were more about Russia, which he loved, than about fighting. When he was in London he continued to give uproarious parties.[48]

Baring had been raised a Liberal, and, having shed his Church-of-England upbringing "with his first teeth," he was gradually being converted to Roman Catholicism by a gentlemanly priest at the Brompton Oratory. Probably for these reasons as well as many others, the friendship between him and Chesterton always meant a great deal to both men. But, as is the case with Chesterton's relationship to both Belloc and Shaw, it is difficult to give the friendship its full due without adding to the legend of triangular fellowship that the Gunn portrait inspired. (This itself is ironic, for the painter almost never had all three men sitting at once.) It plays upon the connection later taken to be the prime one — that they all eventually became Roman Catholic — without examining in any real way the differences among them, or recognizing the fact that their friendships did not form an equilateral triangle.[49] Perhaps more important for understanding how Chesterton arrived where he did is the simple fact that he had many friends; he was never the sole close friend of one person — the only possible exception being the period when he and Bentley had "worn one hat, smoked one cigar."

As his career grew, Chesterton began to learn the economic advantages of the fact that everything a writer had sold once could be sold again. He wrote to his agent, A. P. Watt, to thank him for demanding and getting a good price for work that he did for the fun of it; through his help Chesterton's columns were now regularly being published in books. The first, *The Defendant*, had appeared in December 1901; the second, which was made up of articles from both the *Daily News* and the *Speaker*, came out in October 1902 with the title *Twelve Types*. The twelve were all writers like Jane Austen and Sir Walter Scott, and in each case Chesterton showed his flair for saying something novel about a well-known author. But he simultaneously demonstrated his characteristically slapdash scholarship, which made this book full of misquotations — a flaw that critics both then and now consider the result of sheer, unadulterated laziness.

His basic literary technique was to be a reviewer rather than a scholarly critic, even one who "set out to break all the rules." His essays gave him a chance to comment on the world about him, to share his insights and express his own enthusiasms and concerns. He was also a subtle, well-read person, so he is usually forgiven for his flaws of documentation and for his inability to seriously "stick to the point"; critics still conclude that his understanding is superbly brilliant, eminently worth reading. Some, like his brother Cecil, like to try to prove that Chesterton could only write well about authors he identified with, like Dickens or Stevenson; others are more inclined to accuse him of "medievalism" or "catholicism" when they do not agree with his view of the present. But considering the sheer bulk of what he wrote and the fact that fashions in both literary and historical criticism change, it is a point in his favor that it is hard to write him off completely.

One hallmark of his writing is his refusal to "disenfranchise" his ances-tors, by which he meant that what is newest is not necessarily best, with the obvious corollary that there might be something to be said for a method unlike the current one. In his essay on Scott he insists that the fact that Scott is an uneven writer does not make him a bad one, especially compared to modern writers, who "have learned to arrange their effects carefully so that the only point in which we fall short is in the . . . misfortune that we have nothing particular to arrange."[50] He adds that Scott is considered too long because modern readers have a "consuming desire to get it over . . . [but] he arranged his colossal introductions just as an architect plans great gates and long approaches to a really large house . . . He did not wish to swallow a story like a pill [to do him] . . . good afterwards."[51]

Just as Chesterton was increasing his public, the political scene was beginning to change. The mopping-up operations of the Boer War had run into the twin problems of guerrilla warfare and the internment camps, and the Liberals were busy publicizing them in hopes of getting in office again. At the same time Milner, the civilian head of the British government in South Africa, was determined to "win the war" on terms that would let him reorganize all of southern Africa the way Bismarck had "centralized" Germany. When a settlement was reached at last on May 31, 1902, the Boers agreed to lay down their arms and become British subjects, hoping that in the not-too-distant future they might win more constitutional free-dom from a Liberal government. But in England itself many Pro-Boers were appalled by the peace terms; Kipling's old aunt hung a black flag out of her window and was nearly lynched.

During this last phase of the war, the Quaker George Cadbury had accepted the moral responsibility of becoming sole owner (and financial supporter) of the *Daily News*. He saw this role as a sacred Liberal mission to save the paper "to promote the welfare of the masses," and he did not expect the paper to make him money. He took control in early 1902, and shortly afterwards, on March 3, 1902, there appeared another "new" *Daily News* on the London streets, with a young new editor from the provinces: A. G. Gardiner.[52] At thirty-six, he was less than ten years older than Ches-terton and his friends. He had grown up in a lower middle-class family with a drunken and often unemployed father and a pious mother who kept the family going. He had left school at fourteen to be articled to a journalist, had married young, and was a provincial editor by the age of twenty-three.

To Gardiner, journalism was primarily public service, not a career. Like a good Liberal, he was against landed privilege, monopoly, and the established church. Although he did drink occasionally, he also stood with the Cadbury family for temperance reform. He was a staunch Little Englander who thought imperialism was a senseless distraction — a kind of bread and circuses of the upper classes — used to keep the country from solving its crucial domestic problems in agriculture and industry; he also saw imperialism as an "affront to international morality." As a result, he had a deep-seated mistrust of the young Liberal-Imperialist politicians like Asquith, Grey, and Haldane, but he was a great admirer of the self-made Welsh orator Lloyd George. Gardiner wanted to pay the Members of Parliament and thus free them to vote their consciences and allow poor men to run; he was committed to the idea of more and better educational opportunities for the voting public. Clearly, he and Chesterton not only would see eye to eye on political and social issues, but also would be important influences on one another.

In a town in which the biggest papers were all Tory, the *Daily News* was considered the official Liberal organ, but its Pro-Boer stance had kept advertisers and readers away, and its circulation had dropped to a low 30,000. Gardiner solved this problem by putting out a paper with a new look: new type, new features, and an expanded literary section. Then he hired a talented group of younger writers — Bentley, Masterman, Belloc, Massingham, Hammond, and Chesterton himself — and managed their divers personalities easily with his relaxed, very open manner.[53]

Beginning about July 1902, Chesterton, having served his writing apprenticeship over the past several years, took off like a huge balloon and sailed up over the heads of his contemporaries, so that everyone in London did start asking themselves, "Who is G.K.C.?" His fame was due in large measure to Gardiner, to whom Chesterton therefore would feel a deep sense of loyalty. Gardiner himself wrote several columns for his paper, and in one of them he described Chesterton as "an extravagant figure in every sense, who with his colossal frame, pince-nez, and great waves of hair surging from under his soft, wide-brimmed hat, was ... undoubtedly the most conspicuous figure in the landscape of literary London." He said that he admired Chesterton for his spirit, his lack of self-consciousness, and his humanity, as well as for his versatility: "You may tap any subject you like, he will find a theme on which to hang all the mystery of time and eternity."[54]

Gardiner's portrait of Chesterton has remained one of the pleasanter forms of the Chesterton legend. Nevertheless, though he was a close personal friend and associate of Chesterton's for a number of years, he, too, was guilty of thinking of Chesterton as a talented, delightful child, when events were to show that Chesterton was at least as good a judge of men as

Gardiner. Of course Chesterton was idealistic, but he was far less removed from ordinary life than he seemed to be. But he was certainly absent-minded; particularly as a working journalist Chesterton did not have the reliability to match his charm. The entire *Daily News* staff worried every Friday afternoon until his weekly copy finally arrived, and it never came the same way twice in a row. Chesterton would scribble it on any kind of paper — including wallpaper — and he would "walk it" there, or send it by messenger or cab, which might arrive with or without him. If Chesterton took a cab he frequently had no money, so the staff had to pay the driver.

Since Chesterton was only one of the group of Gardiner's young hope-fuls working together on the newly reconstituted paper, it was an exagger-ation to say that Chesterton alone was "striking a new note . . . of pugnacity and [writing] like a political leader with his eye on the division lobby" — that role was the one played by H. W. Massingham, the Parliamentary reporter. It also is not really true that in his weekly column Chesterton was "preaching war, drink and Catholicism . . . to peaceful semi-Tolstoyian Non-conformists."[55] On the contrary, Chesterton was one with the others, shar-ing their concern about the cause of social justice and arguing only about the best means to obtain it. Like most young reformers (or utopians) these Liberals originally thought that they were only trying to restore a lost liberty, rather than mounting the barricades for revolution. Like the Liberal Party itself, none of them had a positive, clearly defined program, but were united by opposition to Conservative programs or the means used to achieve them.

By 1902, however, Chesterton had "arrived" as a literary lion. A clear sign was that John Morley, both a writer and a senior member of the Liberal Party's establishment, asked Chesterton to write the biography of Robert Browning for the series "English Men of Letters." With the publication of that book — his fifth — in 1903, Chesterton belonged both to journalism and to literature as his times understood both terms. Far from making his name writing about the Boer War, Chesterton became a regular part of the literary scene just as the war was ending and the Liberals were about to regain office for the first time since he was a boy.

79

Chapter Seven

THE PARADOXICAL HERETIC
1904-1905

Literature is a certain attitude or atmosphere, like religion or philosophy. . . . Books are things like boots . . . more important than good literature . . . in the same serious sense that the daily paper is more important . . . because citizenship must be more important than art.

G.K. Chesterton, "On Books,"
the *Morning Post*, October 18, 1906[1]

"**I** have never taken my books seriously; but I take my opinions quite seriously," said Chesterton in his *Autobiography*, confounding or confirming his critics, who based much of their literary judgment of his work upon this single statement.[2] They would have understood Chesterton if they had recognized that his career as a writer was established during a period when many important writers saw their purpose the way he always did: to be reporters on the real world, writing about things that mattered then and there, using their art for that cause. Wells, Shaw, Bennett, Galsworthy — all saw themselves as involved with and influencing events. This is what Cecil Chesterton meant when he talked about his brother being "first and foremost a propagandist," and being proud of it. Later, when the fair dawn of a new era had become a tempest-tossed morning, both his contemporaries and younger writers who had not shared the euphoria of the liberal's sunrise called Chesterton either a fool or a teller of fairy tales. But hindsight written as history does not describe his literary career. It is better to see him as he was — bulking larger and larger against a particular backdrop, the secret of his particular charm lying in his use of paradox, which developed from his instinctive effort to maintain a balance, rational and realistic, in a period full of extravagant emotional reactions.

As a writer Chesterton was always more of a debater than a philosopher. He took a statement that sounded contradictory to fact or common sense and showed it was true, or the reverse; in both cases he stood the world on its head to get its proportions right. It is not very probable that he was consciously using an intellectual system like Nietzsche's; it is more likely that Shaw, who was the new rage of literary and political London, was the one influenced by German philosophy, and that Chesterton instinctively chose to fight Shaw (and Cecil, who agreed with Shaw) with his own weapons.[3]

To be a writer on Fleet Street then was to be both commentator on and participant in the political scene, no matter what one wrote — "art," "finance," or "politics." Among those working there, an open freemasonry existed. The newspapers themselves were influential in determining opinion, and this power created the "romance" and "comradeship" that everyone, including Chesterton, enjoyed. But he was also quite capable of putting in hours of work alone, or with a secretary; he also was never the kind of workhorse he described nostalgically in *A Miscellany of Men* when he said,

> Nothing looks more neat and regular than a newspaper ... [but] nothing ... goes every night through more agonies of adventure, more hairsbreadth escapes, desperate expedients, crucial councils, random compromises, or barely averted catastrophes. Seen from the outside, it seems to come round as automatically as the clock and as silently as the dawn. Seen from the inside, it gives all its organizers a gasp of relief every morning to see that it has come out at all.[4]

Here Chesterton is really describing Bentley's life as a journalist. He put together a daily column of news briefs, wrote editorials, read contributions and cut them to fit the space, and did an occasional interview, staying at work until morning when the paper finally came out.

Both Chesterton and Bentley became writers at a time when concepts about writing and writers were still vague in many ways, and the line was very loosely drawn between "men of letters" and reporters. The difference between a staff reporter and a free-lance was also vague, because most writers did both. In addition, nearly all of them regarded writing itself — literature and journalism — as having a moral purpose, not an aesthetic one.

At that time a change occurred that seemed to point up the social significance of the press: for the first time since Gladstone's government had fallen in the 1880's, being a Liberal meant something again. The reaction against the Conservatives' programs and its leaders was growing so fast that everyone felt the rising tide of voter dissatisfaction that was to lead to the great Liberal landslide of 1906. Predictably, Chesterton gloried in the change. But his brother seriously misrepresented his message and method of delivery when he later insisted that "while most writers ... retain their root point of view all through their lives, while they continue to modify their mode of expression ... Chesterton ... has almost wholly outgrown the opinions which were his when he first emerged into notice, but his method of conveying them has hardly varied by a hair's breadth."[5]

To make his point, Cecil tried to show that his brother had once been a Socialist-Imperialist like Shaw and him (although the bulk of the evidence shows that Chesterton only talked about being a Socialist), and then attempted to prove in 1908 that Chesterton was a Bolingbroke Tory. The truth is that as late as 1913, at a *New Witness* conference, Chesterton was declaring that while he might not longer be an "official Liberal," he was still a Liberal, noting that "it is the other people who are not."[6] He made the same declaration much later at Glasgow University in 1925. From the standpoint of classic nineteenth-century liberalism, he was quite correct. It was really his brother Cecil who gave up his childhood liberalism to swear allegiance to Fabianism, only to become a "Tory Democrat," a Conservative position once personified by Lord Randolph Churchill.

During this period, when liberalism had almost as many meanings as there were Liberals but still provided a useful umbrella of strong political and social purpose, the attitudes that informed Chesterton's personal variety were basically those his parents had taught him. These included an overriding concern for individual freedom, combined with an atypical refusal to become a part of the governing Establishment, and a strong bias toward making a hero, not a pensioner, of the poor. This last part of the Chestertonian creed probably came straight from its chief Victorian source, Charles Dickens, who was also a lasting influence on the Socialists of the day. A reader of Dickens found it hard to feel superior to the remarkable characters Dickens had created, and he absorbed more than a little of Dickens' dislike for the exploitative upper classes. This kind of Dickensian liberalism, combined with the feeling of worth with which the Chestertons imbued their children, seems to have kept Gilbert Chesterton from joining the coteries like the Fabians, the occultists, and the movers and shakers of the political scene. Instead, disillusionment with practicing liberalism made Chesterton turn an emotional political "creed" into his version of the Christian religion. Unlike his younger brother, who as a child experienced neither guilt nor loss, Chesterton did not rebel against the stable elements in a world in which he had experienced both; he simply transformed those elements when he lost confidence in pragmatic politics and politicians.

In the immediate post-Boer War period, a number of contradictory factors made it possible for the Liberals to regain power. Lord Rosebery, an eccentric aristocrat married to a Rothschild heiress, withdrew from politics, leaving the control of the party to Sir Henry Campbell-Bannerman. Like Chesterton, he had been a strong Pro-Boer. The Conservative Party, ignoring the maverick Joe Chamberlain, had passed the prime ministership from uncle to son, both members of the Cecil clan, which had been powerful since Tudor times. This act helped feed Chesterton's suspicions that English politics was a chummy family affair. By 1903 Chamberlain had split the Conservatives with his proposal of tariff reform, advocating protection for imperial goods, which was against the Liberal idea of free trade with everyone; and soon he left politics to his sons Austen and Neville. Two other

Conservative bills helped to unify the Liberals because they, too, defied the old Radical-Liberal stance by establishing state control over two areas which Chesterton saw as inalienably private and personal: the education of children and the right to drink.

The first bill was the Education Bill of 1902, which a Fabian historian, Ensor, called one of the two or three greatest measures of the twentieth century.[7] It represented an effort to create a state school system of both primary and secondary education. It abolished independent school boards, but it also included the Church of England and Roman Catholic parochial schools inside the state system, giving financial control of these schools to elected county councils. The Fabians were good at "taking over" these councils as a part of their effort to establish a collectivist state run by enlightened bureaucrats.[8] At the same time the bill saved these parochial schools from bankruptcy and forced Nonconformist parents to send their children to those schools if there were no others in their area. The parents were not only taxed to support these schools, but Nonconformist teachers were often barred from teaching in them. This bill alone turned a vague feeling of fellowship between Nonconformists and the Liberal Party into an active alliance.[9]

Chesterton had always favored the Disestablishment of the Church of England in Wales (heavily Noncomformist), and he supported their right to educate their own children in their own ways. But he was also aghast at Nonconformist tendencies to see a Popish plot in the bill.[10] Chesterton's basic position was simple and had a Rousseau-like sound. The education of the young was the right of their parents, and neither the state nor any alien sectarian group should be in charge of a child against his parents' will. He therefore supported the Liberal effort to change the bill, and later denounced his own Liberal Party for failing to reform it.

In the spring of 1904, the Conservatives also passed their Licensing Act. Its purpose was to reimburse the owners of public houses whose licenses had been suspended in 1891 in an effort to cut down on the number of pubs. Liberal Nonconformists were in favor of any bill limiting the sale of liquor, while Liberals like Chesterton were against the monopoly of the big liquor companies. Chesterton felt the right to associate with other men in a local public house was exactly like the right of a lord to belong to — and drink in — his private club. For this reason he supported the Liberal position against the bill, which controlled licensing hours, the availability of liquor, and the monopoly of its sales, but he did not support the Nonconformist stand for teetotalism. It was this stand, as well as Cecil's later description of him as a "wine-drinking Catholic writing for a Nonconformist paper" and his public debates with Shaw, who was a teetotaler, that permanently smudged his reputation, making him appear to be a rolling drunk always on a gargantuan debauch.[11]

Meanwhile, during 1902, his new friend Belloc had published *The Path to Rome*, a Stevensonian travel book about a hike he had made across France. In it Belloc gave his personal recapitulation of the romantic idea of a Europe where "once all we Europeans understood each other." Chesterton did come to accept his basic thesis: that Rome is the font of European civilization. At the same time, Belloc himself suffered from a sense of a divided heritage utterly unlike Chesterton's rooted Englishness. As a member of a religious minority, Belloc felt like one of the oppressed, but he also disliked the clannish snobbery and political inertia of the upper middle-class English Catholics. In that sense Belloc was a "marginal" Englishman, but when he went to France, the country of his birth, his John Bullishness and (Dr.) Johnsonian manner made him seem English. The crowning irony was that his writing was little read in France, while Chesterton's work was not only read but admired.[12]

Although he had a growing family to support, Belloc had decided to run for Parliament as a Liberal (M.P.'s were unpaid). Perhaps he hoped to become a Cabinet minister or obtain, via this route, a paid position in government. But it was largely through his subsequent career as a typical Liberal "obstructionist" that Cecil and Gilbert Chesterton saw the workings of Party government. It is entirely incorrect, however, to say that in 1903 either Belloc or Chesterton was disillusioned by liberalism and retreating to his own "medieval" world of imperial popes and craft guilds. Like their friends and colleagues on Fleet Street, they both thought the millennium was on its way, when the enemies of privilege would defeat the old guard, in a Revolution without the "R," and build a New Jerusalem in England's green and pleasant land. Unfortunately, every one of them had a different floor plan for the building.

During the period of 1902 to 1906, the single most important influence on Chesterton's thinking was his editor, A.G. Gardiner of the *Daily News*. If Chesterton had not reflected Gardiner's editorial position, he would have lost his job there sooner than he did. Under Gardiner the *Daily News* was near the top in a fiercely competitive market. Its audience was the wide, hard-to-define "suburban classes whose self-regard and dedication to self-improvement set the tone for the era." To compete with the yellow press of Alfred Harmsworth, who was reaping a fortune using advertising to sell market "entertainment," the *Daily News* "wore a look of dignity . . . consonant with its sense of purpose [though] the impression . . . was one of vitality."[13]

Gardiner pushed for political measures, using the paper to produce a spirit of social reform. He saw his own role as keeping in touch with the Liberal leadership like Campbell-Bannerman and the younger group more oriented toward "social welfare" — people like Asquith, Grey, and Haldane; he also wanted to reach young rising stars like Winston Churchill and David Lloyd George. Like Chesterton, Gardiner was in favor of Welsh disestablishment, ending plural voting, better housing legislation, free public education, and reforms in the poor law, in prisons, and in land-holding rules, especially the rule of primogeniture.[14] Many of these basic tenets, although afterward adopted by both Fabian Socialists and Conservatives, are pure "distributism." For example, one of Gardiner's most strongly held convictions had been documented about this time by J.L. Hammond of the *Speaker*, who, like Chesterton, had come to work for the *Daily News*. This was the idea that the problems of their late industrial society, with its appalling urban poor, were the result of the systematic "exclusion" of small landowners from the land. Hammond's thesis was that enclosures of the eighteenth and nineteenth century had created urban slums, the drop in real wages, the loss of ordinary men's "quality of life," and a decline in agricultural productivity. For an answer Gardiner resurrected the old Liberal slogan as a rallying cry — "Three Acres and A Cow" — for everyman.[15]

The greatest area of potential disagreement between Chesterton and Gardiner lay in Gardiner's admiration for Bismarckian Germany. Chesterton did not want social welfare measures to be carried out by either Shavian supermen or Wellsian samurai; he mistrusted both German philosophy and the arts. Gardiner, on the other hand, was another "Evangelical" reformer who had secularized his childhood piety to push for moderate state intervention, armed with facts and figures like a Fabian tract. Unlike the Fabians, however, Gardiner was strongly in favor of trade unions, and, like Chesterton, supported any cause which allowed the worker to be his own master. Both men adopted the classic Liberal stance that they must be free to criticize their own party when it failed to live up to its promises.

The growing Liberal consensus made for very strange comrades in arms. Gardiner and Chesterton both shared many ideals with another Liberal journalist, H.W. Massingham, who was Gardiner's Parliamentary reporter. Massingham had been raised a Radical by a Methodist father, but had given up religion in favor of Stopford Brooke's variety of socialism, joining the Fabians during the 1890's and becoming a great friend of Shaw. He quit an editorship, however, rather than support the Boer War. Although he had a strong distaste for dogma and party organization, Massingham considered anyone who disagreed with him an enemy, and never had any instinct, as Chesterton did, for seeking a middle ground.

As the leading Liberal editor, Gardiner had to ride herd on a wild variety of prima donnas, from Chesterton, with his strongly developed sense of humor and charming but annoying absent-mindedness, to rigid in-fighters like Massingham and Belloc, to developing politicians like Hammond and Charles Masterman. His combination of writers was rich but unstable, like the Liberal Party they all belonged to, but during these halcyon days before their party took office, they only had common enemies, like Harmsworth and the Conservatives.

By this time Chesterton had decided that the Fabian Socialists were elitists. Many of them were governmental insiders who made good use of knowing the ropes of county and municipal bureaucracies, and had a characteristically English instinct for upward social and educational mobility, which he always mistrusted. In contrast to their programs (detailed for him by Cecil, among others), Chesterton's creed became that of a kind of anti-intellectual intellectual, unimpressed by the sophistry that ends did not matter if "good" was being done.

It was about March 1903 when Chesterton "made" his Fleet Street name by gaily and publicly crossing swords with one of the Socialist old guard, Robert Blatchford. He was the editor of the *Clarion*, one of many small newspapers then afloat, and author of *Merrie England*, the pamphlet that had converted Cecil to socialism. Chesterton became famous as much for the way in which he conducted their debate as for what he actually said, because their discussion wove in and out of the columns of the *Daily News*, the *Clarion*, and several other papers, involved other writers like Conrad Noel, and ended up in a pamphlet called *The Religious Doubts of Democracy*, published near the end of 1903.

Many of Chesterton's arguments sounded like clever verbal tricks, but the real irony of the debate was that while Blatchford said that socialism must be a religion, he mistrusted his fellow Fabians as fact-oriented intellectuals.[16] By contrast, Chesterton for the first time publicly used "liberalism" as "orthodoxy," making use of the Anglo-Catholic arguments of his wife and friends in the Christian Social Union. While they argued about politics and economics, both men shared certain ethical presuppositions about the universe and human nature which were never clearly articulated. Observers felt that Chesterton "won" because he got their discussion on a more rational basis, but he insisted that he was "defending a . . . plain matter of . . . human morals."[17]

The first Blatchford-Chesterton "debate" was about free will. Chesterton's basic method was to attack Blatchford's lack of ordinary common sense, saying that it was impracticable for a man to act before he was clear about his theory of action. He next reduced Blatchford's argument for determinism to absurdity. He told Blatchford not to thunder from his pulpit that a man could not be blamed for anything, because such reasoning should stop a person "in the act of saying 'Thank you' to somebody for passing the mustard." He should not praise a man for passing the mustard if he couldn't help but pass it! He cleverly suggested that Blatchford liked determinism because of the unjust social system that made him "so anxious to forgive that he denied the need of forgiveness."[18] Later in the debate Chesterton was publicly asked four questions which he answered in his *Daily News* column, stating them in his inimitable style:

Are you a Christian? *Certainly.*

What do you mean by the word Christianity? *A belief that a certain human*

being whom we call Christ stood to a certain superhuman being whom we call God in
a certain unique transcendental relationship which we call sonship.
What do you believe? *A considerable number of things. That Mr. Blatchford is an*
honest man. . . . And [less firmly] that there is a place called Japan. . . . I believe a
large number of other mystical dogmas, ranging from the mystical dogma that man is
the image of God to the mystical dogma that all men are equal and that babies should
not be strangled.
Why do you believe it? *Because I perceive life to be logical and workable with these*
beliefs and illogical and unworkable without them.[19]

Chesterton's "Christianity" as stated here is almost a recapitulation of
his position in *Heretics*, published in 1905. Paradoxically, in defending liberalism he found he was defending Christianity, and vice versa — although
he was talking about a rational way of life, not a faith, because he had not
yet subscribed to many creedal elements of Christianity. But this did mark
the beginning of the time when he gave the public a grandstand seat to
watch the stages of his "conversion." The final stage came when he concluded that the Christian Church down through the ages had always managed to keep its balance in a world gone mad, a historical fact that he
thought proved its "supernatural" origin.

One of the reasons why his contemporaries and successors have often
felt like relegating Chesterton to a medieval backwater is that he now
developed a fondness for using theological terms in what they thought of
as ethical situations. This "contrariness" in his use of terminology was what
he was referring to when he said that he owed his success as a journalist
to writing the "wrong" item for the "right" paper. By using terms upside-
down, he made his readers think about what he — and they — were really
saying. At the same time, his predilection for kidding contrasted sharply
with the earnest, Evangelical approach of many of his fellow writers. As
members of the Christian Social Union, he, Cecil, Conrad Noel, Masterman,
and others all took on the duty of lecturing serious-minded audiences. But
one night Chesterton was overcome with mirth when Canon Holland told
his law-abiding audience that he assumed most of them had never been in
jail. In response Chesterton wrote this jesting verse:

I understood him to remark . . .
That half a dozen of his friends
Had never been in quod.
He said he was a Socialist himself,
And so was God.[20]

It was this slightly "tipsy" humor of his that appealed to many readers but
led to misunderstandings about his positions on serious affairs.

In May 1903 Chesterton's first full-length literary biography — about
Robert Browning — was also published. He had written it in the "poor

man's university," the reading room at the British Museum, where deathly silence was the rule; typically, Chesterton drew cartoons to communicate with other scholars. The book instantly won him wide recognition for the brilliant originality of his insights into Browning, but brickbats for his incredibly sloppy lack of detailed scholarship and his breezy, journalistic style.[21]

Chesterton's way of conveying the effect that an author had on him was to sit down and write about him from memory, because ". . . that is what literature is for; it ought to be part of a man."[22] He quoted Browning's poetry from memory and got whole lines wrong, even inventing a line that Browning never wrote. He also illustrated the difference between Browning and Tennyson by translating a Browning passage into Tennysonese and one from Tennyson into Browning-like verse. Even his proofs were covered with whimsical Chestertonian doodles. When the senior editor at Macmillan's found thirteen misquotations on a single page, he predicted disaster.

He was wrong. *Robert Browning* was a fantastic success, reprinted for years; it is still one of Chesterton's best books, as well as a good introduction to the poet. Its very success, in fact, began the debate about whether Chesterton should become a "man of letters" or a "journalist." Like most of his own generation, Chesterton chose to do both at once, risking the epitaph of the "master who wrote no masterpiece."

He developed his own method for writing about another author in *Robert Browning*. He discussed life, literature, and his own ideas about both, gave a few hard facts, provided no dates — but still summed up Browning with justice and panache. He showed that Browning was not a metaphysical philosopher, understandable only to the elite, but a poet for everyone to read. One of the novel points he made was that Browning had a love for the ugly and grotesque, which often tell a story better than the static perfection of a work of art. He also told the story of Browning, the Liberal, and of Mrs. Browning, to whom he gave credit for being not only a fine poet, but also a keen, intelligent observer of her political world. Chesterton admitted that he could identify easily with Browning, who also had grown up in an urban, middle-class London family and had gone to the university there; he suggested this affinity when he said, "If any of us are truly optimistic and believe . . . as Browning did that existence has a value wholly inexpressible we are most truly compelled to that sentiment not by any argument. . . but by a gesture, an old song, a portrait . . ."; in other words, by the bits and pieces of real life.[23]

As a direct result of this "inept" biography, Chesterton was asked in 1904 to accept the newly established professorship of English literature at Birmingham University, one of the nineteenth century's "red-brick universities," modeled upon his alma mater. Since his formal lecturing skills were never highly regarded, it is undoubtedly just as well that he did not try to become a Sir Walter Raleigh or a Professor Ker, but it is interesting to realize that he might have met the young Tolkien had he not preferred to remain a London journalist.

Just before *Robert Browning* came out, Shaw's *Man and Superman* opened in London at the Court Theatre. It was a huge success, thanks to the actor-producer Harley Granville Barker. Shaw was doing well: he had finally made a stable marriage that provided him with a steady income and an upper middle-class lifestyle, and his plays had become very popular. In them, as an apt pupil of Ibsen and Nietzsche, Shaw was dramatizing his Fabian ideas about the destiny of the human race, while his "new woman" was now the personification of his mystic "life force."[24] Although they were not yet linked in the public mind as debaters, Chesterton's philosophy of life was a dramatic contrast to Shaw's "superman" idea. Since both Cecil Chesterton and Conrad Noel had recently become full members of the Fabian Society, Chesterton heard Shavian ideas not only in the theatre, but at home, which gave him a chance to practice his arguments against them.

Chesterton's second biographical study was published a year later in 1904, in the series called the Popular Library of Art. (The growth of a literate public, eager to read and become cultivated, much like our world is eager for self-help books, made these series bestsellers.) This book was a portrait of a still-living painter named G.F. Watts; when his wife read him the book, he declared it was a true and grand judgment of his work. Chesterton's thesis about Watts was that he was born into the nineteenth century, which was self-conscious, and believed itself to be an idea and an atmosphere. Watts sought to mirror his age; he knew that to enjoy life means to take it seriously, that art must not be divorced from ordinary life. Since these sentiments sound very much like Chesterton's own approach, the book is clearly a tribute to the Victorians, whom he claimed as some of those ancestors he did not wish to disenfranchise.

The book also gave Chesterton a chance to tangle publicly with the art "schools" of his Slade days, especially the "art for art's sake" movement he had hated. He presented his own theory of art: that art is a separate language which in its own sphere functions like a language made of words. With art, an artist can draw diagrams and blueprints, preach, or write poems, never using art as a symbol of other symbols, but as a method of making contact with reality. It has been pointed out that in his own fiction Chesterton uses his painter's eye, drawing in lurid, murky, highly visual backgrounds, setting his scenes with a vividly artistic vocabulary — even using his stories to talk about the relationship between art and society.[25]

Although no one now has ever heard of G.F. Watts, the book was highly regarded when it appeared; it illustrates graphically the paradoxical problem of the academic evaluation of Chesterton's work. Many contemporary commentators refuse to consider his popular audience, or his "quaint" idea that the effect art has on the general reader is more important than its survival as a piece of academic equipment. Chesterton clearly wrote in the pre-Eliot period, although Eliot himself paid him graceful tribute on more than one occasion, and himself reflects the ideas of a generation reared on Chesterton. Chesterton's appreciation, his insights, his way of turning his subject upside down to make him stand out clearly — all these are techniques that work but that do not carry the kind of intellectual "clout" that extensive documentation and jargon do. Apart from the references to his own time, there is really nothing Chesterton wrote that cannot be understood today by the ordinary reader, provided he enjoys Chesterton's style. In terms of intellectual respectability, it is also true that "no other writer of this century has been able to elucidate the central ideas of major writers with such clarity and wit, or to place these ideas so clearly against the broadest perspectives of their cultural backgrounds. . . . A reader might do worse than to use [his] essays as a first guide through English literature."[26]

Chesterton's first published novel also appeared in 1904. It is *The Napoleon of Notting Hill*, a pseudo-adventure story for boys without a single woman character in it (proving to some how immature the author was). Its basic theme is the one he proposed in an article, "The Patriotic Idea," published in a collection edited by Lucian Oldershaw. There he wrote, "The patriot never under any circumstances boasts of the largeness of his country but always . . . of the smallness of it."[27] This book reflected Chesterton's political creed, but it also showed an ironic, upside-down world, reversing the scientific utopias of H.G. Wells in which brave new worlds are run by machines and Shavian supermen. Typically, the themes of Chesterton's fiction and poetry are clever satiric echoes of current literary fashions; one depicts a utopia of the past, another an invasion, another a detective who thinks but does not detect, still another a Dostoyevskian fool playing a Shavian superman.

The Napoleon of Notting Hill catches today's reader by surprise not only because it opens in 1984, but because Chesterton was such a good prophet. He saw that empires wax and wane and never provide the kind of local, democratic loyalty men need, and he foresaw that the socialist state would end not with Orwell's Big Brother, but with drabness and boredom. He dedicated the book to Hilaire Belloc, with whom he shared a passionate love of particular places.

In plot and setting the novel is based upon Chesterton's Kensington childhood, a time when he had dreamed about the Campden Hill waterworks and played at knights with a wooden sword and helmet. Brooding over the Boer War, he had come to see that the Progressives wanted to destroy the very places he particularly wanted to preserve. They formed a picture in his mind, where "there was a row of shops. At one end was a public-house . . . somewhere a church. . . . There was a grocer's . . . a second-hand bookshop . . . an old curiosity shop . . . shops supplying all the spiritual and bodily needs of men. . . ." Chesterton said that he realized suddenly "how completely lost this bit of Notting Hill was in the modern world"; his Progressive friends, he said, were only interested in "world-shaking . . . and making events." At that point he discovered that he opposed plutocrats and idealists, "and I drew my sword — in defence of Notting Hill."[28]

Characteristically, Chesterton told this story to his journalist friend Titterton in answer to a question about what had been his greatest temptation. It was a religious question, not a social one — but Chesterton answered it in a social way, showing how the two categories continually overlapped in his own mind. His temptation to sin was to be a part of the "movers and shakers," the power structure, the Establishment, those who "only wanted to do Big Things." It was local patriotism that made him a "populist."

Like Shaw in his plays, Chesterton was trying to create a medium through which he could get his ideas across, letting his "ideas dressed as characters" debate with the other ideas of the time. A born storyteller, he created his own form, a clever, original combination of vivid, mood-setting descriptions of place, wildly romantic and coincidental plots, and Shavian characters who spoke dialogue that Shaw early recognized was very suited to drama. In his best works, Chesterton's style has been called "good-humored Kafka."[29]

The plot of *Napoleon* is an elaborate joke that turns sour. It begins in a drab London where the king is now elected by lottery from the civil service. By chance, however, the newly elected official is Auberon Quin, physically like the cartoonist Max Beerbohm, who is a joker. Quin proceeds to order the dull "socialist" city neighborhoods like Bayswater or Pimlico to build city walls, adopt coats of arms, and raise militia and dress them and their rulers in elaborate medieval costumes, just as if London were becoming a nest of small Italian city-states. Most of the officials loath the costumes and the ceremonies, but one young leader, Adam Wayne, takes the whole prank seriously. When a highway is proposed which would cut through Notting Hill, Wayne calls out his militia to defend itself, captures the waterworks on Campden Hill, and defeats his enemies by threatening to flood London. He becomes their conqueror, a Napoleon, until the other neighborhoods unite against him and destroy his empire.

Typically, Chesterton gives the idea of "pacifism" short shrift, but he also dismisses the kind of imperialism Wayne's excessive patriotism creates. As always, he dramatizes his own instinct toward balance, using the two mismatched heroes, the joker king and the emperor, who meet on the final battlefield. There the king admits to Wayne that the whole idea was a joke, but Wayne accepts this apology, saying that between them they had done a better deed than they knew, for it took a fanatic and a satirist to "lift the modern cities into that poetry which everyone who knows mankind knows to be immeasurably more common than the commonplace. . . . There is no war between us."[30]

The two heroes go off together into the wide world, not only representing the two sides of the human brain, but also acting as personifications
of their author's pursuit of political truth, tempered by his enjoyment of
the possibilities of everyday life. The ultimate confrontation between the
Napoleon and the whimsical king is a fight between earnestness and humor,
which Chesterton suggests must be resolved by the ordinary man, who has
both traits. These two characters might also be labeled "Cecil" and "Gilbert,"
for Cecil was a fanatic greatly given to causes, intolerant of halfway measures
or opposition, who deplored his brother's omnipresent sense of the ridiculous. Interestingly enough, the most ridiculous criticism leveled at *The
Napoleon of Notting Hill* began with Cecil's accusations that in this book his
brother showed a romatic yearning to return to medievalism as a way of
life.

Legends grew up about how this book was written, encouraged by
Chesterton himself, who recognized the value of a "good story." As he told
it, he and Frances were broke, and since she was obliged to manage the
money for them both, Frances played the role of the mother in "Jack and
the Beanstalk," telling him to go do something useful. Chesterton went to
Fleet Street and fortified himself by spending his last ten shillings on food
and drink, then marched off bravely to his publisher's office, where he
outlined the plot of the story and demanded a twenty-pound advance. He
got the twenty pounds in gold sovereigns, and went home and poured them
all into Frances' lap. Sleuths, however, have discovered that Chesterton had
already been at work upon the manuscript, for which he had a normal
contract. This fact is like the one about his writing: though he thought out
what he wanted to say, and did correct his manuscripts, he wanted to be
known for composing quickly and well. Like a schoolboy, Chesterton liked
to appear either a quick study or a dunce — never a grind. The more
probable truth of this particular situation is easy to deduce: when Chesterton
asked for money, he took along with him the part of the manuscript he
had already written, and got the advance that way.

About the time *The Napoleon of Notting Hill* came out, Belloc published
one of his best-known novels, *Emmanuel Burden*, which had run serially in
the *Speaker*. It had thirty-four illustrations which Chesterton had drawn, and
since much later in their respective careers he did other illustrations for
Belloc's books, this collaboration fostered an idea that they were thick as
thieves, sharing one another's prejudices. In fact, Chesterton was also doing
illustrations for other friends, like E.V. Lucas and E.C. Bentley. From now
on, Belloc's influence on Chesterton was destined to decline, since by 1905
he had moved out of London. It was about this time, meanwhile, that the
association between Chesterton and Shaw began to grow. The figure *always*
lurking in Chesterton's shadow, a man first a Shavian and then a Bellocian
disciple, was Cecil.

While his older brother was becoming a well-known literary figure in

London, producing all different kinds of work helter-skelter, Cecil Chesterton, by April 1904, had accomplished an ambition of his own. He had been elected to the Executive Committee of the Fabian Society, whose Old Gang, made up of Shaw, the Webbs, Bland, and some others, hoped the "youngsters" would begin to run the show. A new "comet" on their horizon was H.G. Wells, who had also joined in 1903, while other active younger members were children of the older Fabians — Rosamund Bland, Clifford Sharp, and Amber Reeves. Like Cecil, they were educated, middle-class young activists, upset about social and political conditions, but also convinced the society itself needed a shot in the arm.[31] The very nature of the Fabian Society, however, made it hard to create an opposition, because the Executive Committee had always operated like an oligarchy but within their own ranks were democratic. "Taking control" of the society's machinery would have destroyed it.

Like Cecil Chesterton, Wells gravitated toward the Blands. They owned Wells Hall, a place where Wells said you had to rush to get a bed before anyone else. Mrs. Bland was a "raffish Rossetti"; her husband, "detached and saturnine," was adored by a flock of young females. Cecil seems to have been one of Mrs. Bland's admirers (he always took to attractive, dominating older women), but he also tried his luck with Rosamund Bland. In addition, he became Bland's disciple.[32] Shaw called Bland a "Tory Democrat" who had the hypocritical habit of blackballing Fabian recruits on moral grounds when he was himself an "incorrigible polygamist." Ironically, he was a convert to Roman Catholicism — yet his mistresses and illegitimate children lived with him at Wells Hall.[33] True to form, Cecil outstripped his mentor: he became even more outspoken than Bland himself.

During the summer of 1904, while Cecil went off to the International Socialist Convention at Amsterdam as a Fabian delegate, Frances and Gilbert went to Yorkshire to visit an old P.N.E.U. friend, Mrs. Steinthal. Yorkshire's high, dry moors were better for Frances' arthritis than Gilbert's beloved seashore, so he cheerfully took to walking across the wide-open spaces instead of the beach. At the Steinthals they met a Roman Catholic parish priest named Father John O'Connor, who was curate at St. Anne's a few miles away. He later moved to a parish with the tongue-twisting name of Heckmondwike (which Gilbert used in a poem), ending his career as a Monsignor and Privy Chamberlain to Pope Pius XI.

Within a few years Father O'Connor was to be called the prototype of the famous detective Father Brown, but he really was a small, neat, very talkative Irishman who fancied himself a literary critic. He seems to have been a very capable confidant: no sooner had he met the Chestertons than he began a correspondence with Frances which lasted the rest of their lives. He urged her to persuade Gilbert to be a "man of letters" and write "important books," to stop wasting his time being a "jolly journalist," thereby proving that he did not understand Chesterton the writer at all. It is to her credit that Frances, who liked and trusted Father O'Connor, wrote back that Gilbert only wanted to paint the town red, and all he needed to do that was buckets and buckets of paint.[34] Later, in his book about Chesterton, Father O'Connor wrote that Cecil was the greater man, because he was a fearless fighter; it was a judgment that only Chesterton himself would agree with.

On their first walk across the moors, Father O'Connor did fascinate Chesterton by telling him tales of incredible evil and depravity that he had heard in confession. He showed such great charity and common sense in the face of real sin that it tickled Chesterton's sense of the absurd when two pompous young university students that day at lunch said that Father O'Connor's profession had kept him naive and unspotted by the real world. At once Chesterton began to play with the idea of developing a character like Father O'Connor, who solves mysteries because he can identify with the criminal mind.

His character, Father Brown, who is identified with him today the way Sherlock Holmes is identified with Conan Doyle, shares no characteristics with Father O'Connor except for a few physical ones: he wears a shabby black habit and a flat roman hat, and carries a large umbrella and a lot of brown-paper parcels. Father Brown is Chesterton's Mr. Pickwick, a mouthpiece for his own wit and wisdom. His ordinariness is Chesterton's: he is a man of simple tastes who enjoys simple pleasures. But he is also a shrewd, clever person endowed with extraordinary sensitivity and powers of observation. With this balance of traits, Father Brown is not a mystic, nor is he a very realistic portrait of a parish priest.[35]

Early in 1905 Cecil Chesterton got his first book published. It was called *Gladstonian Ghosts*, and reflected his Fabian stage of development. In it he proclaimed loudly that if "Mr. Gladstone is dead . . . where is the new era? Mr. Gladstone's place has been taken by men who have inherited all his obsolete prejudices — only lacking his abilities."[36] Cecil went on to energetically attack some of his brother's most cherished political groups and principles: Little Englanders, the Liberal slogan of "Peace, Retrenchment and Reform," and "Protestants." At one point he remarked that "it is often possible to get the Tories to pass good measures without knowing it," a comment that echoes the smugness of Beatrice Webb.[37] Apart from sharing a constitutional dislike of "Protestantism," which both saw as a projection of a state religion used to oppress the poor since Tudor times, the brothers had very little in common; they must have had some good arguments.

Shortly afterward, in March 1905, a collection of detective stories called *The Club of Queer Trades* appeared, written and illustrated by Chesterton. Their theme is the idea that Chesterton had already stated in his essay "A Defence of Detective Stories," in which he said that modern man had a great need for romance and adventure which, paradoxically, he can find just around the corner in any ordinary London street. The very first story, "The

Adventure of Major Brown," typifies the rest. The story is about a modern commercial agency that manufactures adventures for people for a price, but the hero, Major Brown, gets mixed up in the adventure by accident. The stories are reminiscent of Sherlock Holmes and Stevenson's *New Arabian Nights*, but the detective in the stories is a former judge who works by intuition; he sits at home and uses common sense to solve the mysteries, while his fiery younger brother dashes about London following up false clues. The villains belong to the upper classes, and resort to little violence; the two brothers are much like Gilbert and Cecil — though in this collection the "knight-errant of modern life" protecting romance and morality is not the actor but the thinker.[38] The tales reflect Chesterton's view of the world, the flesh, and the devil.

During March of 1905 Chesterton participated in a series of public lectures sponsored by the Christian Social Union, which further identified him as a "Christian" spokesman. Frances revealingly recorded this event in her diary as "one of the proudest days of my life."[39] It seems clear that her interest in these "lay sermons" given at St. Paul's Church, Covent Garden, was due more to the state of her husband's religious convictions than to the union's overriding interest in social concerns.

On March 16 Chesterton gave a talk called "Vox Populi, Vox Dei," and on March 30 he spoke on "The Citizen, the Gentleman and the Savage, or Where There is no Vision, the People Perish." His basic message was that an individual must have a philosophical commitment before he begins to change the world; thus the entire Fabian theory of acting pragmatically without worrying about belief was unworkable. By implication, he was suggesting that such groups had philosophical presuppositions that they could not or would not admit to. This was also to be the theme of the essays collected that June under the title of *Heretics*. Among others who spoke was Cecil Chesterton, who was ruthlessly pragmatic, giving a re-working of a Fabian paper on the public utility of free school lunches! His argument was that improving the poor children's diet would make them strong to fight the class war.[40]

Their "sermons" were published in 1906 with the title *Preachers from the Pew*, meaning what today is usually called "the ministry of the laity" or "the priesthood of all believers." About the same time Chesterton's most famous hymn, which is still in many hymnals of all denominations, was published. It carried his familiar message of social concern, with a hope to avoid Cecil's class war, addressed directly to the Lord of Hosts:

> O God of earth and altar,
> Bow down and hear our cry,
> Our earthly leaders falter,
> Our people drift and die. . . .

Tie in a living tether
The prince and priest and thrall,
Bind all our lives together. . . .
Aflame with faith and free,
Lift up a living nation,
A single sword to thee.[41]

It was about this time that Chesterton drew the "40 diagrams" — cartoons — used to illustrate E.C. Bentley's *Biography for Beginners*, a collection of his comic "clerihews." Bentley rewrote these verses from St. Paul days (some of them originally written by Chesterton) because he needed the extra money. The verses' subjects included Jane Austen, Dante, and Cervantes, Don Quixote being one of Chesterton's favorite characters. Chesterton's illustrations were remarkably good; the "imaginative and fantastic pictures . . . showed his extraordinary gift for drawing at its best."[42]

This was the time when Bentley began writing his modern "ballades," which were published in places like *Punch*, the *Speaker*, and, later, the *Eye-Witness*. When he began to make money with them, he, Chesterton, Baring, and Belloc got into the habit of firing them at one another off-the-cuff. According to Bentley, the fact that they imitated Henley's Kiplingesque style was the joke; their aim was to turn imperialism "upside-down." The ballades, usually both topical and satirical, were a form at which Gilbert excelled; and when they became popular, another of Chesterton's talents was publicly acknowledged. The fact that it was he and his old friend Bentley who began this particular activity has since gotten lost in the myth that Belloc, Baring, and Chesterton wrote them as a part of a very early "Roman Catholic" alliance.[43]

The year 1905 was a watershed year, not only for English political life, but for a number of people who mattered in Chesterton's life. Belloc decided to move his large family back to Sussex, where he had been raised. He first rented a house, then bought King's Land, where he lived like a lord of the manor, observing Christmas festively, and making his own wine. As their friendship grew, Cecil Chesterton visited King's Land often, while Gilbert, on the other hand, saw Belloc less and less.

At fifty Shaw was finally a literary lion with a colorful public image; he was known as a skinny, red-bearded man who wore homespun yellow jaeger suits, followed a vegetarian diet, and was always ready to answer questions provocatively. His plays, which were serious but not tragic, reflected his personality. To preach his Fabian gospel he used the "paradoxical" device of inverting stock melodrama. *Major Barbara*, for example, carried Shaw's message that the poor cannot be helped to help themselves but must be directed by men of destiny and power, without "illusions" — or, as Chesterton would put it, without "a view of the universe."[44] The Fabian queen bee, Beatrice Webb, whose background was much like Major Barbara's, held this attitude.[45] This year she had been appointed to the Royal Commission on the Poor Law, and for the first time she was in the public eye.

Meanwhile, Wells had joined the Fabians, and he was much courted by the Old Gang, who saw him as a new celebrity who agreed with their idea of a society run along collectivist lines by a managerial elite. Several of his books had illustrated this thesis, especially *A Modern Utopia*, which was almost a Fabian tract. The Fabians also saw him as a sparring partner for Shaw, complete with his carefully manufactured image of "H.G.," the scientific prophet with lower-class manners and a gift for publicity, a small, sharp man who made things happen.[46] Wells' wretched childhood had made him gloomy, but now that he was rich and getting famous, he began to turn his hopes for an apocalyptic future into an interest in practical politics. He was very much the "New Man," and socially he, like Cecil Chesterton, preferred the Bland menage to the more bourgeois households of the Webbs and the Shaws. But Wells thought the Fabians were too slow and methodical, and in 1905 he made a bold play to turn them inside out, appealing to the newer or younger Fabians. By 1906 the society was embroiled in a civil war, a war that directly affected Cecil Chesterton's subsequent career and therefore, indirectly, his doting brother's life as well.

That June *Heretics* came out, dedicated to "my father." Its tone reflected the seriously inquiring but genial manner of Mr. Ed, although it was his father's own lares and penates Chesterton was attacking: Science and Progress, or the survival of the fittest and the rise of the superman. The book was a collection of his recent essays from the *Daily News*, with a new introduction and summary showing that the arguments going on among the Fabians as well as the intellectual climate around them were matters that he understood well, even if he did not agree with the Fabians' assessment of them.

Heretics is filled with sharp, contemporary allusions to recent events and popular figures, containing a number of capsule sketches of personalities like Joseph Chamberlain, Winston Churchill, and Asquith. It is tied together by its thesis that the very word "heresy" has been turned upside-down: it no longer means being wrong — it means being clear-headed and courageous. Similarly, the word "orthodoxy" now does not mean being right, but being wrong or reactionary, and the new Golden Rule, as spoken by Prophet Shaw, is that "there is no Golden Rule."[47]

In *Heretics* Chesterton made his famous statement that "for a landlady considering a lodger, it is important to know his income, but still more important to know his philosophy." He then pointed out that the old Liberals had removed the gags from all the heresies, so that religious and philosophical discoveries could be made — but the result was that now there was no general discussion about issues. Even blasphemy, Chesterton noted, depends upon belief and fades with it. He suggested that if someone doubted this idea, "he should sit down seriously and try to think blasphemous thoughts about Thor. . . ."[48]

The specific "heretics" Chesterton describes at length are Kipling, Shaw, Wells, FitzGerald (the translator of the gloomy, determinist *Rubaiyat* of Omar Khayyam), Harmsworth of the "yellow press," Tolstoi, George Moore, and Whistler (as well as those on both sides of the Irish Question). All of them are "heretics" because they have philosophies that are "quite solid, quite coherent, and quite wrong." Worse than that, their philosophies all lead to a modern morality which can only point to the horrors of breaking the law; their ideas all led to a "certainty of ill," never to perfection. Chesterton blamed this negative spirit on the intellectual winds blowing from Germany.

Many of Chesterton's comments are very apt, as when he talks about "painting the map red" as an innocent game for children, or says he can "lie awake at night and hear [H.G. Wells] grow . . . [but] it is hard to enter into the feelings of a man who regards a new heaven and a new earth in the light of a by-product." About Shaw he made the discerning comment that he was thought to be a "capering humorist . . . but he is thoroughly consistent." Beneath their modern veneer, Chesterton thought, these heretics were fanatics who wanted to lead messianic cults to replace Christianity as the source of Western civilization; Chesterton himself had become convinced by now that there was no reason to invent a new religion because "everything in the modern world is of Christian origin . . . the French Revolution . . . the newspaper . . . the attack on Christianity. . . ." What actually distinguishes the pagan from Christianity, he pointed out, is that one has "sad virtues," and the other "happy virtues." And Christianity was what was needed now, because "it is at the hopeless moment that we require the hopeful man."[49] He added that the human brain is a machine for coming to conclusions, and the cure for a bigot (or a heretic) is belief. His recommendation was that the world go on a long journey and "seek until we have discovered our own opinions."[50] In *Heretics* Chesterton nailed his theses to the door; he himself recognized that he was already on the long journey that he recommended to others, seeking the roots of his own attitudes.

He stated this fact simply in one of his most famous parables: the one about the monk and the lamppost. A mob in the street wants to tear the lamppost down. The monk, "in the arid manner of the Schoolmen," says,

> "Let us first consider . . . the value of Light. If Light be in itself good" — At this point he is somewhat excusably knocked down. . . . The lamppost . . . is [then] down in ten minutes, and they . . . congratulate each other on their unmedieval practicality. . . . Some . . . pulled the lamppost down because they wanted the electric light; some because they wanted old iron; some because they wanted darkness, for their deeds were evil . . . [but] what we might have discussed under the gas-lamp, we . . . must discuss in the dark.[51]

By December 1905 Chesterton was popular enough to be asked to write another weekly column for the *Illustrated London News*. It was called "Our Notebook," and gave him a much-needed steady income of 350 pounds a year, for which he was so grateful that in later years he refused to allow his agent to ask for a higher fee. In theory he was not to write about politics or religion, although no editor ever succeeded in keeping him off either topic. Gardiner, his editor at the *Daily News*, pointed out that it made little difference: no matter where Chesterton started, he ended up discussing "all the mystery of time and eternity." But in the first published collection of his *Illustrated London News* columns, Chesterton joked that he could not understand people who take literature seriously, but "I can love them and I do . . . [and] warn them to keep clear of this book. It is a collection of crude and shapeless papers upon current . . . subjects . . . written at the last minute . . . and I do not think our commonwealth would have been shaken to the foundations if they had been handed in a moment after."[52]

That same fall of 1905, the Liberal newspapers had been pressing the Tory prime minister, Balfour, to resign and allow a General Election. He chose to do so suddenly, forcing the Liberal leader Campbell-Bannerman to form a Liberal government and then go to the country, or "show his poker hand before he could really play it."[53] Although his help was largely verbal, Chesterton became very personally involved in this campaign.

Chapter Eight

THE ORTHODOX LIBERAL

1906-1908

When next you hear some attack called an idle paradox, ask after the dox. Ask how long the dox has been in the world; how many have believed in the dox; how often the dox has proved itself right in practice; how often thoughtful men have returned to the dox on theory. Pursue the dox; persecute the dox. In short, ask the dox whether it is orthodox.

G.K. Chesterton, the *Daily News*, October 28, 1911[1]

I have not lost my ideals in the least; my faith in fundamentals is exactly what it always was. What I have lost is my old childlike faith in practical politics.

G.K. Chesterton, *Orthodoxy*[2]

THE General Election of January 1906 gave the Liberal Party a startling landslide victory, as well as a very uncertain mandate for action. This event was important in Chesterton's life because several of his close friends ran for office and won, and their experiences as Members of Parliament gave him the personal knowledge by which he judged actual party politics. It was his own observations, not the echoed opinions of others, that changed the nature of his faith in liberalism, causing him to label himself "orthodox" while he called the more pragmatic politicians "heretics." The important thing to recognize is that, in his vocabulary, these two terms were as much political as they were religious.

But at first, in the flushed dawn of a new era, he was as happy as his fellows, and in one column he lightheartedly teased the candidates by discussing the rules for electioneering. The very tone of this article shows the kind of gaiety and hope felt by all his Liberal friends; once they were in the House of Commons, the old would be made new:

> Most of us will be canvassed soon. . . . Some of us may even canvass. Upon which side, of course, nothing will induce me to state, beyond saying that

100

by a remarkable coincidence, it will in every case be the only side in which a high-minded, public-spirited and patriotic citizen can even take momentary interest. . . . The rules for canvassers are . . . printed on the little card . . . you carry about with you and lose. . . . You must not offer a voter food or drink. . . . Whether the voter is allowed to feed the canvasser, I have never been able to inform myself . . . [nor] if there is any law against bribing a canvasser to go away.[3]

He has fun with the rule against impersonating a voter (suggesting one use a disguise kit with a false moustache), but adds, "you must not threaten a voter with any consequence . . . [despite the obvious threat that] a canvasser says if the Opposition candidate gets in, the country will be ruined."

At the end of the article Chesterton sounds a note of high seriousness, prophetically pointing up one of the real problems the Liberals were to face, when he says that historically the House of Commons cannot hold all its elected members, and that traditionally the problem has been resolved by assuming that many will never come. He says that "is a peculiar way to do your duty to king and country." As he knew, his Liberal friends now running for office were fairly itching to do their duty to mankind, and their frustration when this proved to be nearly impossible was what sent them off on wildly different paths: Belloc to decry Parliamentary government itself; Masterman to try to learn to be a practical politician.

Belloc was running for South Salford, a working-class suburb of Manchester with a large Irish-Catholic population. It had been a Conservative seat, but Belloc won with a whopping majority of 852 votes. He had taken great delight in making it perfectly plain to his constituency that he was a classic Radical-Liberal who supported the platform of the 1880's: land reform, free trade, Home Rule for Ireland, Disestablishment of the Church, and free public education — all positions Chesterton held as well. Belloc had informed his constituents that he would vote his conscience in everything. He dared them to vote for him because he was Roman Catholic; at the same time he strongly supported the Nonconformists' fight to defeat the Education Bill of 1902. With foresight he predicted that Chamberlain was in favor of imperial preference (or tariffs on non-imperial goods) not just to keep the empire sound, but also to pay for new social welfare legislation.[4] Like Chesterton, Belloc also supported the Nonconformists' wish to destroy the monopoly of the few large brewers like Guinness, not because he believed in temperance but because he believed in the "little man" who ran a local pub.

Winning the election made Belloc ecstatic; he sent off a telegram to Chesterton and his other friends in London asking them to meet him at Euston Station, saying, "This is a great day for the British Empire, but a bad one for the little Bellocs."[5] Unpaid as an M.P., Belloc could not afford to keep an apartment of his own in London, but rented a room from Maurice Baring near Westminster.

So many other *Daily News* staffers won in the election that Gardiner held a celebration dinner. The one with the greatest potential was Charles Masterman, an old friend of both Frances and Gilbert who had lived in a London slum while establishing his career in journalism. He came from a strongly Evangelical family, but had gone to a public school and to Cambridge on scholarships, where as president of the rival union he had faced E.C. Bentley in debate. He was a gifted, pious "new" Liberal and an Anglo-Catholic member of the Christian Social Union. Sincere to the point of melancholy, Masterman was also becoming a part of the old-boy network; shortly after his election he began to court young Lucy Lyttelton, a member of an "Establishment" family with a network of kinship and connection like that found in the family trees of Beatrice Webb and Virginia Woolf.[6] During the next few years Belloc and Chesterton came to realize that intricate personal interrelationships like these controlled much of the real party power.

The election itself carried ominous overtones that the jubilant Liberals largely ignored. Groups with widely different agendas were among the new Members of Parliament; each group tended to claim the victory as its handiwork. The prime minister, Campbell-Bannerman, managed to put together a Cabinet that included almost all the factions: "Limps," or Liberal Imperialists, like Asquith as Chancellor of the Exchequer; Grey at the Foreign Office; and Haldane, the mystical admirer of Prussian Germany's efficient welfare state, at the Army. To balance them, Campbell-Bannerman put in old Gladstonians like Morley, while adding the young, fiery Welshman David Lloyd George, who had campaigned like a preacher for the Nonconformist cause of free education. For the first time, too, thirty Labour candidates had been elected because they were unopposed by Liberals. Observers in 1905 assumed the Liberals would "swallow up" the Labourites; the opposite eventually took place.

This new House of Commons had many members who were Nonconformists; their church leaders had actively campaigned to get them elected. But these two hundred new members did not sit or vote as a bloc, because the schisms in their interests and priorities surfaced quickly.[7] At the same time, with the huge majority they had, the Liberal Party did not need the thirty Labour votes, nor the Irish bloc, so it did not feel obligated to solve the problem of Irish Home Rule, or to honor any other campaign promise promptly — much to Belloc and Masterman's disgust. In spite of the fact that the Liberal business community had, for the first time, elected a large number of representatives to Parliament, the day of the paternalistic family company was over. It was giving way to larger, more impersonal public companies. A compensating trade union movement now urged its members to identify not with the company's interests, but with their own. In the face of this destruction of his boyhood vision of "Chesterton and Sons," Chesterton himself began to identify with the radical support for trade unions, preferring it to a bureaucratic welfare state.

The final Liberal problem was to be cuckoos in the nest, the primary one being Lloyd George. His stated ambition was to resurrect Joe Chamberlain's Newcastle Program to "steal the Fabian thunder," but he also was described later as having been a "half-human visitor to our age . . . [with] a final purposelessness, mixed with cunning and . . . love of power . . . rooted in nothing."[8] Chesterton was strangely sensitive to all of these political portents, and his essays show his gradual discovery that the roots of his liberalism were not in the Evangelical tradition, nor in Benthamite utilitarianism, now translated into Fabian tracts — they were, in fact, in orthodox creedal Christianity.[9]

Between 1903, when he first fenced with Blatchford, and 1908, when he published *Orthodoxy*, working his way "backwards" from the social justice preached by Dickens and the egalitarian humanism of Whitman, Chesterton "did, like all the other solemn little boys, try to be in advance of the age. . . . And . . . found [he] was eighteen hundred years behind it."[10] It is this statement, made by Chesterton himself, that makes all the assumptions about his early conversion to classical Christianity such myths. One such myth is found in Holbrook Jackson's classic, *The Eighteen Nineties*, written in 1913. In it Jackson talks misleadingly about the somersault of ideas at the very dawn of the twentieth century, "when intellectual consciousness landed on its feet . . . becoming wildly English and frankly Christian in the genius of G.K. Chesterton."[11] Jackson only got to know Chesterton after 1907, but like most of their contemporaries, he accepted Cecil's assertion that his brother had become a Christian convert by about 1895. Gilbert Chesterton, oblivious of dates himself, never tried to set the record straight in so many words, but left clues throughout his writing.

In fact, Chesterton's conversion to Christianity was gradual, not the result of a blinding revelation; his age was full of that kind of mystical emotionalism, and his instinct was to balance it with a rational intellect. Unlike Cecil, he never took the obvious step of being formally confirmed in the Church of England. Instead, during these very busy years in London, as he wrote and met the great people of the period and watched the Liberal Party try to be all things to all men, he came to see that he had instinctively accepted the basic tenets of Christianity, particularly the Fall and the Incarnation. The fascinatingly original aspect of this "conversion" was that the victory of the Liberal Party crystallized in his mind its "classic" principles, which were then so intertwined in his thinking about Christianity that he himself seemed not to know where one began and the other ended, a natural development for a thinker for whom ideas always had consequences. By 1908 his original point of view was to be clearly defined in *Orthodoxy*, a book supposedly about religion, but one in which every aspect of Christianity is talked about in terms of liberalism, because Chesterton internalized the Liberal creeds as a result of the problems that the Liberal Party had after 1905.

What E.C. Bentley, a "converted" Liberal, jubilantly called "Revolution without the R" had won the election. But as the Liberal Party proclaimed its Gladstonian principles, its real mandate was to pass economic legislation to provide a better standard of living, despite the fact that England was losing ground in world trade. The wide electorate who had voted Liberal really wanted more economic opportunities as well as security against old age, sickness, and unemployment — all of which meant creating the welfare state, a goal quite alien to "Libertarian" Liberals like Chesterton.[12]

The Liberals were not the only party with internal troubles. That same election year of 1906 saw dissension within the Fabian ranks as well. In February H.G. Wells read a paper in which he told the society that it was too small, too poor, and too collectively inactive, that it should stop imitating the cautious Fabius Cunctator and play Scipio, who had destroyed Carthage.[13] The younger set felt that Wells was just what they had been looking for to give the society "whoosh and an effective place on the new political scene."[14] Cecil Chesterton was at the forefront of this group, who next urged the Old Gang or the Executive Committee to set up a committee to consider their future. But Hubert Bland in particular objected to Wells, who had talked his daughter Rosamund into running off with him by telling her that she was illegitimate, and that her father was an old rake. Rosamund's fiance, Clifford Sharp, managed to bring her back, but next Wells had an affair with another Fabian child, Amber Reeves, a relationship that formed the basis of his novel *Ann Veronica*. Both Bland and Beatrice Webb took a very bourgeois view of such behavior, and the issue of Wells' influence hung in limbo while he went off on a U.S. tour. While he was gone, Cecil Chesterton unaccountably decided to stick with the Old Gang, turning against his contemporaries in the "Fabian nursery," possibly because he had been interested in Rosamund Bland himself, or because Mrs. Bland and Shaw "wooed" him. This decision, however, cost Cecil his Fabian power base, and meant he had to seek another route to fame and fortune.

It was that spring of 1906 that Shaw and Chesterton apparently first met face to face, although there are as many versions of this meeting as there are about the meeting between Chesterton and Belloc, and it is, as usual, surprisingly difficult to figure out the true chronology of events.[15] Since it is commonly accepted that the two men knew of one another from 1901, when Chesterton had written the article on Sir Walter Scott which Shaw admired, their friendship can be dated from that time, although so far as meeting for lunch or discussion is concerned, it is far more likely that it was Cecil Chesterton, the young star of the Fabians, with whom Shaw was getting together.

During the interval between 1901 and the time of their documented meeting in 1906, they carried on a series of skirmishes in print. In 1905, for example, Shaw wrote a letter to the *Daily News*, complaining that Shakespeare wrote potboilers for hard cash; Chesterton happily picked up his challenge and for the first time called Shaw a "Puritan." He insisted that Shakespeare was an artist in love with words, but also that he had seen the double nature of words, which are also signs meaning something. "Shakespeare," wrote Chesterton, "stands on two legs," combining the matter and the manner, a comment that would apply equally well to Shaw and Chesterton themselves.

April 1906 was the month of their fabled meeting. Shaw's wealthy wife had persuaded the famous Parisian sculptor, Rodin, to do a head of her husband — or, possibly, Rodin had asked the now-famous playwright to sit for him. Chesterton and Oldershaw happened to be in Paris on a short visit, and Oldershaw, typically the promoter of Chesterton's image, brought Chesterton to Rodin's studio to meet both Shaw and the sculptor. They found Shaw, stripped to the waist, talking a blue streak in bad French to the confused sculptor, trying to tell him about the plot of *Major Barbara* and explain the Salvation Army. Oldershaw insisted upon introducing Chesterton to both men, who ignored him, so Chesterton, always an appreciative listener, simply sat and watched Shaw bounce about lecturing Rodin on free trade and the Boer War, convincing the Frenchman that he was both a poseur and a fraud. It is very unlikely that either Shaw or Rodin ever knew Chesterton was there.[16]

This was also the year that Cecil Chesterton, clearly looking about for a new base of operations, joined Conrad Noel in quitting the Christian Social Union to join its new rival, the Christian Socialist League, a more militant and outspoken organization. His older brother, while always interested in and aware of Cecil's activities, was increasingly busy with his own writing career, which involved writing two columns a week, lecturing all over England, and producing a steady stream of books, both fiction and non-fiction. Most of the non-fiction was about literary figures who had social and political dimensions as well, so that in writing these "biographies" Chesterton was also reassessing his own roots.

One of the best known of these books is *Charles Dickens*, published in August 1906. Chesterton, who adored Dickens and knew him by heart, wrote brilliantly about him, and his name was associated with Dickens' name for all of his life. Above all other literary sources, Dickens influenced Chesterton's fundamental political and religious convictions: the Chestertonian liberalism that became his Christianity was derived and nurtured by his acceptance of Dickens' social philosophy.[17]

When Cecil insisted that Gilbert could only write about authors with whom he agreed, he had hit upon a half-truth that was valid enough. They both had heard Dickens at their father's knee, and Gilbert was always loyal — in his fashion — to their own hearth. He also saw his beloved father as a kind of Mr. Pickwick, a true Englishman and the Dickensian character he most admired. Beyond this, Chesterton found value in all of Dickens' work: both its content and its methods affected his own writing. He not only wrote books and articles about Dickens and introductions to his complete works, but he also was president of the Dickens Fellowship and was given Dickens' actual chair (which he did not dare sit in). With his brother and a host of friends he also participated in a public "Mock Trial of John Jasper" from *Edwin Drood*, the last, unfinished Dickens' novel, which today is admired as the beginning of the "modern" detective story.[18]

In 1906, when Chesterton wrote about him, Dickens had no "literary" reputation in England, while on the Continent he was regarded by French, German, and Russian intellectuals as *the* figure in English literature, surpassed only by Shakespeare. Shaw was the only other major English literary figure who admired Dickens as much as Chesterton did; together they formed an alliance to promote Dickens, which became a vital part of their friendship. Like him, they both wrote "social melodrama" that represented society "in a fairly complex and critical way" yet achieved tremendous popular success, giving their readers the "pleasure of seeing the follies of men and institutions combined with the satisfaction of witnessing the triumph of virtue and the punishment of vice." In their day, too, "the basic principle of the melodramatic vision . . . was the primacy of religion . . . [which was] the cement tying together the other social and moral ideas."[19] Both Chesterton and Shaw were reproducing, in Edwardian terms, Dickens' kind of fiction and social vision.[20]

As a knight crusading against relativism and art for art's sake, Chesterton always considered his subjects in their own social context, for in his own way he was as action-oriented as Cecil. His principal defense of Dickens' greatness was his insistence that he was an event in English history, the native version of the French Revolution that was deeply and radically English. Dickens "did not pity . . . or love . . . or champion the people . . . he was the people, so that in his denunciation of the Fleet Prison there was a great deal of the capture of the Bastille."[21] To Chesterton, Dickens also seemed to be the literal, primitive Christian whom Dostoyevsky saw; in addition, he admired Dickens and Gladstone as the twin saints of liberalism.

Quoting (and misquoting), Chesterton explained that Dickens' worth was not to be reckoned in novels at all, but in characters; he pointed out that "his novels are simply lengths cut from the flowing and mixed substance called Dickens . . ." in which any piece will have good and bad parts. For Dickens is "like life . . . akin to the living principle in us and in the universe. . . . He is alive. His art is like life. . . . It cares for nothing outside itself and goes on its way rejoicing. . . ." The problem, Chesterton explained, was that "for our time and taste he exaggerates the wrong thing." Although "exaggeration is the definition of art . . . moderns permit any writer to emphasize doubts . . . but no man to emphasize dogmas."[22]

He insisted that Dickens was a "mythologist rather than a novelist. . . . He did not always manage to make his characters men, but he always managed to make them gods." This stands in direct contrast to Shaw's theory that Dickens' characters are grotesques because that is how a genius sees ordinary men.[23] Chesterton himself preferred early Dickens, especially Pickwick; he also suggested that, ultimately, Dickens' greatest character was himself. He compared Dickens' total body of work to that of Chaucer, who also had painted a superb portrait of English life. Someday, he prophesied, Dickens would come to be seen as the greatest writer of the nineteenth century; at that time when we have traveled a long way along a rambling English road where our travels are "interludes in comradeship and joy . . . all roads [will] point to an ultimate inn . . . where we shall meet Dickens and all his characters and . . . drink . . . from the great flagons in the tavern at the end of the world."[24] It is this kind of romantic summary that Chesterton's detractors call his "medievalism."

Although she did point out one glaringly misstated fact, as well as the predictable misquotations, Dickens' daughter told Chesterton how much she liked the book. Chesterton never bothered to change mistakes in new editions, because for him, a typical journalist, a word written was already as dead and gone as yesterday's newspaper, and he was always too busy to fuss. Frances, too, did some of his proofreading, so a share of the blame is hers as well.

While Chesterton sat in a Fleet Street pub, turning out copy, often with a loud chuckle, politics was in the air about him. His friends on the *Daily News* were beginning to be bothered by the twin facts that the Liberal leadership had not rushed to redeem its campaign pledges, but nonetheless expected new recruits to respond obediently to calls for party discipline. Masterman, the old Oxford Union debater, found Parliament much like the university, but deplored the fact that "we await tomorrow. Everything is coming tomorrow."[25] Belloc, the fighter, had attacked his own party in his maiden speech over its sloth in not stopping the import of Chinese coolie labor to Africa, and he, too, expressed gloom over the stalling on bills affecting education, liquor, and land-holding.[26]

Their glum reactions were shared by the Liberal press for which Chesterton was busily writing. His editor, Gardiner, supported the slogan "Peace, Retrenchment and Reform" without recognizing that there were real incompatibilities between peace (with dreadnoughts to scare Germany), retrenchment (or economy), and reform (social legislation). Most Liberals still thought war with Germany unthinkable; others, like Belloc and Chesterton, mistrusted "Prussianism." Last but not least, the Nonconformists wanted a new education bill, but had no interest in allowing "Papist" Ireland home rule.

As the editor of the nearest thing to an official paper, Gardiner was being forced to stop his typically Liberal habit of criticizing all comers. Most

London papers were Conservative, with several now controlled by Harmsworth, newly made Lord Northcliffe. Like other editors, Gardiner also began to puff Lloyd George as the man to save liberalism because he would act. The great coverage the Liberal press gave Lloyd George at this time helped him to rise very rapidly in the party ranks, but it was this kind of artificial, self-serving relationship between M.P. and editor that made Chesterton say uneasily that "more than I ever did, I believe in Liberalism. But there was a rosy time of innocence when I believed in Liberals."[27]

He was not alone in his growing disenchantment. Other Liberal journalists like H.W. Massingham were far more extreme, insisting that they must criticize their own party or be whitened sepulchres. Massingham called himself a Liberal until his death, arguing that the party had betrayed him. Others, like Gardiner and Masterman, came to feel guilty about betraying the Liberal creed, but also felt themselves betrayed by events and other men.

From March 1905 to November 1906, Chesterton's next novel, *The Ball and the Cross*, was published serially in the Christian Social Union's magazine, *Commonwealth*. The novel was not put out in book form until 1910, but it fits logically between *The Napoleon of Notting Hill*, published in 1904, and *The Man Who Was Thursday*, published in 1908. These three novels have been described as the most representative of all Chesterton's novels because of their themes and the way he related them: in these books the theme of sanity and madness in the world is linked to the theme of wonder and romance, with its ability to change the way in which the world itself is perceived.[28] The characters in these novels are not fully rounded; they are types who represent various political and social positions. Shaw also employed this kind of characterization in his plays, as did their mutual mentor, Charles Dickens.

Structurally, *The Ball and the Cross* has the same pattern as *The Napoleon of Notting Hill*: two protagonists who stand for opposite sides of the political spectrum experience an eventual reconciliation that gives the novel its meaning. They are Turnbull, a feisty redheaded bookseller who is atheistic and "Left" down to his fingertips, and a dark, romantic Highlander named Evan MacIan, who is not only a Roman Catholic but also a Jacobite who wants the Stuart kings restored. They begin a duel which results in a chase all over England, during which both meet a variety of the modern "heretics," and each has a vision of his own utopia that reveals its flaw — that when all social reforms or restorations have been carried out, there will still remain the problem of "original sin"; that is, to bring about their brave new worlds it will be necessary to eliminate all objectors. Although they have very different "political programs," like Quin and Wayne in *Napoleon* and the two brothers in *The Club of Queer Trades*, MacIan and Turnbull become comrades, brothers in arms pitted against a modern world which is like an insane asylum. They learn that their political and social views are closely intertwined with their religious values, and each is converted by the other. It is therefore quite misleading to assert that in this novel only MacIan is Chesterton's spokesman.[29]

The characters' transformation occurs in a comic, wildly unrealistic adventure story which is the Chestertonian version of Wells' science fiction. The book opens with the capture of Michael, an old Bulgarian monk, by a scientist, Professor Lucifer, who flies about in a silver spaceship. Lucifer drops the monk on the ball and cross at the top of St. Paul's Cathedral, leaving him to fall to his death, but the monk instead finds there "some equality among things, some balance in all possible contingencies which we are not permitted to know lest we should learn indifference to good and evil."[30] At the end, Turnbull, MacIan, and the old monk all find themselves locked up in Lucifer's modern, hygienic insane asylum (the world), from which they are rescued by a good French bourgeois, who starts the fire of revolution that returns the world to sanity.

This novel is a Chestertonian fairy tale in which existence itself is always a romantic adventure — here complete with two heroines who are attractive realists, though hardly Shaw's new women. But it is not as perfect a work of art as *Napoleon* or *Thursday*: no doubt due in part to its publication as a serial, *The Ball and the Cross* rambles on too long. Nonetheless, it is an interesting statement of Chesterton's political beliefs (in 1905) about the sanctity of the individual.

Unlike the heroines in Shaw's *Mrs. Warren's Profession*, Ibsen's *A Doll's House*, and H.G. Wells' *Ann Veronica*, Chesterton's women do not yearn to own property, go to the universities, vote, use contraceptives, or be divorced. Neither are they the dolls and playthings of husbands who are arbitrary masters in their own homes; there is a lot of Chesterton's wife and his mother in his heroines. They are guides like Dante's Beatrice, as queenly and demanding as his Virgin Mary, who tells King Alfred "naught for your comfort, Yea, naught for your desire / Save that the sky grows darker yet / And the sea rises higher."[31] They are also like the fairy princess in the toy theatre's high tower: she waited to be rescued, but she probably told the prince how to accomplish this feat, and then took responsibility for making sure they lived happily ever after.

While his older brother was drawing word pictures of the kind of women he most admired, Cecil Chesterton was a part of a Fabian Society battle over leadership which had also turned into a battle of the sexes. On the one hand there was Beatrice Webb, who enjoyed equality with her lower-class husband in public and private, but held strongly Victorian views on sex; on the other hand there was H.G. Wells, the liberator, who was personally enjoying the sexual revolution in the upper middle-class, a change fueled by a generation of improved education and birth control. Wells wanted the society to promote rights for women and enlisted the "Fabian nursery" for his side, while others, like Cecil, felt it was out of place. His typical outspokenness lost him his support, so that by December 1906 Fabians from all over England had come to vote Wells out. The Old Gang spoke up for themselves, while Wells' followers, like Cecil, deserted him. Cecil then was voted off the Executive Committee for his disloyalty to his own age group. Cecil continued for some time to defend socialism against what he called Belloc's "peasant proprietorship" ideas, and both he and Gilbert were to become involved in a new Fabian project.

The great fight as well as the "progressive" temper of the times had caused a boom in Fabian memberships, so that by 1907 the membership had doubled to over 7,000. Two earnest young Fabians from Leeds now appeared in London with a mission. They both were convinced that the Fabians should create a Socialist attitude toward art and philosophy, and they therefore became charter members of the newly formed Fabian Arts Group, which hoped to relieve Fabianism of its "webbed feet." Their names were Alfred Orage and Holbrook Jackson.[32]

The real moving spirit proved to be Orage, whom Shaw called the most brilliant editor England had had for a hundred years, but added that he did not belong to the successful world. Besides belonging to the Fabians, Orage was a member of the Christian Social Union, and admired Ruskin and Morris. An unhappily married schoolteacher, he had been a Theosophist, a follower of Nietzsche, a vegetarian, a dabbler in the occult. He followed these fads with the messianic, humorless spirit of one of Chesterton's "heretics," still looking for an idea powerful enough to change the world.[33] Orage was extremely susceptible to conversion and had a desire to turn his own revelations into universal dogmas; except for his lower-class origins, he was a lot like Cecil Chesterton.

During the spring of 1907 a little weekly called the *New Age* came on the market, and Orage and Jackson managed to buy it with help from Shaw and a Theosophist banker in the City. The paper was announced in the *Fabian News* as a Socialist journal to be run along Fabian lines. This technically identified all of its contributors with Fabianism, although Orage was so eclectic in his tastes that he actually published anyone who had something to say and said it well. The paper's main contributors were the "bohemian" Fabian Arts Group, which met at Clifford's Inn. Cecil Chesterton and Clifford Sharp wrote about politics, Arnold Bennett did book reviews, and Havelock Ellis wrote about Freud. Although Cecil claimed to be Orage's assistant editor, that job was also claimed by Orage's mistress. Part of the charm of the operation was that Orage held open editorial meetings every Monday afternoon at the A.B.C. Restaurant in Chancery Lane, where all the contributors helped to read the proofs.[34]

The membership of the *New Age* staff and the Fabian Arts Group overlapped so much that it is impossible to distinguish between them. There is also no clear evidence whether the "Great Debate" between Shaw and Chesterton began in the pages of the *New Age* or in various London lecture halls, organized by Orage and sponsored by the Fabian Arts Group; the probable answer is that both forms of the debate began at about the same time. It was now that the general format for their debates was created. Shaw, whose allies might include Wells or Cecil Chesterton, faced Chesterton, while Belloc sat in the chair, acting as moderator and moralizing. From the beginning their subject was socialism versus what is now called distributism but what was really Chestertonian liberalism. This friendly association may have given rise to the idea that Chesterton was once a Fabian, which he was not; the Fabians were always his "friendly" foes, about whom he did say, "When I remember the other world against which [the Fabian Society] reared its bourgeois banners of cleanliness and common sense, I will not end without doing it decent honour."[35] Although the "Great Debate" is also said to have started much later, in 1911, with the two men's separate talks at the Cambridge Heretics Club, Shaw and Chesterton must have debated one another onstage long before 1911 — or, at the very least, shared the platform before that time.

In purely literary terms, the "Great Debate" officially started on December 7, 1907, in the *New Age*, with an article by Belloc called "Thoughts About Modern Thought." Chesterton next wrote on "Why I Am Not A Socialist"; next Wells wrote "About Chesterton and Belloc"; then Belloc wrote "On Wells and A Glass of Beer." Finally Shaw got into the act with his famous article on "The Chesterbelloc: A Lampoon," which appeared on February 15, 1908. Their series went on until early in 1909 and got very silly, with articles on "The Shawbox" and "The Chestershaw," all pointing up the fact that it was not anyone's intention then to identify Chesterton only with Belloc.[36] This was the period when Belloc was still a backbencher in Parliament, growing disenchanted with party politics; it was also the last period of time when Chesterton was readily available for Monday afternoon "staff meetings," or Saturday-night arts groups.

Shaw and Wells had already perfected their public "personas," which — much to the cartoonists' delight — they played to the hilt, dressing their parts and making appropriate comments; they were self-created, walking advertisements. Chesterton had become equally dramatic, thanks to Frances, who early in their marriage had persuaded him to don his voluminous cape and soft brigand's hat, and to flourish his beloved sword stick, but to call Chesterton a poseur and forget that his costume was only one among many is ridiculous. Shaw was certainly Chesterton's dramatic match: tall — six feet four — and red-bearded, he dressed in yellow linsey-woolsey suits, and was frequently heard loudly refusing to eat "killed animals." When these two walked together down a busy London street, they were a sight to remember.

In the early *New Age* debates, Chesterton opposed "state" socialism in much the same terms he had used recently in *The Ball and the Cross*. He called it a dictatorship run by a self-chosen elite. He defended the inalienable right of the poor to be themselves, using his favorite hobbyhorses of pubs and education as examples. He suggested that Shaw wished to legislate that all mankind must eat grass. Impishly and poetically, Chesterton kept insisting on a fact the Fabians knew to be true: the working class in England was incurably conservative, so that social change would have to be forced upon them by an educated bureaucracy.[37] He also shared their tendency to prefer the older squirearchy and aristocracy to the new, rich upper middle-class. Wells, the self-appointed scientific prophet with lower-class manners (and upper-class morals), kept insisting they all agreed about the evils of society. But he, too, felt the poor could not be left to run their own lives because, left alone, they would not grow into supermen. Shaw, as usual, had the last word because he invented the "Chesterbelloc," a character whose "Hilary Forelegs" led the greater hind legs named Gilbert; this creation, unfortunately, is all that remains alive of their arguments today.

In spite of this mythological beast, Shaw stated unequivocally that "Belloc and Chesterton are not the same sort of Christian, not the same sort of pagan, not the same sort of Liberal, not the same sort of anything intellectual," and ended with this challenge: "What has the Chesterbelloc to say in its own defense. . . . It is from the hind legs that I particularly want to hear [for Belloc] . . . is up against his problems in Parliament; it is in Battersea Park that a great force is being wasted." It seems to have been Cecil Chesterton, writing about his brother, who first used the term "Chesterbelloc" as if it were the real name of a real animal. As a disciple first of Shaw's, then of Belloc's, Cecil shared Belloc's tendency to regard his brother as weak and ineffectual because he did not "provide weapons wherewith one may wound and kill folly." Still, most people preferred Chesterton's chuckle to Belloc's bite.[38]

From this point on Shaw took Chesterton under his fantastic wing, urging him to write plays, and scolding him for his lack of financial sense. This friendship not only produced the debates and public recognition for which they were famous, but affected both their writing careers. Chesterton did write one play which European commentators said revealed Shaw's influence; he also brilliantly analyzed Shaw in one of his biographical commentaries. In his *Autobiography*, Chesterton characterized their relationship with this observation:

> I have argued with him on almost every subject in the world; and we have always been on the opposite sides, without affectation or animosity. . . . All these differences come back to a religious difference. . . . I think all differences do. . . . The difference is this. . . . Shavians believe in evolution exactly as the old Imperialist believed in expansion. . . . Man has been made more sacred than any superman. . . . His very limitations . . . have become holy . . . and God . . . very small.[39]

The same month that Shaw was lampooning the "Chesterbelloc," Chesterton published his most popular and enduring novel, *The Man Who Was*

Thursday. It now appears that he had been working on it for some time, because it is the story of his adolescence and his romance, turned into another wildly romantic, amusing, but terrifying tale.

In discussing Chesterton's novels it is valuable to use the discarded term "romance."[40] As a literary genre, a romance is neither fantasy nor escape; it is defined by its particular assumptions about reality. Two forms popular today are the western and the detective story, both usually considered second-rate, even if, as was true in Chesterton's day, it is these popular writers who are widely read. Romantic fiction either creates a world that is simpler than reality, or escapes into another time or place; the unpleasant aspects of either love or money are ignored. Dickens was a romancer, and Chesterton was his disciple, writing in allegorical terms about his own time and its controversies.

The frankly autobiographical element in *The Man Who Was Thursday*, subtitled "A Nightmare," is stated very clearly in the dedication to E.C. Bentley:

> This is the tale of those old fears, even of those emptied hells —
> And none but you shall understand the true thing that it tells. . . .
> We have found common things at last, and marriage and a creed,
> And I may safely write it now, and you may safely read.[41]

His particular hell was thoughts of suicide, brought on by the sense of meaninglessness and the lack of self-identity common to bright adolescents; the creed was a combination of liberalism and Christianity. Like many young men in life and in literature, both Bentley and Chesterton had discovered that having a wife to support gave a purpose to their lives, so that it is perfectly true that his archetypal myth was the quest for the Grail — which, for Chesterton, always ended in domesticity.[42] He celebrated this paradoxical discovery in most of his novels.

It is highly appropriate that it is this novel which is usually chosen to prove that Chesterton was not just a "jolly journalist bloated with fermented gusto who wrote tremendous trifles," but someone who felt deeply the dark forces of chaos loose in the Western world. His anarchy sounds very contemporary, but anarchy was also real and intellectually fashionable in 1908. The resemblance of Chesterton's writing to Kafka's, first pointed out by C.S. Lewis, is the result of the kind of allegorical imagination also shaping Wells' science fiction — but in Chesterton's work the atmosphere is absurd, not portentous. Kafka himself had not only read Chesterton's novels but admired them. He is quoted as having said that "he is so gay, one might almost believe he had found God." When asked if laughter is a sign of religious faith, Kafka added, "Not always. But in such a godless time, one must be gay. It is a duty."[43] That is a remark Chesterton might well have made himself.

The Man Who Was Thursday is also a boys' adventure story, complete with costumes and sword fights and a mad chase across Chesterton's boyhood London, described so accurately that a map can be drawn of the trail. It is a political parable of the times that tells a love story patterned after Chesterton's own romance, as well as expresses faith in a universe found to be friendly after all. Its stylistic blending of the format of an adventure/detective story, grotesques like those of Dickens and Browning, and prophecies similar to those of the Old Testament together form Chesterton's personal and authentic method of expression.[44] It is this tone of high levity that has made people call him a "metaphysical jester," or a fool for Christ — or even, in Father Ronald Knox's phrase, the author of a Pickwickian *Pilgrim's Progress*. But the book is also a dramatization of the ideas in *Orthodoxy*, which was written at the same time, as well as a sharp, topical commentary on the underlying dangers in social reform itself.

The story is told within a frame of "real life," opening with a grim and lurid sunset in Saffron Park where the hero, a poet named Gabriel Syme, has come to a social discussion group like the ones the young Chestertons enjoyed. He meets another poet, an anarchist, who has an intelligent sister. The two poets argue about the meaning of life; then, as they leave the meeting to walk home, they fall into a wild adventure upon which hinges the fate of London. When it is over, Syme wakes up to find that he is still quietly walking in a sleeping, early-morning London, but his whole outlook on life has changed:

> Dawn was breaking over everything in colours at once clear and timid. . . .
> A breeze blew so clean and sweet, that one could not think it blew from the
> sky; it blew rather through some hole in the sky. Syme felt a simple surprise
> when he saw rising all round him . . . the red, irregular buildings of Saffron
> Park.[45]

At this point he again meets the poet's redheaded sister, whose memory had sustained him during the nightmare. The sister is an "Impressionistic," thematic version of Beatrice who leads Dante out of Hell, so her figure is as important, in terms of Christian symbolism, as that of the gigantic Sunday, leader of the anarchist cell. Sunday, the criminal who is God, is described like Chesterton's High Master at St. Paul's School. His anarchists are known by their code names, which are the names of the days of the week, suggesting both the days of creation as well as the gods of pagan mythology. All are ultimately revealed to be policemen, dedicated to the preservation of society — like their chief, who enlisted them in the crusade.

Although *The Man Who Was Thursday* was a great influence on an entire generation of readers, many younger ones like Father Knox ignored its political, or public, message that the elite of the world easily despair and then join conspiracies to destroy the world. But when it was initially published, its theme was very contemporary, because in 1908 anarchists, like our terrorists, really existed. During this pre-war period, six heads of state were murdered by what has been called "The Idea," a dream of a stateless society without government, law, or property, where a man would be as free as God meant him to be.[46] This idea had made established society sense violent revolution in the air, for those tried for these murders insisted they were only creating a better world. Chesterton, therefore, was portraying a growing political tenseness that was felt even in England, where Liberal promises and programs were being stalled by the increasing obstruction of the House of Lords, as well as by division among Liberals over priorities. As the reformers became depressed over the future, irrational violence was building.

Chesterton saw Belloc glumly commuting from Sussex to Westminster, aware that his chances of party preferment were nil, but as obstreperous as always; Masterman, meanwhile, was about to join the old-boy network by marrying Lucy Lyttelton, herself a connection of the new Liberal prime minister, Asquith. A self-made, middle-class lawyer, Asquith was a highly competent man but also a trimmer, just as Chesterton had said.[47] Liberals like his editor Gardiner also began to see Asquith had no policy except to stay in office. As a result, Asquith valued capable young comers like Masterman, who soon became Parliamentary Secretary for the Local Government Board, and by 1912 was Undersecretary of State in the Home Office under young and newly married Winston Churchill. By contrast, a back-bencher like Belloc, who refused to support intervention in the Belgian Congo and spoke against the new Liberal Education Bill because it would hurt parochial schools, was no use at all. To Chesterton, who watched their careers, it seemed that as Belloc grew less "manageable," Masterman grew more so.

Cecil Chesterton's anonymous biography of Gilbert, called *G. K. Chesterton: A Criticism*, appeared during 1908. Its strange mixture of insight and argument, myth and fact was polemically heightened to make its subject more like a Shavian superman with comic overtones. Its broad portrait of Gilbert as a wine-bibbing, wife-dominated, portly hero whose ideas came from the Middle Ages was probably the greatest single influence on Chesterton's subsequent biographers. The book's misuse of chronology was adopted uncritically first by Titterton and then by Gilbert himself, who never had any head for dates, finally becoming "gospel truth" in Maisie Ward's book. It is also possible that Cecil deliberately patterned his description of his brother's career after that of another noted writer, Charles Dickens, who had flashed on the London scene when he was quite young and had become a celebrity within a year.[48] Ironically, the very attitudes he insisted were Gilbert's were those he himself was coming to adopt.

Frances and Gilbert suspected almost immediately that Cecil had written the book, because the very structure of the arguments echoed his endless debates with his brother. It was also dedicated to "MLC — the wittiest woman in London," who could easily be Mrs. Chesterton. Knowing Cecil was always in need of work (he borrowed money from them when they could hardly afford it), the Chestertons said nothing. In any case, it would have been ridiculous for Gilbert Chesterton to try to prove that he was not as much of a celebrity as his brother claimed he was. Besides, there was some excuse for Cecil's deliberate heightening of the "literary lion scene": it was true that now other noted men and society hostesses wanted to meet or entertain the Chestertons. A case in point is H.G. Wells, who, having known Cecil, was becoming acquainted with Gilbert, and who, like virtually everyone else who knew Gilbert, remained fond of him until his death. Frances' diaries are full of descriptions of meeting such people on various social occasions, most of which she found exhausting.

During the summer of 1908 Gilbert and Frances rented a house at Rye, "that wonderful inland island, crowned with a town ... like a hill in a medieval picture."[49] They turned out to be neighbors not only of the great Henry James, the expatriate, proper American novelist, but also of Wells, who had a place called Spade House nearby. He filled it with guests, among them romantic, rebellious young women and a Swiss governess for his sons; his second wife, understandably, appeared "under a strain."

Henry James was the grand old man of the area, the master who Chesterton said reflected the "grey twilight of the Victorian Age," a most amusing criticism of someone who was to be the "new" author whom Virginia Woolf's generation chose to copy. Chesterton would not have been surprised by this topsy-turviness in the literary world, for he had long known that "progress" was an illusion; but he would have had little patience with their egotistical tendency to say that the only subject for fiction was their own consciousness and its sensations. He himself was an acute observer of James, whom he saw as an American who had reacted against America by steeping his psychology in everything that was antiquated and aristocratic. James's Lamb House was the seat of a long-dead patrician family, whose portraits James "treated as reverently as family ghosts"; his fictional characters were similar, "delicate and indisputable," so "we cannot help but admire the figures that walk about in his afternoon drawing rooms; but we have a certain sense that they are figures that have no faces."[50]

James's equally famous brother William, a psychologist, was visiting him. He wanted to meet the Chestertons, but his brother felt they must first be introduced. He was very reproving when William put a ladder up to the garden wall to peek over at Chesterton's house; fortunately, Wells showed up at this point and introduced them. Shortly afterward Henry James came to pay a formal call, and while they sat making polite conversation about literature, with James augustly deploring the fact that Shaw's plays had no form, there was a loud shout from the garden: "G-i-l-bert!"

Chesterton felt it must be Belloc — it was his foghorn voice — but Belloc was supposed to be in France. He appeared, however, dirty and footsore, with a friend with whom he had walked from Dover to Rye. Now he loudly demanded food and drink. Commenting on this incident later, Chesterton said that although Henry James was supposed to be subtle, this situation was "too subtle" for him: "Here on the other side of the tea table was Europe . . . dirty and unwashed, shouting for wine . . . unbelievably a Member of Parliament and an official of the Foreign Office." James's reaction was pure American, Puritanical disdain.

Chesterton and Wells found they enjoyed one another's company and shared an enthusiasm for "larks." They invented a game called "Gype" which they commented on in their newspaper articles, but the whole point of the game was precisely that it had no point. They also shared a love of toy theatres and collaborated on several plays designed for them, including one about the celebrated report of the Poor Law Commission that featured puppets of Beatrice and Sidney Webb. This camaraderie also produced Chesterton's interesting assessment of Wells: he felt that Wells' main problem was that "he always seemed to be coming from somewhere rather than going anywhere," reacting too swiftly to everything and being continually in a state of reaction.[51]

A collection of Chesterton's essays from the *Illustrated London News* called *All Things Considered* appeared in early September of 1908. Its title had been suggested by another journalist friend, E.V. Lucas, who wrote some celebrated guidebooks to London. In the introduction Chesterton answered Cecil's complaint that he played the buffoon by explaining that "the chief vice [of these essays] is that so many of them are very serious; because I had no time to make them flippant."[52] Beneath the veneer of flippancy and paradox, Chesterton (in most of the essays) is talking about the political concerns of the day, such as oligarchy, patriotism, education, and the growing fondness of intellectuals for Eastern mystical cults.

On September 25, 1908, Chesterton next published *Orthodoxy*, which he correctly labeled a "slovenly autobiography." The chapters in *Orthodoxy* correspond very closely in subject matter to his last book, the *Autobiography*, which might be labeled a "slovenly reminiscence." Having dedicated *Heretics* to his father, he appropriately dedicated *Orthodoxy* to his mother, who represented the dictatorial but democratic tyrant of home and hearth, high priestess of the world's certainties and ruler of its most important dominion. Although Cecil had scooped his brother by getting his book into print earlier that year, it is Gilbert's book that has remained a minor classic.

Those who want to read Chesterton's writing backwards to prove that he was born a Roman Catholic have tried to turn *Orthodoxy* into a Newman's *Apologia Pro Vita Sua*, but it is really no such thing. It neither reflects certain convictions about the nature of the Church which he later came to accept, nor functions primarily as a piece of Christian apologetics. It was the answer to a challenge, a call to debate, issued not only by critics of *Heretics* but also by Cecil, who was becoming convinced of the validity of Roman Catholicism and liked to use his brother as a sounding board.

In *Orthodoxy* Chesterton was characteristically seeking a useful balance between a rationality that caused intellectual arrogance and despair, and a romanticism without roots that had gone wild. He was not delivering an exposition of Thomist theology, but defending both the romance found in ordinary life as well as the usefulness of reason for understanding it.[53] When he repeats his parable from *Heretics* about the old monk and the lamppost, then, he is not really defending the monastic way of life.

Orthodoxy has remained popular with ordinary readers because it is based upon Chesterton's discovery of a traditional faith in his own thoughts and background. Its basic organization reflects his purpose, which was to combine his experience and his reflections on the human condition into a story that illustrates how his Liberal ideals, once developed, turned out to be what Christianity had stated in its ancient creeds.[54] (His brother had been absolutely correct when he predicted that his older brother would never turn against his own roots.)

Chesterton chose to tell this tale in a series of dramatized scenes, the first of which is probably the most famous picture he ever "drew." The story is told in his inimitable style, combining the Western Christian tradition of the quest for one's own soul, the focus of the stories of King Arthur as well as of Dante and Bunyan, with the unmistakable flavor of heroic adventuring to strange new worlds more reminiscent of Defoe and Swift and Robert Louis Stevenson. He began,

> I have often had a fancy for writing a romance about an English yachtsman who ... discovered England under the impression that it was a new island in the South Seas. ... The man who landed [armed to the teeth and talking in signs] to plant the British flag on that barbaric temple which turned out to be the Brighton Pavilion ... looked rather a fool. ... But if you imagine that he felt a fool ... you have not studied with sufficient delicacy the rich romantic nature of the hero. ... His mistake was really the most enviable mistake and he knew it. ... What could be more delightful than to have ... all the terrors of going abroad combined with all the ... security of coming home again?[55]

He added, in his typically conversational tone, "This seems to me to be the main problem for philosophers, and ... is the problem of this book. How can we contrive to be at once astonished at the world and yet at home in it?"[56] His sense that the world was a moral battleground had helped him fight to keep the attitude that has been labeled his "facile optimism," so that he could recover the wonder and surprise at ordinary life he had once felt as a child.

His next stage involved encountering Christianity through other people who were Christians, who helped him realize that "I am that man in the yacht. ... I did try to found a heresy of my own; and when I had put the last touches to it, I discovered that it was orthodoxy."[57] His "orthodoxy" is based on the fact that Christianity gave him both a view of the universe and a way to act, while its "proof" for him came from the criticisms made of it by his fellow moderns. He describes the contemporary world as a madhouse, as he did in *The Ball and the Cross*. In it the skeptic believes everything begins and ends in himself, so that his friends are a mythology he has made up. Just as the circle is the symbol of reason and madness, so the cross is the symbol of mystery and health, but it is "idle to talk of the alternative of reason and faith. Reason itself is a matter of faith. It is an act of faith to assert that our thoughts have any relation to reality at all. . . . The thought that stops thought [is] . . . the ultimate evil against which all religious authority was aimed."[58]

As Chesterton talks about "orthodoxy" or "Christianity," however, it becomes clear not only that he is using the term to make an analogy rather than a dogmatic statement, but that the roots of his use of it come from liberalism. For example, in the middle chapters he describes how he was a pagan at twelve and a complete agnostic at sixteen, but still had retained the "doctrine" of his childhood. This was the creed of liberalism, which stressed that things common to all men must be more valuable than things peculiar to some men, and that the political instinct is one of the things men have in common, like falling in love. "Liberalism" had also taught him that the most important things must be left for men to do themselves: mating, rearing the young, establishing laws for the state — and he insisted on enfranchising his ancestors as well, on listening to the voice of tradition. In all these analogies, it is very important to pay attention to Chesterton's personal use of terms. His use of words like "usury," "imperialism," "orthodox," or "heretic" are all quite private, owing something to ordinary definitions but always carrying certain idiosyncratic elements that are Chesterton's alone. This is one reason why it is unsafe to assume that "characters" like the "Virgin Mary" in his early works stand exclusively for the person defined by Roman Catholic dogma.

Chesterton felt he had learned to be a "Liberal" in the nursery when he was taught fairy tales, which expressed the ordinary person's experience of the surprise and wonder of life, but which required obedience to certain incomprehensible rules like "Be home by midnight" as a condition of happiness or fulfillment. Then, having since childhood also believed that the world contained "magic" (mystery, wonder, or sometimes a miracle like Cecil's birth), he began to think it involved a magician: where there is a story, there must be a storyteller.

As an unhappy teenager, Chesterton next had come to terms with the idea of suicide. He had to decide if it were a "right" or a "crime." Modern and ancient philosophers said it was a right; Christianity said it was the destruction of a universe, and he chose that definition. From this point he began to separate "God from the cosmos" and see the world as His creation. He discovered the "Christian" idea that God was a creator who had written a perfect play; then He had left it to human actors, who made a mess of it. (He dramatized this idea in his last play, *The Surprise*.) Finally, Chesterton had come to realize that we are the survivors of a wreck that sank before the story began, which explains why he could be both at peace with the universe and yet at war with the world — in other words, this is his usual, pictorial way of describing the truth of the Fall.[59]

Modern philosophers had told him that he was in the right place, but Christianity told him he was in the wrong place, and he suddenly felt much better:

> I had been blundering about . . . with two huge and unmanageable machines . . . the world and the Christian tradition. I had found this hole in the world — the fact that one must somehow find a way of loving the world without trusting it — . . . [and] I found this projecting feature of Christian theology, like a sort of hard spike, the dogmatic insistence that God was personal, and had made the world separate from himself. The spike of dogma fitted exactly into the hole in the world. . . . Once these two parts of the two machines had come together . . . all the other parts fitted . . . with an eerie exactitude . . . [and] the thing [Christianity] . . . had revealed itself as a truth-telling thing, that is, a way to live.[60]

In telling his own story Chesterton also dealt with most of the modern complaints against historic Christianity: the sociological concept that the legend of a dying and living God had appeared over and over; the solipsistic insistence that all one can know is what one personally feels; the stoic's idea that life is real, life is earnest and must be endured; and the utopian idea that the rich are trustworthy. He concluded that democracy is derived from the doctrine of original sin. "Orthodoxy" became one of his names for Western Christendom, whose chariot flew through the ages, knocking heresies flat, and reeling — but managing to stay upright. He ended the book on a characteristic note by suggesting that the gigantic secret of Christianity is humor, a joyful gaiety and mirth shared by Christ himself.

At the age of thirty-four Chesterton publicly called himself an "orthodox" Christian in this fashion, but he did not become a devout member of a parish. He continued to allow Frances to perform those duties for both of them, while he remained a variety of the genus Protestant in which everyman is his own theologian. While his book is built upon symbols, such as "fairy tales" or "tradition" or even "Christianity," it is not based upon the symbols Cecil had used, like the toy theatre or the J.D.C. But those symbols did reappear years later, when Chesterton himself sat down to write his *Autobiography*, presumably with Cecil's book in hand. Ironically, he himself was one of those persons who read interpretations back into his life.

But *Orthodoxy* was a more historical account than his *Autobiography*; it realistically tied together Chesterton's religious convictions and his political concerns. In defending classical liberalism from within and without, he discovered Christian tradition, which gave him an older basis for the twin beliefs of his childhood: that all men are made in the image of God and that all men fell. Christianity also described a world in which epic actions had meaning, where circumstances were not determined in advance, so that even if many battles were lost, the ultimate war would be won. His view of orthodoxy did not accept the "negative" way of other Christian mystics, nor any Eastern concept of oneness with the universe, or hope of nirvana. Instead, he used it to make a strong pragmatic statement about the value of expressing the obvious, while defining what the obvious really was.

That year, as Gilbert and Cecil each drew his highly individualistic "portrait of the author as a young man," Frances Chesterton suffered another family tragedy which changed all their lives. Her younger brother, Knollys, had always been subject to spells of depression; like Frances, he had suffered a severe attack over their sister Gertrude's death. Recently he had become a Roman Catholic and had begun using Father O'Connor as his "father confessor," but this did not cure his depression, either: one Sunday evening he committed suicide by drowning himself in the sea.

Like all responsible people, Frances was stricken with guilt, and Gilbert suddenly found that, once again, he was absolutely necessary to her emotional stability. As he wrote to Father O'Connor, marriage must be a sacrament because even a man like himself could sometimes be indispensable; at the same time "he never feels so small as when he really knows he is necessary." The general public always saw Gilbert as ludicrously dependent on Frances, who tied his tie and found his tickets; and it was true that all their married life, like a typical older sister, she fussed over him and coped with innumerable family crises. But when she suffered this loss immediately after an operation she had in hopes of being able to get pregnant, she needed Gilbert's undivided time and attention. In fact, she always had a need to feel needed, but the Fleet Street life was not one which, on the whole, gave her much of Gilbert's time.

Whatever her precise motivation, she did seize this chance to ask Gilbert to move to the country, where she could have a garden of her own and he could work at home. It was not a totally unreasonable request, but it meant changing the patterns of their lives and friendships, as well as leaving the center of action — a change Frances may well have thought necessary for Gilbert's own health and peace of mind. In any case, in typical Chestertonian fashion, Gilbert agreed to the move, but it was not actually accomplished for another year.

Part Three

WHAT'S WRONG
WITH THE WORLD?

1909-1913

Today's "human comedy" still remains unwritten. . . . We know little of the forces fermenting in that strange laboratory which is the birthplace of the coming time. We are uncertain whether civilization is about to blossom into flower, or wither . . . whether we are about to plunge into a new period of tumult and upheaval . . . [a] prolongation of the present half-lights and shadows . . . [or] whether a door is to be suddenly opened, revealing unimaginable glories.

C. F. G. Masterman in a postscript to *The Condition of England*, 1909

A book of modern social inquiry has a shape that is . . . sharply defined. It is always . . . stating the disease before we find the cure. But it is the whole definition and dignity of man that in social matters we must actually find the cure before we find the disease. . . . [In] modern social discussion, . . . the quarrel is not merely about the difficulties, but about the aim. We agree about the evil; it is about the good that we should tear each other's eyes out. . . . I have called this book "What's Wrong With the World" but the rather wild title refers only to one point, What is wrong is that we do not ask what is right.

G.K. Chesterton, *What's Wrong With the World*, 1910

Chapter Nine

THE HOME OF JONES

1909-1910

I asked the man . . . where the next train went to. He uttered the pedantic reply: "Where do you want to go?" And I uttered the profound . . . rejoinder, "Wherever the next train goes to." . . . It went to Slough. . . . From there [we] set out walking . . . [passing] through the large and quiet cross-roads of a sort of village . . . called Beaconsfield . . . and we said to each other: "This is the sort of place where some day we will make our home."

G.K. Chesterton, *Autobiography*[1]

GILBERT and Frances had made this amusing excursion, using the railroad system like a Ouija board, sometime earlier, so that when Frances needed a change of scene, they had a real place in mind. To move out of London would signal that Chesterton was no longer "just" a day-to-day journalist like Bentley, who must be near his office, nor a free-lancer like Cecil, obliged to keep finding new markets; it was also a common middle-class practice to move to a "country" home near London. Other writer friends of his — like Shaw, Belloc, and Wells — had already done so, seeking peace and quiet for more productive writing, as well as a place to invite their frequent company. Entertaining guests was the job of the writer's wife, while he hid in his study to write; and although Ada Jones criticized her hospitality, Frances seems to have functioned very well in the role of hostess. In addition, she read Gilbert's material, criticizing it, sometimes even copying it and proofreading it as well.

Predictably, moving to a place like Beaconsfield seemed to Cecil Chesterton as bad as living in Bedford Park; he found "bedroom suburbs" both phony and bourgeois. The comments both he and his future wife made show that they took this move personally, assuming that Frances had the ulterior motive of separating the brothers and trying to make her husband over into a "man of letters." Ada even hinted that Frances was angling for a Liberal title in the event that new peers had to be created. (It is difficult to imagine Chesterton accepting a title in return for helping to pass Liberal legislation through Parliament.)² But it is true that the move was made largely for Frances' sake, and had the inevitable result that the two brothers saw less of each other.

As other, more disinterested commentators pointed out, Chesterton had changed. He was grossly overweight, and seemed to move more slowly, slowed down even further by his unfailing humor and courtesy, which meant that a walk along Fleet Street was characterized by a thousand interruptions that waylaid him and disrupted his thoughts. But there was one thing the move did not change: Chesterton never quit being a part of the working press, although, as Bentley pointed out, he could have stopped writing his weekly columns and settled down to be a poet and biographer. Instead, his move to Beaconsfield only intensified his struggle to get the columns done on time.³

In certain ways the Chestertons' move came at a good time. Fleet Street itself was alive with tensions and troubles of which Chesterton, and probably Frances, too, were only too aware. By 1909 the golden age of journalism was already gone. The profitable London papers were all Conservative, and it was increasingly difficult to launch a new paper. Chesterton sardonically observed that the ordinary journalist was more and more becoming "a man who wrote things on the backs of advertisements."⁴ The only exception to this decline in the "free" press was the *Nation*, which had taken the place of the dying *Speaker*. Its new editor was H. W. Massingham, the archetypal Liberal journalist — bright, opinionated, and very emotional, with a sense of mission but no sense of humor.⁵ Chesterton wrote for the *Nation* now and then, but he and Massingham did not really get along well, partly because Massingham was inclined to take every statement literally.

In organization, the *Nation* was very much like the *New Age,* run like a family affair. Both were lively, controversial, and comprehensive, and the names of their contributors overlapped. Neither paper was circulated widely nor did more than stay alive financially. The *Nation*, however, not being a Fabian offspring, got more respect as the "pure voice" of liberalism. During the next few years Massingham arbitrarily decided that Chesterton was lost in the Middle Ages, and his judgment gave currency to this attitude all along Fleet Street. What he really was objecting to, however, was Chesterton's use of Christian "orthodoxy" as the philosophical basis for liberalism. This position was anathema to Massingham, who as an ex-Evangelical was now intrigued by the Blavatskian kind of Eastern "nirvana."

Bigger and better newspapers were in trouble, too. As early as 1907 George Cadbury was talking about selling the *Daily News* if his son Henry could not make it pay, so that the editor, Gardiner, was increasingly uneasy about his own future. At the same time his temperamental writers like Chesterton and Massingham accused him of not acting independently of the Cadburys. (The paper was derisively known as the Cocoa Press, because the family fortunes were founded upon the chocolate made from their cocoa plantations in Angola.) In 1907, for example, Gardiner was accused of not standing up for "the freedom of the press" when he stopped a writer from calling the Cadburys "slave-owners." Shortly afterward Chesterton wrote a column defending a Liberal backbencher who had denounced the open sale of titles, a practice that had begun about 1890 to fill party coffers, and that now was becoming really blatant.[6] Gardiner suppressed Chesterton's column because he felt the *Daily News* must support the government. Furious, Chesterton protested that the backbencher was being "humiliated and broken for telling the truth," and that this was the "hypocrisy of public life [which means] the secret funds and the secret powers are safe." When Chesterton then begged Gardiner to let him write a letter to the editor in support of the backbencher, Gardiner did agree to that, and published it.

Although they remained close friends, Chesterton becoming godfather to Gardiner's son, the seeds of trouble were sown, and a year or so later Chesterton was protesting that "you allow Massingham [as Parliamentary reporter] . . . to damn and blast the Liberal Party . . . [and] if I have to follow the Liberal Government . . . I cannot write for the paper." He added that sooner or later he and Gardiner would have a row about "right and wrong" because liberalism "must allow for open questions."[7] Unquestionably, from Gardiner's point of view, Chesterton, Massingham, and the rest were being very idealistic; unquestionably, too, they considered this kind of "open questioning" to be a vital part of the Liberal creed, one which they must defend at all costs, against all comers, even their closest friends. This situation was not helped by Shaw's taking advantage of every public occasion to taunt Chesterton with being "Cadbury's property."[8]

In the end, caught in the crossfire between his paper's owners, the problems of the Liberal leadership, and the public's right to know, Gardiner pleased no one. He had also begun to suspect that his Liberal heroes — Winston Churchill and Lloyd George — were more interested in their own careers than the good of the country or the party. No wonder Chesterton sensed the Fleet Street he had idolized (and idealized) was being destroyed, something he clearly stated in a poem which is *not* about his sorrow at moving to Beaconsfield but a bitter word play on the fact that in medieval times the Fleet was a prison[9]:

> *When I came back to Fleet Street. . . .*
> *. . . not in peace I came. . . .*
> *All buried things broke upward;*
> *And peered from its retreat. . . .*
> *[Telling] the secret of the Street. . . .*
> *[that] the street's a prison [and]. . . .*
> *All that they leave of rebels*
> *Rot high on Temple Bar. . . .*

Where they, and I, and you,
Run high the barricade that breaks. . . .
And shout to them that shrink within,
The prisoners of the Fleet. [10]

The practical political problems arose not on Fleet Street, but in Parliament. The prime minister was caught between the demand for social legislation and a lack of money to finance it, and also plagued by the fact that Liberals disagreed among themselves over priorities. Chesterton, for example, was eager for Irish Home Rule and land reform, but very cool to old-age insurance or a totally state-controlled educational system. The splits within their ranks had not yet been faced by the Liberals because most of their bills did not make it through Parliament, largely due to the Conservative majority in the House of Lords. Every time the Lords vetoed a government measure, the Liberal papers told Asquith to "go to the country," oblivious of the possibility that he would come back with a weaker party, not a stronger one. Hence his pet phrase, "Let us wait and see." [11]

Into this political vacuum stepped the bright young speechmakers, Churchill and Lloyd George, who borrowed Fabian techniques and introduced social legislation by administrative fiat. The battle lines were still further confused in February 1909 when the Majority Report of the Royal Commission on the Poor Law was issued, reflecting an attempt to get all administration into the hands of the municipal officials. Its position was undermined by the famous Minority Report, "the Webbs' Utopia in a Blue Book," which was published by the Fabian Society. [12] The Webbs wanted a minimum national standard of living and paupers classified by need, not by name. Its famous signatories were Beatrice Webb and the M. P. George Lansbury, both Fabian Socialists. To push for the acceptance of their far more extreme proposals, the Webbs now founded a National Committee for the Break-up of the Poor Law, among whose celebrity sponsors was Chesterton himself. [13] He, of course, had been emotionally conditioned by Dickens to loathe the Poor Law and its workhouses. But, unhappy at the idea of a new "aristocracy" of bureaucrats, Chesterton was not likely to be anything but an uneasy ally for the Webbs in the long run.

All kinds of Liberals — from Belloc to Chesterton, from Bentley to Masterman — were convinced that there must be a crusade to break the power of the House of Lords which they saw (especially with the increase in the sale of titles to rich businessmen) as a plutocracy of stolen riches, not an old established and landed aristocracy. Increasing the popular outcry against the Lords was also a way to keep the unstable Liberal coalition together, and a fateful step toward a showdown was taken that April 1909 when Lloyd George introduced his "People's Budget." It was designed to provide money for an expanded Navy and to pay for his newly established old-age pension system; the budget also represented "punitive taxation." It became celebrated through Lloyd George's famous Limehouse Speech about "the rich."

While all these political alarms were sounding and he was making plans to move to Beaconsfield, Chesterton was developing his friendship with Shaw, discovering what they had in common, particularly their view that the world was a moral place. That August, Chesterton published his biographical study *George Bernard Shaw*. It was a remarkably able book that provided a look at the relationship between the two men, as well as demonstrated Chesterton's insight into the workings of Shaw's personality.[14]

Like all Chesterton's studies, the chief purpose of this book was to study Shaw's intellectual position by showing his relationship to his background and his times. When it was published, reviewers kept saying that it showed how much Shaw and Chesterton agreed. In fact, Shaw and Chesterton asked the same questions of society, but they got quite different answers.[15] Using Chesterton's terminology, he was "orthodox," while Shaw was the "heretic." Shaw kept telling Chesterton to quit pretending to believe in God, while Chesterton replied that if Shaw did not rediscover the reason for believing in God, the human race was lost. When Shaw suggested that it was necessary to abolish private property because it caused poverty, Chesterton retorted that he must solve the problem of poverty by restoring property to ordinary men, by which he meant not just land, but a decent wage and the right to work — in short, their right to be their own masters.

In his portrait of Shaw, Chesterton took Shaw's public image and turned it upside-down. He pointed out that the bumptious Shaw was really a shy man, as well as a "Puritan," by which Chesterton meant a sober, ascetic person who believed in determinism. He showed that Shaw was also a pragmatist, using facts and figures the Fabian way to sell socialism as a scientific salvation for the human race. He denied that Shaw was paradoxical, or comic, or socialist, but said that he was in deadly earnest, "a respectable gentleman of the Middle Classes, of refined tastes . . . [whose] great defect is . . . that lack of democratic sentiment [illustrated by his remark that] 'I have never had any feelings about the English working classes, except for a desire to abolish them and replace them with sensible people.' " If it were not enough to insist that an outspoken Socialist was really bourgeois, Chesterton also demonstrated that Shaw was a "heretic" because of his insistence on consistency carried to its logical conclusion, uninformed by ordinary common sense.[16] Beneath Shaw's puckish exterior, Chesterton detected the instincts of a crusader who was also an Edwardian mystic, with his vision of a "Life Force" which could create supermen. He stated that Shaw did not write problem plays because he never gave both sides equal time; he also showed no respect for the two cornerstones of ordinary lives: tradition and convention.

Shaw was long-winded because he was quick-witted, but Chesterton disagreed with the critics who felt that Shaw's lengthy prefaces gave away the moral, saying that the reader or viewer needed to know the precise background of a Shavian hero, just as he needed to know that Shaw was a "Puritan, an Irishman and a Progressive," even if he spilled out of these categories. In fact, said Chesterton, Shaw had used himself as a model for his own superman.

He concluded with this gleeful summary:

> Most people either say that they agree with Bernard Shaw or that they do not understand him. I am the only person who understands him, and I do not agree with him ... [but] however he may shout profanities ... there is always something about him which suggests that in a sweeter and more solid civilization he would have been a great saint of a sternly ascetic ... type. ... He is literally unworldly. ... All the virtues he has are heroic virtues. Shaw is like the Venus de Milo; all there is of him is admirable.[17]

Ironically, Shaw spent the next thirty years of his life trying to keep the critics from seeing how well Chesterton understood him. His initial defense was to ridicule Chesterton's insights and make them insignificant by harping upon Chesterton's misquotations and missing facts. He suggested that the biography could not be valid because it did not contain long critical examinations of his work, although in fact it has an orderly and systematic discussion of his plays and literary techniques, aimed at Chesterton's usual audience: the ordinary, educated reader. Basically, Shaw intimated that the study was no good because it was not written the way he would have written it. But, in the review which he wrote for the *Nation,* he admitted that "this book is what everybody expected it to be: the best work of literary art I have yet provoked ... and I am proud to have been the painter's model." But he added slyly, "All the same, it is in some respects quite a misleading book."[18]

The next book Chesterton published was another collection of topical essays from the *Daily News* called *Tremendous Trifles,* whose very title is now used to suggest his image as a Toby Jug buffoon.[19] Recently it has become accepted policy to counteract this misleading image by insisting in Freudian fashion that lurking beneath Chesterton's rotund exterior was a slender melancholy trying to escape. But both extremes are too neat, too simple; they leave out much he was trying to say. This is also true of the label "metaphysical jester," used to suggest that he wished to make men laugh to make them see.[20] A true metaphysical jester was Nietzsche, who was also insane; there was nothing insane or psychotic about Gilbert Chesterton.

A good antidote for such "heresies" is to read *Tremendous Trifles.* It is full of echoes of other works Chesterton wrote in the same period, and it illustrates the important themes repeated in all his writing, as well as adds to his ongoing "slovenly autobiography." Stylistically, these essays are neither so paradoxical nor so convoluted as one is led to expect. Usually they are cast in story form, and in tone and outlook they are close cousins to his

Father Brown stories, which, seen from this perspective, then become just another form of Chestertonian narrative art.

The essays sound as if he were chatting with a friend, and the paradox or epiphany he wants to convey is a part of the structure, not a verbal twist. The subject matter and treatment of the essays show that everything he wrote did fit together because his outlook on life was unified. But they do not illustrate the simplistic corollary, often repeated, that Chesterton had developed all his ideas by 1900 and never again changed his mind. What remained the same was his personality, which he had learned to display openly in his work. When reading these essays in the light of the time in which they were written, as well as noting their "eternal" qualities, it is helpful to quote Chesterton, who remarked that "the usual way of criticizing an author who has added something to the literary forms of the world is to complain that his work does not contain something which is obviously the speciality of someone else."[21]

Tremendous Trifles has been labeled a "bitter" book, but it should be remembered that Chesterton was writing these columns for Gardiner's paper during a period of growing uneasiness. Many of them show an insight embodied in a joke on himself for not looking closely enough at the world around him, though often, as he does look more closely, he no longer sees the best of all possible worlds. He said that these "fleeting sketches ... amount to no more than a sort of sporadic diary ... recording one day in twenty which happened to stick in the fancy ... whose purpose is to help [my] fellow men exercise the eye until it learns to see the startling facts that run across the landscape as plain as a painted fence"; and in these sketches he described many things that the conventional vision then denied. One of his most acute perceptions was this line: "This is the tragedy of England; you cannot judge it by its foremost men."

More typical is the tone of the essay called "A Piece of Chalk." He had set off for a day's sketching, armed with brown paper and chalk, not to draw the scenery before him but "the fertile dragons of his imagination" — only to find that he had no white chalk. He explains that white chalk is necessary to philosophy because it is "not a mere absence of colour; it is a shining and affirmative thing. ... The chief assertion of morality is that white is a colour [for] virtue is not the absence of vices ... [but] a separate and vivid thing." Then he suddenly stood up and roared with laughter — at himself — for "I was sitting on an immense warehouse of white chalk. The landscape was made entirely out of white chalk. ... I stood in a trance of pleasure, realizing that this Southern England is not only a grand peninsula, and a tradition, and a civilization, it is something even more admirable. It is a piece of chalk."[22]

This "trifle" has all the flavor of Chesterton's insights. England has a moral character that is expressed in the most "primary" color. She is really built upon virtue and worthy of his instinctive national pride, which is neither elitist nor imperial. There is nothing bitter about this "vision," nor is it shallow. It takes a kind of second sight to see this wonder in the ordinary fact of a chalk downs.

Other essays point out the difference between his outlook and the "Eastern" mysticism that was flourishing among intellectuals. Chesterton was never in sympathy with the "sects" like the occult Brotherhood of the Golden Dawn; his adolescent experiences with Oldershaw and his brother had probably taught him a lesson. Still, he felt the universe was mysterious, and he liked to call this quality "magic," as he did when he declared that "mysticism keeps men sane. As long as you have mystery, you have health. . . . The ordinary man has always been sane [because] . . . he has always had one foot in earth and the other in fairyland."[23] He makes the same point in "The Perfect Game," describing the time when he had been losing a croquet game and made three perfect hits only after it became too dark to see.

Some essays, like "The Diabolist," are frankly autobiographical; others relate to the political situation, as does "The Riddle of the Ivy." In this essay he makes a mocking list of the things that are better in England, including the specially English kind of "humbug," shown when the Tory leader Balfour said that the House of Lords must be preserved "because it represents something in the nature of a permanent public opinion . . . above the ebb and flow of the parties." Chesterton says tartly that Balfour "is simply a poet [who] knows that nearly all the Lords who are not Lords by accident [by birth] are Lords by bribery . . . dunces whom he has himself despised and adventurers whom he has himself ennobled."[24] This is not bitterness, but partisan Liberal politics. But England was Chesterton's home, despite his quarrels with it; of an inn in France, he said, "This is the wrong end of the world for me."

By October 1909 the Chestertons had finally made the move from Battersea Park to Beaconsfield, the small town about twenty-five miles west of London that lay at the edge of the great chalk downs that Chesterton called the exposed skeleton of England. This move gave him an appreciation for the countryside, unlike his love of London and the city, that increased his sense of identification with ordinary men. Far from removing him from "real life," living in Beaconsfield helped him gain an understanding of the closely knit, gossipy nature of small towns, as well as the far more orderly hierarchy of social classes. He delighted in the strange byways of small-town history, pointed up by Beaconsfield's Old Town and New Town; he identified with the average suburbanite's wish for a home of his own. He described this hope in his first full-scale book of social philosophy when he said, "The ordinary Englishman has been duped out of his . . . possessions in the name of Progress. . . . [He] is a man who [is] kept perpetually out of the house in which he had meant his married life to begin. . . . The idea of private property . . . one man one house . . . remains the real vision and magnet of mankind."[25]

The Chestertons first rented a small house called Overroads, which was surrounded by pleasant fields slowly being converted into subdivisions. As Chesterton said later, he had lived in Beaconsfield from the time it was almost a village until the time it was almost a suburb, but "it would be truer to say the two things . . . still exist side by side."[26] He went on to joke that he had once planned to sum up the differences between the two towns in a work called "The Two Barbers of Beaconsfield." According to him, "It was to be a massive and exhaustive sociological work, in several volumes," showing that the two barbershops belonged to two different civilizations.[27]

As this joke shows, Chesterton thoroughly enjoyed becoming a part of the local village scenery; predictably, he made friends wherever he went. The life Cecil thought he could only experience among "laborers, ploughmen and poachers" Gilbert found in the barbershops, which he patronized daily because — so the story went — he was too absent-minded to shave himself. In fact, it was probably a good excuse for him to get a little exercise, as well as a chance for him to do some of the "mooning about" that hid his intense concentration.

After they moved to Beaconsfield, Frances organized Gilbert's life. It was during this time that Gilbert sent Frances the famous telegram reading, "Am at Market Harborough. Where ought I to be?" and she telegraphed back, "Home." She now took complete control of their finances, giving Gilbert an allowance that his brother felt was paltry — but since Cecil not only lived free at home but still borrowed money from his family, his judgment means little. It was in fact widely known that Gilbert was a fool about money. He had, for example, sold the rights to *Orthodoxy* for one hundred pounds *before* telling his agent, and Shaw's constant refrain was that he failed to demand for his work what the market would bear.

Chesterton still appeared in London to settle contracts, debate, or visit his family, but he now spent the majority of his time in Beaconsfield. He and Frances were weekend guests at friends' homes, and attended parties such as the annual J. D. C. dinner (which now included the members' wives). They themselves had a great many guests, and held parties — parties that were famous for the charades and silly dressing up and plays, often complete with nonsense rhymes, as well as the productions of Chesterton's toy theatre.

Chesterton was working harder than ever, but in the morning, when he reluctantly went to his study to write, he was once caught tossing a paper bird out the window to shoot it with a bow and arrow; once he sent an enormous paper snake down the front stairs. He might wander out in the garden and aimlessly attack defenseless bushes with his sword stick; and there was the time that Father O'Connor returned from the village to find him crouched on all fours on the roof of the garden house. These interludes apparently helped cure his writer's block. Habitually, once he thought out what he was going to write, he quickly wrote it down or dictated it without making many changes. When he finished his weekly columns, some secretary or visitor would have to make a flying trip by bicycle to catch the last London train, while Frances called and arranged to have the article picked up at the station. No doubt Chesterton rather enjoyed these weekly "scares" and resisted efforts to get him better organized.

He had a succession of secretaries over the years, chosen more for their personalities as members of the family circle than for their secretarial skills. Many were amateurish, often friends or neighbors who were inept or slow and did a multitude of odd jobs, like walking the dog. Ada Jones waxed very eloquent over them, declaring that these people were hired because Frances was such an individualist that she was "drawn towards local products and little shops." Ada would have hired a capable female from a bureau.

Her comments, however, make it seem likely that even the courtly Gilbert must have found being polite to Ada something of a trial. When she waspishly adds that the move to Beaconsfield revealed Frances to be the "eternal voice of woman summoning man from the tavern," she illustrates her ignorance. Chesterton did not want a wife to pub-crawl with him and be one of the boys; he did want one to call him home from the pub because he wanted a home to go to. His attitude highlights his reaction to the extreme suffragettes. He felt the sexes were created differently for the preservation of the human family, which was the divine cornerstone of society; and, like most Englishmen, he also preferred to hobnob with other men.

His first novel had been typed by a Battersea neighbor, Mrs. Saxon Mills. When she refused payment Frances bought one of her children a new coat. His first real secretary, Nellie Allport, had to write everything down in longhand, and this may have been one reason why he dictated slowly — though the reason may also have been that he often wrote two pieces at one time, writing one himself and dictating the other. He typically worked from about ten A.M. (he hated to get up in the morning), with short breaks for lunch and tea, until dinner at 7:30. The family and any guests they had went to bed around 10:30 at night, usually leaving Chesterton still up, pacing about, thinking out his next day's work. He was certainly not leading a lazy life, but he made absolutely no effort to remember ordinary details like clothes, haircuts, tickets, meals, where he was or where he was going. These were all Frances' job, together with keeping the household together and solvent; she was also his most constant reader.

There was a constant succession of visiting children, for both Frances and Gilbert adored children and took on other people's whenever given a chance. These visitors never felt ignored because of Chesterton's work. Small Peter Oldershaw called him "the Big Uncle" who roared and padded about like a lion. Once when he was sick Peter got postcards from Chesterton with a special poem and a serialized weekly story about a boy who pulled a rope and found it tied to a bear. Nicholas Bentley remembered the time when he was in the garden with Chesterton, who recited his poem "Lepanto" to him for his approval. All of the children remember that Chesterton never acted as if they were smaller or less important than he.

A charming remembrance of the way in which children regarded both Chestertons appears in Aidan Mackey's recent book, *Mr. Chesterton Comes to Tea, or How the King of England Captured Redskin Island.* It is a story Mackey made up to match a series of pencil drawings made long ago by Chesterton for two little girls he knew. Each time the Chestertons came to tea, the story was "continued" for the girls. Mackey's version is a delightful mixture of all the incredible and scary stories Chesterton wove to amuse his younger friends, very much like the elaborate productions he staged for them with his toy theatre, complete with handpainted puppets and props.[28]

In fact, Chesterton went out of his way to be kind to both children and adults. He talked in public and private much the way he wrote, effortlessly tossing off epigrams and entertaining comments, but also making everyone about him feel they had contributed to the conversation. He would take a remark by the smallest or shyest person, toss it about, embroider it, turn it upside-down, and then give it back, saying that this was just the point he needed for his next article.[29] He had the knack of making whoever he was speaking to feel a million times wittier than he had ever guessed himself to be.[30]

In Beaconsfield the Chestertons soon got a dog. The first one, a Scottie, was called Winkle; the second was named Quoodle, whose namesake is a major character in the novel *The Flying Inn,* published in 1914. In an essay for the *Daily News,* Chesterton wrote about the pleasures of having a dog:

> I have found that nearly all things not evil are better in experience than in theory. . . . Take . . . the innovation I have of late introduced into my domestic life . . . a four-legged innovation. . . . I have always imagined myself to be a lover of all animals, because I never met any animal I definitely disliked. . . . One loves an animal like a man, instead of merely accepting the animal like an optimist, . . . but there is something deeper in the matter . . . only the hour is late, and both the dog and I are too drowsy to interpret it. He lies in front of me curled up before the fire. . . . I sit on one side of the hearth. . . . Somehow this creature has completed my manhood. . . . A man ought to have a dog. . . . Those other four legs are part of him. . . . Before evolution was, we were [because] the civilized dog is older than the wild dog of science. The civilized man is older than the primitive man. . . . We feel in our bones that we are the antiquities. . . . Faintly against the fading firelight can be traced the prehistoric outlines of the man and the dog.[31]

They also had cats, one of whom helped himself to Chesterton's breakfast bacon, but this did not bother Chesterton at all. He became notorious for slipping the dogs tidbits under the table, and asking wistfully if the family thought the current pet really liked him. This behavior was much on a par with the children's recollections of his doing things like taking off a slipper, slapping the tea table, and saying firmly that he was "putting his foot down" so they could stay up longer or have a special treat.

Not long after the Chestertons had moved to Overroads, an adjoining field (with a shade tree under which they liked to picnic) was about to be sold to a laundry. Since Chesterton had remarked one day that he wanted to build himself a house around that tree, they bought the field, and a few years later constructed a brick-and-timber studio there at the "top of the meadow" where their plays and parties were held. Eventually they converted the studio into their home, Top Meadow, where they had a beautiful garden full of blooms for Chesterton to stab with his sword stick in a fit of creative frenzy.

Chesterton was often away, speaking to groups all over England. Traveling to and fro by train, he would stuff his pockets with detective stories from the railroad stand and then fall asleep, after politely asking a fellow traveler to wake him up at the right stop. But he liked to come home. Partly, no doubt, because he had grown up in a happy family where his father was usually home, working in his den, he and Frances never developed the problem he made fun of in one essay about Ibsen. In it he described the "complaint" of the upper middle-class against marriage by saying, "If two married people moon about in large rooms all day long, it is highly probable that they will get on each other's nerves . . . but in actual human monogamy, the two people are not always together. . . . Half the affectionate married couples of the world are perpetually parted lovers . . . like the postman and his wife."[32]

The issue of women's position in society had been developing an undercurrent of hysterical discontent which erupted a year later on Black Friday, November 18, 1910, when there was a riot outside Parliament. The movement had begun in the Liberal 1870's (Chesterton had been in favor of women's rights as an adolescent), but was aggravated now by the economic fact that there were more women than men and few career opportunities for middle-class women. In addition, public opinion was divided over the reform of the harsh divorce laws, the issue of contraceptives and the falling birth rate, as well as the right to vote. The times reflected Freud's patronizing question: What does woman want? Woman is not sure herself.[33]

Politically, the Establishment, like the Church of England and the courts, was against suffragette reforms, while the Liberal Party paid lip service to women's right to vote but dragged its feet on implementation. This kind of confusion was reflected in the position of Chesterton and his friends. Cecil, though running around with a "New Woman," was now echoing Belloc's position, which had some truth in it — that most of the suffragettes were rich, idle women bored by their lives, while the mass of ordinary women did not want "equality" at all.[34] They both saw the suffragette demands as "elitist" rather than truly representative of women's wants. Masterman, more and more a comer in Liberal Party councils, was theoretically in favor of women being educated like men, but he thought the political power of the suffragette movement was being wielded less to facilitate equality than to obtain power and glory.[35] His attitude was shared by Winston Churchill and other Liberals, who recognized the women's rage and violence as a method of political harassment that could only damage the Liberal Party — and their own careers.

Chesterton himself undoubtedly saw Belloc's "elitist" argument as valid, but he would not have been too impressed by Masterman's growing desire to stay in office at any cost. He felt instinctively that the great majority of women had no yearnings for the vote nor for the kind of drudging office work Frances and her sisters had done. Typically, he stated his views in a whimsical manner, with the result that either he is not taken seriously, or, even more ironically, he is accused of being a proponent of views that he shared with most of his male contemporaries.

Based upon his own experience, especially with his mother and his wife, he made this observation:

> Women [are] not kept at home in order to keep them narrow; on the contrary they [are] kept at home in order to keep them broad . . . to play at five or six professions, . . . and so come almost as near to God as the child when he plays at a hundred trades. . . . Women [have] a harder time than men; that is why we take off our hats to them [while] modern women defend their office with all the fierceness of domesticity. . . . That is why they do office work so well; and . . . why they ought not to do it.[36]

Parenthetically, it might be added that this position is a strange, typically Chestertonian amalgam of something stated much later by Dorothy Sayers, when she accused men of having taken all the interesting jobs away from women. It is also an attitude typical of more contemporary Englishmen like Lewis, Tolkien, and others — this idea that a woman's place is in the home, and that a man's need for companionship and intellectual challenge is best satisfied by other men.[37] The reason for Chesterton's having such attitudes can be clearly traced to his own upbringing and domestic felicity.

Chesterton also drew prophetic analogies from the contemporary scene. For example, in an *Illustrated London News* column he discussed the wild campaign for votes that led to militant feminists attacking ministers, breaking windows, and chaining themselves to fences, and to feminist prisoners going on hunger strikes.

He compared their behavior to the young Indian Nationalist movement started by Indira Gandhi's grandfather, commenting that "the principal weakness of Indian Nationalism seems to be that it is not very Indian and not very national. . . ." He went on to explain that it would make more sense to him if an Indian patriot declared that he wished India had always been free from white men in all their works — if he said, "if you do not like our sort of spiritual comfort, we never asked you to. Go . . . and leave us with it." But instead, Chesterton pointed out, the Indian was saying "with increasing excitability, give me a ballot box. Provide me with a Ministerial dispatch-box. . . . I have a heaven-born claim to introduce a Budget."[38]

A struggling young Indian student named Mahatma Gandhi, who was living in London, read this *Illustrated News* column, and it changed history. He not only observed and adopted the militant tactics of the suffragettes, but he also began his campaign for native Indian dress, language, and customs.[39] London then was a superb training ground for would-be revolutionaries; its models included the militant upper-class English ladies, the trade unionists with their developing fondness for violent syndicalism, the Irish, still deprived of Home Rule, the Unionists, and the conservative House of Lords.

Another "Revolution without the R" occurred in Parliament on November 30, 1909, when the House of Lords, filled to capacity with the "Backwoodsmen" or peers who rarely came to Westminster, voted down Lloyd George's so-called "People's Budget." Two days later the Liberal House of Commons passed a resolution that "the action of the House of Lords in refusing to pass into law the financial provision of the year is a breach of the Constitution and a usurpation of the rights of the Commons."[40] This action by the House of Lords now forced a General Election.

Historians still argue about whether the handling of this budget was a deliberate attempt to force a showdown with the House of Lords, or designed to circumvent them by going past them to the country.[41] The true Socialists argued that this budget was not going to "make the rich poorer and the poor richer," which was their definition of good legislation. Massingham at the *Nation* was already screaming editorially at the cowardly Liberal Cabinet, who had not been willing to tackle the Lords head-on, echoing Belloc's opinion that the Establishment, Liberal or Conservative, had no real intention of reforming the House of Lords along the lines of his austere Republican principles. Belloc showed his lack of faith by running for election as an Independent.[42] On the whole, Chesterton seems to have been less suspicious than Belloc of the intentions of the Liberals, and to have supported the "crusade" with his usual openheartedness in the way that Gardiner and Bentley did, as part of the campaign for the old cause of land reform and putting an end to "privilege."

On January 15, 1910, in his *Daily News* column, Chesterton declared that "this is the one historical election that I have seen since I was born, and perhaps the only one I shall see before I die."[43] The Tory papers echoed his idea, saying it was the most important election since 1832, while the *Daily News* called it a return to the civil wars under Cromwell in the 1700's. At the same time the budget was nowhere near as popular as its proponents like to claim, and the Lords, insisting they were giving the country a chance to declare its position, were not seen as villains by everyone. Like other events in history, its grays became black and white with the passing of time.

The election results preserve this picture very ironically. In January 1910 the Liberal Party was returned to office with a slim majority that now did depend upon the Irish Nationalist bloc and the Labour members. The Conservatives had made great gains, so the House of Commons almost mirrored its situation during Gladstone's days, when Irish Home Rule had driven the Liberals from office, and every roll call had carried the seeds of party disaster. The party still had its hardcore Radical and Nonconformist supporters, but, in general, the country's mood was a mixture of boredom and impatience, which meant that to stay in office and keep its allies together, the Liberal Party would have to go forward with the crusade against the Lords, then establish Irish Home Rule.[44] The difficulty was that to reform the House of Lords the Liberals needed the support of King Edward VII, and it was not clear that they had it; and the Irish supporters whose votes they needed would only vote for the budget, which they disliked, if given Home Rule.[45]

Belloc had won re-election as an Independent, while supporting Lloyd George's budget as a step toward equalizing land ownership, but he deeply mistrusted Lloyd George, seeing him as a master of demagoguery and the willing slave of the Liberal plutocrats. He sensed that Asquith and his Cabinet were uncertain of what to do about the peers; he and his new protégé, Cecil Chesterton, were writing the book that outlined these suspicions.[46]

Published in 1911, their book was called *The Party System*. Its thesis was simply that there were not two parties, but one, because the "frontbenchers" like Asquith and Balfour, Churchill and Smith, were such close friends, so interrelated by blood, marriage, and education, that they left the majority of the M.P.'s disenfranchised and the country unrepresented.[47] In the book both authors carried on their nasty habit of making personal attacks on people like Charles Masterman. They called him a self-serving would-be member of the Establishment who voted one way as an M.P. and another way once he was a Cabinet minister, without regard for principle. They abused him in print, went to his election speeches and heckled him, and finally rejoiced openly when he lost his seat and his career was ruined.

Chesterton himself was terribly distressed by their behavior, and apologized for it to Gardiner. Long afterwards he suggested that his friend Masterman had never been able to get away from the spirit of the age which he called Puritanism, "a dark, pessimistic frame of mind that retained a sort of feeling of the perversity of the gods. . . . He was also an organizer and liked governing. . . . His pessimism made him think that government had always been bad . . . and was now no worse than usual . . . [so that] to men set on fire for reform [Cecil and Belloc] he came to seem an obstacle and an official apologist, but the last thing he wanted was to apologize for anything."[48] As usual, Chesterton did not confuse the doer with the deed; he and Masterman remained friends, despite circumstances that involved them in a political scandal a few years later. Nevertheless, though Chesterton deprecated their manner of attack, Belloc and Cecil were right, both about the leadership of the major parties as well as about Masterman's tendency to gloss over clear-cut improprieties among his fellow party leaders, to enjoy being "on the inside looking out."

Chesterton's novel *The Ball and the Cross* appeared in book form in February 1910. Its twin protagonists, Turnbull and MacIan, who are also comrades in arms, probably reinforced the popular idea that Shaw and Chesterton were public adversaries with an identical "comic touch."

In May, as Halley's comet made one of its historic passes over England, Edward VII died. He had been very distressed at the pressure Asquith had been putting on him to promise to appoint enough new Lords to get the budget through Parliament; now the Liberals were faced with a new king, George V, who was regarded as inexperienced, proper, and dull. To make matters worse, the new king felt strongly that the whole constitutional crisis had shortened his father's life.

The Liberal leaders promptly spent the summer "proving" the truth of Belloc's thesis. They held a series of secret, highly irregular meetings with their opposite numbers in the Conservative Party, trying to make a deal that would avoid another General Election over the issues of the House of Lords and Irish Home Rule. All the Liberal newspapers and the Irish, the Labour bloc, and even some diehard Unionists (who were pro-Ulster) protested publicly, but the meetings went on until November. In them Lloyd George played the role of "radical populist," suggesting the solution was a coalition government, while Balfour was fighting to keep control of his own party.

That same June Chesterton's first book of social and political commentary appeared, called *What's Wrong With the World*. Like most of his important works, Chesterton wrote it in answer to another book, in this case responding to Charles Masterman's *The Condition of England*, published in 1909. In his book Masterman stood for most of the Liberal positions Chesterton supported, but in a "new" Liberal way; he was clearly beginning to lose his nerve and become, like his party, paralyzed and apprehensive about a future in which he could not quite accept the Collectivist's kind of social action.[49]

Masterman had described the various classes and prescribed for their faults in a somewhat Olympian manner, making Chesterton's more democratic attitude interesting by contrast. Masterman, for example, saw the suburban man in his villa (on the hill) looking down on the poor (in the plain), feeling he was being taxed to help less hardworking types get free aid. But instead of sympathizing with the suburbanite, he made this pronouncement:

Suburban life has ... little conception of social services, no tradition of disinterested public duty. ... The individualism of the national character [is] unchecked by the horizontal links of the industrial peoples, organizing themselves into unions, or by the vertical links of the older aristocracy with a conception of family service which once passed from parent to child.[50]

Chesterton dedicated *What's Wrong With the World* to Masterman in a long, friendly letter in which he said the book was a shapeless, inadequate creation to give to someone "who has written one of the really impressive visions of the moving millions of England ... but I think you politicians are none the worse for a few inconvenient ideals. ... You will recognize the many arguments we have had ... [but] most of all there exists ... [a] friendship which, please God, will never break."[51]

Masterman himself, despite his bureaucratic stance, was never the prototype for either member of Chesterton's celebrated Socialist and Tory duo, Hudge and Gudge, both of whom were full of theories about how to house the rest of the country "without considering what kind of a house a man might like for himself. In short, they did not begin with an ideal and therefore were not practical politicians." The Conservative in Chesterton's parable persuades himself that "slums and stinks are really very nice ... [and] the habit of sleeping fourteen to a room is what has made our England great," whereupon he turns into "an apoplectic old Tory." Meanwhile, Chesterton's Socialist has convinced himself that "those maniacally ugly buildings [projects] originally put up to ... shelter human life grow more and more lovely [for] ... man is really happier in a hive than in a house." He becomes a "lean vegetarian with a gray pointed beard and an unnaturally easy smile, who goes about telling everybody that at last we shall all sleep in one universal bedroom." Chesterton then pleasantly confides to the reader that "I am neither a Hudgian or a Gudgian," also suggesting that there is a strange similarity between those two gentlemen's positions.[52]

In answer to the visions of Masterman and Shaw, Chesterton tries in this book to express in social terms the Christian-Liberal ideal of equality he had explored in *Orthodoxy*. These two books, the most significant ones he wrote between 1905 and 1914, represent different approaches to his defense of the rights of the individual, as well as a typically Chestertonian attempt to upend the picture of the world to make people look at it, and to restore a much-needed balance to ideological positions.

What's Wrong With the World is a series of related essays on the economic, moral, and political themes of the day, but it has a sustained argument like *Orthodoxy* rather than the pasted-together feel of *Heretics*. It begins with a chapter called "The Remedy," which gives a farcical description of a typical Fabian tract, full of tables about the "decrease of crime among Congregationalists, growth of hysteria among policemen and similar ... facts"; it finally suggests Chesterton's thesis — that "in social matters we must actually find the cure before we find the disease."[53] His reason for this upside-down idea is that "when things don't work, you need the thinker . . . [for] it is wrong to fiddle while Rome is burning, but it is quite right to study the theory of hydraulics."[54]

Chesterton goes on to attack the contemporary wisdom that considered the working classes a great problem but never saw them as people. He was actually fighting three different groups at once: the humanitarians, upset that a third of the country was starving while the rich were extravagant; the Liberal reformers, who wanted to regiment the poor for their own (and the country's) good; and the Fabian Socialists, who wanted to "collectivize" everyone.

This book has rightly been called "vintage Chesterton," full of his sparkling energy, immensely readable and quotable, written in his simple and deceptively casual manner.[55] It stands in stark contrast to the sergeant-major, tour-de-force argument of Belloc's book on the same general subject, *The Servile State,* partly because Belloc found all men fools and Chesterton loved them all. This is Chesterton's vision for humanity, his utopia, but his angle of vision is always as one of the ruled, not one of the rulers.

By using parables and his own method of paradox, Chesterton shows the interconnections between current politics, economics, and social thought; then, by reducing them to some of his amusing examples, he demonstrates their relationship to "the servile state." In Part One he talks about the poor in terms of housing, work, and self-respect; in Part Two he discusses imperialism, or plutocratic manipulation of markets, and its effect on jobs. In Part Three he discusses feminism, and in Part Four he talks about education, both being different aspects of the problem of the family; Part Five is his description of utopia. As usual, he used facts that were not perfectly correct, or left facts out, but he drew a very convincing picture of the world as he saw it. He also pointed out that since society was made by man, it can be reconstructed upon any plan that ever existed; like a clock, it can be put forward an hour, or turned back two. What the book really does is argue, effectively and amusingly, for a position, a way of looking at the world, which is distinctly unlike those he was debating.

Like much of what Chesterton wrote, it also has an unconsciously prophetic touch, for much of what he says about the welfare state makes more sense now than it did in 1910.[56] According to his theory of history, it is what one does that matters, not whether one is considered "advanced" or "backward," for there is no revolution that is not also a restoration, and all the men in history who have done anything for the future have had their eyes fixed on the past: "Tomorrow is the Gorgon: a man must only see it mirrored in the shining shield of yesterday. . . . A true free-thinker is he whose intellect is as much free from the future as from the past. He cares as little for what will be as for what has been; he cares only for what ought to be."[57]

In talking about the ordinary man's home, he said that this was the only place where man had the freedom to do as he liked and be himself, to be creative by painting the walls purple or by growing dandelions in his yard. He wanted everyman to have his own home and support himself without being someone else's wage slave; his chief argument against what he called imperialism was that gigantic industrialism and international high finance by their very nature required specialization and hierarchy, so they tailored the man to the job, not the job to the man.

In talking about women, Chesterton reversed the old nursery rhyme to say "the queen is in the counting house, counting out the money, The king is in the parlor, eating bread and honey." (This certainly sounds like his own household.) What he meant was that women are natural rulers, but are not democratic; therefore they should rule the more important sphere, the home, and leave the world to men.

In talking about education, which he saw was the necessary root of any utopia, he pointed out that everyone is a teacher, no matter what he may say, and therefore everyone shares the very trait so many moderns profess to disapprove of: authority. When people talk about separating dogma from education, they have forgotten that dogma is education, and that if a teacher is not dogmatic, he is not teaching. To illustrate what he meant he told the story of a nice little boy brought up in a Nonconformist, middle-class home; he is taught to love his country, say his prayers, and wear his Sunday best. Next he is handed over to Fagin, who naturally teaches him to drink, steal, lie, and wear false whiskers. Were the same little boy to be given to a vegetarian Socialist, he would end up not eating meat; a Tolstoian pacifist would teach him not to love his country. "In fact," Chesterton concluded, "there are no uneducated people, [there are] only . . . people . . . educated wrong."[58]

He went on to say that modern educational theories consisted of two ideas, neither of them of much use. The first was a desire to give a public-school education to the poor, when what they should learn is the traditions of their own parents — "beer and liberty" — instead of having "soap and socialism" preached at them. The other idea was to give girls a boys' education. He took the miseducation of the poor one step further to argue vehemently against the legal practice that allowed the state to take charge of poor children who were judged mentally defective in order to prevent them from reproducing; the state could also send its representatives into poor homes to cut off the children's hair if they had lice, a practice to which the bureaucrats would not dare subject the rich. His denunciation of the whole idea of eugenics was very much ahead of his time; so was his constant concern that there be one law for all.[59]

In the last part of the book he attacked what he called the "Calvinist" theory of utopias, which assumes that earthly life is not the drama but the epilogue. What he meant was that "Puritans" like Shaw rejected as superstition the idea of being judged after death, but were still quick to defend the doctrine that man is judged before he is born. In other words, the Progressives all believed in a variety of predestination, or determinism. Chesterton insisted that such determinism had existed long before the North was Christianized, and since the time of the Reformation it had been slowly creeping back into the European consciousness in the form of realistic novels (like those of Zola) and problem plays (like Ibsen's).

This is the first time that Chesterton dwelt at length upon his idea that the Protestant Reformation was a symbol of economic exploitation, as well as of the destruction of a civilization organized to give the individual considerable control over his own life. This particular view of the world of the late Middle Ages was one Chesterton shared with many other radical Socialists and intellectuals of the period, like young Tawney and his old friend J. L. Hammond, who were now engaged in redressing the balance of history against the nineteenth century's admiration of the efficiency of the Tudors, the Stuarts, and the Whigs.[60]

His own conviction about the "truth" of history he summed up in another vivid picture. He pointed out that an idea has not been disproved simply because it has been defeated. He said that many of the largest efforts of history — like the French Revolution and the Roman Catholic Church — had been frustrated in their full design and have come to us as gigantic cripples; "the world is full of these uncompleted temples. . . . History does not consist of completed and crumbling ruins. . . . It consists of half-built villas abandoned by a bankrupt builder. This world is more like an unfinished suburb than a deserted cemetery."[61]

In this book Chesterton did not climb out on a limb and try to saw it off; he tried to balance on the limb, seeking the golden mean. For example, he refused to condemn popular literature like westerns and thrillers, but he also saw no reason to hand Zola to infants. He even dared to say that he saw a real value in the Victorian idea of literature as something that could be read aloud in the family circle. This attitude clearly put him in the "old fuddy-duddy" position at a time when European culture was invading London and destroying what the avant-garde called "British insularity." Along with sex, censorship was a hot topic among intellectuals, and moderation was anathema to their belief in creative expression, which they defended in scientific terms.[62]

Chesterton did not believe that the future would evolve a new kind of man, for he accepted the dogma of Christianity that human nature is a given. He also never assumed that there was anything especially golden about the "good old days." He ends his discussion of utopias on a serious note, suggesting that politicians should learn to take people as they are — women as handy, thrifty, hard, and humorous, and children as full of energy — while working to find a way to help the poor who were too poor to be domestic. He warns the Conservatives that the Socialists, given the chance, will turn England into a beehive for them, but if they want a truly domestic country, they themselves will have to submit to a burden far heavier than any People's Budget, and distribute their lands and wealth as sternly and sweepingly as the French Revolution did. Finally, he closes on a Bellocian note, saying he has this horrible suspicion that Hudge and Gudge are secret partners because one wants women workers because they are cheaper and the other calls this work "woman's freedom to live her own life."[63]

As if to point up the fact that he was beginning to fill the public role not only of reporter but of prophet, that November of 1910 Chesterton published another of his short biographical sketches. This one was about the strange eighteenth-century visionary poet and painter, William Blake, who had rhapsodized about the horrors of industrialism — "those dark Satanic mills" — and called for building (or rebuilding) "the New Jerusalem in England's green and pleasant land." Chesterton was supposed to be discussing Blake as an engraver and painter, but typically he began with Blake's ideas.

He was not very enthusiastic about the strange verbal thrusts of Blake's poems, noting that "we always feel that he is saying something very plain and emphatic even when we have not the wildest notion what it is." He compared Blake's visions to the eclectic, creeping Orientalism so popular at the time, particularly the cults that denied individuality and wanted to "dissolve" people into a cosmic unity. He also equated Blake and his eighteenth century with the "art for art's sake" period at the Slade, not liking Blake's confused visions; but he was very impressed by his draftsmanship. The book demonstrates Chesterton's premonition that there was about to be another period of "private" art, a retreat to impressionistic techniques and idiosyncratic symbols with relative values, again reflecting a period of social and political uncertainty.[64]

The times were summed up in the immortal phrase of Virginia Woolf, herself a typically rebellious member of the younger generation of the upper middle-class: "On or about December 1910, human character changed." For the English intellectuals at the universities and in London, 1910 did mark the very moment when English attitudes toward Englishness, the Continent, and tradition changed radically, giving a new illusion of "progress."[65] In terms of literature, Woolf went on to complain that Edwardian novels had left her feeling she must do something, "join a society, or more desperately, write a cheque"; they were not works of art, "complete in themselves."[66] She said these writers were not suitable models for a young writer, so she and her contemporaries turned back to the old master Henry James and his disciple Conrad, later to Joyce and Lawrence as well, confident that these writers were the vanguard of a new world. This bore out what Chesterton had suggested in *The Napoleon of Notting Hill* in 1904: the more things change, the more they stay the same. But it was to be the Bloomsbury group's followers who wrote the prevailing myths about this time.[67]

Only a month before, Chesterton had published another book of newspaper columns from the *Daily News* called *Alarms and Discursions*. In it he had written amusingly about himself as a Cockney becoming "the Village Idiot ... a spectacle and a judgment to mankind." He had learned that "I do not dislike the country, but I like the town more. Therefore the art of happiness ... suggests that I should live in the country and think about the town. I have found the house where I was really born ... from which I can see London afar off."[68] This note of nostalgia for a Fleet Street that is no more corresponds to the temper of the times, which historian Peter Rowland recently described:

> Distance invariably lends enchantment and the years immediately preceding 1914 have come to be wistfully regarded as the sunshine days of the twentieth century. ... The legend runs ... [that] every moment ... was devoted to implementing social and constitutional reforms in every sphere ... [but] somewhere along the line ... the story does not ring quite true ... [and] one is driven towards the conclusion that the erosion of support for the Liberal Party [after] 1906 arose from the fact that it was doing too little rather than too much.[69]

Although the fact was not realized for another decade, the great dream of Liberal revival and reform was dead in 1910, and at least one Liberal was better off viewing the debacle "from afar."

Chapter Ten

THE SECRET PEOPLE

1910-1912

Smile at us, pay us, pass us; but do not quite forget;
For we are the people of England, that never have spoken yet. . . .
We hear men speaking for us of new laws strong and sweet,
Yet is there no man speaketh as we speak in the street.
It may be we shall rise the last as Frenchmen rose the first,
Our wrath come after Russia's wrath and our wrath be the
worst.
It may be we are meant to mark with our riot and our rest
God's scorn for all men governing. It may be beer is best.
But we are the people of England; and we have not spoken yet

                            G.K. Chesterton, "The Secret People"[1]

THAT December of 1910 the prime minister told the new king that there must be another General Election — the second in a year, the third in five years — because no compromise had been worked out with the Conservatives over the issue of the House of Lords.[2] The official Liberal line was that this was a crusade to end "the Peers against the People," while the Conservatives were having problems with how much support they wanted to give their own program for tariff reforms, even though they were united against Home Rule for Ireland, and were widely supported in this position.

For Chesterton the election was significant for two reasons: it was probably the last time he could in good conscience vote Liberal; and Belloc, convinced by his own arguments that Parliamentary government was a cabal by both parties, chose not to run at all. Afterward, E. C. Bentley, who was raised a Tory and reverted to that position after the war, reported sadly that in working to destroy the power of the Lords, they had engaged in "a dirty fight."[3] He meant (and Chesterton agreed) that they had helped to destroy the older, more humane aristocracy, which took some interest in the plight of the poor, in favor of a totally self-serving bureaucracy.

Bentley's attitude was echoed in Chesterton's very sarcastic poem called

"The Revolutionist: or Lines to a Statesman," in which he baited a Tory M.P. who had been insisting that he was in the thick of the fray while the "revolution" was going on. He told the M.P. that he "would not revolutionize a rabbit," and ended by saying,

> Walter, be wise, avoid the wild and new!
> The Constitution is the game for you. . . .
> If you goad these grey rules to break,
> . . . see that you do not wake
> Death and the splendour of the scarlet cap . . .
> The thunder of the captains and the shouting,
> All that lost riot that you did not share —
> And when that riot comes — you WILL be there.[4]

Chesterton was verbally mounting the barricades himself, sympathetic to the irrational violence and revolution that were becoming more apparent; far more of a Radical than a Liberal, he happily engaged in the "crusade." But the General Election in December produced the same stalemate between Conservatives and Liberals as before, in spite of the fact that the Liberal Party had now won three elections in a row. To party leaders, the situation seemed clear-cut enough at the time: with the help of Labour and the Irish and the king, the Liberals would pass the Parliamentary bill curtailing the power of the Lords, and move on to build utopia.

The electorate was actually dividing into new socio-economic "nations." During this period the rural poor, the middle class, and the suburban groups were becoming more conservative, while the industrial urban poor stayed Liberal for now, identifying with its radical elements but also keeping an eye on Labour as it waited in the wings.[5] The social fabric was coming apart at the seams, and within the Liberal leadership there were also divisions whose differences peaked over the war, so that this 1910 victory was ultimately fatal to the party.[6]

Although the Liberal Party did accomplish a number of its stated objectives during this period, it was losing the support of some of its members like Chesterton, who disagreed with the way in which it tried to solve society's ills; it was also threatened by a rising tide of revolution, of a refusal to reason together that was destroying the pre-war "consensus." In spite of his old-fashioned attitude about social legislation, Chesterton for a number of reasons supported these outbursts so long as they related, like the trade union movement, to the basic economic and social facts of life for the ordinary worker. For example, he was not bothered by the increasingly disruptive strikes that upset Fabian ideas of decorum and legislation; he was pleased to have the trade union-Socialist alliance breaking down. At the same time he mistrusted the methods and the disingenuous attitude of Winston Churchill and Lloyd George, who were liberalism's most progressive spokesmen.[7]

Increasingly influenced by guild socialism, Chesterton now saw the unions were the only way the ordinary industrial worker could have some control over his job, which constituted the only form of "property" such a man had. It appealed to him far more to think about the workers owning their own company than to have them work for faceless, international conglomerates (the "usurers"), and he sided with the men when troops were called out against strikers in 1910. The *New Age* also supported guild socialism editorially, interested in halting the growing power of the state and diffusing the social responsibility.[8]

Its chief proponent at this time was a Christian Socialist named Penty, who had lived in the United States; there he had seen unions that were industry-wide with skilled and unskilled workers. In theory, at least, these workers were free of the fear of unemployment, had foremen they chose, created their own profits by their own productivity, and did not have massive bureaucratic interference.[9]

Guild socialism's economic and social concepts were not only supported in the *New Age* by Orage (with whom Chesterton was still in contact), but also by an old Fabian friend, George Lansbury, editor of the new *Daily Herald*. Both papers were considered to have "deserted" the Fabian cause for "medievalism," so about this time Cecil's friend Clifford Sharp was made editor of a new venture of the Webbs, the strictly Fabian publication called the *New Statesman*.

There were other signs of society's nervous sense of change besides confused political alliances: aimless violence proliferating among the suffragettes, the Irish, and the workers; and the avant-garde's attitude about theatre, literature, and the arts. There was a widespread taste among intellectuals for esoteric religions and cults, related to their interest in psychic phenomena and sexual freedom — interests that carried an overtone of decay to anyone with strong ethical standards like Chesterton or his friend Masterman, a sign that the upper classes were ripe for destruction. Many of the cults were ascribed to the East, but the leaders were often Christians, such as the well-known proponent of Platonic mysticism, Dean Inge of St. Paul's Cathedral.

A classic study of their attitudes was written by Evelyn Underhill, a lady not unlike Beatrice Webb. Mrs. Underhill was well-off, childless, and intellectually curious, married to a man who did not mind what she thought or wrote so long as she also maintained his upper middle-class home and social life. She was born and bred a member of the Church of England, but she did not return to it as an adult until after the war. During this interval, Mrs. Underhill studied and expressed her own brand of mysticism; she assumed she was on a romantic, individualistic quest for her own soul. Chesterton wrote of her that she felt "two worlds were better than one."

Her own idea was that a dim consciousness of the beyond leads mankind to question outward things, using a kind of higher instinct which is "an

149

anticipation of the evolutionary process."[10] According to Mrs. Underhill, the initiates of mysticism are able to see things that are "mean and insignificant" in ordinary life as "luminous and grand," bathed in divine radiance. This is not a world that Chesterton could or would accept; it denies the idea of the Incarnation, which had become his philosophical justification for the brotherhood of man. Mrs. Underhill did feel that her "two worlds" could be reunited by "self-surrender." She shared Beatrice Webb's romantic tendency to focus personally on certain symbols, such as the Virgin Mary, and to revel in the atmosphere of old cathedrals.[11]

Fundamentally, they were both latter-day Theosophists, followers of Annie Besant, who had proclaimed that "there was only one religion in the world, that all faiths were only versions or perversions of it," and that "the universal church is simply the universal self. . . . We are really all one person." Chesterton wanted to love his neighbor "because he is not I," while he felt the "divine center of Christianity . . . threw man out of it in order that he might love it." His reaction to this kind of all-embracing universalism was related to his wish that the average man be allowed to run his own life.[12] It would appear, then, that the true "medievalists" in 1910 were these lady mystics.

Mrs. Underhill's book, *Mysticism,* was published in 1911, and it was a huge literary success. In it she not only defined "the mystical experience" but wrote the history of its Western and Eastern exponents. Its basic thesis was that mysticism is an experience that involves man in a unique adventure in which the important thing is the experience itself.

The prevailing philosophical theory at the universities was still Hegelian; it insisted that "immanence" was the ultimate reality, that the world and human consciousness could be identified with the divine. A great popularizer of this "new theology" — which, of course, was almost exactly like the kind the Chesterton boys had heard preached in the 1880's — was R. J. Campbell, who combined it with his version of socialism, planning to build the Kingdom of God in this world as a corporate utopia. Dean Inge and Mrs. Underhill were in a somewhat different way trying to "reunite" Christendom by ignoring the institutional church; as the Dean explained, mysticism would solve the religious problems of the people who need a belief that "will not rest on tradition or authority or historical evidence, but on the ascertainable facts of human experience. . . ."[13] In other words, he was proposing a very pragmatic, Fabian-like approach that one might do great things or have marvelous "experiences" without having a theoretical basis for them.

But since the time he first met Frances, Chesterton had been under the influence of the orthodox Anglo-Catholics like Bishop Gore and Conrad Noel. They had responded to this eclectic heresy's challenge by taking the Incarnation as their battlecry for social justice, to safeguard both the divinity of Christ and the sacraments themselves. It was their view that Chesterton upheld, both in politics and religion, refusing to be impressed by Henri

Bergson's "elan vital," which translated into Shaw's "Life Force."[14] Chesterton's own thoroughgoing acceptance of the basic Christian tenets is underlined by his writing during this period, especially his Father Brown stories, *The Flying Inn,* and his play, *Magic.* The crucial problem for him came as he began to realize he must separate his religion from his politics, or be willing to call them by new names, since "Liberal" and "Christian Socialist" were gradually ceasing to mean what he felt they must mean. In this respect, the person who most clearly "embodied" the problem came to be Charles Masterman.

About this time Belloc and Cecil published *The Party System.* In it they not only explained that real political power now rested in the Cabinet, but also stated emphatically that all the leading politicians were corrupt, willing to cover up for one another, and easily "bought for a price."[15] Their thesis was not without support: during that entire period the same names kept cropping up, associated with both public and private roles — Rufus Isaacs, Herbert Samuel, Sir Edward Carson, Lloyd George, Winston Churchill, F. E. Smith, Asquith, Haldane, and the Webbs. Leadership was held in common, as it were, by a very few, who then had the opportunity to make places for their own friends and relatives. This had probably always been true, as it is still somewhat true today.[16]

In view of his upbringing and education, it seems inevitable that Chesterton, who could see both Belloc and his brother as men of intelligence and good will anxious to serve mankind, should increasingly become what is known today as an "anti-intellectual" intellectual. He based his dislike of castes or cliques upon his heritage of a broad middle class comprised of neither "snobs nor prigs." Gradually, as he began to lose the attention of the Establishment, Chesterton substituted for it a wider, more ordinary reading public which corresponded to his "ideal ordinary man."[17] The process was not so much a result of a conscious decision as the way that events and his career were to carry him. It is harder to describe the manner in which Cecil Chesterton's opinions were to carry him from one extreme to another, except as a series of "conversions" triggered more by particular people than by conviction; he was always more inclined than Gilbert to be — or want to be — a mover and a shaker, and hence more inclined to the role of do-gooder. Perhaps, like Belloc, he was also angry at his very lack of power.

A number of the specific accusations made by Belloc and Cecil Chesterton were accurate, if spiteful. Among them was their concern over the party coffers and the secret fund, which only helped Liberal candidates approved by the leaders, and the sale of peerages, which had become commonplace — especially to wealthy businessmen; many of the real noblemen had gone into business to recoup their family fortunes.[18] Since both parties did these things, inevitably there was a general Parliamentary "consensus" to let well enough alone. On a different front altogether, Belloc's strong prejudice against Germany and her imperial plans, which both Chestertons agreed with, found some support in two ways: in the concern of Grey at the Foreign Office to consolidate England's position with allies like France, and also in a strange wave of "invasion novels," the most famous of which was Erskine Childers' *The Riddle of the Sands*.[19] Unionist Tories and Imperialists of all varieties were worried about the kaiser's plans, and the People's Budget had as one purpose raising enough money to build more dreadnoughts. Pro-German Liberals like Gardiner were most unhappy with this attitude, in spite of German gunboat diplomacy.[20] The suggestion of an international conspiracy among the very wealthy Jewish financiers and German imperial interests, however, was more a conviction of Belloc and Cecil than Chesterton himself. The difficulty is that they all wrote for the same papers, and from now on all of their views are lumped together, a grouping encouraged by the fact that over the next twelve years all three became known as Roman Catholic spokesmen.[21]

In the meantime the "Great Debate" between Shaw and Chesterton went public in a new way. On May 29, 1911, Shaw spoke to the Heretics Club at Cambridge University on "The Religion of the Future," a talk published sometime later that year, as was Chesterton's reply.[22] Shaw cheerfully told the students that God had died during the nineteenth century; but he was manufacturing a new god for the twentieth century, his "Lifeforce," adding that "we are all experiments in the direction of making God."[23] His atheistic audience seems to have misunderstood him, but the comments he made about Darwin's banishing God from the world were picked up by the national newspapers with the headline "Christ a Failure." The Heretics Club happily elected Shaw to membership, then decided to ask Chesterton to "reply."

The invitation that Chesterton accepted was not really a chance to debate, since he and Shaw spoke on different days, but it was the first encounter of theirs that was carried "live" in the major media and published afterward in book form. Chesterton spoke on November 17, 1911; he began by asking, "How could Mr. Shaw blaspheme by saying that Christ . . . had failed in England when the remark is obviously true? I happen to believe . . .Christianity is the true religion, but I do not believe for one moment that . . . England is a Christian country. . . . Mr. Shaw is something of a Pagan himself, and like any Pagan, he is a very fine man."[24]

In all their debates Chesterton never did become the smooth and polished orator that Shaw was. He usually arrived late, made comments about his size (by 1911 he weighed 270 pounds), and carried a bunch of scribbled notes on odd bits of paper, at which he would peer nearsightedly. Bending his head to look at them, he muffled his high-pitched voice and his pincenez fell off. He blew through his moustache and chuckled amiably at his own wit. By contrast, Shaw was punctual and well-organized, a lean, dapper man with a gorgeous Irish voice and the gestures of an accomplished actor.

He had a way of throwing back his head and swaggering that was very effective onstage, while his actual seriousness and sincerity still shone through, proving that Chesterton was right when he said that "socialism is the noblest thing for Bernard Shaw; and it is the noblest thing in him."

Chesterton, however, was very gifted at repartee, able to get past Shaw's guard. He had already discovered that an audience liked him better if he rambled on in a conversational tone, so he simply did so, talking more or less off the top of his head. During most of their debates, as contemporaries admit, the question of "who won" depended upon the political or religious views of the onlooker.[25] Their publicized appearances together, which continued, on and off, until 1927, also showed that in many ways they were temperamentally similar, both appearing to be comics while deeply serious about their ideas.

In this first published encounter Chesterton announced that Shaw had his facts wrong and was no democrat; then he asked his audience which they preferred, "the absurd baby God of Shaw's kicking in the cradle, or the great King who prefers his knights to be chivalrous and free."[26] Having made his position quite plain, he answered hecklers and questioners in what the *Cambridge Daily News* called the "most enjoyable part of the evening." Shaw was very delighted with the publicity they got, and invited Chesterton to lunch to plan a series of debates. By November 30, 1911, he had gotten them onstage together at the Memorial Hall in London.

This was a period in Shaw's career when he badly needed a new diversion. His plays, no longer being produced at the Court Theatre by Granville-Barker, were not the success they had been; the Fabian Society was again having internal rows; and his marriage was less happy than before. Chesterton thus provided him with a much-needed outlet; in fact, the debates enhanced both of their public careers.[27] These subsequent debates were held under Fabian auspices, with strict rules that annoyed both men. Belloc was again invited to be chairman as he had been in their earlier *New Age* debates, but he was not supposed to do what he did best: interrupt with sardonic comments of his own. Shaw and Chesterton were to stick to the point, too, and to talk a specified length of time. Even so, they managed to have a lot of fun, teasing one another and amusing their audiences.

On November 30 their topic was "The Democrat, the Socialist and the Gentleman." Shaw announced that a "Democrat who is not also a Socialist is no gentleman,"; the alternative to a gentleman is like "a cad to a Socialist" or "a Democrat . . . [to] an idolator." He then gave a brilliant textbook definition of democracy. Chesterton then rose and said, "I don't know whether I am a gentleman, I am sure that I am a Democrat, and that Mr. Shaw is not a Democrat [and] . . . I don't know what is the social rank of a person like myself who presumes to be a gentleman and not a Socialist, compared to the social rank of the gentleman who is a Socialist and not a Democrat, like Mr. Shaw!" Then he gave clever definitions of democracy and socialism, slightly different from Shaw's, and the two men spent the rest of the evening debating their points of disagreement.[28]

Chesterton defended the ordinary man's right to property as a sine qua non of democracy, a right that meant freedom, while Shaw defended collectivism and state ownership of the means of production. Both agreed on the need for change — or, as Chesterton put it, "I cannot understand why so dextrous and brilliant a debater . . . wasted so much time . . . attacking the present system of industrial England . . . . Who except a devil from hell ever defended it. . . . I object to his Socialism because it will be . . . devilishly like Capitalism."[29]

That summer, encouraged by the reception to *The Party System,* Belloc started a weekly paper, with Cecil as his assistant editor. It was called the *Eye-Witness*, and its first issue came out on June 22, 1911. The two men had gotten some financial support, but the paper never attracted much advertising because its editorial policy was anti-big business. Chesterton's actual contributions to the paper consisted almost entirely of the satirical ballades that he, Bentley, Baring, and Belloc had been writing to one another for their own amusement. Chesterton's name helped sell the paper — and its existence eventually changed his life.

It had been their friend Baring who, with Belloc's help, had put out one issue of the *North Street Gazette* in 1908 (the year he also converted to Roman Catholicism), planning to "expose all the public scandals save those which happen to be lucrative to the proprietors." Baring now suggested that the *Eye-Witness* was the *North Street Gazette's* offspring, but this was not altogether true; the *Eye-Witness* was in deadly earnest, a result of the pairing of Belloc and Cecil.[30] The two men not only admired one another's prose, but were both temperamentally men of action with a taste for combat. As Gilbert Chesterton put it, their partnership was made inevitable by their "temperaments of a . . . rapid and resolute sort."[31]

Other newspapers like the *Manchester Guardian* or the *Daily News* were being kept alive by their breezier, less significant sister papers, but that did not stop the pair from hoping to establish, unaided, their own voice on Fleet Street. When the *Eye-Witness* was sharply criticized for its unnecessarily strong and slangy language, Chesterton defended their schoolboy shrillness by saying that their paper's "novelty and originality [came from] the social convention that English politics were not only free from political corruption but almost entirely free from personal motives about money. . . ."[32] His comments point up the fact that the *Eye-Witness* was not founded to expound the socio-political theory ultimately known as distributism, but to be an anti-Establishment sheet, harassing ministers like Masterman who had "betrayed" the Liberal cause.

Since the two men also began to attack the Liberal Party's social legislation, they often took contradictory positions or joined in strange alliances.[33] Their idiosyncratic stance, similar to that of many of their fellow editors, demonstrates that affinities and alliances and "party" labels were all in a state of flux. At various times, the paper supported the pro-Unionists on Ireland and the Syndicalists on trade unionism; always it was very strongly and unpleasantly anti-Semitic, partly because of Belloc and Cecil's personal antipathies, and partly because of Belloc's more objective judgment that the Dreyfus affair had destroyed the nerve of the French Army, and that the Rothschild family had put France's economy in jeopardy. Cecil could also name any number of assimilated Jewish Liberal politicians who he felt had "bought" their positions in society and government.[34] Then, as now, the topic was almost impossible to discuss politely or altogether fairly. Only once did Gilbert Chesterton take their strident, rather nasty tone — when he spoke publicly to a Jewish politician who he felt had wronged him and those close to him beyond apology.

Two things need to be remembered about the Jewish question in England up to the time of the postwar knowledge of the Holocaust. Apart from artistic society and the "jet set," which prided themselves on a kind of cultural broadmindedness, accepting of such things as mixed marriages, the English have always viewed Jews as "different," tending both in literature and life to label them by race. The best that can be said about Chesterton, then, is that he was representative of his own culture: he was typical of most English writers from Charles Dickens to Agatha Christie. Their social behavior was clearly conditioned by the very insularity that Englishmen — Chesterton included — have always been proud of. But in no sense of the word can Gilbert Chesterton be called a "Jew baiter"; in his private life he did have close Jewish friends.[35]

The *Eye-Witness* did a good job of shouting about specific social abuses that were real, if sometimes overplayed in its columns. Its concern was usually with a legal system that had one law for the poor and another for the rich. Chesterton's contributions were like his "Ballade of an Anti-Puritan," whose message was a dig at "progress" and the "simple life" as expounded by various politicians. It ended with the refrain, "I feel a little bored/Will someone take me to a pub!"[36]

Many of their Fleet Street friends were also contributors, but two in particular were to be associated with the Chestertons, and not always to their reputations' advantage. The first was Titterton, who wrote for the *New Age*; though he idolized Gilbert, he himself was a highly prejudiced and feisty individual with a curious lack of good judgment. The second was Father Vincent McNabb, who was often found in the paper's dingy offices on John Street; he seems to have been much involved in Cecil's conversion to Roman Catholicism. Father McNabb was a Dominican devoted to the causes of Irish freedom, Roman Catholicism, and the simple life, which in his case meant wearing homespun robes and refusing to use a typewriter because it is a machine.[37] Belloc and Cecil Chesterton were men after his own heart. Father McNabb and Gilbert agreed passionately on one cause:

their crusade to stop the practice of "eugenics," which, in the name of both progress and evolution, gave the public control over the "unfit" to keep them from reproducing.[38] This was far from being an idea spawned by the Nazis; at this period the idea of breeding a superior race was a popular position of English intellectuals, backed up by some very malicious laws.

Cecil Chesterton acted as assistant editor, and he was a good editor, far superior to either Belloc or his brother, but in his articles he sometimes showed a lack of judgment — particularly in a political column that he signed "Junius," after an eighteenth-century journalist who ferreted out corruption in high places. On August 3, for example, he bitterly attacked Masterman for supporting government bills to further his own career, in spite of the fact that there has never been any evidence that Masterman was venal in any way, except that, as Gilbert suggested, he found he was good at government and wanted to go on doing it. Cecil, however, went on to insist that it was perfectly safe for him to attack Masterman or any other bureaucrat who had been "jobbed into a salaried post" because there were no laws of libel; they were only what some other political hack said they were. The only thing a journalist needed to decide was if "the man you are attacking is likely to . . . face the ordeal of cross-examination in the witness-box." The only person convinced by Cecil's reasoning seems to have been his brother, who mentions it in his *Autobiography*. Belloc's biographer suggests that it would have been better for his character and peace of mind if he had not spent the next few years attacking public figures personally, also suggesting that much of the blame must rest with Cecil, who encouraged him.[39]

The paper also provided a place for Belloc to expound his ideas about the need for a redistribution of land as a basis for a better society. This was an old Liberal position, summarized in the slogan "three acres and a cow." Belloc now linked the concept with the French peasant proprietors, who were heirs of the "redistribution" of the French Revolution, as were other European countries, particularly Poland. Like Chesterton, he also was greatly influenced in his conviction that such a land scheme could work by the success of the 1903 Irish Land Bill. This bill had been written by their Conservative Anglo-Catholic friend George Wyndham. It let the government buy out large Irish landowners and restore the land to their tenants for annual payments less than their current rent. Passed to take the place of Home Rule, this bill had worked well after a fashion — until the Unionists, both Irish and English, began to regard Ireland as a part of the empire.[40] In recommending this concept, Belloc and Chesterton were not harking back to "the good old days"; they were using as their model a recent program, visible and viable. But it confused his friends and enemies alike when Belloc also supported the "last ditchers'" efforts to preserve the House of Lords. He did so largely because he felt, truly, that the Liberals really would not *reform* the Lords, while more peers would mean more manipulation of the Commons.

The battle between "old" and "new" liberalism over social legislation was begun by the reform of the Lords, but the real warfare started over Lloyd George's Insurance Bill, which was passed in July 1911 but did not go into effect until July 1912. Although Chesterton was not as actively engaged in attacking the government as Cecil and Belloc, he, too, regarded this bill as the opening wedge of the servile state. He also typically telescoped the time of its passage and its implementation, assuming that by the time of its passage he had quit writing for the *Daily News*. [41]

This bill marked the end of the very uneasy alliance between the Liberal Party and the Labour M.P.'s, while unions represented the only power that could be used against both the owners and the government. It was in this radical mood, echoing the strong "direct action" spirit of the time, that Chesterton and his friends were ready to man the barricades for a general strike. They still saw the unions as a variety of friendly societies with their own self-managed insurance programs and their craft orientation.

While Belloc had his own economic reasons for opposing this compulsory tax, which provided sickness and disability pay for about two million workers, Chesterton's negative reaction can be summed up under his symbolic, philosophical term "Prussianism."[42] To him, the name "Bismarck" meant what we think of when we use the Orwellian term "Big Brother." But contemporary opposition to this bill was not along party lines. Although part of its provisions had been written by William Beveridge, a protégé of the Webbs, they disapproved of it because it demanded some support from the individuals covered, while, at the other extremes, Lord Northcliffe of the Tory Press also attacked it.[43] This rather "unnatural" alliance suggested to Chesterton that the ordinary man and the older aristocracy had more in common with each other than with the professional do-gooders of either party.

Meanwhile, the great Liberal "crusade" to reform the House of Lords had actually been accomplished that August on a day when the temperature reached one hundred degrees, but the momentum for grassroots reform had just about died out.[44] Nonconformist leaders like the Cadburys had begun to doubt the wisdom of the press "marrying" a particular political party, which left room for the self-serving politicians like Lloyd George and Winston Churchill. Even the maverick Liberal editor Massingham now openly deplored the fact that the party system could not save the country, while a series of dangerous incidents with the German navy had transformed him from a Prussian admirer into a rabid foe of the kaiser and his ambitions. In short, many of Chesterton's attitudes were shared by his contemporaries.[45]

On July 7, 1911, Chesterton published a collection of short stories that proved to be — paradoxically — the most important of his career, because they provided him with lasting fame. It was Virginia Woolf, who represented the antithesis of Chesterton's social and religious values, who stated emphatically that to survive, all great artists must create a memorable character. Chesterton had now done so in the person of Father Brown. This collection, called *The Innocence of Father Brown,* was dedicated to his old J. D. C. friend Waldo D'Avigdor and his wife, Mildred, who lived near the Chestertons in the country. Although Chesterton wrote his Father Brown stories hastily (like almost everything else he wrote), often to finance other projects, they contain some of his most gorgeous "word painting," and are shaped by the two things that mark his best work: his personality (evident in the narrator and the protagonist), and his ideas, which were always moral concerns told like fairy tales. A columnist recently said, "There have been priest-investigators since G.K. Chesterton's Father Brown . . . [but he] was the progenitor and by far the best of the species [because he] was interested in ideas."[46]

Continuing efforts to divide Chesterton's writing into categories of "good" and "trashy" or between his roles of journalist and man of letters have never worked, because he was always both artist and propagandist simultaneously.[47] At the same time it isn't true that he or his writing, including "Father Brown," did not change under the impact of new events and experiences. As a whole, however, the Father Brown stories represent some of his most characteristic positions, political and social as well as moral and religious. These stories show Chesterton's un-English distaste for caste: in them aristocrats and plutocrats are often crooks, while society's invisible men — people like postmen and waiters — are taken for granted and therefore unseen.[48] Unfortunately, the fact that Father Brown is a Roman Catholic priest has been misused as a building block in the campaign to make Chesterton a lifelong Roman Catholic writer.

As a character Father Brown had an ancestor in the older brother of *The Club of Queer Trades,* who liked to contemplate human nature to solve mysteries instead of scouring London for clues. Intuition, based on common sense rather than on logical deductive reasoning, is the keynote of Father Brown's method. Many of the plots involving him are derived from Edgar Allan Poe's "The Purloined Letter," in which a clue is hidden among other things similar to it. In Chesterton's stories, however, clues are hidden in a highly romantic way, as they are in "The Sign of the Broken Sword," in which a battlefield is covered with corpses to hide one murder. Most of the stories have a moral atmosphere that has been compared to that of Dickens' novels; they also play quite strongly on the idea of the "unfamiliar in the familiar" found in Dickens' last unfinished novel, *The Mystery of Edwin Drood.* These stories also have the same kind of moral seriousness found in Shaw's plays of the same period.

It would probably amuse Chesterton greatly to have critics defending his literary reputation with the Father Brown stories, but it is true that his fictional style is often better suited to shorter forms: he liked to telescope events and to set the scene in broad strokes, without detailed description.

In these stories he could concentrate on a central idea, like an ordinary view of the world that provides the root of real understanding.[49] Although the character of Father Brown developed into Chesterton's mouthpiece rather than a realistic parish priest, he also represents his creator's conviction that God comes to man, not man to God, which is a central idea in all of his writing, the concept he labeled "the Incarnation."[50]

Much comment has arisen over the origins of Father Brown, but Chesterton himself emphatically stated that when a writer creates a fictional character,

> he fits him out with ... features meant to be effective in that setting. ... He may have taken ... a hint from a human being. But he is not thinking of a portrait but of a picture. In Father Brown it was the chief feature to be featureless. ... His commonplace exterior was meant to contrast with his unsuspected vigilance and intelligence. ...[51]

The problem of identification arose chiefly because Chesterton did borrow some intellectual qualities from "my friend Father John O'Connor," who then developed the mistaken idea that Father Brown resembled him. The really interesting aspect of the Father Brown stories, however, is not where Chesterton got the idea for them but what he made of it: he used these stories to keep in touch with the general reading public while promoting his own ideas. The result has been interesting: although he was declared "reactionary" by the literary establishment long before he died, these stories have lived on and have won him long-lasting critical attention.[52] Another compliment paid him was John Dickson Carr's creation of Dr. Gideon Fell, who is Gilbert Chesterton brought to life.[53]

This collection of stories destroys another myth about Chesterton: that he never changed his mind after 1901. In that year he had written about the detective-story writer as the "real poet of the city and the detective the romantic hero who is the protector of civilization ... who helps the public see the poetry of city life."[54] This early essay of his is endlessly quoted by other practitioners of the detective art, including Howard Haycraft and Dorothy Sayers. But by 1911, when Chesterton published the first Father Brown collection, his detective had developed into someone who is neither the knight of law and order nor a gentleman in any way identified with the Establishment. In fact, Chesterton's idea of using a shabby little Roman priest guaranteed that his character would be denied the normal, upper-class acceptability granted to the most poorly paid of the Church-of-England clergy.

In these short tales, Chesterton was also writing very pointed, apt political commentary which is often missed today. George Orwell, for example, found in Chesterton's writing "an apolitical world gone mad." The most exquisite irony is one that only Chesterton himself could savor — his contemporary acceptability among "the murder intelligentsia," who, recognizing his egalitarianism, confuse his ideas with those of the welfare state.[55] He was always accused of a childish affection for blood and gore, and it is true that he did think that a socially stratified society, run by samurai, for example, was worse than murder. But a careful rereading of this original collection shows his real preoccupations, stated in many a sharp comment, like those in "The Queer Feet," in which Mr. Audley, "never having been in politics, . . . sometimes . . . embarrassed the company by . . . suggesting that there was some difference between a Liberal and a Conservative."[56]

It has often been pointed out that Chesterton did not always keep to the rules of fair play with the reader, but this casualness allows him to ignore everything except the particular theme he wants to develop. If a reader accepts the story's basic premise, Chesterton also provides clues so obvious that he can walk the thin line between being too fantastic and too absurd.[57] Now that what is called "formula literature" is attracting more critical attention, his stories are seen as giving a new vitality to his stereotypes, as well as expressing his underlying moral conviction that all problems have a clear and rational solution. Moreover, as a mystery writer Chesterton clearly does reflect the twentieth century's recurring social cycles of public guilt and reform.[58]

Many of these early stories are dramatizations of *What's Wrong With the World,* and they contain thinly veiled, topical allusions which would have made them particularily salty to his contemporaries. His viewpoint can be clearly illustrated by comparing his story, "The Invisible Man," with H. G. Wells' novel of the same name. In Chesterton's story there is no upwardly mobile young scientist exploring the outer limits of the universe for what he can gain, but a social statement that many members of society are "invisible," like his murdering postman, who "has passions like other men." Another story, called "The Queer Feet," is about a useless "Establishment" club in London in which a man who wants to steal its special silverware pretends to be a waiter among the clubmen, and a clubman among the waiters. The members protest that a gentleman never looks like a waiter, but in fact they all wear identical evening dress, so from that time on the clubmen are forced to wear green to prevent confusion.

This particular story employs a narrative technique that Chesterton used a great deal in his later writing: "playing" the role of narrator within the story. Here he explains that ". . . since it is . . . unlikely that you will . . . rise to find the Fishermen [clubmen] or that you will . . . sink low enough to find Father Brown, I fear you will never hear the story at all unless you hear it from me."[59] The irony inherent in the tale is reflected in the fact that these club members, like the Members of Parliament, may call themselves "fishers of men" in the New Testament sense, but of course the true fisherman is Father Brown. The club has a vast number of ceremonies but no history and no object; its "talk was that strange, slight talk which governs the British Empire. . . ."

This story also gives more than a hint of Chesterton's "uncharacteristic bitterness," which shaped his forthcoming essay collection called *A Miscellany of Men*. It illustrates the fact that Chesterton, like many of his generation who were feeling a sense of increased alienation and isolation, was deeply uncertain about the way his world was moving. It is fitting that Father Brown, born in this troubled period of time, should have proved to be Chesterton's passport to the future, representing not the blind certainty of a dogma, but characteristic concern for the ordinary person.

Chesterton's next response to the sense of chaos and crisis besetting his fellow intellectuals was to finish a work that a number of critics have called his masterpiece. This is his long narrative poem about the Saxon king Alfred, *The Ballad of the White Horse*. It is almost unread today, but it was so well known during his lifetime that it was quoted, with no attribution, on the front page of the *Times* the day that Crete fell in World War II and the English feared Germany might actually win the war.[60] Whether it is a superb example of public poetry or a ghastly imitation of older forms depends upon the reader's critical point of view or his religious assumptions. Many of those who read it today take it to be a private paean to the Virgin Mary, a personal mystic vision of heavenly things; those who dismiss it label it a jolly journalistic flirting with medieval history. For a biographer, the poem's value lies in what it says about its author's state of mind and his view of the world at the time when it was written. But it also seems as if the issue of its literary merit may eventually be resolved in its favor, since one of the recent great masters of English poetry has praised it.[61]

The basic faith that this poem publicly proclaims is still the Chestertonian mixture of liberalism and Christianity described in *Orthodoxy*; it is not in the least specifically Roman Catholic. His "Virgin Mary," apart from his use of legends about her that were part of Alfred's story, is a typical Chestertonian heroine, demonstrating the eternal "womanly" qualities in time of danger: acting caring but stern, exhorting men to go and do their duty, no matter how challenging, while she maintains civilization at home. The poem is an expression of Chesterton's lifelong romantic conviction that it did not matter if an individual won so long as he fought as hard as he could and never gave up. As Chesterton saw it, victory had come again and again to the Christian side because, as it says in *The Song of Roland*, "Christians are right; pagans are wrong," and because Christians keep struggling even when they are defeated. The whole point of using Alfred as an English Christian hero was that he "would dare anything for the faith, he would bargain in anything except the faith," by which Chesterton meant that Alfred took his mission — not himself — seriously. Therefore, the vital historical event, as Chesterton saw it, was not the great victory at Ethandune, but the baptism of Danish Guthrum. His baptism, along with his chiefs, ensured that although a century later there was a Danish king ruling in England, "he got the crown, but he did not get rid of the cross," and England remained a Christian realm.[62]

While Chesterton was working on the poem, he and Frances hired a car and drove as far as the marshes in Somerset, where legend said Alfred had hid and burned a peasant's cakes; they also viewed again the great prehistoric white horse of chalk cut out of the Berkshire downs, which is above the battle site. The poem's white horse thus unites a very private symbol from Chesterton's past and his favorite image for England herself — a piece of chalk — in a narrative clearly meant to carry both connotations. The ballad itself is based upon three legends about Alfred the Great which were a part of Chesterton's own childhood, straight from the pages of Dickens' *A Child's History of England*. The poem also has overtones of Kipling's *Puck of Pook's Hill,* published in 1906, in which Alfred is described as a leader who has come down to us "because he fought for the Christian civilization against the heathen nihilism." Alfred also appealed to Chesterton because he was a younger son, sincere and hardworking, but not charismatic — a George V, not an Edward VII. Although Chesterton used stories not considered historical, Alfred *was* a historical king, so this poem gave him a chance to combine his pictorial and historical imaginings into a unified whole, with the message that "Alfred is no fairy tale; His days as our days ran."[63]

Differing with the informed historical opinions of his day, Chesterton insisted that the English were not a race of purebred Teutonic supermen, but a mixture of Roman, Celt, and Saxon, not to mention Danish. Alfred's army was also made up of ordinary men who would fight heroically for their own homes, whereas, in the jargon of the time, the invading Vikings were clearly "fitter," more "Progressive." In many ways they were a perfect symbol of the supermen so admired by Shaw, ushering in a "new day."[64] Evolution was on their side, but Alfred ignored that fact and gathered his scattered troops for a final assault even though all their leaders had fallen; and he won. But he did not win England lasting peace, for God's universe does not "bid the bold grass/ Go, and return no more." On the contrary, the weeds will creep back and recover the great image, which must then be painstakingly scoured again. The poem ends with a description of the returning Vikings that is a message to his own time:

> They shall not come with warships
>> They shall not waste with brands,
> But books be all their eating
>> And ink be on their hands. . . .
>
> By this sign you shall know them
>> That they ruin and make dark. . . .

> When is great talk of trend and tide,
>   And wisdom and destiny,
> Hail that undying heathen
>   That is sadder than the sea.[65]

His faith expressed in this long poem is as much "liberalism" as it is "Christianity" because it is political and social, not eschatological in emphasis. Unlike most of his contemporaries, who had given up on Christendom and were hoping for some "sign" from the East, Chesterton still steadfastly held up the image of Western civilization, refusing to despair, because that was what he called sin. He dedicated the poem to Frances, whom he said "brought the Cross to me," a simple statement of fact; the poem was always one of her favorites. In writing it, Chesterton had abandoned his usual writing habits: he had revised this poem over several years, changing obvious images to more subtle ones, removing much of the "olden talke," and improving the loose, irregular beat of his ballad style.[66] It was published as a complete work on August 31, 1911.

The poem received mixed reviews from the start. His friend Maurice Baring, who reviewed it for the *Eye-Witness,* took him to task for not imitating Coleridge more closely, even though Chesterton's own "Jack the Giantkiller" tone was apparent.[67] It was a time when literary tastes were changing, and in general, except among ordinary men, ballads were "out." By 1914 what we still call "modern" was thoroughly established in England, from airplanes to Russian ballet, but that culture was increasingly a private affair to be appreciated by upper middle-class bohemians who had university educations and considered themselves Socialists, though without much interest in such a public thing as politics.

In the meantime, the passage of the reform bill for the House of Lords now meant that the Liberal government was obligated to pass a Home Rule bill to repay the Irish for their support. Such a bill was duly introduced in April 1912, but in the interval the Unionists, who stood for the "territorial integrity" of the entire British Empire, had joined the Ulster Orange Society to form a Unionist Council. The Conservatives had gotten rid of the aristocratic Balfour and now had for a leader Bonar Law, who was committed to the destruction of the Liberal Party, a far cry from Belloc's theory of collusion between the two Front Benches.[68]

Into this increasingly unstable scene, in which Liberals like Chesterton and Masterman alike both still hoped for a Gladstonian revolution, came a new leader "to beat the Orange Drum" to keep all Ireland English. On September 23, 1911, the barrister Sir Edward Carson became head of their new "army." He belonged to the Anglo-Irish squirearchy, but he had been called to the English Bar. He had become a household word in 1895, when he destroyed Oscar Wilde in court, an event Chesterton remembered vividly. Dour and relentless as a cross-examiner, he looked like a "puritanical pirate," with dark eyes brooding over a long jaw and heavy chin. By 1912 he and his followers had signed, in their own blood, a bowdlerized version of the old Scots Covenant called the Ulster Sacramentum, pledging to defeat the "conspiracy" to establish Home Rule.[69]

From the point of view of many Liberals, including Chesterton and the editors of the *Eye-Witness,* the Carson slogan that "Home Rule was Rome Rule" was vicious nonsense aimed at destroying the Liberal Party. But it became more and more obvious that the vicious personal attacks in the press, the heckling at the meetings, and the gun-running could all lead to civil war. The prime minister was accused by many fellow Liberals of caring only to stay in office, but it is probably fairer to say that Asquith saw his delaying tactics on the Home Rule Bill as the only way to save the country.[70] Inevitably, the splits inside the Liberal Party grew larger.

The Fabian Old Gang was equally upset at the failure of government to remain calm, because the last thing they had wanted was bloody barricades and revolution, whether by the masses or by aristocrats. Shaw's play *Heartbreak House* reflected their gloom.[71] By contrast, Gardiner at the *Daily News* let Erskine Childers (who was later shot to death as an Irish patriot) write a series supporting Home Rule; Massingham at the *Nation* criticized Asquith for toadying to Lloyd George, whose motives he now suspected, while reacting violently against the militant feminists, who by now had taken their battle to the streets.[72]

Although he did not support the women's radicalism, Chesterton did support the militant workers' demands, even in the face of the great railway strike of August 1911, which showed the country how paralyzing such a stoppage could be. He voiced no objections, either, when the miners joined in a combined strike the following March, and then began to form the Triple Alliance, a coalition of miners and railroad and transport workers who were planning a general strike for August 1914. He expressed his reaction in a poem, "The Song of the Wheels," which he wrote on a Friday and Saturday in August 1911. The poem ended with this wild shout:

> Call upon the wheels, master, call upon the wheels,
> Weary grow the holidays when you miss the meals. . . .
> If a man grow faint, master, take him ere he kneels,
> Take him, break him, rend him, end him, roll him,
>   crush him with the wheels.[73]

Several months later, in February 1912, Chesterton published a novel called *Manalive,* in which he celebrated again one of his earliest themes: the joy of being alive. (During 1911-12 he was actually at work on a novel about the proposed general strike, but because of his illness he put it in a drawer and forgot about it until a general strike occurred much later, in 1926.) *Manalive* is clearly a much earlier work, possibly the final version of his first novel, for he began writing it when he was still working at Fisher-Unwin.[74]

It is both a variation of the detective story as well as an allegorical comedy, with ideas dramatized in rapid, symbolic incidents typical of Chesterton's fiction. Its story is clearly the early Chestertonian "gospel" about the need for romance and adventure in modern life. The hero, Innocent Smith, is both a fool for Christ and a kind of self-portrait; he keeps "acting out" the way to look at life with fresh vision. In spite of its thematic origins, the published book is more of a realistic drawing-room comedy than are his other earlier novels. It has a neat, two-part structure, and takes place mostly in one locale. It is set in a suburban boardinghouse, which is the "Home of Jones," a place where ordinary people live.[75]

What is clearly symbolic is the wind that blows Innocent Smith over the wall into the garden to rejuvenate this group of young people who have adopted the attitudes of the times. The wind is the Holy Spirit, for the young curate (modeled after Conrad Noel) calls it "a great gale . . . by Him who made His Angels winds. . . ." Smith himself is accused of burglary, bigamy, blasphemy, and murder. Actually, his crimes are not really crimes at all: for example, he is "accused" of offering to kill a suicidal intellectual (who runs away); of courting and remarrying his wife repeatedly; and of landing at Brighton Pavilion after roaming the world. The public courts would have put Smith in a madhouse, but these people solve his "crimes" far more competently by holding the mock High Court of Beacon in the boardinghouse to try his case. But it is really Smith's accusers who are on trial, getting an education in politics and morality; in this way Smith's outlook is preached to the wide world. This "court" not only illustrates Chesterton's feeling that the real English courts were controlled by the powerful, but also dramatizes his conviction that the home is the place where society should solve its problems.

Manalive has clear thematic connections with Chesterton's other work, especially *The Man Who Was Thursday* and *The Wild Knight*. Its unusually tight dramatic structure may owe something to Shaw's repeated effort to get Chesterton to write a play, something he was about to do most successfully.

Chapter Eleven

HIS BROTHER'S KEEPER

1912-1913

It is the fashion to divide recent history into Pre-War and Post-War conditions. I believe it is almost as essential to divide them into Pre-Marconi and Post-Marconi days. . . . I think it probable that centuries will pass before it is seen clearly and in its right perspective; and that then it will be seen as one of the turning-points in the whole history of England and the world.

G.K. Chesterton, *Autobiography*[1]

IN February 1912 Chesterton published a little book in the Home University Library Series called *The Victorian Age in Literature*. This book has rightly been called a "masterpiece of arrangment, of suspension, and counter-tension, whereby names are lifted in large webs of interreacting influence."[2] Yet it so frightened the editors of the series that they prefaced it with an explanatory note, saying, ". . . this book is not put forward as an authoritative history of Victorian literature. It is a free and personal statement of views and impressions made by Mr. Chesterton at the Editors' express invitation." Once again, Chesterton had proved impossible to categorize, because he discussed the Victorian giants within the frame of their era. As a result, the book is "pure" Chesterton at his best; it has stayed in print, and can be called another of his minor masterpieces.

In *The Victorian Age* Chesterton summed up (at the appropriate moment in his own life and that of his country) where he had come from in order to discover where he had arrived. He examined his own Victorian roots and acted very Victorian by being extremely "anti-Victorian." His thesis was that the age was best understood as a compromise between the rising forces of rationalism and the waning faith of an earlier age. To him, the typical Victorian who began the age was the historian Macaulay, while the typical representative at the end of the age was Huxley, the scientist. "Macaulay took it for granted that common sense required some kind of theology, while Huxley took it for granted that common sense meant having none. Macaulay never talked about his religion: but Huxley was always talking about the religion he hadn't got."[3]

The whole book is clear, amusing, beautifully written, and brimming with Chestertonian one-liners that have been quoted ever since, such as the crack that "Matthew Arnold kept a smile of heart-broken forbearance, as of the teacher in an idiot school, that was enormously insulting." Also well-known is his observation that "the Oxford Movement was a bow that broke when it had let loose the flashing arrow that was Newman," as is the comment that earned him Thomas Hardy's undying enmity: "Hardy became a sort of village atheist brooding and blaspheming over the village idiot."

The book marked a summing-up of his own thoughts as well as the end of a chapter in his writing career, for he wrote no more literary commentary of this kind again until 1927. His point about the Victorian Compromise — which he said consisted of a combination of middle-class religion and economics joined to aristocratic political forms — was that it had been attacked by his own heroes, the English "revolutionaries" such as Dickens, Ruskin, Carlyle, and Newman, with the formula "Christianity and liberalism." Their attack, however, destroyed the compromise and shattered the Victorian world, which broke into two parts: socialism and imperialism, reflected in the literary figures of Bernard Shaw and Rudyard Kipling. For Chesterton the moral to be learned from the period was plain: "The Victorian Age . . . thought that commerce outside a country must extend peace; it has certainly often extended war. They thought that commerce inside a country must certainly promote prosperity; it has largely promoted poverty. But for them these were experiments; for us they ought to be lessons."[4]

While Chesterton was summing up his background and its moral deficiencies, the Liberal government was trying to cope not only with the domestic atmosphere of "perpetual anxiety and alarm," but also with the threat of war.[5] Public concern over this possibility had been reflected in invasion novels like the one by Childers and the one by Wells called *The War in the Air*. There was also a novel by Saki which had the kaiser ruling from Buckingham Palace, and a very funny spoof by young P. G. Wodehouse, in which a Boy Scout named Clarence saved England from simultaneous invasions by Germans, Russians, Muslims, the Swiss Navy, the Chinese, and the Barbary pirates.[6] In his next novel, *The Flying Inn*, Chesterton would produce his own version of the invasion story, showing his talent for combining "pop art" and philosophic ideas and commentary.

Concern over England's military unpreparedness was gaining ground, not only among the Conservatives but among the Liberals as well. Many of them were now prepared to desert the isolationist Little England position, "open diplomacy," and protests against military expenditures, because from 1910 to 1914 Germany had built eleven dreadnoughts to England's thirteen. That February the war minister, Haldane, was sent to Berlin to try to arrange an agreement to limit the arms race. His mission had come about at the suggestion of two friends: Sir Ernest Cassel, a Jewish, German-born London financier whose daughter was to marry a cousin of the king; and

Albert Ballin, head of the Hamburg-Amerika Line, another Jewish financier whom the kaiser called his friend. Haldane's mission was a failure because the Germans insisted that England must promise to stay neutral in any continental war in return for arms limitation. The London press was very vocal about its disapproval of the very idea of the mission, sarcastically labeling Haldane "the Minister for Germany." One of his nastiest critics was Conservative editor Leo Maxse of the *National Review,* who was always passionate in his devotion to certain causes and rabid in his opposition to others, with no middle ground.[7] All Fleet Street talked loudly about the fact that Cassel and Ballin were Jewish. Speaking of this period long afterward, however, Chesterton commented, in typical fashion, that he never forgot that England had betrayed Haldane by charging him with betraying England.[8]

In much the same belligerent spirit of their peers, Belloc and Cecil Chesterton at the *Eye-Witness* were still looking for chances to prove that a small clique ran England for its own advantage, a clique possibly financed by Jews. One regular feature of their paper was called "Lex v. The Poor," which rang the changes on the injustice that legal penalties for the rich and the poor were never the same. They also fought the Mental Deficiency Act, which allowed two doctors to take a child from his parents and lock him up if they thought he was mentally incompetent.[9] But now a real scandal had developed which was to become Cecil Chesterton's greatest crusade. The episode known as the Marconi Affair was never completely explained, but it was a matter of violent public concern for over eighteen months, and helped to destroy the Liberal Party. It also left England, on the brink of war, without a telegraph system.[10] It greatly affected Gilbert Chesterton because it confirmed his growing distaste for and distrust of politicians — even his friends — and it threatened Cecil's actual freedom.

The Marconi Affair had really begun in 1911 when international unrest made the government decide to build a chain of state-owned telegraph stations throughout the empire. These stations would come under the jurisdiction of the post office, whose Postmaster General, Herbert Samuel, was one of the Liberal Party's Jewish leaders; but the contract to build them had to be ratified by the House of Commons. Bids to build the network were gotten from two companies, and on March 7, 1912, the Marconi Company's bid was accepted provisionally, until voted on by the Commons.

The managing director of the Marconi Company was Godfrey Isaacs, whose brother, Sir Rufus Isaacs, a successful Jewish lawyer, was the Liberal Attorney General as well as a close friend of Mr. Samuel. The fact that three of the principals were Jews added to the eventual unpleasantness and uproar. In fact, the Isaacs family was convinced that the entire episode represented blatant anti-Semitism.

Sir Rufus had already taken silk at age thirty-seven, had been the M.P. for Reading, and had become the Liberal Solicitor General and now Attorney

General, in which post he was in line for the Woolsack, or the position of Lord Chancellor of England, the top legal job in government. This august post, however, had been given to Haldane that June (as a result of the publicity about his efforts in Berlin), but Asquith made Sir Rufus a member of the Cabinet to keep him in the government. His brother Godfrey, on the other hand, had been involved in numerous business deals and was reputed to "love power." He became director of the Marconi Company because he got along well with the inventor. Right after submitting a bid to the government, Godfrey sent out a circular to the company's shareholders claiming he had won the imperial contract, although the government was free to choose another system it if found a better one. He then went to America, where he was also a director of the American Marconi Company, and reorganized that company. He came home to England in April 1912 with 500,000 shares of the American Marconi Company to sell.

He next offered to sell some shares to his brothers, Sir Rufus and Harry Isaacs, but Sir Rufus declined on the grounds that it would be inappropriate for him to buy them from a director of a company with whom the government was negotiating. Harry, however, bought about 50,000 shares and then sold Sir Rufus 10,000 of them. Sir Rufus now sold 1,000 shares to Lloyd George, the Chancellor of the Exchequer (the number-two man in the Liberal government), and 1,000 shares to the Liberal Party Whip, who was in charge of the party's war chest (the secret funds). On April 19, 1912, the stock of the American Marconi Company was put on the open market for about twice as much as these Liberal politicians had agreed to pay. The next month they all bought and sold more shares (on paper), and the Chief Party Whip bought another 3,000 shares for the party.

Clearly, the shares of the American Marconi Company went up because it was assumed that the English company would get the English contract. No one was bribing the ministers, but they were certainly given the chance to make a killing based on inside information. It was also particularly unattractive that the country's chief financial minister, as well as its Attorney General, whose job it was to determine the legality of government actions, and the Chief Party Whip, all had their hands in the till.[11] What little was known about the situation at the time bore all the earmarks of the basic *Eye-Witness* premise: that the government was guilty of cupidity and collusion. But the situation was not public knowledge on Fleet Street until mid-July of 1912.

During the interval, Cecil Chesterton, who had recently made the Belloc family his new chief mentors, often visited them and got lectured about his soul by Elodie Belloc. One day, after talking to her all night, Cecil went back to London and sought out the same Father Bowden at the Brompton Oratory who had converted Maurice Baring. Shortly afterward, on June 7, 1912, he was re-baptized at the Oratory as a Roman Catholic.[12] Judging from the effort that Gilbert Chesterton later made to explain his own similar actions, the Chesterton parents were not enthusiastic about Cecil's decision.

To say that at this point Gilbert was also ripe for conversion "telescopes" the events of his life. In 1912, although he was convinced by experience that belief in a personal God was the only way of life that worked in a decadent world, Chesterton was an acknowledged Anglo-Catholic; his thinking owed little to Roman Catholicism.[13] But unquestionably the conversions first of Maurice Baring and then of his beloved brother had an emotional effect on him. Through them he also became aware of the kind of daily self-discipline demanded by Roman Catholicism, habits at this point so alien to his upbringing that they may have been the source of Belloc's often repeated statement that Chesterton was not good convert material. Certainly Belloc's conviction needs to be taken seriously in the face of more romantic efforts to prove his friend a Catholic all his life.[14]

At any rate, not only did Belloc admire Cecil's writing more than Gilbert's (he never actually read much that Chesterton wrote), but they both shared "a streak of that fanatical intolerance which seems to be fertilized, not by profound convictions, but by personal animosities . . . to hold a grudge against the universe, the world, and you in particular."[15]

Midway through 1912 Belloc published his most important book, *The Servile State,* which made it possible for him to change Cecil's political and economic views.[16] Its publication was timed to coincide with the implementation of the National Insurance Act, and its message was simply that the creation of the welfare state was the creation of the servile state. Belloc foresaw an upper class controlling the means of production and a proletariat who depended upon them for wages and unemployment compensation. To him, the control of the means of production was the control of life and liberty itself; capitalism and socialism were just different names for the same thing — the all-powerful state. The only difference would be that under socialism these slaves would have the "security which the old capitalism did not give them."[17] Chesterton agreed with Belloc's defense of liberty at the expense of security, particularly because the new Liberal legislation would establish a benevolent despotism imposed by the upper classes and the government on the lower classes only.[18] In terms that are strangely Marxist-sounding, both Belloc and Chesterton kept harping on the fact that this kind of social legislation would create wider and wider class distinctions between the doers-to and the done-to. (In their thinking they were closer to the Fabians than the Tories.) Their own Radical-Liberal background, with its ideal of a society entirely made up of a self-sufficient "middle class," put the freedom to choose far ahead of the freedom from want. In an era that might be described as "post-welfare state," it is possible to argue that their prophecies are finally coming true.[19]

Since this is the point at which it is customary to label them both "medievalists," it is interesting to discover that their basic economic understanding of English history was "revisionist," but along strictly Socialist lines. Belloc illustrated his basic thesis by reference to a period in the Middle Ages when he believed that there had been widespread ownership of the means of production. It was the time when the urban workplace had been dominated by the craft guilds, when the peasant could not be evicted from his land and had the right to share the "commons," which were later enclosed by the big landlords. He stated that "this *distributive* system . . . was guaranteed by . . . cooperative bodies, binding men of the same craft . . . or village . . . together; guaranteeing the small proprietor against loss of his economic independence, . . . while it guaranteed society against the growth of a proletariat. . . . The restraints upon liberty were . . . designed for the preservation of liberty. . . ."[20] This "Chesterbelloc" fantasy of the past was an acceptable historical analysis at the time.

The famous *Fabian Essays,* first published in 1889 and never out of print thereafter, stated that "the Catholic Church developed . . . the widest and freest system of education the world has ever seen before this century; Protestant individualism in England shattered the Catholic Church; founded the modern land system upon its confiscated estates; destroyed the medieval machinery for charity and education."[21] Chesterton and Belloc's old friend and Liberal editor, J.L. Hammond, as well as the Fabian historian R.H. Tawney, all endorsed this approach, admiring the late Middle Ages and downgrading the Reformation, the Tudors, the Stuarts, and the great Whigs of the seventeenth and eighteenth centuries who had created "Parliamentary government" for their own self-interest. It might be argued that it was the Fabians who wanted to rebuild the monolithic structure of the Roman Catholic Church under the guise of collectivism, while, like true Edwardians, Belloc and Chesterton really wanted to restore their idealized nineteenth century that favored family businesses in which workers could help be responsible for their own welfare. But Chesterton also called owning property "the art of democracy," and he was not willing to give up the right of the individual "for the greatest good of the greatest number." Unlike his Fabian friends, he gave the "ordinary" people credit for knowing how they wanted to live.

Meanwhile, during that summer of 1912 Belloc was proving to be a capricious, fussy, nervous editor. By July, bored by the job and overworked because of his many other writing projects, he resigned his editorship to Cecil and sold him his shares as well. An editor in his own right at last, Cecil Chesterton took over with boundless enthusiasm, running the paper, as Belloc wrote Baring, "always with vigor, not always with discretion."[22]

Many of the Chestertons' friends contributed to the *Eye-Witness* for nothing, and chief among them was Gilbert himself, whose name helped to sell the paper. Two of his best-known "topical" poems appeared there after Cecil had taken over. One, "The Shakespeare Memorial," begins, "Lord

Lilac thought it rather rotten/ That Shakespeare should be quite forgotten."
The other, "The Horrible History of Jones," goes like this:

> Jones had a dog; it had a chain
> Not often worn, not causing pain
> But, as the I.K.L. has passed
> Their "Unleashed Cousins Act" at last
> Inspectors took the chain away;
> Whereat the canine barked, hurray!
> At which, of course, the S.P.U. . . .
> Were forced to give the dog in charge
> For being Audibly at Large.[23]

At this time Chesterton's poetic fame rested more on narrative poems like "Lepanto." This poem, which every schoolboy used to know, was published in the *Eye-Witness* on the anniversary of the great battle waged against the Turks by Christians under Don Juan of Austria, which kept the Ottoman Empire out of Europe. It was extremely popular and recited everywhere, with loud approval given to its refrain of "Don John of Austria is going to the war!" Its final apotheosis came in 1915 when John Buchan, spy-story author and Tory politician, wrote to tell Chesterton that the men in the trenches had shouted the poem as they went over the top. Since Chesterton had always admired *The Song of Roland*, sung to lead the Normans into battle at Hastings, it is hard to imagine a compliment more to his taste. Above all, he saw himself as a public poet, not a private recorder of his own moods; he was writing for men in a group, sitting around in a pub or at a party, drinking and singing songs as he and his friends liked to do.

On July 20, 1912, as the Marconi contract was being placed before the House of Commons for formal debate and passage, which would be supervised by the junior minister, Charles Masterman, the gossip circulating about it in the City and the drawing rooms of the West End was suddenly written up in the *Outlook*. This paper suggested that the contract represented another South Sea Bubble, an eighteenth-century scandal in which the ministers had been impeached.[24] On August 8, Cecil Chesterton joined in the press attack, quickly assuming pride of place as the loudest spokesman for both the public interest and those M.P.'s who wanted to debate the contract openly. Masterman had the ticklish job of keeping the contract from being debated, for fear of bringing down the Liberal government itself, while the fact that Sir Rufus and Lloyd George did not reply to the charges being printed convinced Cecil that the "whole of the press . . . was in league to conceal corruption or too craven to expose it." Other Fleet Street papers like the *Daily News*, which were genuinely afraid for the Liberal Party's tenure in office, reproached Cecil for his language, but, as Belloc again wrote Baring, "Nobody believes anyone did anything wrong except a couple of hundred gossiping bankers in the City and some eight to ten thousand in the West End."[25]

The government did not want to drop the contract with the Marconi Company in favor of that of its rival, a German company, but no one is sure how early Asquith knew that his chief ministers had been playing with the shares. The prime minister had said privately that answering the press attacks would only help the circulation of papers like the *Eye-Witness,* but the people who contributed articles to the *Eye-Witness* were a small but influential group, much read, so it was hard to believe that men with nothing to hide would not answer the charges made. That fall Cecil went on trumpeting his accusations, in a style that was "invective, lively and pungent"; he received no answer, which further built his self-confidence.[26]

Fleet Street itself was very unsettled that year, uncertain of its own future. That September, for example, Bentley left the *Daily News* to go to work for the *Daily Telegraph,* which he felt was still maintaining its "independent position." What he meant was that Gardiner had begun to edit his copy to make it match the official editorial policy. Before he left, Bentley had also begun a secret project: writing a detective story in order to win a contest that offered fifty pounds as first prize. He had never before written a full-length book, but now, walking back and forth from his home in Hampstead every work day, he developed a plot. He decided that he must have a hero who was a "recognizable human being," and made a list of items that were absolutely necessary to include: a perfect alibi, chasing about in motor cars, a detective who fails when the amateur succeeds, and a crew of regulation suspects. He reluctantly decided to include a love interest, too.[27]

In mid-1911, when Bentley had carefully thought out his plot, he and his wife met the Chestertons in Paris, and Bentley outlined the plot to Chesterton as they sat together in a hotel lounge. Characteristically, Chesterton was full of admiration and urged Bentley to go ahead and write it out, saying that he wished he had thought it up. The legend that Chesterton had made a bet with him that he could write a book was untrue, as Bentley later pointed out, because Chesterton never made bets.

The book, now known as *Trent's Last Case,* was a milestone in detective-story writing. It came out later in 1913, charmingly dedicated to Chesterton:

> The only really noble motive I had in writing it was the hope that you would enjoy it . . . [and] I owe you a book in return for *The Man Who Was Thursday* . . . [and] I said I would when I unfolded the plan of it to you surrounded by Frenchmen [but also] because I remember the past.[28]

It seems especially fitting that Bentley and Chesterton celebrated their affection publicly with two such masterpieces. It is also fitting that Bentley chose to continue his work as a journalist, not quitting and living off the profits of his book, which he could have done.

Trent's Last Case was hailed for being "startlingly original ... with a liberating influence ... a good plot, a love interest integral to the story, real flesh and blood characters, but most of all [for] its good writing ... with so light and so sure a touch."[29] Bentley's attractive heroine, Mrs. Manderson, is a perfect Chestertonian heroine: she chooses love "in a setting where there was always creative work in the background ... men and women with professions or arts ... ideals and things to believe in and quarrel about. ..."[30] She is the woman in *What's Wrong With the World*: she is able to out-think the boyish Trent, who admires her for it, and she is feminine and talented; she even has a delightful sense of humor that matches his ability to "piffle so well." All those who argue about Chesterton's view of women need to take into consideration the fact that Mrs. Manderson is an interesting and well-rounded character in her own right, and is clearly a product of the society that Chesterton knew. Furthermore, it should be remembered that the "new" women of 1912 were either throwing rocks through the plate-glass windows of the *Daily News,* or creating havoc, like Ada Jones at the *Eye-Witness*, or behaving in sexually irresponsible ways.[31]

That October of 1912, just before the formal Parliamentary debate on the Marconi contract began, Chesterton published another collection of essays called *A Miscellany of Men*. It was the last group to be gathered from the *Daily News,* where he had become unhappy. These essays have been called "bitter" because they are aimed at the people who run things:

> [Their] powers and privileges have grown so world-wide and unwieldy that they are out of the power of the moderately rich as well as of the moderately poor. ... The things that change modern history, the big ... loans, educational philanthropic foundations, the purchase of numberless newspapers, the big prices paid for peerages, the big expenses ... incurred in elections ... are getting too big for everybody except the misers: the men with the largest of earthly fortunes and the smallest of earthly aims.[32]

While the accusations have a strangely contemporary ring, they were echoed in the Fleet Street press generally, as well as in places like *Trent's Last Case,* in which the murder of a plutocrat had multiple consequences:

> In Paris a well-known banker walked quietly out of the Bourse and fell dead upon the broad steps among the raving crowd of Jews, a phial crushed in his hand. In Frankfurt one leapt from the Cathedral top. ... Men stabbed and shot and strangled themselves. ...[33]

This is clearly a picture of the closely connected, evil world of high finance.

In these essays Chesterton is mourning the loss of Bentley's "Revolution without the R," and his loss of belief in politicians. In one essay he describes a spontaneous fire at Beaconsfield, in which good timber was destroyed at the very time when junk was being collected for a bonfire in honor of the coronation of George V. He calls the two fires symbolic of the world:

Just as there are two fires, so there are two revolutions. And I saw that the whole mad modern world is a race between them. Which will happen first, the revolution in which bad things shall perish, or that other revolution in which good things shall perish also. . . . One is the riot that all good men . . . really dream of . . . when we shall take tyranny and usury and public treason and bind them into bundles and burn them. And the other is the disruption that may come prematurely, negatively, and suddenly, in the night, like the fire in my little town.[34]

In this essay Chesterton sounds like a major prophet, talking about the wheat and tares being gathered at the last day, and the unexpected arrival of the Bridegroom. Still, the elegiac tone of the essays is contemporary, reflecting the reactions of his peers. Although his young friend Nicholas Bentley later described this time as "the age of innocence," that was not how his father and adopted uncle saw it at the time.[35]

Two days after the book's publication the House of Commons began to debate the Marconi contract. There had been a vigorous "coaching session" beforehand, during which Sir Rufus Isaacs explained repeatedly to Lloyd George just what it was he had done with his Marconi shares. Charles Masterman was present at this very private session and recorded the scene in his diary with great good humor, saying that Lloyd George was "rather endearing" because he, the Chancellor of the Exchequer, was in a "perfect fog" about what he had done.[36] Masterman's relaxed attitude about the situation goes a long way toward making the Chestertons' accusation about him justified, for he had never been the sort of person who normally would have thought it funny for a minister to behave this way. Either he was enjoying his importance as the minister who must get the contract passed so much that he didn't care about the gravity of the situation, or, as Chesterton suggested, he loved the maneuvering itself.

The testimony that the ministers gave to the House of Commons makes fascinating reading, because they neither lied nor told the whole truth. Sir Rufus and Herbert Samuel both declared that they had never dealt in the shares of that company (taken by the Commons to mean the English company), a statement that was quite true. That their shares were in the sister company was a fact that was never brought out. Lloyd George histrionically flew into a public rage, demanding to be charged openly with a crime, not questioned about rumors — and then sat down again without saying or denying anything.[37] The son of Sir Rufus later wrote that Asquith had ordered his father to deny everything to save Lloyd George, while Masterman wrote in his diary that, even so, Asquith had been very upset, saying, "I cannot save him." Staying in office was Asquith's main concern, and this was probably the reason that Isaacs and Samuel felt that if Lloyd George had not been implicated, they, as Jews, would have been thrown to the wolves.

The Liberal press, afraid of destroying its own party, was as divided over the whole issue as the Liberal Party itself. Gardiner, for example, had already sadly come to the conclusion that Lloyd George was an opportunist, but he still joined in the effort to whitewash him. The more rigid and doctrinaire Massingham maintained such an objective and critical attitude in his editorials that Lloyd George accused him of treachery; long afterward Chesterton complimented Massingham on his upright stand.[38]

As the tumult from the press and Parliament grew louder, those who publicly supported Lloyd George felt that they had done so much for his cause that he was indebted to them. One supporter who felt this way was Winston Churchill, whose wife reminded him later, when he needed support, that "Lloyd George is in . . . your debt . . . for Marconi."[39] Although the Conservative press generally attacked the Liberals, Lord Northcliffe supported the accused ministers at Churchill's request. (Both men were later furious to discover that Lloyd George had bought more than one group of shares.) The chief leader of the Conservative press was Leo Maxse of the *National Review,* who was as stubborn and opinionated a Tory as Massingham was a Liberal. Both were given to vicious personal attacks. (Maxse's sister was married to a cousin of Balfour, whom Maxse had helped to drive from office with the slogan "Balfour must go."[40])

At this critical juncture, the backer of the *Eye-Witness* went bankrupt, and the paper was about to fold. Cecil Chesterton could not bear to give up both his first editorship and what promised to be a real fight, so he went to his father and asked him to be the paper's backer. His wife insisted that he had never before asked his father for a penny, which may well have been true; on the other hand, he had let his parents house and feed him for thirty-three years. Mr. Ed agreed to support the paper, whose name was now changed to the *New Witness*.

Cecil rushed to Ada to tell her, "It's all arranged, I'm going to have the paper and there's only one thing left to settle. I want you. . . ." She cut him off, assuming this was one more marriage proposal, but it was not: Cecil wanted her to be his assistant editor.[41] She accepted eagerly, and the pair was launched on a joint career of seeing how much trouble they could stir up on Fleet Street — once they overcame the problem of getting out the first issue, with creditors taking away the furniture as they wrote. Under their mutual control the *New Witness* was resolutely egalitarian, referring to Lloyd George as "George," F.E. Smith as "Smith," even after he became Lord Birkenhead, and Sir Rufus Isaacs as "Isaacs."[42]

It is hard to judge how accurate the accusation is that Ada played "a sinister and influential part" in the paper's stepped-up Marconi campaign, or that she was the brain behind most of Cecil Chesterton's subsequent excesses. But it is true that her flair for writing good copy was compromised by her reporting real events as if she were producing a soap opera.[43] Her friends, like Titterton, were very loyal, but it is interesting to note that a comparatively objective reporter has said that "one can only conjecture what [Gilbert's] highly talented but intensely loyal circle made of her."[44]

One of Ada's first editorial acts was to try to persuade Cecil to fire the secretary, who promptly promised to sue. The family lawyer wrote hastily to Gilbert Chesterton, begging him to intervene, claiming that if the secretary went and Ada remained, "the paper cannot last three weeks!" Chesterton and Belloc both rushed to town to stop Cecil, but they did not even try to get rid of Ada, although the lawyer had added that she was an impossible person to have in charge of a newspaper.[45]

The next public event in the ongoing Marconi Affair was the Cabinet's forced establishment of a Select Committee of Inquiry to hold hearings, which began on October 25, 1912. Its composition was strictly along party lines, with the Liberal members having a majority. From this point on, Liberal candidates or speakers were heckled with shouts of "Marconi, Marconi!"[46]

Chesterton's public role at the *New Witness* was still as a writer of topical verse. Some of those he wrote at that time are among his most famous, including his drinking songs, which were later published in his novel *The Flying Inn*. These songs are some of his very best, like the one Shaw heard the younger Fabians singing loudly one night after a meeting:

> Old Noah he had an ostrich farm and fowls on the largest scale
> He ate his eggs with a ladle in an egg-cup big as a pail. . . .
> And Noah he often said to his wife when he sat down to dine,
> "I don't care where the water goes if it doesn't get into the wine."[47]

Another favorite begins, "Before the Romans came to Rye or out to Severn strode/The rolling English drunkard made the rolling English road."[48] And the canine "hero" in *The Flying Inn* was to declare,

> They haven't got no noses;
> The fallen sons of Eve;
> Even the smell of roses
> Is not what they supposes
> But more than mind discloses
> And more than men believe. . . .[49]

These poems helped to give the public the idea that Chesterton was a "rolling English drunk," when his real point was again the Whitmanesque ideal of comradeship in the ordinary man's club, from which he should not be driven in the name of health, hygiene, or heredity.[50]

Many of Chesterton's poems were sharper than knives, like the "Song of Right and Wrong," which got him fired from the *Daily News,* and his harsh condemnation of Parliament as "the city set upon slime and loam" in the short poem called "Who Goes Home?" Because of these angry poems, both his contemporaries and his biographers tended to assume that *whatever*

Cecil Chesterton printed, his brother agreed with. But Gilbert Chesterton was never a "good hater"; to him, the means used to reach an end was as important as the end itself.

Meanwhile, the Parliamentary Select Committee took its time calling witnesses, and Cecil grew increasingly convinced that he had hit upon a great international conspiracy that had corrupted the entire government, though there was never any evidence of this. But when nothing much happened he got bored, and by January 1913 his paper had launched an attack in another direction — an attack on the business record of Godfrey Isaacs. On January 9, the *New Witness* published a list of twenty bankrupt companies with which Godfrey Isaacs had been associated. Not happy with the mere publication of the "Ghastly Record," he — or Ada, for at his trial he swore he had not done it — sent men wearing sandwich boards plastered with copies of the *New Witness* to march up and down before the Houses of Parliament and Isaacs' office, and to follow Isaacs about London.[51]

Then, on February 12, 1913, Leo Maxse was called to testify before the Select Committee, and the whole situation was brought out into the open. Maxse testified that he was surprised at the ministers' not volunteering that they had had no transactions in the shares of *any* Marconi Company. Two days later a French newspaper, *Le Matin,* misquoted Maxse as saying that Samuel had bought shares in the *English* Marconi Company before the contract was settled and had resold them for 400 percent profit.[52] The French paper had the facts so garbled that there was widespread suspicion that their editor had been put up to running this version because it could be so easily disproved. This suspicion was fed by the fact that Samuel and the two Isaacs promptly hired the best prosecuting lawyers in London, the Conservative Unionists Sir Edward Carson and F.E. Smith, to start libel proceedings against *Le Matin.* The prime minister reluctantly agreed to let them follow this course, while the conservatives in Parliament were angry with Carson and Smith because they had made it more difficult to attack the Liberals in the Commons. The English public by now was not only shocked by the affair, but felt it had been played for a fool.

During this French libel suit the three ministers for the first time publicly admitted that they had dealt in *American* Marconi shares while the English company was negotiating with the government. (It was not until May that it came out that the Party Whip had also bought shares for the secret party fund.)[53] In the meantime, Cecil had gotten his heart's desire; he was sued for libel by Godfrey Isaacs, the only principal in the case who was not a member of the Liberal government. Isaacs also briefed Sir Edward Carson and F.E. Smith.

When the summons was served on Cecil at the *New Witness* offices, he had it framed to hang on the wall and took his entire staff to Fleet Street's El Vino for a round of draught champagne to celebrate. He then proudly editorialized in his paper, saying, "We are up against a very big thing. . . .

You cannot have the honour of attacking wealthy and powerfully entrenched interests without the cost. We have counted the cost; we counted it long ago."[54]

The preliminary hearing was held at the Bow Street Court on February 26, 1913, with Cecil insisting upon being his own lawyer. He argued for an adjournment on the grounds that he had not yet been called to testify before the Select Committee, but the magistrates ruled against him and called the case for February 28. When the Select Committee actually called Cecil on April 28, he suddenly refused to testify, but Belloc did testify on April 24, following Cecil's orders to describe him as solely responsible for all of the *New Witness* articles, although Belloc also publicly shared the blame.[55] It has been suggested that Cecil was protecting Ada, who had certainly had a hand in all that happened.

Cecil now displayed an astonishing inability to appreciate the simplest legal points. He believed what he had vaingloriously written about there being no laws of libel, so that he never saw himself in real danger until it was too late. His method of acting as his own lawyer was to use debater's tricks, trying to turn the tables and make himself the accuser and Isaacs the defendant. That was not the charge, and his tactics did not work. He was not "stupid, but conceited and arrogant. . . . All of his life he had shone in debate . . . [and thus he] probably thought he could outwit the lawyers on their own ground, so he had not bothered to learn the legal points on which the argument turned."[56]

While Gilbert Chesterton publicly joked about the situation, it was obvious to his friends that he was absolutely appalled by it. He was also having professional problems, which came to a head just as Cecil was being summoned to trial. Increasingly disturbed by Gardiner's editorial timidity, he had gotten himself into trouble with both his editor and the Cadburys with his "Song of Right and Wrong," which included this verse:

Tea, although an Oriental,
Is a gentleman at least;
Cocoa is a cad and coward. . . .[57]

Since in Fleet Street jargon the Cadburys' newspapers were called the "Cocoa Press," this verse cut a little too near the bone. Chesterton was upset about the effort of the *Daily News* to keep the Liberals in office at any price, but the fact that his brother was bravely daring the government to do its worst and getting no support from the "cads and cowards" was a part of his trouble, too. Chesterton was even more upset when Gardiner wrote to him personally to say that he had too much respect for Chesterton's sense of decency to suppose he would stoop to so "gross an outrage" against those with whom he had been associated in journalism for years. Then Gardiner asked him outright to "correct" the impression the poem had made, making it clear that Chesterton was being given a chance to "resign."

Chesterton contritely replied that he had not meant anything personal, but also that "it is quite impossible for me to continue taking the money of a man who may think that I have insulted him. . . . I see no other course but to surrender my position on the paper quite finally." Because Gardiner loved Chesterton, he was saddened by Gilbert's decision. In the next letter Chesterton responded by saying that he had never accused the Cadburys of being anything but nice to him, and never of being hypocrites. He added the significant comment that "I believe my friends right about politics, but wrong about people."[58]

The regular income which Chesterton had gotten from the *Daily News* had to be replaced, and the *New Witness,* with his own father backing it, was still not breaking even.[59] As a result, Chesterton had begun to write regularly for the *Daily Herald,* run by his Socialist friend George Lansbury. This paper had been born during a printer's strike a year earlier, and its basic outlook was syndicalist, with a bias favoring the trade unions.[60] The editorial tone of the paper was as shrill as the times, but Lansbury accepted contributions from a wide variety of people, including Belloc and Mrs. Pankhurst, the militant suffragette, and the paper's philosophical position was not yet hardened enough to exclude Chesterton, who was also very angry at the country's leaders.[61] After 1914 Chesterton broke with the paper and its policy because Lansbury was a pacifist, although he was also very much against the warmongering of the Northcliffe papers.[62]

Adding to Chesterton's fears for Cecil was the curious coincidence that he, too, had become involved in a libel suit. In a letter to Father O'Connor, Frances wrote that not only were they all afraid that Cecil might get a long prison sentence (in criminal libel cases the defendant is either fined or imprisoned), but that Gilbert had been served with a summons for libel by Sir William Lever, having said in print that the Lever Soap Company's model worker city, Port Sunlight, was nothing but a slave compound. His libel suit was a civil suit, but Shaw was concerned enough to offer not only to explain Chesterton's statement to the company, but also to provide financial assistance with the court costs.[63] This case was settled out of court, but it did not add to Chesterton's peace of mind.

When Cecil appeared in court again on February 28, Mr. Ed and Gilbert persuaded him to bring the family solicitor, although he continued to be his own spokesman. Cecil insisted on pleading not guilty, but the judge again ruled against him and said the case must go to a jury.

On May 27 Cecil Chesterton walked cheerfully into the Old Bailey for the case of *Rex v. Chesterton*, bringing his tense and terrified family in his wake. His parents were so upset at the idea of seeing their son in the dock that they would not go into the courtroom, so while they sat outside with Frances, Gilbert and his Uncle Arthur took turns sitting in court and coming back to report. Ada Jones flew about, alternately enjoying the court scene or working to get the paper out; she actually brought Cecil some proofs to check during the lunch break.[64] The courtroom was jammed with Fleet Street reporters, and the judge was a member of the Phillimore family, whose estate had been managed by the Chestertons for three generations. Gilbert Chesterton took this fact quite personally, although other observers felt the judge was stern but fair. Godfrey Isaacs' mother sat in court each day, glaring at Cecil.

Cecil was still determined to handle his own case. Since he had refused to testify before the Select Committee, everyone expected him to produce fireworks in court. But quite the opposite happened. Whenever Cecil cross-examined a witness, Sir Edward quickly objected, and his objections in almost every instance were upheld by the judge. Chesterton later tried to insist that Cecil was tried on the "legends" about the case, which were that he was denouncing ministers for dabbling in the stock market and that the whole attack was blatant anti-Semitism. In reality Sir Edward first demolished Cecil's wild charge that the ministers had connived to have the government enter into a contract for the benefit of Isaacs' brother, and then insisted that Cecil was claiming that Godfrey would have been prosecuted for his management of various companies if his brother were not Attorney General. Finally, he reduced to absurdity Cecil's arguments about Godfrey Isaacs' business mismanagement by saying that the Marconi contract had been approved by "almost every expert in the government service," and he was therefore not sure "how far this charge of corruption really goes. Would the committee have to talk to . . . the Colonial Office, the Board of Trade, the Treasury, the India Office, the Admiralty, the War Office?"[65]

Sir Edward next brought out one of the famous sandwich boards and demanded to know "whether men were entitled to libel and slander and hunt men out of their business." F. E. Smith then rose and let Herbert Samuel testify that he had never discussed the Marconi contract with either Isaacs brother; then he let Sir Rufus testify that he did not think he had acted "corruptly." Godfrey himself testified that he had not talked about the Marconi contract with his brothers before it was awarded, and said he had not been a total business failure. At this point Cecil insisted upon taking the stand himself to prove he was not afraid of Sir Edward Carson, but he had no real evidence to offer in support of his accusations, no valid witnesses to call.[66] Observers saw Cecil suddenly draw back and almost apologize when the judge asked him point-blank if he accused the Isaacs brothers and Samuel of perjury.[67] Cecil's attorney tried to persuade the jury that he had acted as a public-spirited citizen in publishing his accusations, as well as in sending his sandwich men to chase Godfrey Isaacs about London, and when Gilbert was called by the defense, he bravely told the judge that he "envied" his brother's position as a defendant in the dock.

But on Saturday, June 8, the jury found Cecil guilty on five counts of the six-count charge. For each count he could have been sent to prison for one year, as well as fined. Cocky as ever, Cecil had sent Ada to buy him some pipe tobacco for a last smoke before he went to his prison cell, but the judge "only" fined him one hundred pounds plus all the court costs, which amounted to an additional 1,500 pounds. Cecil and Ada and their followers in the courtoom thought that the verdict was a victory and gave a loud cheer, which astonished the judge. As it turned out, Cecil did not have enough money to pay the fine, and had to pass the hat to get out of jail.[68] The best summing-up of the entire case was done by Shaw, who wrote tartly that "it was a silly business begun to show that there was nothing to choose between a Cabinet Minister and Titus Oates, and provoking a counter-demonstration that there was no difference between a Cabinet Minister and George Washington."[69]

Chesterton has been accused of remaining obsessed with this case all the rest of his life,[70] but historians agree that the real facts show that the Liberal Party covered up the sordid behavior of its members to save its tenure in office. The fact that the scandal ended by personally threatening Cecil was a dreadful thing to his brother, as was the fact that people like Charles Masterman and Gardiner took it so lightly. It also showed that the law was not concerned with protecting ordinary people against government corruption; it proved that the ministers themselves were "brutes who refuse them bread" and that newspapers were "liars who refuse them news."[71]

Only four days after Cecil had been sentenced, the Select Committee made its official report, which was adopted by a purely party vote. It declared that the Liberal ministers had acted in good faith. Northcliffe's *Times* called the report a "pailful of whitewash"; the Minority Report, written by the Conservatives, declared that Sir Rufus had committed a grave impropriety, and that all the ministers who had bought shares in this private deal had not been open with their own party, the House of Commons, or the country.[72] Their motion to censure these ministers, had it passed, could have toppled the Liberal government. Sir Rufus might not have gone on to become the Marquis of Reading, Lord Chief Justice, and Viceroy of India; Lloyd George might not have become prime minister, nor Sir Herbert Samuel leader of the Liberal Party.

Chesterton had a final personal difficulty with the Marconi Affair that he never quite articulated. At the crucial moment, when there was a strong case for corruption and shady practices against the ministers, his brother had not only failed to bring a workable charge against them, but had patently lost his nerve. This was a heavy blow to Chesterton, because he shared Cecil's romantic notion of himself as a crusader par excellence. This situation is probably part of the reason that Cecil worked so hard to join in the actual fighting of World War I, and why Chesterton acted as if his death had occurred in combat: they shared a need to prove that Cecil was fearless. At the same time, Chesterton blamed the Liberal Party leadership for not telling Germany that if it threatened France, England would intervene. He felt this "cowardice" had caused the war.[73]

It was ironic that, when Cecil died in 1918, Godfrey Isaacs was involved in yet another libel suit. It was then that Chesterton wrote the famous "Open Letter to Lord Reading," a blistering diatribe in which he told Isaacs that he, Chesterton, was a happier man because his brother was dead. But perhaps the final justice occurred in 1925, when Isaacs died. It was then made public that under his management the Marconi Company had suffered heavy losses from unwise investments.

Part Four

THE OUTLINE OF SANITY
1914-1936

The practical tendency of all trade and business today is towards big commercial combinations, often more imperial, more impersonal, more international than many a communist commonwealth —things that are . . . collective if not collectivist. It is all very well to repeat distractedly, "What are we coming to?" . . . The obvious answer is —Monopoly. . . . Now I am one of those who believe that the cure for centralization is decentralization. It has been described as a paradox. There is apparently something elvish and fantastic about saying that when capital has come to be too much in the hand of the few, the right thing is to restore it into the hands of the many. . . .

Capitalism is . . . a very unpleasant thing. . . . When I say "Capitalism" I mean . . . that economic condition in which there is a class of capitalists . . . relatively small, in whose possession so much of the capital is concentrated as to necessitate a . . . majority of the citizens serving [them] . . . for a wage. . . . The Socialist would put it in the hands of even fewer people; but those people would be politicians. . . . A Socialist Government is one which in its nature does not tolerate any true and real opposition. . . . The Government provides everything; and it is absurd to ask a Government to provide an opposition. . . . Opposition and rebellion depend on property and liberty. . . . Those rights must be protected by a morality which even the ruler will hesitate to defy. The critic of the State can only exist where a religious sense of right protects his claim to his own bow and spear; or at least, to his own pen or his own printing-press.

G.K. Chesterton, *The Outline of Sanity*, 1926

Chapter Twelve
THE WAR THAT WILL END WAR
1914-1918

*I have lived through the times when many intelligent and ideal-
istic men hoped that the World War would be an introduction
to the World State. But I myself am more convinced than ever
that the World War occurred because nations were too big, and
not because they were too small. It occurred especially because
big nations wanted to be the World State. But it occurred, above
all, because about things so vast there comes to be something
cold and hollow and impersonal. It was NOT merely a war of
nations; it was a war of warring internationalists.*

G.K. Chesterton, "On War Memorials"[1]

Although the world did not explode in war the moment that Cecil
Chesterton was declared guilty, Chesterton felt the imminence of disaster; he was exhausted by the demands of his own career and his concern
over Cecil, and weighted down by Fleet Street's sense of doom. It was only
afterward that he saw that the Marconi Affair had signaled the end of
Gladstone's Liberal Party, which assumed that public morality protected
private rights, and in which the rulers tolerated opposition and rebellion
against themselves. Now, bitterly mistrusting his own leaders, Chesterton
needed from that time on to take up arms against any "monopoly" that
destroyed private property and personal liberty. He also fought to keep free
his own weapons, "the pen and the printing press." Once again he had
committed himself to leaning against the world to keep it balanced against
heresy.[2]
    Chesterton was almost relieved by the actual outbreak of hostilities,
because it gave a strong sense of direction to his defense of the living roots
of liberalism, which was "Christendom." Between 1914 and 1925, Chesterton
"took the cross" exactly as the original Crusaders had done, for it was in
those terms that he came to see his new role as a working, day-to-day
journalist and editor. For him, as for most of his contemporaries, this world
did crack up in 1914, so that from then on he was a kind of jolly Saint

Augustine, writing about the City of God among the ruins of Rome. At the same time, however, he did not spend his time on eschatology, but tried to be heard in the marketplace of ideas, not so much to push his program for economics or social reform as to insist on a standard of ethical concern.

There were, however, warnings that Chesterton was physically and mentally overwrought. The night the Chestertons opened their studio at Top Meadow, Chesterton — tired and possibly a bit drunk — fell and broke his arm. About this time he also reluctantly agreed to getting new front dentures. In addition, from Christmas 1913 through the spring of 1914, he had a serious attack of bronchitis that nearly developed into pneumonia. These problems were heightened because he reacted with acute sensitivity to any illness — the result of his father's attitude toward sickness and his sister's tragic death.

By now Chesterton's friendship with Shaw had become more intimate, and Shaw had taken to needling Chesterton on every occasion about writing a play. He informed Chesterton that it was no use answering him in the *New Age*, because he would not stop his attacks on Chesterton's reputation as essayist, journalist, critic, and liberal unless he contributed to the English drama. Shaw even wrote out a scenario that he thought was appropriate for Chesterton, which is now in the British Museum. In it, Saint Augustine returns to England to see if it is still Christian, meeting a worldly Bishop of Blackfriars, a Liberal politician, and a Press Lord Carmelite. On October 20, 1909, Shaw had written him a letter beginning, "Chesterton, Shaw Speaks! Attention." He *demanded* that Chesterton write the play, and offered not only to pay him for writing it but to finance its production.[3] Possibly unwilling to become Shaw's protégé, and very busy, Chesterton still did not respond to this friendly debating opponent who was also taunting him about being "Cadbury's property."

By April 1912 Shaw was writing directly to Frances, telling her he was coming to visit them to read them his newest play. This was *Androcles and the Lion,* which Shaw called a "religious harlequinade." Shaw instructed Frances to put on an act, saying she wished her husband would write plays like that, and threatening, if he did not, to "go out like the lady in *A Doll's House* and live her own life, whatever that dark threat may mean."[4]

Not long afterward Chesterton apparently did sit down and write *Magic*, the only play which he saw produced in his lifetime. It is a very Shavian play, which led European critics to conclude that Chesterton was Shaw's disciple. Like Shaw's plays, *Magic* has a plot that turns on coincidence and contrivance, and spare characters that are based on "types"; its dialogue shows Chesterton's talent for drama. As Shaw put it, "Mr. Chesterton was born . . . with all the essential tricks of the stage at his finger ends; and it was delightful to find the characters which seem so . . . ragdolly . . . in his romances became credible and solid behind the footlights."[5]

Thematically, the play is a dramatized version of Chesterton's impulse as a teenager to sin by playing God, a demonstration of pride that inevitably brings evil with it. It tells the story of a wandering "conjurer" who is tempted by the heroine's brother — a crude young H.G. Wells type just back from America — to perform "magic" as a kind of parlor trick in the drawing room of a duke. When the conjurer onstage turns a red light blue, however, he finds that the spirits have "turned the tables on him," obeying his impudent call upon the fiends.[6] To keep the skeptical brother from going mad, the conjurer lies, then bitterly tells the other characters that "a half hour after I have left this house you will be all saying how it was done," meaning that they will all deny this reality of evil by explaining it away scientifically.[7] In his denial the conjurer is "redeemed" by the heroine, who, like a true Chestertonian heroine, turns their relationship, which was based on a fairy tale, into something "that comes true," so they can live happily ever after.

The star character is the heroine's uncle, the duke, a fuzzy-minded, aristocratic Mr. Malaprop who invariably ends a comment with a non sequitur, the most famous being the line "Modern man and all that. Wonderful man, Bernard Shaw!" He is "Liberal" in every way, as is demonstrated in the opening scene: he gives a check to a Christian Socialist clergyman for his "model" pub, which is being established to teach Englishmen to drink decently, then turns around and gives another check to an atheistic doctor who is starting a league to oppose the pub.

Shaw had a fit later on when he discovered that Chesterton had sold the original manuscript of the play for a song; he wrote to Frances that "in Sweden where marriage laws are comparatively enlightened ... you could obtain a divorce on the ground that your husband threw away an important part of the provision for your old age. ... In the future, the moment he has finished a play ... lock him up and bring the agreement to me. Explanations would be thrown away on him."[8]

Magic opened at the Little Theatre in London on November 7, 1913, and everyone who was anyone was there. It was a great success, acclaimed by the critics and loved by the public, and it ran over one hundred performances. Even disapproving members of the agnostic intelligentsia such as George Moore and Frank Harris admired its successful mixture of metaphysics and melodrama.[9] The final word lies with Chesterton himself, who wrote his own review of *Magic* for the *Dublin Review* in January 1914:

> The author of *Magic* ought to be told plainly that his play ... has been treated with far too much indulgence in the public press. I will glide mercifully over the most glaring errors, which the critics have overlooked — no Irishman could become so complete a cad merely by going to America — that no young lady would walk about in the rain so soon before it was necessary to dress for dinner. ... The Secretary disappears half way through the play. ... By the exercise of that knowledge of all human hearts which

descends on any man . . . the moment he is a dramatic critic, I perceive that the author of *Magic* originally wrote it as a short story. It is a bad play, because it was a good short story. . . . The drama is built on that grander secrecy which was called Greek irony. . . . The audience must know the truth when the actors do not know it. . . . It is a weakness in a play like *Magic* that the audience is not in on the central secret from the start. . . .[10]

In a way Chesterton was quite right: *Magic* played more convincingly than it reads.

While Gilbert was ill at home that Christmas, Ada and Cecil, with a host of other Fleet Street regulars, were getting ready for what was probably the greatest Fleet Street happening of their day: one of the many episodes of pre-war fun which Chesterton called "friendship and foolery" and looked back on nostalgically. This was the Mock Trial of John Jasper, which took place on January 7, 1914, at the King's Hall, Covent Garden. The Lay Precentor of Cloisterham Cathedral in the County of Kent, he was tried for the murder of Edwin Drood, Engineer — a trial based, of course, upon Dickens' last, unfinished novel, *The Mystery of Edwin Drood*. Sponsored by the Dickens Fellowship, this project had a very large and celebrated cast of characters. Chesterton had agreed to play the Judge, Cecil was the Council for the Defense, Ada Jones played Princess Puffer, an old hag who ran an opium den, and her brother Charles was a lawyer's clerk. The foreman of the jury was Shaw, and the jury was composed of people like W.W. Jacobs, Belloc, G.S. Street, and William Archer.[11] The amateur actors did not use prepared scripts, but made themselves familiar with the unfinished novel. Ada and Cecil, for example, spent Christmas Eve at 11 Warwick Gardens, with Cecil coaching Ada in preparation for her cross-examination.

The London papers gave the trial a great deal of publicity, and the house was sold out. During the actual performance, which lasted over four hours, every actor wore a period costume including Mr. Justice Chesterton, who was appropriately attired in full legal regalia. Opinions differed, however, about whether all the actors took the Mock Trial in the right spirit. Ada Jones was very indignant because Shaw, as foreman of the jury, interrupted the proceedings, made jokes, and had the gall to rise, when the jury was to retire to determine the verdict, and say that their verdict was manslaughter against John Jasper. The jury, he said, had reached their verdict during their lunch break! But Chesterton, in his bewigged role as the judge, took Shaw's irreverent behavior in very good spirit, and himself delivered a short, witty speech in which he committed everyone but himself to jail for contempt of court.

Chesterton's next novel, *The Flying Inn*, came out on January 22, 1914, with an affectionate dedication to the artist Hugh Rivière, who had painted a portrait of Chesterton "in his big Inverness cape with that massive head . . . [and] big mane of brown hair, his hat on the grass and a favorite sword stick brandished against the sky." Rivière was very touched by this gesture, and commented later that he thought Chesterton himself was a draftsman with a great and free grasp of form and character. He remembered seeing him take out an old envelope and cover it with extraordinary sketches of characters, ". . . some in medieval dress, and some modern, two or three clever heads of G.B. Shaw and others clerical and political and imaginary."[12] Riviere added that often when they dined Chesterton was finishing an article for which a messenger boy was waiting in the hall, and Chesterton never noticed what he ate or drank because he was so busy thinking and talking. This is not the picture of a drunkard, but such absent-mindedness was not good for Chesterton's general health.

The Flying Inn made use of the drinking songs which Chesterton had written for the *New Witness*. It was also his version of the pre-war invasion novels, which typically represented a "polemical" statement of what was wrong with England, as well as suggested a war scare.[13] Chesterton did not follow the typical scenario, in which English unpreparedness was explained by the mental deficiency of her lower-class recruits; in his book, the ordinary Englishman saves England from her "puritancial" and "imperialist" politicians with their snobbish elitism nurtured by their adoption of "Islam," or the East. His polite drawing-room fakir who has society by the nose is called Misysra Ammon, or the Prophet of the Moon (a prophetic echo of a present-day Pied Piper). Critics who regard this book as bitter or too fanciful ought to realize that the seer Rabindranath Tagore, whom the intellectuals called "the wisdom of the East personified," was at that time enjoying a wild social success: he was knighted, and also won the Nobel prize for literature. What is most ironic is that Massingham, the Liberal editor who considered Chesterton "lost in the past," wrote that Tagore's teaching was of the "utmost importance to our time . . . the voice of the East . . . speaking in parables and spiritual songs to the hard and coarsened ear of the West."[14]

In Chesterton's novel, the prophet is a "little owlish man in a red fez, weakly waving a green umbrella . . . who [had] some fad about English civilization having been founded by the Turks. . . ." He convinces the peer whom he converts to Islam that "he is right at the root. There is a kind of freedom that consists of never rebelling against Nature. . . . They understand it in the Orient better than we do in the West. . . . It is all very well to talk about love in our narrow, personal romantic way; but there is something higher than the love of a lover or the love of love . . . the love of Fate."[15]

The Flying Inn is a romantic adventure story, typically Chestertonian, with touches of satire and social irony. To keep his pub open, an ordinary, middle-class English pub-keeper named Humphrey Pump teams up with a rebel Irishman named Dalroy. Dalroy has just lost his small island kingdom of Ithaca in a peace settlement between England, Germany, and the Turk. The same English minister who engineered the "peace" treaty—Lord Ivywood (who is a convert to the East) — has now gotten legislation passed in England that outlaws drinking. But by a curious twist, the Parliamentary bill has left open the possibility that "if a place has an inn *sign*, it will also have [his] gracious permission to really be an inn." Pump's pub sign, the "Sign of the Old Ship," is "a square wooden board ... decorated with a highly grotesque blue ship such as a child might draw, but into which Mr. Pump's patriotism had insinuated a disproportionately large red St. George's cross." Determined to take advantage of the law's loophole, the two picaresque English heroes "fly" with this sign, roaming about England by cart, carriage, and automobile, and stopping wherever it is safe to put up the sign and sell drinks from their keg of rum.[16]

Certainly this novel is amusing: the drinking songs are funny, and so are many of the scenes, such as the one in which the dog Quoodle brings Dalroy into Lord Ivywood's "harem" of doting society ladies, known as the "Simple Souls." Nonetheless, it is also perfectly true that this novel is sharp in tone. Throughout it are suggestions of Chesterton's real despair with Parliamentary government and the irrational "Mooniness" of high society's "religious" ideas. He savagely portrays the upper classes, journalism, and the intelligentsia, showing that it was *their* aristocratic arrogance which left England unprepared to defend herself — either against herself or against an enemy from the outside.[17] But *The Flying Inn* also sings the praises of the ordinary English, the "secret people" of Chesterton's poem.

In the novel, Lord Ivywood has become totally isolated from ordinary people, becoming an Eastern fanatic who says that "the world was made badly ... and I will make it over again."[18] He is contrasted with the silly (or simple) poet Dorian Wimple, who dramatically wakes up to the needs of others when his own chauffeur faints from hunger because the poet has been too busy to let him eat. Since Lord Ivywood has betrayed "Christendom" by allowing the Turks "to be encamped in English meadows ... [a] thing that had never been ... nearer than some leagues south of Paris, since ... Carolus ... the Hammer broke ... backwards at Tours ... [that] green standard of the great faith and strong civilization which has so often almost entered the great cities of the West....," Dalroy's army of ordinary men march on Parliament as if it were the Bastille, then go on, like Alfred's army, to defeat the "Vikings" in what is clearly a Chestertonian revolution.[19]

If, on the one hand, *The Flying Inn* is a jovial, fantastic book, with a triumphant victory against the enemies of the people, it carries, on the other hand, the message of Chesterton's great dismay at the kind of government England had and the way the world was going. It contains specific examples of things that had concerned Chesterton, from Prussianism and international "Jewish" imperialism to issues like the Chinese laborers imported into the Rand. Lord Ivywood is the archetypal doctrinaire politician, aristocratic and revolutionary, inhuman and courageous, against whom Chesterton is issuing his call to revolution.[20] But it would be patronizing to suggest that *only*

Chesterton was suffering from mental weariness, and that he had no clear idea of what hope might have relieved it.[21]

One of the clearest indicators of the temper of the times was Shaw's play *Heartbreak House*, which he began in 1913 but did not finish until after the war began. "It expressed his contempt for a society which was as doomed as a set of first-class passengers chattering . . . while the sinking ship settled in the water." The ship itself was "this soul's prison we call England"; its passengers were "useless, dangerous, and ought to be abolished."[22] (This might be Chesterton's description of Lord Ivywood.) Shaw was referring to the Fabian Old Gang's feeling that their great effort to bring secular salvation to England had failed. Ordinary men would not create a new moral order, and they had no clear-cut successors except the radical young Coles, who were Guild Socialists looking forward to an apocalyptic general strike. Shaw had a faint hope that the slate might be wiped clean by war and a new world built from the ashes, but he knew that world holocaust was a dreadful price to pay for this rebirth.

In early 1914 England's domestic and foreign affairs were growing more chaotic, although there was no series of diplomatic crises that foreshadowed the outbreak of war as there was to be in 1939. Historians now tend to agree with Chesterton that too many things were left unsaid which might have made Germany step back from the brink. At the Foreign Office, for example, Grey was keeping his commitments secret even from part of the Cabinet.[23] The most pressing domestic problem was the Liberals' Home Rule Bill for Ireland. It had been introduced twice since 1912 and passed twice by the House of Commons, but failed to pass the Conservative House of Lords. Then in March 1914 the Irish issue suddenly shifted to a question of the army's loyalty. It seems to have been a method seized by the Conservatives to win a battle they were not sure of winning in the House of Lords. Many army officers were Unionists, sympathetic to the idea that Ulster, or *all* Ireland, was English.[24] There was also Sir Edward Carson's Ulster Volunteer Force, an army the public thought to be 85,000 strong, and armed to the teeth.

Winston Churchill, trying to prove he was not a secret Unionist like his father had been, ordered the Third Battle Squadron into position off the coast of Ireland. Then the general in charge there gave his men the odd idea that if there was war, they need not obey orders but could "disappear" without losing their army commissions. By the afternoon of March 20, a group of fifty-seven officers in the Third Cavalry Brigade stationed at Curragh had informed their chief that they would accept dismissal rather than move against loyal Ulster — something no one had ordered them to do. This was the so-called "Curragh Mutiny," which Asquith, calm as ever, called a "strike," but the Liberal papers loudly blamed him and Haldane (now Lord Chancellor).

To make a badly handled matter worse, the Liberals lost a series of by-elections that spring, among them that of Charles Masterman, whose promising career was ruined because he could not go on holding a Cabinet post without a seat in the Commons. To his old friends like Chesterton, it seemed as if Masterman had been deserted by his "masters"; in fact, when Lloyd George came to power a few years later, that was exactly what did happen as Masterman tried repeatedly, without success, to be re-elected.[25] The Irish problem, meanwhile, kept growing, and by July 24 — the very day that the Cabinet heard about the Austrian ultimatum to Serbia — the situation in Ireland was considered out of control.

Earlier that June, Chesterton had engaged in another wild frolic that, in retrospect, took place in a different world. His version of the episode was that out of the blue Shaw appeared at his door in Beaconsfield on June 6, proposing that Chesterton join him, William Archer (the music critic), and Lord Howard de Walden in making a movie. It would be directed by Shaw's theatrical friend Granville-Barker and produced by Sir James Barrie of *Peter Pan* fame. What actually happened was somewhat more formal, for Granville-Barker had issued invitations to his chosen actors, "a few piratical spirits," to spend a weekend making a movie for their own amusement.[26] The actors were to pretend to be cowboys, completely costumed in chaps, boots, and hats, and swinging lassos. When Chesterton asked Shaw just what the joke was, Shaw helpfully replied that the joke was that nobody knew what it was.

Chesterton soon found himself in an Essex brick field being rolled around in a barrel, being lowered over a cliff with ropes, and lassoing "wild" ponies that nuzzled him for sugar lumps, while movie cameras ground away and the director shouted commands like, "Register self-sacrifice!" and "Register resignation!" All four actors were put on one motorcycle, whose wheels were spun to make it appear to be moving, while Sir James Barrie stood about, smoking a pipe and watching his friends make fools of themselves.[27]

When this location shooting was over, the actors were told that Barrie had arranged a dinner at the Savoy Hotel, where he would explain what was going on. In the "conspiratorial manner" of an Oppenheim or Edgar Wallace, Barrie had plotted the dinner to be a huge formal affair attended by everyone important in London, from the prime minister to Sir Edward Elgar, who told Frances Chesterton, "I suppose you know you're being filmed. . . ." Chesterton noted that *she* was not brandishing a champagne bottle, but that some of the guests were showing a "marked relaxation from the cares of State."[28] After dining they all adjourned to the hotel auditorium, where Shaw delivered a savage oration denouncing both Barrie and Granville-Barker, concluding by drawing an enormous sword which he waved about. This was the signal for the other three cowboys (who had been coached) to leap from their seats, waving swords of their own, and chase Shaw offstage through the scenery. Soon afterward Chesterton got a friendly note of apology from Barrie saying the whole project was being dropped, a solution which somehow seemed to Chesterton to suit the times in which "if the Cowboys were . . . struggling to find the road back to Reality, they found it all right."[29]

It must have been about this time that a schoolboy named Malcolm Muggeridge, the bright son of a Fabian Society member, was taken by his father to a dinner in Soho where Chesterton was being entertained. Muggeridge said this was an occasion of inconceivable glory. Fascinated, he observed the enormous bulk of the guest of honor, with his great stomach and plump hands, the pince-nez on its black ribbon almost lost in the expanse of his face. When Chesterton delivered what he thought was a good remark, he blew into his moustache with a kind of wheeze, like a balloon losing air. Young Muggeridge did not follow what Chesterton was saying, but he persuaded his father to wait outside until Chesterton left so he could see "the great man make his way down the street in a billowing black cloak and old-style bohemian hat with a large brim."[30]

But such pleasant events were to become only memories. On July 28, 1914, Franz Ferdinand, the heir to the Austro-Hungarian empire, was assassinated by some Bosnian extremists in Sarajevo, Serbia. The average Englishman thought very little about this eastern edge of Europe, where since 1912 (and earlier) a group of small nations had been fighting over the remains of Turkey's European empire. These countries — like Greece, Serbia, and Rumania — were underdeveloped nations trying to grow, each sponsored by a different Great Power looking for "spheres of influence." The Russians, badly beaten in 1905 by the Japanese, were supporting the Slavic countries, hoping to get Constantinople, and France wanted to get back Alsace-Lorraine from Germany; while the ancient Austro-Hungarian empire was fighting gradual dismemberment. The kaiser kept engaging in acts of provocation, as German philosophers talked about war as a "biological necessity." In the background, international financiers of France, Germany, and England, a number of them Jews like Cassel and Ballin, fought each other in world markets for new places in which to invest.[31] (None of those with special interests foresaw a war that would drag on, reducing Europe to secondary world status, destroying her characteristic institutions like the monarchy and the empire, while giving a clear field to "democracy" and women's rights.[32]) At the same time the International Socialist Movement was trying to organize the workers of the world to ignore any call to arms. Shaw, for example, supported the conscientious objectors, and although he was given very bad press for his convictions during the war, to the postwar generation his ideas seemed contemporary.

The formal European alliances — the Triple Alliance composed of Germany, Austro-Hungary, and Italy, and the Triple Entente composed of Russia, England, and France — made Europe like an armed camp, where the German High Command wanted to fight the "inevitable war" at the "right time," confirming all of Chesterton's worst suspicious about them. At the same time Chesterton's own attitude about war was that the "only defensible war is a war of defense." And a war of defense, by its very definition and nature, is one from which a man comes back battered and bleeding and boasting only that he is not dead.[33]

As the invasion novels had already pointed out, the most immediate threat Germany posed to England was that she might take control of the Belgian channel ports, from which an invasion could be easily launched. In the end, then, it was not just the "sacredness" of Belgian soil over which the English went to war, even though the rights of small nations played a big part in the reaction of many Liberals like Gardiner, Masterman, and Chesterton, as well as Lloyd George, who made it his crusade.[34]

The day that a group of young Bosnian anarchists called The Black Hand murdered the Austro-Hungarian heir in hopes of freeing their country, Germany told the aged emperor that it would stand behind him, but the English were too busy mourning the death of Joseph Chamberlain to pay much attention. The Liberals were bewailing what glory their party might have won had Chamberlain stayed faithful, while the Conservatives wept for a man who should have been prime minister, who would have given unity to the nation and meaning to the empire.[35] Next Austro-Hungary sent Serbia a list of demands; Serbia accepted all but the one which violated her own sovereignty, so on July 28 Austria declared war on her. By July 29 the Russians had mobilized and demanded English and French support; on August 1 Germany declared war on Russia, and by August 3 the French had declared war on Germany.

During this incredible period, when country after country ordered up her troops and declared war, the Liberal government was split between the old Liberal Imperialists like Asquith, Grey, Haldane, and the naturally warlike Churchill, and the Little Englanders, who were for peace; the rest, like Lloyd George and Masterman, were caught uneasily in the middle. (Masterman was still in the Cabinet as a kind of "temporary" minister.) Masterman later wrote that it was a company of tired men who for a dozen hot summer nights tried to avert war and keep Europe from "falling to pieces like a great house falling."[36]

On July 31, Grey asked both France and Germany to respect Belgium's neutrality, but the German High Command planned to be in Paris in a fortnight, which required that their armies dash through Belgium. On Sunday, August 2, the Germans invaded Luxembourg, and Grey told France that if the German fleet came into the Channel or the North Sea, England would fight. On August 3, Grey spoke to Parliament and sent Germany an ultimatum to get out of Belgium. By 11 P.M. on August 4 the Germans had not replied, so Big Ben tolled and the crowds began to sing; England was at war.

Most Englishmen reacted by being wildly excited. Ada Jones and Cecil Chesterton, for example, shared the popular view: they had been afraid Grey would give in to the Germans and were delighted he did not, although they were surprised to find the German and Austrian waiters in their favorite restaurants tearful; later, they disliked having London overrun with Belgian refugees. While Shaw loudly declared that Belgium's neutrality was humbug, Fleet Street's Liberal editors like Massingham and Gardiner were agreeing with the Chestertons, who saw the issue as an article of faith: small nations must not be invaded, swallowed up, nor put through the horrors of war for a great power's ambitions.

Like Belloc, Cecil Chesterton felt very strongly about the purpose of the war, which he saw was to root out all "Prussianism" from Western civilization. In his book, *The Prussian Hath Said in His Heart*, he developed a new variation on the old Liberal theme that there was a natural Teutonic blood alliance with democratic institutions, a myth still alive in the Rhodes scholarships of the empire-builder; he turned the myth upside-down to show that "the war was inevitable [because] . . . of the political and military power of Prussia, the character of the Prussian monarchy, and the spirit of those who directed the policy of the German Empire. Prussia . . . [is] incompatible with a civilized and Christian Europe. Sooner or later the one had to be crushed."[37] The book has a graceful and witty preface by Shaw, who says of Cecil, "where he will come out in the end I do not know . . ."; it is dedicated to Gilbert, "in memory of many arguments and an alliance." Although Gilbert's attitude was never as bloodthirsty as Cecil's, he never adopted the point of view of other Liberals like Massingham, who, discouraged by years of carnage, eventually supported a negotiated peace and an agreement that everyone was at fault.[38] As in most things, Chesterton remained loyal to the original idea involved.

Fleet Street itself not only lost hundreds of reporters to war, but also suffered shortages of paper and ink, so that the newspapers had to charge more for fewer pages, and the bigger papers did better by comparison. Northcliffe's *Times* kept its size but its price rose to threepence, while Gardiner's *Daily News* rose to a penny and shrank to half its size, losing many of his favorite features. Gardiner refused to print stories of war atrocities, a staple item in Northcliffe's yellow press, at the same time gradually losing his hope that the sacrifice would not be in vain.

At the *New Witness* (while Chesterton struggled with increasing ill health), Cecil and Ada Jones were plunged into campaigns on behalf of the ordinary soldier and his wife, who were never given the same treatment as officers. They also hunted for shady businessmen making profits from government contracts, fussed at the new, stricter drinking laws, and, best of all, enjoyed almost weekly rows with their own printers, who felt much of their material was high treason under DORA, the wartime Defense of the Realm Act, which gave the government almost complete control over the individual's rights. This act did establish that "such rights were neither inherent nor inalienable," which was anathema to all good Liberal idealists.[39]

The war itself brought a kind of collectivism that was almost beyond Fabian belief. Not only did the state run the railways, the mines, and the merchant marine, but DORA gave England a taste of secret police, spies, and surveillance, while many determined Socialist pacificists had a hard time of it in jail.[40] The coming of the war also stopped the general strike, which, like Chesterton's novel *The Return of Don Quixote*, was "shelved" until 1926. In addition, the Liberals managed to buy the cooperation of the Conservatives: they promised the Conservatives — who were ready to fight a civil war in Ireland — that the issue of Irish Home Rule would be a dead letter until the war was over. Meanwhile, women took advantage of the manpower shortage to break into fields in which they had never worked before, hoping to win the vote and other rights as a reward for a job well done. Wartime England was, in truth, a world turned upside-down.

Chesterton himself was physically unfit for fighting, which may have intensified his boyish admiration for "battles and barricades." He is accused of failing to see the "utter disparity between . . . swordplay, or . . . heroic fighting in the streets of London, and that nightmare of guns, gas, barbed wire and trenches." Stories about him center on anecdotes like the one about the young lady on Fleet Street handing out white feathers, who demanded to know why Chesterton was not out at the Front. He replied, "My dear madam, if you will step round this way a little, you will see that I *am*."[41]

But Chesterton's view was more balanced than such stories suggest, something made clear by his comments on this war, in which he lost his most precious possession. He shared the not uncommon feeling that this was a crusade against the barbaric Hun, fought for that bundle of concepts and identities that constitute Western civilization. But in his *Autobiography* (written when another world war was imminent), he also says that to tell a soldier defending his country that "it is the War That Will End War is like telling a workman, naturally rather reluctant to do his day's work, that it is The Work That Will End Work." He added that the war "settled exactly what it set out to settle . . . [not] to put a final end to all war or all work or all worry. . . . We only said that we were bound to endure something very bad because the alternative was something worse." He concluded that the war had saved Beaconsfield,

> . . . not an ideal Beaconsfield, not a New Beaconsfield with gates of gold and pearl descending out of heaven from God, but Beaconsfield. A certain social balance, a certain mode of life, a certain tradition of morals and manners, some parts of which I regret, some parts of which I value . . . [were] . . . menaced by the fate of falling into a complete and perhaps permanent

inferiority . . . to another tradition. . . . The men whose names are written on the Beaconsfield War Memorial died to prevent Beaconsfield from being . . . overshadowed by Berlin.[42]

Both his calmer, more judicial tone and his consistent attitude make Chesterton seem considerably saner about the war than someone like H. G. Wells. Wells had been spending a romantic bank holiday with his mistress, Rebecca West, who gave birth to their son Anthony the day the war broke out; although surprised by the event, Wells at once named it "The War That Will End War." He adored the idea of change destroying the old and stable to create the new, so he now accepted the idea of a crusade against Germany and got into a raging row with Shaw, who, as a determined pacifist, made public fun of the Allies' moral pose. Wells called the young Fabians who were conscientious objectors — including Bertrand Russell, Lytton Strachey, and Clive Bell of the Bloomsbury group — "shirkers and screamers," an insult for which they never forgave him.[43] By about 1916, however, Wells had become less jingoist and far more critical of the "endless" war that was being waged so inefficiently. Chesterton, on the other hand, clearly saw the war as a part of the endless fight to "scour the White Horse," and was constitutionally unable to back down because of the cost.

By October 1914 the Kaiser's "splendid little war," which was supposed to end quickly because the cost of modern arms was so high, had settled in trenches along the Marne. The Western Front stretched from Belgium to Switzerland in a rigid line marked by barbed wire, bomb craters, and rats. The English fleet had bottled up the German navy, but no sooner had Russia opened the Eastern Front than Turkey came in on Germany's side, making England nervous about her imperial lifelines. This in turn brought on Churchill's ill-fated Dardanelles expedition, which killed the poet of the "early" war, the young Fabian Rupert Brooke, who has been called the "last Liberal" because he associated war with glory, not horror.[44]

That same October Chesterton's second collection of Father Brown stories, called *The Wisdom of Father Brown,* was published. It was dedicated to his old friend and brother-in-law, Lucian Oldershaw. These stories had previously been published in *Pall Mall Magazine*; another collection like this wasn't published again until 1926. Unlike the stories in the first collection, which all took place within the British Isles, these have settings ranging across Europe, and involve treason, curses, bandits, and murder. Like all the Father Brown tales, they have a "once upon a time" narrative style which misleads readers into thinking them removed from the topical irony Chesterton wrote as "journalism," but these stories are all crisp and biting, very much commentaries on the times.

One, for example, called "The Purple Wig," opens with a description of a Fleet Street editor — a caricature that Gardiner might have called libelous if it had appeared in the *Daily News*:

Mr. Edward Nutt, the industrious editor of the Daily Reformer, sat at his desk. . . . He was a stoutish . . . fair man. . . . His movements were resolute, his mouth firm and his tones final; but his round, rather babyish blue eyes had a bewildered and even wistful look. . . . It might be truly said of him, as for many journalists in authority, that his most familiar emotion was one of continuous fear; fear of libel actions, fear of lost advertisements, fear of misprints, fear of the sack. His life was a series of distracted compromises between the proprietor of the paper . . . who was a senile soapboiler . . . and the very able staff he had collected to run the paper. . . .[45]

This story then becomes a savage tale of how this editor knuckles under to the proprietor, first chopping up a story that he assigns about a certain noble lord, then removing the phrase "Romanist priest" and substituting "Spiritualist." Finally, when it turns out that the so-called aristocrat with a hereditary secret is actually a rich Jewish lawyer who has had the "extinct" peerage revived for him, the editor writes the journalist, "Dear Finn, You must be mad; we can't touch this. . . . Old Soap Suds was sick enough at not getting his peerage last year; he'd sack me by wire. . . ." The story ends with the editor "automatically and, by force of habit, altering the word 'God' to the word 'circumstances.' "[46]

Perhaps the most interesting story of the group, however, is the last one, which is called "The Fairy Tale of Father Brown." Most improbably, Father Brown is discovered in the "picturesque city and state of Heilig-waldenstein . . . one of those toy kingdoms of which certain parts of the German Empire still consist. It had come under the Prussian hegemony . . . fifty years before. But in merely looking at it one could not dismiss that impression of childishness which is the most charming side of Germany."[47] The land is forcibly annexed by Bismarck, who sends as a ruler "Prince Otto of Grossenmark." But his plans for taking advantage of the tiny kingdom's mineral riches are ruined when he is accidentally killed by his own order — a parable (or prophecy) about the kaiser and the Prussian state.

Late in October 1914 Chesterton made a trip to Oxford University to speak "in defense of the English Declaration of War" to a huge crowd of undergraduates. He was feeling terribly ill, and afterward recalled nothing except that he had spoken for the right side. He remembered coming home and trying to write Shaw a letter, drafts of which exists today, saying,

> You are, my dear Shaw, face to face with certain new facts but you still try to treat them as if they were old frauds. . . . With the millions of British at this moment Belgium is not a pretext, but a passion. . . . You are out of your depth . . . for you have jumped into this deep river to prove that it was shallow. . . . We support the Government because the Government *represents* us. . . .[48]

But the suggestion that Shaw and Chesterton's friendship was irreparably damaged because of their disagreement over the war fails to take into account the serious rift that occurred later, when Chesterton became a Roman Catholic.

Writers and journalists quickly found themselves being recruited to work for what was basically a ministry of propaganda. That September Chesterton had attended a meeting run by Masterman, who had been given the job of establishing this department, innocuously known as "Wellington House." His staff included authors like Barrie, Bennett, Galsworthy, Conan Doyle, Hardy, and Wells, as well as Fleet Street editors like Gardiner, Garvin, Spender, Strachey, and even Chesterton's literary agent, A. P. Watt.[49] Not only was their work done secretly so that the English public knew little or nothing about it, but their writing itself was published in neutral countries like America and Spain without attribution, so that it would be taken seriously. For example, Chesterton's pamphlet *The Barbarism of Berlin*, which came out in November 1914, appeared in Spain with the title *The Concept of Barbarism*. The chief purpose of Wellington House was to persuade America not to enter the war on Germany's side, and then, if possible, to persuade her to enter it on the Allies' side. A good deal of what was published by Masterman's group was translations, but Chesterton's contributions were really his own brand of war propaganda. One such book was *The Crimes of England*, in which he tried to convince his reader that it was England's fault that she had encouraged Prussia's growth to the point where she had become a viper in their bosom; another was his slight eulogy of the dead general Lord Kitchener.

When the government became a coalition, Masterman's group was put under John Buchan first, then Sir Edward Carson, and ultimately, the press baron Lord Beaverbrook. Fortunately for Chesterton's peace of mind, it was never run by Lord Northcliffe. Obviously, from start to finish Wellington House was a strange, somewhat furtive operation, but to attack what Chesterton wrote for it seems futile; it was the only way in which he could support the war. Propaganda written under such circumstances is seldom counted as contributing to a writer's chefs d'oeuvre, but instead is thought of as a part of the history of past times — something that might be said, for example, about the writing of people like Stephen Spender and George Orwell in the thirties.[50] The opinion Chesterton had of the "Prussians" he had held for a long time, but it was the war that led to his writing entire books on the subject.

Cecil Chesterton and Ada Jones were still enjoying the war. They had appeared at Beaconsfield one day that fall before Gilbert became ill, finding the town full of soldiers and boy scouts, and the Chestertons entertaining the vicar and some old ladies. While Cecil took his brother off to his little study to argue, Ada marched outside to admire some goats being raised "for the war effort." The couple returned to London that evening just in time for the first zeppelin bombing raid; afterward they vented their journalistic ire on the fact that the government did not publish the damage done nor a list of casualties. That November, Ada got a commission to write about the condition of the military hospitals across the Channel in Boulogne, and Cecil insisted upon coming with her. Their enthusiasm was somewhat dampened when they found the hospitals filled with wounded boys suffering from trench feet and trench fever, a result of the unsanitary conditions on the battleline. But Cecil seized this chance to propose to Ada once again, this time with a new angle. Despite the fact that he, like Gilbert, was very overweight, and also suffered from Bright's disease, he was wild to go and fight and kept trying to enlist.[51] Now he asked Ada if she would marry him if he succeeded in becoming a soldier, and she agreed. They had just returned to England when Cecil found out that his brother was terribly ill.

The strains of the past year and the outbreak of war combined to make Chesterton a prime candidate for a physical breakdown. He was overweight, overworked, and very anxious at a time when Frances herself was not at all well: she suffered from attacks of neuritis and arthritis of the back, which meant she sometimes had to spend days in bed. One day in November of 1914, their doctor was called to see Chesterton and found him lying almost across the bed, which had broken down from the weight of his body dropped across it. Shortly after that there were nurses around the clock at Overroads, and by Christmas Eve of 1914 Chesterton had slipped into a coma in which he stayed, with occasional spells of lucidity, until Easter, 1915.

No one has ever completely explained what caused this illness. It may have been bronchitis and malfunctioning kidneys, caused by his overworked heart and bad circulation; or it may have been "gout all over his body" — Father O'Connor's curious diagnosis. His doctors were afraid that his brain would be damaged, so he had to be kept absolutely quiet, and for a long period only Frances and the nurses entered his room. His weekly column for the *London Illustrated News* was taken over by Belloc, himself under terrible strain because he had lost his wife earlier that year; now he was as worried as ever about money, and had a houseful of children to raise alone.

It was during this strange interlude, when the outside world and the war stopped for Chesterton, that Frances spent her time either watching over him, praying for him, or sitting downstairs, patiently correcting the proofs for *Poems*. This was a new collection drawn from his books and articles, scheduled to be published in April 1915. She found this an especially poignant task, since they had together decided which of his poems to her they would include, leaving out the ones they felt were too private.[52]

During the worst part of Chesterton's long illness, a curious little drama was played out which also has never been completely explained. Frances was in the habit of writing regularly to people whom she found sympathetic listeners, among them Father O'Connor and Mrs. Wilfred Ward, the wife of the well-known editor and publisher (and mother of Chesterton's biographer Maisie). They were both people who kept Frances' letters (which were later made available to Maisie Ward), and they were also both ardent Roman Catholics who appear to have had more than a little evangelistic zeal. When he learned how ill Chesterton was, Father O'Connor took the initiative to write to Frances and tell her something intriguing. About three years earlier (around 1910 or 1911), Chesterton had told him he was thinking of joining the Roman Catholic Church. There is no reason to doubt Father O'Connor's word, except there is some possibility that he was misinterpreting what Chesterton had said, something he had done in other instances.

This single letter has been used to prove that Chesterton was "really" a secret Roman Catholic in his heart long before he formally joined the Church. The actual facts make this an unlikely possiblity. True, since his parents had been upset when Cecil joined the Church in 1912, their reaction alone — not even counting Frances' feelings — might have prevented Gilbert from taking such a step. On the other hand, many Chesterton commentators fail to see the similarity of the doctrinal positions of the Anglo-Catholic and the Roman Catholic Church in the areas that mattered to Chesterton. The differences that he cared about lay primarily in matters of daily discipline and habits as well as in a certain lack of social "acceptability," an un-Englishness, and the time was not ripe for him to regard those as a hair shirt he personally must wear.

At any rate, poor Frances was very upset, for on the one hand she wanted to give Gilbert a chance to convert if he wanted to, but on the other hand, she knew that his parents would never forgive her if she acted on her own authority. She also realized that the resulting publicity from a deathbed conversion would be worldwide. Oddly, she wrote Mrs. Ward for advice, and that lady promptly communicated with Father O'Connor, whom she did not know, virtually giving him his marching orders to go to Beaconsfield. But when he arrived, Frances resolutely refused to let him see Chesterton until God restored him so that he could decide himself what to do. When Chesterton was better, neither he nor Frances mentioned the subject to Father O'Connor, who sensibly let it drop.[53] But from this point onward there were increased attempts on the part of the spokesmen for Roman Catholicism in England — especially in its literary and journalistic circles — to insist that Chesterton was one of them.[54]

While Chesterton still lay desperately ill, Cecil took off on a trip to America, where he had been invited to debate the Allied cause. He lectured in New York, Buffalo, and Chicago, where he enjoyed America's "fresh and violent" culture, in which the "police shot down strikers but the strikers bombed the police."[55] But he also went to Virginia and Tennessee because he became fascinated by the South, which he considered "a new civilization." He was especially intrigued by the race relations problem, proposing that "repatriation" might be the best solution, and he was clearly against any "miscegenation."[56] In New York his main debate was titled "Whether the Cause of Germany or That of the Allied Powers is Just."[57] Cecil's defense was the official Liberal one — that Austria and Germany had tried to crush smaller nations. His opponent, Viereck, editor of *The Fatherland,* claimed only Shaw understood that England was both afraid and envious of Germany. He also attacked Cecil for having said (in print) that the wealthy English Jews should all be put in concentration camps and made to chop wood, insisting that in Germany Jews were treated as regular citizens, and that it was the English and Russians who were getting ready to hold pogroms.

Cecil had left Ada to edit the *New Witness*, with help from its various contributors like Titterton. Belloc, who was writing about the military campaigns for *Land and Water*, continued to write Gilbert's *London News* column, and contributed articles to the *New Witness* as well. But Belloc wrote to Baring — now a major on the Western Front — that if Cecil did not try to make the *New Witness* more diversified it would probably fold, adding that there ought to be a list of people in politics that the paper "kept off of."[58]

In the war, 1915 was a year of stalemate. The English had the German navy bottled up, her colonies captured the German colonies, and an economic blockade of Europe was established. But the Russians' Eastern Front was bogged down, and the casualties on the Western Front were ghastly. When Baring wrote Chesterton shortly after Easter to tell him how good it was to see his name on his column again, he also sent a list of all the friends he had lost from his Eton and Oxford generation. (England's toll was heavy: when the war finally ended, one in eleven men in the age group between twenty and forty-five had been killed, and men of fifty were being called up.)

That April, *Poems* was published, and in early August a small book called *Wine, Water and Song* appeared, a collection of the songs from *The Flying Inn.* Apart from writing his weekly column and regaining his strength, Chesterton was chiefly involved in writing a series of books, articles, and pamphlets for his propaganda job under Masterman: in the next few years he produced *The Crimes of England* (1915), *Letters to an Old Garibaldian* (1915), *Lord Kitchener* (1917), and *A Short History of England* (1917).

Nineteen-fifteen was also a watershed year for English government, which was drastically changed by a number of events. Accusations about atrocities and a lack of supplies — as well as what amounted to a witch-hunt against Germans — were being generated by the Northcliffe papers as well as by Maxse at the *National Review*. This clamor was greatly increased when the Germans sank the *Lusitania* in February. Now their outcry was for "conscription" — the draft — an appalling idea to Liberals, to whom it meant a standing army, individual coercion, and, ultimately, dictatorship. By May, when Haldane had to say that the government was willing to consider conscription, the Liberal papers all tried to pillory him. Then there was another public uproar about the munitions shortages, and Asquith had to change his Liberal government into a coalition government — or be thrown out of office. To the horror of the Liberal press, Haldane and Masterman were put out of office, and Northcliffe and Maxse claimed credit for their demise.[59] But the excuse Asquith used was yet another personnel problem; Churchill's attempt to hit the Germans "from behind" through Turkey had failed miserably, so he resigned and joined the army, leaving room for Conservatives in his wake. The real winner of this maneuvering was Lloyd George, who was seeing that supplies got to their destination on time. In retrospect, this coalition government — with Lloyd George as War Minister and the Conservatives' Bonar Law at the Colonial Office and Baldwin at the Admiralty Office — foreshadowed the decline and fall of the Liberal Party. To observers like Cecil and Belloc, it also was a clear case of "party system" politics as usual.

The *New Witness* assumed that Northcliffe was using his paper empire to gain power for himself, and that Lloyd George was Northcliffe's "man." Chesterton himself wrote in July to Bentley, congratulating him on the fact that his *Daily Telegraph* "continued to be almost the only paper that the crisis has sobered and not tipsified." Chesterton signed off by saying, "Gott strafe 'Armsworth."[60] But the *New Witness* also agreed with Northcliffe on fighting the Germans to the bitter end, and to some extent went along with his efforts to keep Liberals like Isaacs or Samuel from being the dominant English group at the peace table. By contrast, Gardiner and Massingham were coming to dread the idea of destroying Germany by total surrender, and also feared what the Conservatives might do to the peace.[61]

By January 1916 a conscription bill had been passed; then that spring the German armies almost burst through the Allied lines at Verdun. At Easter 1916 came the Irish "Rising" with the Sinn Fein, who had plotted with the Germans. The Germans, however, sent no help to the rebels, many of whom were then executed as traitors. To Liberals like Masterman and Chesterton, the Irish right to Home Rule was an article of faith, so that the "Rising" was not treason; nevertheless, it would have been disastrous if the Germans had obtained Irish bases.[62]

As he grew better, Chesterton received so much fan mail that he and Frances hired a new secretary named Freda Spencer, who was quite young and pretty. Although she was not the best typist — she labored on a Corona typewriter named "Ursula" — she could manage to do a letter or an article, which was helpful. She was fun to have around the house, acting much like a daughter to the couple, whom she called "Uncle Humphrey" and "Aunt Harriet." To show his affection for her, Chesterton wrote verses in which he pretended that there was a wild romance going on between Freda and the dark gentlemen on his box of cigars named Julian Alvarez.

In October 1916 Cecil Chesterton published another propaganda book called *The Perils of Peace*, in which he called for the total destruction of Germany as a Great Power. More importantly, he also achieved his heart's desire: he was accepted by the East Surrey regiment, although classified only as "B2" — fit for home service. Military life improved his health enough so that he was soon made a "B1," and then, because of his mother's Scottish ancestry, was allowed to transfer into the Highland Light Infantry, where his uniform included a Scottish bonnet and kilt. He got along well with his fellow privates, who did not expect to find gentlemen in the ranks, least of all one who spent his spare time sitting in a pub with a drink at his elbow, finishing articles for his paper.

Cecil's departure for the army meant that Chesterton for the first time in his life became an editor. Apparently no one thought that Ada alone could cope "for the duration," possibly because the *New Witness* was in deep financial trouble. This concern is illustrated by a letter from Cecil on *New Witness* stationery, in which he says, "My brother, Mr. G.K. Chesterton, has consented to undertake the Editorship during my absence. . . . I have every hope, especially with my brother's name upon it, that it may be self-supporting."[63] So, despite the fact that he had barely recovered from his serious illness, and the additional fact that Frances did not want him to take the job, Chesterton, inevitably, did what Cecil asked. He took on both the editorial and the financial responsibility for the paper for the rest of his life, seeing it as a sacred duty — so sacred he did not even pay himself a salary, for, as he put it,

> I became an editor. It would at any time have seemed to me about as probable or promising that I should become a publisher or a banker or a leader-writer on *The Times*. But the necessity arose out of the continued existence of our little paper . . . which was passionately patriotic and Pro-Ally, but as emphatically opposed to the Jingoism of *The Daily Mail* [Northcliffe's popular paper]. . . . When my brother went to the Front, he left his paper in my hands, requesting me to edit it until he returned. But I went on editing it; because he did not return.[64]

No one, including Chesterton, ever made a secret of the fact that he was a very poor editor. Living in Beaconsfield, he was not available every day to mind the store or the staff, and he was too absent-minded to be good about details, and too much of a peacemaker to enjoy the quarrels the paper's articles often caused. Nevertheless, he was the one who made the paper survive. He used his own income to keep the paper going, writing most of the editorials himself, as well as a weekly page of comment called "At the Sign of the World's End," which alone probably sold the paper. In addition, if there were empty spaces, he simply sat down and wrote a poem or a short article to fill them. Ada Jones, with the help of Titterton and a sixteen-year-old girl nicknamed "Bunny," was in charge of getting the paper out, and she ought to have been able to make up for Chesterton's shortcomings there.

The kind of row Chesterton often had to smooth over was like the one that developed when the writer Ford Madox Ford (who had changed his last name from "Hueffer" because of anti-German sentiment in England) was given a hard time in a review. Wells then wrote to scream at Chesterton about it. Chesterton wrote Wells a pleasant letter in response, but stood up for the efforts of the *New Witness* to allow freedom of the press — even for poor or unfair reviews. Calmed down, Wells really did not want to fight with Chesterton, and accepted his apology.

By December 1916, Lloyd George had taken control of the government and forced out Asquith, who had just lost his son on the Western Front. Lloyd George's national government now included the Conservatives Bonar Law, Milner, Curzon, and a new press lord from Canada (Lord Beaverbrook), as well as F. E. Smith and Sir Edward Carson. Considering that Chesterton had every reason to mistrust these men, his editorial reminding the public that "George" had a "piebald" reputation was very mild. Other editors like Gardiner, increasingly dispirited about the way things were going, were unhappily aware that under Lloyd George, Northcliffe had a "national press" with which he virtually ran the government. Using appallingly unscrupulous methods, Northcliffe was destroying both the country and Fleet Street simultaneously, because "mythology and the newspaper cannot co-exist."[65] Chesterton's comment on this was that the yellow press "spread panic and political mutiny and called them patriotism and journalistic enterprise . . . which my friend Bentley . . . described as England being stabbed in the back. . . . [My] little group was fighting upon two fronts: the Hohenzollerns and the Harmsworths."[66]

The failure of the Somme Offensive in 1916 and Germany's decision to go all out in submarine warfare brought the United States into the war in 1917. About that time Chesterton went on a trip to Ireland to help recruit volunteers for the war, for he felt strongly that imposing the draft on Ireland would be insanity. (The articles he wrote then were collected and published in 1919 as *Irish Impressions*.) His experiences there convinced him that the old 1903 land act of George Wyndham had done a great deal of good for the general population, helping to re-create a stable Irish peasantry instead of landless agricultural slaves.[67] This idea was vividly illustrated for him by a drive down a road where on one side small farmers had gotten a good harvest gathered in, and on the other, it was rotting in the rain. When he was told the rotting harvest was caused by some strikes, he said, "You may curse the cruel Capitalist landlord or you may rave at the ruffianly Bolshevist strikers; but you must admit that between them they have produced a stoppage, which the peasant proprietorship a few yards off did not produce. . . ."[68]

During 1917 another piece of Chesterton's "war propaganda," his small eulogy for the dead general Lord Kitchener, was published, as well as another collection of his essays, culled from the *Daily Herald*, which he had left when it remained pacifist in 1914. This book, one of his least popular, was called *Utopia of Usurers*. "Usury" was Chesterton's own term for international high finance acting immorally on its own behalf. Considering when these articles were written, it is not surprising that they are labeled bitter, anti-Semitic, and reactionary, although there is reason to believe that bankers and businessmen had been manipulating world events. It should be remembered, too, that Chesterton was also talking about any kind of "collectivist" action which was really against the common good, from Tudor enclosures to beer monopolies. In these articles he strongly supported a revolutionary re-distribution of land, even if it meant outright confiscation, reacting against what he perceived to have been great uncaring inequalities.[69]

His brother Cecil had continued to fight to go overseas, and in June 1917 he finally was rated "A1." He got three days' leave, caught a train for London, and when he arrived at midnight woke up Ada to say they were getting married.[70] Given one hundred pounds by his parents, he bought a Special License, got a new uniform, had lunch with Shaw, bought his future wife a ring — and left all of his purchases in the cab going home. It took the entire *New Witness* staff to get him ready the following day.

Cecil and Ada were married twice: first in a Registry Office, and then at Corpus Christi Church in Maiden Lane. Ada's brother and niece were there, as well as Gilbert and Frances and their parents, plus Belloc and his mother and Conrad Noel. A gay luncheon at the Cheshire Cheese followed, attended by Fleet Street friends who made speeches; one was given by Sir Thomas Beecham, the conductor, who was an admirer of Cecil's fighting journalism and a financial backer of the *New Witness*. Early the next morning Ada accompanied Cecil to Sandwich, where the embarkation camp was located; she stayed in a hotel there, joined by his parents, until he was piped onboard. Then she returned to London to rent them a Fleet Street flat. Not much is known about Cecil's overseas experiences, except that he was at Ypres and Etaples and was never wounded, but often ill from conditions in the trenches. He was invalided home early in 1918 and promised his wife he would not go back, but during the summer of 1918 when the war was going badly and manpower was short, he volunteered again.

That October of 1917 Chesterton's *A Short History of England* was published; he began with a wry preface saying that the only reason he was writing a history was that other histories were "written against the people," who were "either ignored or elaborately proved to have been wrong."[71] This history was his most important piece of propaganda. It is a piece of "re-education," not meant for the ordinary reader but for Chesterton's peers, the ones educated at Oxford to believe in the prevailing "Teutonic" theory of history. The book is also the opening salvo in the postwar "teaching war" that he was to wage with H. G. Wells.

In *A Short History* Chesterton tries to restore a balanced viewpoint by leaning over backward to get people's attention. There are those who criticize his insistence on the idea of an England formed by Roman civilization, then nurtured by the medieval Roman Church, which spawned the merchant guilds and the system of holding land in common; but they have not studied the books against which Chesterton was making a debater's case. They assume he is simply echoing a Bellocian idea about the good old medieval days, when in fact both he and Belloc are talking as post-industrial, nineteenth-century radicals.

They are arguing against the historical school led by Stubbs and Green, whose outright worship of Germany was so lopsided that it ignored any other factors of national life. Green's *History of the English People*, for example, begins with the claim that "the Fatherland of the English race" is lower Hanover, where "our ancestors with their fierce, free energy . . . took part in the general attack of the German *race* on the Empire of Rome. . . ."[72] In his sarcastic response to this idea, Chesterton remarked, "It is perhaps permissible to disagree with . . . Green when he says that no spot should be more sacred to modern Englishmen than . . . Ramsgate where the Schleswig people . . . landed . . . [but] it would be rather more true to say [this landing] was nearly . . . the end [of our island story]."[73]

Even more specific than Green is Stubbs, the father of the Parliamentary theory of history, whose thesis is that the House of Commons began in Teutonic forests:

> The English . . . are a people of German descent . . . [with] the elements of the primitive German civilization and the common germs of German institutions. . . . We owe the leading principles . . . worked out in [our] constitutional history . . . to the Germanic races [before whom Roman civilization fell]. . . . The constructive elements of our life are barbarian or Germanic. . . .[74]

Since these were the standard versions of history, it is small wonder that Chesterton thought their thesis should be modified for men going into battle against armies that could *clearly* claim to be descendants of those all-powerful German barbarians. One would suspect that both Stubbs and Green would have recommended unconditional surrender, so that Beaconsfield could be overshadowed by Berlin.

In opposition to them, Chesterton now offered in his history what Belloc had offered earlier in *The Servile State*, the "Fabian or Socialist" version of English history, with one important addition. He — like Belloc — accepted the beliefs of the Roman Catholic Church as much as he admired its organization. The book's final chapters are an attack on the Bismarckian welfare state, which he called a "relapse of the barbarians into slavery," but he was also debating Wells' proposals to evolve mankind into something "higher."[75] Wells himself, having abandoned his early position of intense patriotism, was now very war-weary, and preferred thinking ahead to his dream of lasting peace. It was in this mood that he wrote in 1916 what is "as near a war journal of the nation . . . as one can hope to find," the novel *Mr. Britling Sees It Through.*[76] Mr. Britling first is hysterical with excitement, then gradually grows despondent, until finally he begins to hope for a new scheme of things in which a League of Free Nations will "order the world aright." This millennium will not come through "corrupt and footing politicans," nor the ordinary individual, but through those "who for the good of the species, believe in and obey the Master, the Captain of Mankind."[77]

Wells, a child of his age, was having another conversion, and by 1917 he had published his strange book, *God, The Invisible King*, in many ways a forerunner of the historical theories he would later try to prove in his *Outline of History*. In it he rejected the avenging God the Father of his childhood and accepted God the Son, the Superman, whose task is to impose upon the world a Wellsian New Jerusalem.[78] To help accomplish this goal, Wells applauded the Russian Revolution, which he said was needed to bring in the new age; then he joined the League of Nations Society of the Bloomsbury group. But when the peace treaties with their secret agreements did not turn fine words into fine deeds, Wells was disillusioned once more, and he ultimately chose for himself the postwar role of "educator" — of the human race. Watching Well's progression through the public attitudes of the moment, Chesterton inevitably placed himself in the front against Wells' sentimentality. He refused to call a "cynical criticism" of England "internationalism," and he distrusted the idea of the "League for the Abolition of Nations," because, like the Oriental ideal of religion — individual personalities melded into a harmonious whole — it claimed that there could be no peace as long as there were independent countries. The strikingly different positions of the two men were about to put them on a collision course once again.[79]

Chesterton had dedicated *A Short History of England* to Freda Spencer, who left the Chestertons shortly after the book came out to become secretary of her old school. She was replaced by a neighbor of the Chestertons who first had to learn how to type before she could begin the job. She discovered that the best way to get Chesterton to start working in the morning was to come in and begin typing loudly.

Meanwhile, the war finally came to an end at the eleventh hour of the eleventh day of the eleventh month: November 11, 1918. It was a rainy day in London when Lloyd George greeted the hysterical mob at No. 10 Downing Street; Big Ben boomed for the first time since the war began. Everyone, including Chesterton, took the moment to have an almost religious significance. To him it was important because the French general Foch had struck his final blow for Christendom near Chalons, where Christendom "had broken the Huns a thousand years before." But in England "the politicians continued to beam benevolently upon us; new noblemen continued to spring into life from . . . obscure commercial soils; there were . . . flourishing economic ventures . . . and all the powers of . . . mergers and newspaper combines, that now rule the State, rose slowly into their present power and peace."[80]

Almost before the celebrations were over, Chesterton was dealt his own stunning blow. Cecil was hospitalized near Boulogne with nephritis. He had been ill for some time, but until the Armistice actually occurred, he refused to report sick. His wife now received a telegram from the War Office, four days late, telling her how ill he was, but since she was only an enlisted man's wife, there was no way for her to go to him. She turned to their friends in Fleet Street, but it was Chesterton who got hold of Maurice Baring, who made it possible for her to go. She arrived only a few days before Cecil died.[81] When she wired the news to Gilbert, he was so overcome that he had to have Frances call his parents.

Ada was the only family member there when Cecil Chesterton was buried in a French military cemetery on December 6, 1918. A requiem was held for him in London on December 14 in Corpus Christi Church, where he had been married. Father Vincent McNabb preached what Belloc long afterward said was the most striking sermon he had ever heard, which so impressed his skeptical friends that they frequently spoke of it. Its central theme was Cecil's overriding passion for justice.[82]

Chesterton was so overcome by grief that he did something more characteristic of Cecil than himself. In the same issue of the *New Witness* in which he mourned Cecil, he printed his scathing "Open Letter to Lord Reading" in his column, "At the Sign of the World's End." In it, Lord Reading — about to go to Versailles with Lloyd George to write the terms of the peace treaty — is bluntly criticized:

> Are we to set up as the standing representative of England a man who is a standing joke against England! ... Are we to lose the war which we have already won. ...[83]

Chapter Thirteen

THE LESSER EDITOR

1918-1925

A portrait is impossible; as a friend he is too near me, and as a hero, too far away.

G.K. Chesterton in his introduction to
Cecil Chesterton's *A History of the United States* [1]

. . . the work which he put first he did before he died. The work which he put second . . . he left for us to do. There are many of us who will abandon many other things, and recognize no greater duty than to do it. . . .

The future belongs to those who can find a real answer to [this postwar pessimism]. . . . The omens and the auguries are against us. There is no answer but one; that omens and auguries are heathen things; and that we are not heathens. . . . We are not lost until we lose ourselves. . . . We, who have been brought up to see all the signs in heaven and earth pointing to improvement, may live to see all the signs pointing . . . the other way. If we go on, it must be in another name than that of the Goddess of Fortune.

G.K. Chesterton as quoted by Maisie Ward in *Gilbert Keith Chesterton* [2]

Hardly were the great guns silenced for the Armistice than the general public showed itself to be both vindictive — listening to Lloyd George's electioneering cry of "Hang the Kaiser" — and melancholy. Victor and vanquished alike sensed that a world had gone and there was nothing good to take its place. It was no comfort to realize that the changes in society had only been accelerated by the war, for to many people it seemed a catastrophe. [3]

Neither Chesterton nor his old friends and colleagues in the Liberal Party (with its lack of a united leadership) could share in the euphoria of an H. G. Wells, the perpetual adolescent, or the optimism of the younger generation — young people like Leonard Woolf and Malcolm Muggeridge, who were convinced that the League of Nations would make "war as obsolete as dueling."[4] Most Liberals mistrusted Lloyd George's motives, while some of them mistrusted his ability to outsmart the other negotiators, fearing it would be "business as usual."[5] To Chesterton, "business as usual" meant more international wheeling and dealing, all the more horrible as the returning veterans came home to find themselves jobless and the country in a postwar slump. It was at this time that Chesterton permanently assumed Cecil's responsibilities on Fleet Street, now dominated by Lord Northcliffe but soon to be run by the mass-production methods of Lord Beaverbrook. (As a result, Liberals Masterman and Massingham would, in a few years, find themselves "outsiders" on their home turf.)[6]

Chesterton's grief over his brother's death was not his only motivation; he never would have retired completely to the quiet of Beaconsfield. But Cecil's death meant Chesterton had to go on being an editor at a most unpromising time. Nevertheless, while Belloc had declared after the Marconi Scandal that "I have ... refused to take any further part in any attempt to cleanse what ... is beyond cleansing [the government]," Chesterton never made statements like that.[7] His intellectual need for balance always led him, in his own way, to commitment, which in turn meant communication.

As a result, in a period that was disillusioning for many people, especially his own beleaguered Liberal Party, Chesterton managed to maintain his equilibrium, not too surprised at the extremes to which Lloyd George and his associates would go, not startled when Wells became an advocate for the League of Nations or Shaw for Bolshevist Russia. It is the essential paradox of his life that from now on, in comparison to his own contemporaries, he should be classified as a reactionary. The chief reason for it was his conversion, which the "pagan" humanists of the period felt pushed him over the border into fantasy land.

A good example of the kind of telescoping that insists that he was the same man in 1905 that he had become by 1925 is Frank Swinnerton's assessment of him. A younger literary figure, typically "Left," he liked Chesterton but admired Shaw. He first lumped Chesterton with Belloc as if they were a pair of Siamese twins, then stated (in a clear parody of *A Short History of England*) that Chesterton advocated a return to the past:

> The world is in a very bad way ... but it was once — in the Middle Ages — in a very good way. ... All the ills of Modern England arise from the ... dissolution of the monasteries by Henry VIII. ... It is one thing to say that the world is wrong ... but when, instead of proceeding to say that the world can be set right by something new, a man says it can only be set right by a return to something old, he is thrown into a defense of the past.[8]

Chesterton's answer, typically poking fun as he makes his serious point, is this:

The modern innovation which has substituted journalism for history . . . has ensured that everybody should only hear the end of every story. . . . Newspapers not only deal with news, but they deal with everything as if it were entirely new. Tu-ankh-amen [whose tomb was discovered in the early 20s] . . . was entirely new. . . . Journalism never thinks of publishing the life until it is publishing the death. As it deals with individuals, it deals with institutions and ideas. . . . The public . . . is being told of all sorts of nations being emancipated. It has never been told a word about their being enslaved. . . . It is very exciting, like the last act of a play to people who have only come into the theatre just before the curtain falls. But it does not conduct . . . to knowing what it is all about. Most modern history, especially in England, suffers from the same imperfections as journalism. . . .[9]

Meanwhile, Ada Chesterton wanted to work her grief for Cecil out of her system by barnstorming across uneasy Europe as a roving reporter. According to her, Cecil had always said that Poland was the key to postwar Europe, so to Poland she promptly went, sending back dispatches and enjoying her rather dangerous adventures. Chesterton typically wished her godspeed, though he was left to run the *New Witness* with the help of Titterton and Bunny, and to get over his own grief as best he could.

At first, Titterton says, Chesterton did not come into the office very often, although he "never exhibited his grief," nor did it keep him from his unfailing habit of being courteous and kind "because he liked people and liked being with them and because, for all his sorrow, he thanked God for being alive. . . ."[10] Titterton's comments make it plain that, in a very real sense, Chesterton was reliving his teenage troubles. He was devastated, the world was despairing — but he was committed to being thankful for being alive. At this time, as it had been earlier, his rational commitment was an act of faith as well as a rejection of the artistic fantasy of playing God.

Soon, however, Chesterton's job as editor began to help him. Titterton explains that Chesterton became glad to come to town: it was "Little Gilbert's Half-Holiday," and he boarded the train feeling "very larky and wicked." Titterton fondly describes the days when Chesterton came to the dingy little offices at No. 20 Essex Street, looking like Father Christmas: he would be wearing his famous hat and cloak, holding a bedraggled cigarillo in one hand, his beloved sword stick in the other, and would act faintly surprised and apologetic for having strayed there, but happy to see them all. This description not only shows how the staff felt about Chesterton, but also makes it clear that it would never have worked for Chesterton and his sister-in-law to run a paper together for very long, because they ran things so differently, and staff loyalty would have been strained. A part of his postwar "restlessness," which was the excuse given for his more extensive travels, probably stems from that fact.

When he came to the office, Chesterton usually brought in a few pieces for the paper or then and there wrote what they needed. Pulling sheaves of paper out of his voluminous pockets, he would sit down in the editor's chair to gaze at the model of a ship in full sail and doodle cartoons all over his notes. He would chat with the staff about the next issue, saying he rather thought they might do this, or that, "if they didn't mind." If he did not come to London, he would call from Beaconsfield (and he hated the telephone; usually Frances did the phoning for them both). Titterton could then imagine him in his small, cluttered study, his desktop littered with manuscript and typescript and drawings and books, as he diffidently asked, "What have you got for next week?"

Other contributors wandered in and out of the office, some polemical Roman Catholics like Father McNabb or Eric Gill, the sculptor who eventually became the art editor; others were a part of the "regular" Fleet Street crowd, like Jack Squire, John Drinkwater, and Desmond McCarthy. A regular was Raymond Radclyffe, one of the most verbally abusive of the reporters, who called potential advertisers "dirty crooks." Titterton himself was inclined to be drastic and foolhardy in his statements (probably reminding Chesterton of Cecil). He loudly proclaimed a dislike for foreigners — Jews, Scotsmen, Irishmen; he also converted from socialism to both "distributism" and Roman Catholicism.

The first postwar election justified all the forebodings of Chesterton and his Liberal friends. Lloyd George cleverly called a General Election for December 14, 1918, planning to take advantage of the Armistice by having another "Khaki Election." He had sounded out Labour's leaders as well as Asquith, leader of the "independent" Liberals, before deciding to run again in a coalition with the Conservatives. Liberal candidates who joined them got party help: others did not. Lloyd George campaigned on the emotional issue of "Hang the Kaiser" and a demand for stiff German reparations. At the *Nation* Massingham called it "a sinister election," predicting that Lloyd George had destroyed the Liberal party, and took his paper over to Labour's side in support of Wilson and the League of Nations.[11]

The coalition won a landslide victory, while Masterman and Asquith both lost their seats, and the defeated and divided Liberals bitterly realized both that the peace treaty would be vengeful and that Lloyd George was still in command — a man who had become incredibly venal, selling honors to fill the party coffers with price tags like 15,000 pounds for a knighthood and 140,000 pounds for a barony. The ultimate irony was that Lloyd George was now a pawn of Northcliffe and the Conservatives, and the ideological winner in the end was Labour.[12]

That this election made it impossible for the Liberals to muster a united party in the postwar period is a fact that historians have long used as proof of the working out of Hegelian dialectic — in other words, proof that the "laws of history" made it inevitable that there should be a new party alignment, with the Conservatives (who continued to uphold king, country, and, especially, empire) faced by the new "counter-elite" of the rising Labour Party, which picked up most of the Liberal intellectuals, particularly the articulate young from the universities. But recently it has been suggested that this pattern was not inevitable — that without Lloyd George as its leader, the Liberal Party of 1918-19 might have gone on in the postwar period holding the balance in the name of the "middle class," a term which Masterman bitterly said had lost its magic by 1922.[13]

For personal reasons, Chesterton in particular could not accept Lloyd George as his party's leader, but he continued to call himself a Liberal in what by the end of the twenties had become almost a party of one.[14] He explained what he meant by this label in his speech as the Liberal candidate for Rector of Glasgow University in 1925, when he told the assembled students (who did not elect him),

> The men who began the historic moment towards liberty in the American and French Revolutions set up something that could stand indefinitely against the Governing Class and even against the Government. It was the Citizen, or, in another aspect, the Free Man. . . . They were not Whigs, they were not Socialists. . . . They desired to back the small man against the big man, and equally, against the big group. They desired the man to influence the State, but his influence on the state depended upon his independence of the State. . . . The Radical [Liberal] is not a rather slow Socialist. Nor is he a rather fast Tory.[15]

Looking back, Chesterton suggested provocatively that, while men's attitudes about the war changed very quickly, underlying English social structure did not change at all. He symbolized this continuity in his ironic story of the great Beaconsfield "battle" over a fitting war memorial. One side wanted to put up a cross, the other to build a clubhouse for veterans:

> There was a huge paper Plebiscite in which hardly anybody knew what he was voting for, but which turned up with a narrow municipal majority for the building of the Club . . . [which was actually never done]. . . . When the whole fuss was over, the rector of the parish raised a quiet subscription . . . and put up a Cross. Meanwhile . . . the chief landlord of the neighborhood . . . casually informed the ex-service men . . . they could use a hall which was his property, for their club . . . and so in the end the whole matter was decided at the private discretion of the Squire and the Parson, as it was in the days of old.[16]

The conclusion one must *not* draw from this remark is that Chesterton, in his dotage, had become a great admirer of the squirearchy or English social class structure. What he did do was come to the conclusion that there was something to be said for noblesse oblige when compared with plutocracy and meritocracy.

The minute the war was over the Irish had "voted" themselves independence, precipitating civil war (the Troubles). The I.R.A. and the Black and Tans joined in a bloody guerrilla war, while Lloyd George tried to get an agreement on a two-parliament government. Liberals like Chesterton were appalled by the carnage and violence, as well as by the idea of a divided Ireland.[17]

Having seen the celebrations in Paris over the signing of the Treaty of Versailles, Ada Chesterton had returned to London by the summer of 1919. She claimed that she did not immediately go back to work for the *New Witness*, but set up her own eastern European news service, which was especially concerned with Poland. (She and Chesterton both felt that the Treaty had shortchanged Poland in favor of Germany.) But Titterton tells a different story: he claims that when Ada returned, his job disappeared. This may have happened while Ada ran the *New Witness* when Gilbert and Frances left on a trip, which was necessitated by Frances' physical condition: the doctor had told Chesterton that Frances was in bad health and needed to spend most of the winter in a warmer climate. Ada's taking over was also a temporary solution to a two-fold problem: Frances was undoubtedly unhappy at the prospect of her husband assuming the editorship permanently, and Chesterton had to decide what he was going to do about Ada's conviction that Cecil's memory and work were *her* job.

E.C. Bentley arranged the trip for the Chestertons through his newspaper, the *Daily Telegraph*. They were to travel to France, south to Egypt, and across it to the Holy Land, coming home by way of Rome. Chesterton was to write a series of articles, as well as make speeches and behave like the celebrity he was. The major problem was getting official military permission to go to Jerusalem. Chesterton wrote to his old friend Baring, as "a man who knows everybody; do you know anybody on Allenby's staff . . . who would know anything about it? I only want to write semi-historical rhetoric on the spot."[18] Baring did know someone, who spoke to someone else, with the result that very soon Baring got a letter from Allenby himself, the English general in command of Palestine, assuring him that the Chestertons would be given every aid to visit his command as well as to see Jerusalem.

In December 1917 Chesterton's imagination had been caught by the daring exploit of T.E. Lawrence, friend of Arab sheiks, and General Allenby, who captured the city of Jerusalem. Over Mount Zion there now waved, for the first time since the 1500s, the banner of the Cross. As it turned out, this trip was to become Chesterton's personal symbol of "taking the Cross" in the Crusader's sense, both in terms of his editorship and in terms of his acceptance of Roman Catholicism. As overt acts of self-commitment, both things were closely related to his love for Cecil and the obligation he felt to take his place. Both actions were on Chesterton's mind as he traveled; both actions also represented a commitment that was going to be very hard on his wife.

But the trip was not, as other biographers have suggested, a pilgrimage that had "Rome" as its manifest destiny, or that represented Chesterton's personal road to Damascus. Chesterton was a more complicated person than that suggests and his decisions were also made on a more ordinary, pragmatic level than this kind of phrase implies. There is considerable evidence from his own letters that had his brother lived, he might never have felt the need for what he called "the iron ring of Catholic responsibilities" in what was his final "acted out" parable.[19]

The Chestertons went by train through France, seeing for themselves its devastated, bombed-out villages, the mud and debris of war, and field after field of pale military crosses. Then they crossed the Mediterranean to Egypt, where they observed the pyramids, the Sphinx, and the "English sightseer." In the articles he was sending back to the *Daily Telegraph*, which he said were little more than bits of an "uncomfortably large note-book," Chesterton had the pleasure of ruminating about both the differences between East and West, Islam and Christianity (which he symbolized with his dog and his donkey), and the origins of their different civilizations.[20] By the time he had reached the East, he was also having a marvelous time telling the English what was wrong with the way they went about being tourists. According to Chesterton, the proper "philosophy of sight-seeing" requires that sight-seers stop comparing "the alien with the ideal," since they do not compare themselves to the ideal "but identify with it." They criticize the world, but never themselves, and as a result their reactions are not realistic enough. The solution Chesterton proposes is to view sights with historical humility. "Whether or no the superior person has a right to expect the unexpected, it is possible that something may be revealed to him that he really does not expect."[21]

Chesterton himself was startled when he reached Jerusalem. He had expected to find it cosmopolitan, although not the "New Jerusalem of charity and peace," or to be disappointed with it as a place profaned, or awed by it as a place dedicated or doomed by its mission. But what he found was quite different:

> the Jerusalem of the Crusaders ... a medieval town, with walls and gates and a citadel, and built upon a hill to be defended by bowmen. ... I had an overwhelming impression that I was walking in the town of Rye ... mixed with the memory of the Mont St. Michel, which stands among the sands of Normandy ... and it reminded me, if not specially of the cross, at least of the soldiers who took the cross.[22]

He had never "fancied it might be possible to be fond of it, as one might be fond of a little walled town ... of Normandy ... or Kent."[23] Jerusalem had the wonder and charm of ordinary life; it and its history, he saw, were real.

All evidence suggests that Chesterton's perception of Jerusalem as a crusader's town strengthened his sense of mission about taking Cecil's place. His act of "taking the cross" was to join the only branch of Western Christianity that was still militant, both a gesture and a form of self-discipline.

In discussing the current situation in Jerusalem and Palestine, Chesterton continued to see it as an example of the kinds of nationalism that Europe represents. He talks about the Crusades as wars of "self-defence" — i.e., patriotic wars fought against attackers who had tried to conquer Christendom. Then he defines once more his theory of history:

> [Neither] the notion of a New Jerusalem in the future . . . [nor] the notion of a Golden Age in the past [are correct]. . . . It is not necessary to idealize the medieval world but merely to realize the modern world. . . . Everything in the past is praised if it had led up to the present and blamed if . . . [it] led up to anything else . . . [but] we have come to the wrong place. . . . We may or may not see the New Jerusalem rebuilt . . . on our fields, but in the flesh we shall see Babylon fall. . . .

In explaining how the actual loss of Jerusalem and the failure of the Crusades affected Europe, Chesterton makes it quite plain that to him "medieval society was not the right place . . . it was only the beginning of the right road . . . but it died young."[24]

To anyone who views both secular and sacred history as inevitably interrelated, what Chesterton says about the relationship of Jerusalem and its history to Western civilization is not fanciful. But his whimsical way of stating things made his contemporaries and later readers take him lightly and refuse to see the factual truth in his comments. For example, he concluded his discussion of the Crusades with the remark that whether they were right or wrong, it was now a fact that "even the wise understand . . . and the learned [are] enlightened on a need . . . which a mob in a darker age had known," that "no practical or even temporary solution [can be found] for this sacred land, except to bring it again under the crown of Coeur de Lion and the cross of St. George."[25]

He was referring to the problem of Palestine; by 1920 the League of Nations would give England a mandate to rule that country. In the interval, the famous Balfour Declaration (used later as a justification for both the guerrilla warfare of Israelis and the United Nations' establishment of Israel) had been issued by the ex-prime minister, acting as part of Lloyd George's coalition government. It stated that England favored the establishment of a national home for the Jewish people and would do everything in its power to accomplish that goal, "it being clearly understood that nothing shall be done which may prejudice the civil and religious rights of existing non-Jewish communities in Palestine or the rights and political status enjoyed by Jews in any other country."[26] This statement was issued because Lloyd George, a Nonconformist, was greatly interested in "freeing" Jerusalem, as well as in finding the Jews a home. (As in so many things, he and Chesterton shared the same Liberal "agenda.")[27] Chesterton, of course, had always seen Europe itself in terms of liberalism's nation-states, as families related by language and customs. Imperialism and internationalism were two sides of the same coin: they both involved coercion and tyranny of the individual in the name of the super-state.[28]

As a logical consequence of this attitude, Chesterton thought that, since Jews were Jews and "as a logical consequence [were] not Russians ... Roumanians ... or Englishmen," the solution to the Jewish question in Europe was to establish a national homeland of their own.[29] At the same time Chesterton had always disliked assimilated Jews who were part of the international plutocracy, men like Cassel and Rufus Isaacs, and it bothered him that Herbert Samuel had enlisted Lloyd George in the Zionist cause. In the last chapter of his published notes, Chesterton discussed "The Problem of Zionism." The *Daily Telegraph*, however, chose not to print this part, and Chesterton referred to their decision in his preface, saying that "it might be worthwhile for England to take risks to settle the Jewish problem; but not to take risks merely to unsettle the Arab problem. ..." In this final chapter he explains that "he and his friends have always been accused of Anti-Semitism," although he had recently seen more blatant anti-Semitism among those who were "anti-socialist." He insisted that he greatly preferred "the Jew who is revolutionary to the Jew who is a plutocrat."[30]

The problem remains that it offends most readers to have Chesterton talking about Jews as a separate group, which he suggests ought to be visually and legally still more separate. The answer that his attitude was not uncommon and had some historical justification cannot be used effectively in our post-Holocaust world.[31] His real concern about international financial power wielded by and for Jews sounds fanciful, in spite of today's well-known lobbies for Israel in most European countries and in America, and his insistence on singling them out racially sounds like Hitler's "final solution." The fact that he did not approve of the concept of a master race, which had been a major German philosophical concept most of his life, is never put forward in his favor. Perhaps the only thing that will justify his remarks and still be considered valid today is the fact that the state of Israel exists, and most of the world believes it was a good idea to give the Jewish "race" a land of their own.[32] But when Israel was established no one heeded Chesterton's warnings about not despoiling or destroying the Arab's rights in the same country. He also would have been unsympathetic with the Israeli conviction that Jerusalem was their capital city; to him it is the capital city of Christendom, a holy place that should remain an "open city."

Chesterton concluded his trip by claiming the privileges of a "pilgrim," proud of the fact that the "fighting Christian creed" was the one thing that had been in the mystical circle "by which everything begins and ends in the mind ... and had broken out of it and become something real. ..."[33]

Although the book that came out of his news dispatches was predominantly political, it was clearly religion that was much on his mind.

On their way home the Chestertons came by way of Rome, where they met Mrs. Wilfred Ward and her daughter, members of the English Roman Catholic "literary establishment." For some time this group had been trying to "win over" Chesterton to Rome, the part of Christendom where he really belonged. They were among those who saw his long approach to Roman Catholicism as "easy and gradual," although, as he wrote afterward, the difference between an "admiring approach and decision" is not a matter of gradation and shades, but "of a passage between sundered worlds."[34] These women themselves might have made Chesterton's choice more difficult, for they were clearly convinced that only "politeness" toward Frances, who seemed hostile to their welcoming cries, was stopping him from converting.[35] Like Ada Chesterton, the Wards took Frances to be one of Chesterton's own "Puritans," a woman who believed in plain living and high thinking, justification by faith and not by works, and a religious self-discipline that was personal, not externally imposed. Their assessment was probably correct.

It is perfectly true that Chesterton knew how much Frances would dislike his taking such a romantic step, and how very much she would loathe the publicity that would follow it. In some ways, then, it is more surprising that she followed him into the Church than that he followed Cecil there. All three of their actions seem to represent a psychological chain reaction, in which each in turn is convinced that by refusing to sign up under the most explicitly "anti-pagan" banner in the modern world, he is demonstrating the sin of pride. In other words, one's personal religious preference ought not to loom so large before Armageddon.

Maurice Baring was back in England, working on a Proustian autobiography as well as beginning to write his highly stylized, strangely religious novels. He was the person to whom Chesterton confided most of his religious scruples. Unlike Father O' Connor or the Wards, or Belloc with his negative reactions (he was arrogantly convinced that Chesterton "romanticized" religion), Baring had joined the Church as an adult and, more important, had found there the strength to continue living, though his personal world had been devastated.[36] He had the gentleness and charm and impish humor that Chesterton needed, and he, too, understood Chesterton's anguish at becoming less "English" by joining Rome.

Baring may well have introduced Chesterton to Father Ronald Knox, who became his "confessor." Father Knox had shown more of the priest than the layman in his own decision. His father had been an Evangelical bishop of the Church of England. One of his brothers was an Anglo-Catholic priest; the others, an editor of *Punch* and a loud atheist. Knox was a classics scholar, who at Eton and Cambridge had developed an Anglo-Catholic piety which disintegrated when he began to worry first about the syncretism of Protestant churches, then the validity of the sacraments, and finally his own ordination. By 1919 Knox had become a Roman Catholic priest; he ultimately was given the task of translating the Old and New Testaments for the Roman Catholics. A versatile man, he was also a witty writer of mysteries as well as spoofs on serious scholarship. He proved to be a very effective and receptive counselor to Chesterton, whom in his university days he had considered an "oracle."[37]

Once back in England in April 1920, Chesterton took over from Belloc the writing of his *Illustrated London News* column and began again to try to keep the *New Witness* alive. The previous November his book on Ireland, *Irish Impressions*, had been published. Along with declaring his hopes for a more widespread distribution of land among small farmers throughout the British Isles (a program Lloyd George had been trying to get his Cabinet to approve), Chesterton had proclaimed himself, like Ireland, "in revolt in most ways against the British government." He had also reacted sympathetically to the Irish people's demand for their own culture and language.[38]

Interestingly enough, Chesterton's old antagonist and debating opponent, H. G. Wells, had decided that the politicians and professionals building a new world order were not doing it to suit him, so he also had gone back to his favorite role as "preacher to the world." In his latest version of utopia, Wells was offering the postwar world salvation by history. His ideas had been foreshadowed in his wartime version of the Book of Job called *The Undying Fire*, in which the Great Teacher shows mankind how they rose from the beasts. Now he planned to be more systematic in what he saw as his "lifework."

Taking the basic design he had been repeating for over thirty years, Wells went to work to gather the details to support his thesis and make it readable. He got together a group of experts to catch his scholarly errors, while he and his wife did most of the research, using the *Encyclopaedia Britannica* and some other general source books.[39] The result was his famous best seller, *The Outline of History*, which began appearing in bi-weekly installments in October 1919 with the subtitle "A Plain History of Life and Mankind." It had the kind of popular success Arnold Toynbee's *A Study of History* enjoyed after World War II; it was reprinted in 1920, 1923, and again in 1925.[40]

Like Toynbee's work, Wells' book was even popular with scholars because, in spite of many errors, "it had sweep, re-living the entire life of Mankind in a single emotional experience." It developed Wells' basic idea of a rhythm in history, of nations rising and falling like species, each owing its triumph to a ruling elite, which in turn is displaced by a bureaucracy, which destroys that civilization. Wells, reading into the past the story of his own time, was convinced that the barbarians were at the door, so a new elite must be developed. He was its prophet, writing its secular Bible, one that began with creation and ended with his favorite version of the new

Jerusalem, although he added the pious hope that "he has added nothing to history."[41]

Although the real "answer" to *The Outline of History* was to be written by Chesterton himself in a few years, Belloc answered first, attacking Wells for the superficial nature of his criticisms of the Roman Catholic Church. A clue to Belloc's complaints can be found in Wells' chapter titles: his commentary on the period of the Crusades was called "The Western World at its lowest ebb," and his discussion of the Renaissance was titled "Europe begins to think for itself." But most comment was very favorable, so much so that Wells became a kind of world pundit whose opinion on Lenin was taken seriously. By 1922 he had decided to join the growing Labour Party and the next year ran as a Labour candidate. Both Belloc and Chesterton were asked to comment on his candidacy by the *Daily News* (which had just fired their old editor, Gardiner, for his outspoken criticism of Lloyd George). Typically, Belloc said Wells was admirably suited to the House of Commons, while Chesterton said that if Wells had a good idea, the last place in the world where he would be allowed to express it was the House of Commons.[42] In this single set of responses, the basic personality difference between the two old friends is made clear.

Chesterton had written a number of essays about divorce for the *New Witness* two years earlier, when there was considerable public discussion about changing the divorce laws; now, on January 20, 1920, they were published as *The Superstition of Divorce*. As always, Chesterton's basic argument was that the family is the cornerstone of society — not because a family is a group in which a person may do as he pleases, but because it is a group in which he must get along. All of the essays turn on an intriguing paradox: "Many quite disinterested people say that they want divorce without asking themselves whether they want marriage." Chesterton claims that marriage itself will continue to be considered the responsible way of life by the Roman and Anglican Churches, by the conservative peasantries, and a large section of popular society "with the result that two different standards will appear in ordinary morality and even in ordinary society." He sees divorce as another part of the modern tendency to want to try every situation when what society needs in art and in ethics is to make a choice and stick to it, using its "creative power in the will as well as in the mind."[43] Inevitably, his support of "rash vows" did not sound like choice to the intellectuals; to them choice was more a matter of having one's cake and eating it, too.

In addition to his weekly column and the writing and editorial work he was doing for the *New Witness*, Chesterton wrote many introductions to books, particularly to the works of Dickens. That June of 1920, to mark the fiftieth anniversary of Dickens' death, he had a little book of appreciation privately printed. That summer he also put out a very small book of amusing poems that had first appeared in the *New Witness*.

The poems were versions of the nursery rhyme of "Old King Cole," done in the style of Tennyson, Yeats, Whitman, and Browning. Originally they were written to be sold at a local bazaar for the benefit of the Beaconsfield Convalescent Home. Happily, they prove that Chesterton was not spending all his time deeply concerned about the state of the world or the state of his soul. The Whitman version begins, "Me clairvoyant/Me conscious of you, old comrado"; the Yeats reads, "Of an old King in a story/From the grey sea/Folk I have heard." Swinburne, his other youthful idol, is mocked in these lines: "In the time of old sin without sadness/And golden with wastage of gold/Like the gods that grow old in their gladness/Was the king that was glad, growing old."[44]

Although the *New Witness* was draining his personal coffers, Chesterton had gone along with Ada's impassioned plea to keep the paper alive, allowing her to come to work for nothing to help the situation.[45] As a consequence, Chesterton's career suffered in terms of books he might have written, and the situation clearly upset Frances, whose arthritis of the spine had become considerably worse. It therefore was partly to replenish the family treasury and partly to distract her that Chesterton agreed to visit the United States, that golden land in the West that loved to fete literary lions.

Before they set sail in October 1920 he published *The Uses of Diversity,* essays from the *New Witness* and the *Illustrated London News*, as well as his articles on his trip East in a book called *The New Jerusalem*, which included the previously unpublished chapter on Zionism. (The *Daily Telegraph* had refused to print it.)

In *The Uses of Diversity*, one essay is particularly interesting. "The Irishman" was triggered by Chesterton's attending an Irish play in which, for a change, an Irish actor played the part of an English gentleman (the usual twist was an English actor playing the part of an Irish servant). Discussing Anglo-Saxon relations in the essay, Chesterton made the apt remark, often quoted out of context, that "unless people are near in soul they had better not be near in neighborhood. The Bible tells us to love our neighbors, and also to love our enemies, probably because they are generally the same people."[46] This was, in fact, a highly appropriate comment about Chesterton's own reactions to America.

Part of Chesterton's attitude toward America was a result of Cecil's influence. Cecil's *A History of the United States* had been published in 1919. In it, he freely admitted his debt, which was considerable, to the longer history written by Woodrow Wilson, now not only president but a Liberal "hero" because he defended small nations. Like Gilbert, Cecil took America's foundation to be the "creed" which was stated in the Declaration of Independence, calling for an essential equality, to which Cecil opposed "Prussian" elitism.[47] Beyond that, however, Cecil had borrowed Wilson's thesis, which defended the Jim Crow South as Jefferson and Jackson's ideal agrarian society, now destroyed by the industrial robber barons of the North. Chesterton inevitably agreed with Cecil's dislike of plutocrats, whether or not he swallowed the racism inherent in Wilson's Black Zionism. Today Cecil's history is virtually unreadable because of the virulence of his racist remarks.[48]

The pleasant tone of voice in which Chesterton himself described America is perfectly illustrated in his next collection of Father Brown stories, *The Incredulity of Father Brown* (1923), which contains a number of tales set in the United States. "The Arrow of Heaven" opens with his genial narrator's voice telling the reader, "It is to be feared that about a hundred detective stories have begun with the discovery that an American millionaire has been murdered; an event which is, for some reason, treated as a sort of calamity. This story, I am happy to say, has to begin ... with three murdered millionaires, which some may regard as an embarras de richesse."[49]

This story goes on to describe — ostensibly through the eyes of Father Brown — what the Chestertons experienced when they first arrived in New York:

> When Father Brown first stepped off an Atlantic liner on to American soil, he discovered ... that he was a much more important person than he had ever supposed. ... America has a genius for the encouragement of fame ... and he found himself held up on the quay by a group of journalists, as by a gang of brigands, who asked him questions about all the subjects on which he was least likely to regard himself as an authority, such as the details of female dress and the criminal statistics of the country that he had only that moment clapped his eye on.[50]

Chesterton's tour of the United States proved very successful. Just by being himself, Chesterton captivated America's public and proved to be a journalist's delight. He disliked reading the strange headlines that American reporters devised for his comments, but otherwise he was amused by his quips as recorded in the press. He had always been gifted at debate and repartee, and now he had what amounted to a worldwide audience for cracks such as, "I do not plan to go farther west than Chicago, for having seen Jerusalem and Chicago, I think I shall have touched the extremes of civilization." He repeated his conviction that the two countries, England and America, were quite different, and that it was an appreciation of the difference which was the whole point of trips, insisting cheerfully that "travel narrows the mind," which was a good thing, for it gave a person real basis for understanding the differences.

He declared that he loved both America and its lecture halls full of females who got more beautiful as they got older. He also was enchanted to discover not only that American men dressed to be comfortable rather than to prove they were gentlemen, but that the American public was very unpunctual. It gave him a "sort of a dizzy exaltation to find [he] was not the most unpunctual person" at his own talks. He liked discovering that the American childhood classics upon which all well brought-up English children were raised, like *Little Women* and *Huckleberry Finn*, were truly representative of their country; but he commented, after staring at the neon lights of Broadway, "What a glorious garden of wonders this would be to anyone who was lucky enough not to be able to read."[51]

He refused to follow Sinclair Lewis's elitist "Henry Jamesianism" and despise *Main Street*, but when Chesterton met Lewis at Marshall Field's State Street store in the rare book department, they liked one another. John Drinkwater wrote about the incident, describing Chesterton as "a large man, . . . only described by the adjective *fat*. Thick mop of hair. Baggy striped trousers, morning coat and white vest." The writers sat down to talk books and Chesterton "stated that he . . . was sure he had autographed more than six thousand books, pictures, postcards. . . . His manager had to fight people off him." Then someone suggested that they write a play together, an idea Chesterton happily agreed to when he learned there was something rare besides books in the safe (whiskey). Lewis named their play "Mary, Queen of Scotch," and Chesterton said that if he wrote the first act it must be a detective play about a mysterious murder: "There's nothing like a nice murder . . . to get real human interest into the play. . . ." He said Lewis could arrive at the solution and write the happy ending to a plot which he sketched out to be the story of "an American ex-distiller from Peoria found dead in his hotel, hit on the head with a quart bottle."[52] (A more serious opinion lurked beneath this jesting: Chesterton considered American prohibition to be the epitome of social hypocrisy in action. As he described it, well-to-do Americans were only too happy to agree with him, discussing it at their dinner tables over the nuts and wine. "They were even willing, if necessary, to dispense with the nuts.")

Frances kept newspaper clippings detailing their entire trip, which she did not enjoy as much as Chesterton did, preferring the parts of America that reminded her most of England, like Boston and the South. She was horrified to discover that she was the "wife of a great man. . . . It never bothered me before." In turn, the reporters, listening to Chesterton's pronouncements about the equality of the sexes, were greatly amused to find that his "unemancipated" wife had a mind and voice of her own (something that should have been obvious from Chesterton's books).

His American audiences noticed that Chesterton was always better in debate than in lecture, that he "liked to get down into the audience and have a sort of heart-to-heart talk in his high-pitched voice with its wheezy chuckle." Clearly his personal presence was even more striking than his personality in print. This fact helps explain his enormous popularity during his lifetime, which critics find hard to believe when they examine his writing, especially when he is discussing his own pet ideas or concerns. Perhaps most attractive was his natural humility, which made him cheerfully reply, when asked which of his works he considered the greatest, "I don't consider any of my works in the least great."[53]

The Chestertons sailed for home on the liner *Aquitania* on April 12,

1921. Back home in England, Chesterton was elected president of the Dickens Society, and was consequently presented with the master's chair (which he did not sit in for fear it might break). He had no books published that year, but continued to be extremely busy with his journalistic jobs.

With the extra money he had made in America, he and Frances were able to convert Top Meadow into their home. They added a wing with a kitchen, a tiny bathroom, and small bedrooms at the top of a narrow, winding stair. Built piecemeal, at first only a studio and den, the house was somewhat strange architecturally, but had a charming, comfortable atmosphere. It resembled a Ruskin-like cottage with its low, plastered walls and many handmade details, like the ironwork fastenings for the casement windows. Chesterton still had his little cubbyhole of an office to work in there, with a door that let him sneak out to the garden unobserved to chop the heads off flowers.

Ada Chesterton characterized Top Meadow as "utterly lopsided in design — half being for a giant and the other half for a gnome," because the original stage became the dining room, perched above the rest of the studio, which was turned into a living room with a high, raftered ceiling. It was filled with bookcases and easy chairs and had a huge open fireplace where Frances liked to sit. At Christmastime both a crèche and Chesterton's toy theatre were displayed, and the curtain of the dining-room stage was pulled back to display the festive food. Sitting onstage, Ada complained that she always felt that the curtain might go up any minute on the family at dinner, or that a maid ought to say an important piece of dialogue when she brought in the meal, or that an audience should appear below to applaud Gilbert's epigrams. (Her comment suggests that Chesterton dominated the conversation, something others say was completely untrue.)

In 1921 Shaw produced his first postwar commentary, a companion piece to Wells' *Outline of History* called *Back to Methuselah*; it was a sign of the times, an indicator of how the old battlelines were re-forming. It was about his life force, or "Creative Evolution," and he, like Wells, chose Eden as the starting point for his treatment of religion from 4004 B.C. to 31,920 A.D. The play took two or three nights to perform, possibly, as Chesterton suggested, to prepare the audience for the idea that, by taking thought, they could live for two or three hundred years.[54] Originally *Back to Methuselah* was even longer, because it included a section called "A Glimpse of the Domesticity of Franklyn Barnabas," Barnabas being one of two brothers, an ex-clergyman and a biologist, who felt human life must be lengthened so that "you can change political conduct through the whole range which lies between . . . eat and drink for tomorrow we die, and the long-sighted and profound politicies of the earthly paradises of More, Morris, Wells and all the other Utopians."[55]

This part of the play, which was not published until 1931, contained a full-length Shavian portrait of Chesterton called "Immenso Champernoon."

Shaw insisted it was a failure, but in fact it is clever and lifelike, and does "give a hint or two as to what the original . . . was like in the first half of his career when . . . he began . . . as a convivial immensity with vine leaves in his hair . . . and in middle life slimmed into a Catholic saint. . . ."[56] This remark shows that not all his contemporaries saw Chesterton as "innately" Roman Catholic, although another character in the play does comment about Immenso's possible conversion, declaring, "You are always defending the Church of Rome and I live in daily fear of your joining it just for an intellectual lark."[57]

Immenso is "a man of colossal mould, with the head of a cherub on the body of a Falstaff . . . friendly, a little shy, and jokes frequently enough to be almost always either still enjoying the last or already anticipating the next. . . . He is careless of his dress and person. . . ." One character says, "Imm here [is] by way of being a pundit and is really only a punster." Immenso replies, "So be it. You may say the same of Plato, of Shakespeare, at all events, I keep to the point . . . ," whereupon another character retorts, "I know your trick of never arguing, but simply talking every idea out of my head except your own. . . ." When his sister calls him a great fat fool, he replies, "Why is England still England? . . . [because] the frankness of the British family relation provides me with a sister to remind me that I am a great fat fool."

The play pits Immenso against one of Shaw's dangerous heroines, a Mrs. Etteen, who pretends to be a vamp but is really a Major Barbara crusading for the Life Force. Mrs. Etteen (standing in for Shaw) accuses him of flirting: "Mr. Champernoon, you are the most incorrigible flirt in England. . . . You flirt with religions, with traditions, with politics . . . the Church, the Middle Ages, the marriage question, the Jewish question . . . with the hideous cult of gluttony and drunkenness. . . . You pay [your opponent] the most ingenious compliments . . . but behind her pretty paint you loathe [her] flesh and blood."[58] Shaw lets Chesterton defend himself in Champernoon's response:

> I deny that innuendo. . . . I was in a Liberal set . . . a Protestant set, an atheist set, a Puritan set. I have everything to lose by defending the Church and the Middle Ages, by denouncing Puritanism, by affirming the existence of God . . . [but] why do I uphold the Church . . . [knowing] as much of [its] crimes as you do? Not for what the Church did for men, but for what men did for the Church. . . . The past is as much a part of eternity as the future. Beware of ingratitude to the past!

His wily oponent insists these gifts for the Church were for people, not for a pack of men trying to persuade others they are demi-gods by wearing black clothes. Then she suddenly shouts, "Are you listening? I know! You are thinking how you can work all this into an article!" and Immenso says, "Damn it, I am. Touché."[59]

This is a delightful, realistic portrait of Shaw and Chesterton. Shaw is still convinced in 1921 that there is a historical condition called "Progress" that will solve the riddle of creation, while Chesterton is convinced that the riddle of creation has been solved already by the Incarnation.

In terms of the immediate political situation, it is one of the ironies of history that Chesterton could stomach neither Lloyd George nor his works, because in a number of areas their Liberal and Christian backgrounds made them seek the same goals. For example, Chesterton, too, thought that belief in the League of Nations was ridiculous, but he sided with France against Lloyd George, who wished (*after* he had won the 1918 election by sounding bloody) to keep Germany strong at the expense of new countries like Poland and Czechoslovakia.[60] Lloyd George thought Poland's postwar attacks against both Germany and Russia proved Poland could never be the needed buffer between those big powers; to Chesterton, Poland had an embattled quality of life which, combined with its Catholic mystique and candidacy as a possible "peasant republic," made him love the "idea" of Poland, egged on as he was by Cecil's memory and Ada's strident advocacy.[61] (England's declaring war against Germany in 1939 in the name of Poland's territorial integrity would have seemed to him a typically paradoxical twist of fate — as well as the right thing to do.)

During this period there were many strikes and a rising jobless rate as England's postwar industrial base lagged in productivity and lost its international markets, and agricultural prices slumped. Chesterton would have approved of Lloyd George's real effort to begin "distributism" with a scheme for land redistribution (which his Cabinet thought too costly). But Chesterton was against the government's putting down the unions, which were a major support of the Labour Party. He would have been completely against the agreement among major labor leaders that the mines and the railways, taken over by the state during the war, should remain "nationalized" — though, again, not precisely for Lloyd George's reasons. Lloyd George said there was no proof miners would work harder for the government than they did for the owners, that it was all a ploy to give control of the mines to the union leaders; Chesterton would have been quite willing to try that.[62]

But Chesterton would not have wished Lloyd George to build a new Centre Party (beginning with himself and Winston Churchill and including useful Conservatives and Liberals, all of them united against the Bolsheviks) because he did not trust the man himself, nor did he want to see the death of the Liberal Party itself. Since the independent Liberals and Lloyd George's group failed to agree, in by-election after by-election Liberal was fighting Liberal, and often, as a result, a Conservative or a Labourite won.[63]

Then in 1922 Lloyd George took two Gladstonian positions: he set up the Irish Free State, with Ulster left a part of England, thus "solving" the issue of Home Rule; and he tried to stop the Turks from taking Constantinople. The Conservatives were so angry at his Irish solution that they refused to stay in his coalition government, forcing a General Election, and no one in England wanted war over a principle. Although no one in England really expected this result, the fact is that when Lloyd George failed to win the 1922 election, the Liberal Party itself never held office again.[64]

There was also a recognizable relationship between this approaching "death" of Liberal England and the "death" of the free press.[65] Writers like Gardiner, Massingham, and Masterman, no longer close friends with power, now like Chesterton, reflected more upon public opinion instead of guiding it. By 1923, on the new Fleet Street of the mass-produced papers of the trust press-lords like Beaverbrook, Chesterton was the only "free" Liberal editor left at large; in some ways he was the only Liberal left. Masterman, for example, still liked holding office. Finally, admitting he felt like Cardinal Newman before joining the Church of Rome, he agreed to run for Labour in 1923. The party won, and he held office in the first short-lived Labour government — but he did not like working with them, and he could not accept the Russian totalitarian state, so he spent the rest of his life (four years) on the verge of a nervous breakdown.[66] Haldane, on the other hand, "a Liberal with vaguely Collectivist principles," found it easier to be a "vague Collectivist with Liberal ideals." But Haldane was no more a real Socialist than Masterman or Gardiner, nor were they by any stretch of the imagination Bolshevist. It was not Chesterton alone who found his "party" had left him.[67]

In February 1922 Chesterton published a group of notes and articles about eugenics which he had written before the war. The book was called *Eugenics and Other Evils* and structurally resembled his earlier sociological study, *What's Wrong With the World*. In the preface to the reader he explains that there was a time when this theme was the topic of the hour, but that changed:

> Then the war came and he thought no Englishman would ever again go nosing around the stinks of that low laboratory. . . . [But] it has gradually grown apparent that the ruling class in England was still proceeding on the assumption that Prussia is a pattern for the whole world . . . [though] they can offer us nothing but the same stuffy science, the same bullying bureaucrats and the same terrorism by tenth-rate professors that have led the German Empire to its recent conspicuous triumph.[68]

With these accusations Chesterton was tackling head on one of the most "respectable" scientific ideas of the twentieth century: to improve the human race by selective breeding, preventing anyone who was a less-than-perfect physical or mental specimen from reproducing. Originally formulated by Francis Galton, this evolutionary theory became widely accepted during the hysterical stir created when the urban slum boys turned out to be unfit for the army during the Boer War, whereas the upper classes, in better shape, had a far lower birth rate.[69] English writers and scientists began to suggest forcible sterilization, segregation, and the removal of "imbecilic" children from their parents, while they opposed welfare legislation because it did not encourage the survival of the fittest.

Under Cecil Chesterton, the *New Witness* had been loud in its protests, almost a lone voice crying in the wilderness against this inhumanity of man to man, although the Roman Catholic Church was also publicly opposed to all such "final solutions." Now in the postwar world Chesterton was one of the most outspoken opponents of the kind of attitude which produced Huxley's *Brave New World.*

As usual, Chesterton pushed his argument to an absurd extreme by means of very graphic stories, such as "The True History of a Tramp," a tale of homeless men who slept by the Thames and were arrested for having no beds. He was trying to show his fellow intellectuals that they were only serving the cause of the employer, who, having created the unemployables in the slums, wanted a good excuse to get rid of them. Even more appalling to Chesterton was the fact that "Liberals" had adopted the ideas, betraying individual human rights in the impersonal name of "humanity"; as he put it, "It does not send food into the house to feed the children; it only sends an inspector into the house to punish the parents for having no food to feed them."[70] Before the war he had denounced the Mental Deficiency Act, which allowed feeble-minded children to be locked up for life on the signature of two doctors; now he demonstrated that the definition of feeble-mindedness was so vague that it could apply to anyone. (This theme reappears in his novel *The Return of Don Quixote*, which he began in the pre-war period.) He thought the concept was much like prohibition in America — a legalized method of depriving the poor of something that the rich had without question.

One amusing chapter in his book, called "The End of the Household Gods," is built around a London music-hall song: "Father's got the sack from the water-works/For smoking of his old cherry-briar;/... 'Cos he might set the water-works on fire." Chesterton elaborately explains the sociological meaning of each phase of the song under sermon-like headings such as the following:

> I. *Father.* This word is still in use among the more ignorant and ill-paid of the industrial community ... the badge of an old ... convention called the family. ... But it is overlaid with more artificial authorities: the official, the schoolmaster, the policeman, the employer. ...

The book also has an index in which he lists such subject headings as "*Bolshevists*, and proletarian art" (spelled BOSH); "*Delusions*, concrete and otherwise"; and "*Doctors*, limits to their knowledge."[71] One strongly suspects that Chesterton himself made the index, much in the manner of his beloved Dr. Johnson and his dictionary.

That spring of 1922, while Top Meadow was being rebuilt, Chesterton's beloved father became very ill. Mr. Ed had been quietly failing for some time, but since he had always been inclined to fuss about his health, his family had not taken the signs too seriously. Frances and Gilbert did try to visit his parents fairly often, and Ada Chesterton dropped in nearly every weekend, because she had become fast friends with Cecil's mother. Still, they were unprepared for Mr. Ed's sudden death. Chesterton, who since infancy had found illness and death terribly depressing, had adored his father. Now, besides having to cope with his grief, he found he was obliged to be the head of the family and undertake all of its business affairs. His father's funeral was held by one of his Grosjean cousins; then the whole family returned to 11 Warwick Gardens for tea. But neither Gilbert nor his mother did anything about sorting out his father's den, which was left untouched until after his mother's death, filled with the memorabilia of Mr. Ed's hobbies and his two sons' careers.

On top of all this, the Chestertons' lease at Overroads was up in June, so they were obliged to move into Top Meadow before it was completely finished. Frances had been laid up with an attack of arthritis, so poor Chesterton, the most unlikely man to supervise a move, had to get her — bedridden and with a nurse in attendance — and their things from one place to the other.

Throughout this time of trouble Chesterton had been corresponding regularly with both Father Knox and Maurice Baring, wrestling with them and with his own conscience over his decision to join the Roman Catholic Church. By July 1922 he had made his decision. He had hoped that Frances would join him, but so far she did not want to, although she confessed to Father O'Connor that Chesterton's indecision was making him very difficult; no doubt she knew he felt guilty at what seemed to be an act of desertion. He was well aware that his father and mother had not been happy about Cecil's conversion, though his father's death probably lessened his worry over parental approval. But he also realized that such a gesture on his part would receive tremendous publicity, most of it unkind and uncomprehending. Many would insist that he had been a Catholic all along; some would gloat as if he had been saved from infamy; others would act as if he had been sent to perdition.[72] The Roman Catholic press made it sound as if Chesterton had not been a well-known Christian apologist for the past ten or fifteen years.

All of the public noise and confusion made taking the step an even braver act than most people realized, because Chesterton, with a strong sense of mission, was deliberately taking on a role which to many observers seemed wrong. The act itself, then, could destroy the very reason for his gesture, because many would no longer take what he said seriously. When asked why he had converted, he invariably replied, "For my sins," and one of those sins was knowing that what he did had a public effect. To discourage his possible backsliding in the cause he had accepted for Cecil, and to increase his own self-discipline as a soldier, he deliberately chose to act out his conviction about the state of the world. He had made the same kind of gesture as a young man in the early 1900's, but now he saw the necessity of "taking the cross" in such a way that he was "standing up to be counted," assuming the public posture which identified him as a part of a particular community, just as he had suggested Jews be distinguished by distinctive clothes.[73] By joining the Roman Catholic Church, however worldwide its body, Chesterton was becoming the proud, naturalized citizen of an endangered small nation, a nation not highly thought of in England.[74] In this way, Chesterton was also reaffirming his sense of identity with the "secret people." He amiably put up with the fact that the Roman Catholic Church made use of him, taking comfort from also being a part of a special, world wide family.

Just as Belloc had mistakenly thought that Chesterton loved only the "romantic" idea of the Church, so Maisie Ward reported that people were amazed that Chesterton "took the cross" without Frances, because she and Father O'Connor thought he would need Frances to keep him straight about the Church's habits of discipline. They ignored his own testimony that he had sought out that very "iron ring of Catholic responsibilities" as the outward and visible sign of his inner commitment to the "one fighting form of Christianity."[75] In *The Thing* — the book Belloc liked best, and one of his most polemical defenses of Roman Catholicism in England — Chesterton put it this way:

> It is precisely because I do sympathize and agree with my Protestant and agnostic fellow countrymen, on about ninety-nine subjects out of a hundred, that I do feel it a point of honour not to avoid their accusations . . . when . . . my co-religionists are being pelted with insults for saying that their religion is right.[76]

There was yet another aspect to his decision. All his life Chesterton felt he was surrounded by a humanistic, pagan world; it was that very concern that had led him to try to express in his work a belief in an external reality, as well as to insist on the unity of life and art.[77] He saw his role as a writer in terms of the symbol of the bridge-builder, Pontifex, a role played by the poet and the priest, whose obligation is to communicate the divine using "morality, religion, and expression."[78]

The postwar Church of England was being changed by a strong modernist movement. Its great pre-war period of social concern had lost its impetus, like the Liberal Party, and a planned revision of the *Book of Common Prayer*, which was meant to draw together the Anglo-Catholics (with their emphasis on the sacraments) and the ecumenical group, floundered before the "deep-Protestantism and anti-Papal" temper of the ordinary Englishman. Chesterton had recently spoken at an Anglo-Catholic Congress at the Albert

Hall, and he had sensed that the Church's underlying confusion was not resolved by the "mystical" approach of people like Dean Inge and Evelyn Underhill, which lacked rational arguments.

At the same time the Roman Catholic Church in England had developed a "middle class" of its own, educated in its private schools and colleges at Oxford and Cambridge, so that it was beginning to be intellectually and socially "respectable."[79] These circumstances were peculiarly fitted to making the best use of Chesterton's talent for going on the offensive to convince his fellow countrymen that "the modern world, with its modern movements, is living on its Catholic capital."[80] The fact that Chesterton's support of the faith always had a very "Chestertonian flavor" does not minimize the kind of moral support he and Belloc provided, which in turn helped to create the "Catholic literary revival" with writers like Waugh and Greene, as well as the world in which Eliot and Auden flourished.

Chesterton was received into the Roman Catholic Church on Sunday, July 30, 1922. The parish in Beaconsfield was using a dance-room in the Railway Hotel as a chapel; after Gilbert's reception the Chestertons began helping the building campaign for the parish church (where they are buried). Chesterton had called Father O'Connor to Beaconsfield to officiate at the rite, quite possibly because Frances liked him; and he brought along Father Ignatius Rice from Douai. Frances waited outside while they heard Chesterton's confession; then, in her presence, they re-baptized him in accordance with Roman Catholic custom, and left the couple together in the church.[81] Apparently Frances was still weeping when they left, but Chesterton, having taken the plunge, was in childlike high spirits all day.

In his *Autobiography* it is his baptism as an infant that Chesterton mentions, although he describes his conversion in terms of his childhood, in which confession, penance, and absolution "by definition [let] a Catholic step out again into the dawn of his own beginning and look with new eyes across the world to a Crystal Palace that is really of crystal." He felt that his belief had restored his sense of wonder by bringing him back to the "ancient conception of humility and the thanks of the unworthy. . . ."[82] Originally he had seen his father, creator of the toy-theatre world, as Pontifex, but now he saw Christ as the bridge-builder, as well as Claviger, the Bearer of the Key, "which was given to him to bind and loose when he was a poor fisher beside a small and almost secret sea."[83]

Typically, Chesterton *wrote* to his mother to explain his decision, identifying it with Cecil—an accurate association, because it still seems possible he would never have so committed himself if he had not felt he was his brother's keeper. Baring was overjoyed by the news; Belloc had been so disapproving of the whole thing that he tried to stop Father O'Connor from going to Beaconsfield, but after Chesterton's commitment he held his peace.[84] The most offended of Chesterton's old acquaintances was Shaw, who was apparently dreadfully upset by Chesterton's decision because he had thought he and Chesterton shared basic religious assumptions. He wrote bitterly to him, "This is going too far. I am an Irishman and I know . . . your ideal Church does not exist and never can exist within the official organization. . . . I find the spectacle [of] . . . the [confession] box, your portly kneeling figure . . . incredible, monstrous, comic."[85]

Chesterton took Shaw's attack in his usual good-natured way; after all, he had expected this kind of attitude, and he understood Shaw's own Irish roots so well that he could also understand this antipathy. But Shaw apparently had brooded about Chesterton's defection so much that, the following year, when they met at a friend's house one night, they actually got into a row — and their exchanges were taken down in shorthand by Shaw's future biographer.

Shaw lost his temper and demanded to know if Chesterton was drunk. Although visibly taken aback at the nastiness of Shaw's tone, Chesterton responded jokingly, but Shaw ignored him, launching into a full-scale diatribe against Chesterton's entire career, questioning his motives and blaming him for being influenced by Belloc, who "turned your pranks into prayers, your somersaults into sacraments, [so] you turn and rend the Eugenics, whose sole crime is that they prefer healthy babies. . . . You fell . . . upon the Jews. . . ." Apparently even Shaw now began to hear what he was saying and, calming down a bit, added, "And yet we all know perfectly well that you aren't half as bad as you paint yourself." Chesterton retaliated by saying that only a Puritan would think that a compliment! Their debate continued for some time, but most people there felt that, of the two, Chesterton was more constructive, honestly trying to help Shaw see why he had acted as he did, while Shaw went on attacking the Church. In the end Shaw said, "I see. Heads you win, tails he loses, all the way," and Chesterton replied with a chuckle, "Precisely."[86]

In September 1922 the collecton of Chesterton's articles about his trip to the United States, called *What I Saw in America*, was published. In it he reiterated his basic conviction that the first thing any normal traveler thinks when he visits a foreign land is how "grotesquely different" foreigners are, and insisted that the "first principle is that nobody should be ashamed of thinking a thing funny because it is foreign; the second is that he should be ashamed of thinking it wrong because it is funny."[87] He made fun of the idea that modern communications were bringing nations closer together, reminding his readers that most bitterly fought wars had been between little nations that lived too close for comfort. He felt that international friendship could only flourish if individual countries recognized and respected each other's differences, or, as he said in the sharp poem from his "Songs of Education," written for the *New Witness*:

> The earth is a place on which England is found,
> And you find it however you twirl the globe round;
> For the spots are all red and the rest is all grey;
> And that is the meaning of Empire Day.[88]

That October *The Ballad of St. Barbara* was published; it was a collection of poems, most of which Chesterton had written during the war. The book, dedicated to Frances, is named after a poem about the Flanders fields and the patron saint of the artillery. This poem pictures Rome as the defender of Christendom over the ages against the barbarian. The collection also includes his poem about Poland, which talks about the "eagles that were double-faced . . ./And in their track the vultures come," and a poem about London that predicts postwar Luddite riots in which "London Bridge is broken down, broken down/. . . a flying dream of thunder-light/Had shown beneath the shattered sky a people that were free."[89]

Generally Chesterton expresses bitter concern over the failure of England's rulers to live up to the effort made by her soldiers, a completely appropriate theme for someone of the "older" generation unable to respect the "men in charge." The bitterest poem of all is his "Elegy in a Country Churchyard," in which he says, "They that fought for England. . . . They have their graves afar./And they that rule in England,/In stately conclave met,/Alas, alas for England/They have no graves as yet."[90]

The Ballad of St. Barbara came out two days after Lloyd George's coalition government fell from power, temporarily destroying the chances of his "co-conspirators" Isaacs and Samuel to keep high offices, but Chesterton, of course, did not agree that "thus ended the reign of the great ones, the giants of the Edwardian era and of the war; and the rule of the pygmies . . . began, to continue until 1940."[91] That opinion, widely held, came from outspoken Winston Churchill, who not only was one of Lloyd George's cronies, but also tried to be both Gladstone and Joe Chamberlain, deserting party and friends repeatedly.

Chesterton's views on post-Marconi politics were illustrated in his next book, *The Man Who Knew Too Much.* Although it has been called the first of his "distributist" novels, it is really Belloc's *The Party System* dramatized. As is true for each of his later books, "novel" is something of a misnomer — the book is a collection of interlocking stories with one protagonist, like the Father Brown series. The hero of the stories is Horne Fisher (the man who knew too much), who is related by blood or marriage to everyone else in the Establishment. The structural element threading through all the stories is the political education of young Harold March, who observes the fortunes of Horne Fisher and draws his own radical conclusions. The protagonist is starkly realistic, complicated and well-rounded. The suggestion that he is meant to be a portrait of Maurice Baring is very unlikely, because they really had only one thing in common: they both had Establishment backgrounds that they would be unable to betray.[92]

Fisher knows it does not matter who wins elections — the same inner circle always rules — so when he wins, he resigns without taking his seat and wears a special costume of sackcloth and ashes to dramatize his dilemma.

A member of the ruling elite, he despises it but cannot betray it, although it betrays him in a "medieval" way, making him the sacrificial scapegoat who pays for the sins of his class. His young disciple March concludes that "it might do no harm if he blew the whole tangle of this society to hell with dynamite," and goes off to join the revolution.

Then, in an odd twist, Fisher's solid family of scoundrels begins to carry out reforms, suggesting that revolution is often brought about by those who dread it most — rather like Chesterton's view of the French Revolution.[93] Fisher was disillusioned when he realized that he could not bring any crimes home to the criminals because they were too highly placed to be punished, but in the end the local squire and the local doctor — the squirearchy — show a genuine concern for their own people. The doctor actually believes what the peasants say, asking the others, " 'Could you not have trusted a little these peasants whom you trust so much. . . . Have you ever thought what all the work of the world would be like if the poor were so senseless as you think them?' " The squire answers, " 'In many ways they are our betters, but I still could not accept anything in their evidence.' " They see the doctor's rather "sinister smile" for the last time: " 'Quite so,' he said, 'but you would have hanged me on their evidence.' "[94]

This quotation alone shows that this book — written in the year of Chesterton's conversion — has to do with religion. Belief is always a religious topic for Chesterton; here it is his ethical attitude toward economic and political reality that is important to him and to his reader. Horne Fisher is actually a kind of political counterpart of Father Brown who shares his essential secret: he understands sin because he is himself a sinner.[95] The final note struck by the book is not the hopeless pessimism of someone who sees himself doomed to be a prophet without honor, but far closer to a suggestion not to sell the common people short, an idea that ties in with the political change that put Lloyd George out of work and gave the government over to "pygmies."

The same tone of serious realism appears in the collection of *New Witness* essays called *Fancies Versus Fads*, which was published on September 6, 1923. A characteristic essay is the famous one on "Milton and Merrie England," in which Chesterton maintains that Milton, far from being a proper Puritan, was an artist whose greatness "is in a style . . . [which] is usually separated from its substance." *Paradise Lost* may be a religious poem, but one which "can hardly justify the ways of God to men . . . when its most frequent effect is . . . to make people sympathize with Satan."[96] Chesterton points out that very few people today sit down to read Milton "in a direct devotional spirit," the way in which they still read his less well-known contemporaries like Herbert, Herrick, and Traherne. From there he discusses English literature, illustrating his historical theory that "it was the political triumph of the Party [of Cromwell] . . . that suppressed the testimony of the populace and the poets. . . . English history has moved away from English literature. . . . And it is for the sake of English literature that I protest against the suggestion that we had no purity except Puritanism, or that only a man like the author of *Paradise Lost* could manage to be on the side of the angels."[97] In essence, he was calling Milton one of the clerks who divided poetry from popular language.[98]

One month later, in October 1923, Chesterton published one of his enduringly popular books, the story of one of his boyhood heroes, Saint Francis of Assisi. Like Chesterton's other biographical studies, the book is short on dates and long on understanding. Written for the People's Library, it gave him a delightful chance to reconsider someone dear to him in the light of his adult Christian convictions:

> . . . [Though] long ago in those days of boyhood my fancy first caught fire with the glory of Francis of Assisi . . . at no stage of my pilgrimage has he ever seemed to me a stranger . . . [but] the problem of St. Francis was that Francis could be described as the world's one quite sincere democrat . . . or not only as a human but a humanitarian hero . . . without raising any religious question at all. . . . [Or one could] stamp the whole history with the Stigmata . . . 'til in the modern mind St. Francis is as dark a figure as St. Dominic. . . ."[99]

Chesterton proposed to "put myself in the position of the ordinary modern outsider and inquirer . . . by approaching the great saint's story through what is . . . picturesque and popular . . . [to] leave the reader the consistency of a complete character."[100] Being Chesterton, he then sets Saint Francis clearly in the context of his own town and time, making him the symbol of the sunrise that ended the "fast and vigil" of the Dark Ages. He also insisted that Saint Francis is first of all a poet ". . . [who] clearly chose to be a fool for Christ."[101]

His own "medieval" term for Saint Francis is one he borrows from the saint: a troubadour or "jongleur de Dieu," who performs a kind of acting-out of the romance of courtly love. Saint Francis was a living version of the acted-out parable which Chesterton himself recognized as one of the great teaching methods, one he had just deliberately performed himself. Chesterton loved Saint Francis for personifying the thankfulness we feel for "the towering miracle of the mere fact of existence if we realize that but for some strange mercy we should not even exist."[102] These ideas reveal that Chesterton was about to go out to tilt at the world's windmills again, as well as at the men who thought they made both windmills and wind. He was to become "the Charlie Chaplin of theology and the Walt Disney of the religious parable."[103]

But, though Chesterton appreciates Saint Francis, he identifies Cecil, not himself, as his disciple. Cecil was always the active one who, in Chesterton's terms, might also have been said to have "walked the world like the Pardon of God," seeing "all the stale paganism that had poisoned the ancient world . . . worked out of its social system."[104] Not only was it Saint Francis' purpose to "tell men to start afresh and . . . turn over a new page . . . it was clearly part of that particular childlike cheerfulness that [he] should paste down the old page that was all black and bloody. . . . The coming of St. Francis was like the birth of a child in a dark house, lifting its doom. . . ." This comparison is clearly a reference to his brother.[105]

In a letter he wrote to Bentley when there was a death in his family, Chesterton had made it plain that these old events in his own family *always* affected him strongly. He wrote:

> . . . I think of you even in the ordinary way far more often than any stranger would believe possible, considering how our work keeps us apart, therefore, how much I am thinking of you now. It resurrects all our past in a way quite undescribable; away back to the time I knew you first, and away even beyond that, to the time when my own childhood was in a kind of shadow, from the loss of my little sister. . . .[106]

This statement plainly reaffirms Cecil's role in his life.

Meanwhile, during 1923 Lloyd George, still an M.P. but out of office, had made a very lucrative deal with one of the syndicated press associations for a column; it was published worldwide and netted him 30,000 pounds the first year.[107] Since he was also sued for breach of contract for writing his *Memoirs*, other journalists like Chesterton must have been well aware of the fact that Lloyd George was getting rich at the expense of them and their party. This fact became particularly bitter because, during May 1923, the *New Witness* failed, while Stanley Baldwin, the epitome of the ordinary man, now succeeded Bonar Law as Conservative prime minister. Chesterton, driven by his feeling that he must keep a paper going in Cecil's name (assisted by Ada, who had been working for him without pay), kept on a skeleton staff and paid the office rent while he considered what to do. He also tried to raise money to help the paper along, using his share of his father's estate.

Everyone was full of advice, much of it conflicting, although the general idea was that he develop a new paper that would be more "general and literary" than Cecil's sheet, making all the use it could of Chesterton's continuing popularity as a writer. Shaw suggested that he simply call such a paper "Chesterton's," an idea Chesterton found terribly egotistical, but he could see the sense of Shaw's other suggestion that he imitate Dickens' *Household Words*, providing a little bit of something for everyone. Shaw also made the crack that he supposed Chesterton would have to stand for some sort of policy, although such papers were only read by their "constituents" — but otherwise to get a readership Chesterton would have to write a new "Father Brown" every week. When the new paper finally began publication, that was what Chesterton did: he wrote a Father Brown story whenever they needed money. In the interim period when Chesterton had no paper to edit, Frances was very happy: she liked to have him at home in Beaconsfield, writing books, finding time to play with their many nieces and nephews, adopted and otherwise, who came to stay, and joining in the social life of Beaconsfield itself. Frances probably hoped that her husband would never find enough financial support to resume publication.

Politically, England had come to a strange new crossroads in her history. In December 1923 a General Election was held to settle the old issue of free trade, which was still a rallying cry that united Lloyd George's National Liberals and Asquith's Independents. The problem was a depressed economy, a society in which there were 13,000,000 unemployed. The election was a strange "draw." The Conservatives had lost their majority, and Labour, running hard in an effort to become the true opposition party, was next, leaving the Liberals in the middle, holding the balance of power. They were divided over whether to help the Conservatives form a government and then vote them out, or support Labour and do the same, but Lloyd George pushed for supporting Labour. As a result, on January 21, 1924, England had her first Labour government in which Liberals like Masterman and Haldane took posts, while in the background the Liberal leaders fought over how to reform their party.[108] But when Labour "recognized" the Soviet Union and had to call another election in 1924, the Liberals' disunity gave the Conservatives power until 1929.

Chapter Fourteen

THE RETURN OF DON QUIXOTE
1925-1928

We alone . . . are likely to insist . . . the average respectable citizen ought to have something to rule. . . . We alone . . . have the right to call ourselves democratic. . . . It is . . . with a somewhat sad amusement that I note the soaring visions that accompany sinking wages. . . . I am quite content to dream of the old drudgery of democracy, in which as much as possible of a human life should be given to every human being. . . . And indeed I do believe that when [men] lose the pride of personal ownership they will lose something that belongs to their erect posture and to their footing and poise upon the planet. . . .

G.K. Chesterton, *The Outline of Sanity*[1]

The Daily Mail cannot really try to destroy Trusts; for it is . . . part of a Trust. The Daily Herald cannot really try to defeat Bolshevism, for its most sincere backing is among Bolshevists. . . . But for me there is a third course: and no other paper will defend or even discuss it.

This . . . has been called "Distributism," signifying that it hopes to distribute private property more equally. But if I were to call this paper "The Distributist Review" . . . it would . . . suggest a Distributist is something like a Socialist, a crank, a pedant, a person with a new theory of human nature. It is my whole point that my solution is simply human, and it is the other solutions that are dehumanized. It is my whole point that to say we must have Socialism or Capitalism is like saying we must choose between all men going into monasteries and a few men having harems. . . . Any title defining our doctrine makes it look doctrinaire. . . . At the same time I want a title that does suggest that the paper is controversial . . . that will be recognized as a flag . . . and the nearest I can get to a symbol is to . . . fly my own colours.

G.K. Chesterton, "Apologia," *G.K.'s Weekly*, November 8, 1924[2]

IN his *Autobiography* Chesterton was to comment that he had "always suffered from the disadvantage . . . of not altering my opinions fast enough. . . . Obstinacy of this sort . . . has all sorts of disadvantages in dividing an individual from his contemporaries."[3] His point was clear by 1925 when Stanley Baldwin, the "plain man" of politics, took over the government again with a large Conservative majority and a Cabinet filled with members of the old-boy network who had all turned their political coats several times.[4] Baldwin had one major aim: to prevent Labour and the Liberals from uniting and, if possible, to get rid of Lloyd George. Chesterton's loyalty to the Liberal Party had to be more philosophical than pragmatic, but loyal he remained. At the same time, Chesterton's preference for ordinary people made him agree with the English, who liked Baldwin for his pedestrian manner, and he, like Baldwin, had no desire for Liberals to join Labour.

By now Chesterton was also facing the literary generation gap created by the war. The younger "intellectuals" who had not actually fought were disenchanted with the peace, partly because they had veterans for teachers and partly because of "war literature" like the poems of Siegfried Sassoon, Wilfred Owen, and Robert Graves. As the decade went on, their feelings were expressed by books like Aldous Huxley's *Point Counter Point*, Evelyn Waugh's *Decline and Fall*, Virginia Woolf's *Mrs. Dalloway*, Hemingway's *A Farewell to Arms*, and Remarque's *All Quiet on the Western Front*. T. S. Eliot's *The Waste Land* became their Bible.[5]

Chesterton could recognize Eliot's "world picture": it was another form of the decadence and despair he had fought before in the fin de siècle mentality at the Slade. *The Waste Land* conveyed the hopelessness of an intellectual community with no sense of comradeship, each individual member being grimly determined to establish his own private world. Because this mood prevailed, the old politicians were being allowed to run things as they liked while the young licked their private wounds, the kind of situation that Chesterton always protested against.[6] Unfortunately, his contact with "intellectual" audiences was hindered by current politics. The old party system was ruling, while the "counter-elite" was gaining power as its ranks swelled with the children of the Fabian nursery and the Bloomsbury group. Young, impressionable Stephen Spender put it this way:

> There was an underlying left-wing orthodoxy of the writers, which went back to the end of the First World War and . . . earlier . . . to the Fabian Society. . . . Their Socialism was based on hatred for members of an older generation conservative or liberal . . . [who had] sent young men out to war

... on sympathy with men in the ranks ... on admiration for revolutionary movements ... pacifism, political and sexual, resentment at the attempt of the Conservatives [to] crush the Russian Revolution and ... dislike of the British Empire.[7]

According to Spender, there was no "orthodoxy of the Right." He accepted Pound, Yeats, and Eliot, but labeled them "conservative" spokesmen because they looked back to the classical tradition of Europe with a view Spender called "medievalist and romantic," not for any connection with Stanley Baldwin's party.

Young Spender was a lemming, always in the swim of intellectual fashion, but his brighter contemporaries like Auden were also "heretics" by Chestertonian definition: humorless, hooked on single ideas, fanatical, now private but soon to become passionately public in their concerns. Graham Greene, a part of that generation "saved" by Chesterton, later remarked how ironic it was that a generation hung up on the puns of James Joyce objected to Chesterton's style; the fact was they did so because their parents had read him. But he went on to declare that Chesterton was "too good a man for politics. ... He saw things in absolute terms of good and evil [while] he succeeded as a religious one, for religion is simple."[8] This kind of summing up puts Greene himself in the position of an elitist or a "Titanist" who, like Eliot later, champions the clerks against the commoners.[9]

During the later twenties, Chesterton did try to speak to this younger "elite" and had some success, although by and large his new audience was the rather clannish Roman Catholics, whose very support made him anathema to "Protestant," "Puritan," and "Pagan." By invitation he ran three times for the honorary position of head of a major university. He lost all three elections, but gained a hearing for his definition of liberalism because it was under that party label that he ran.

His first campaign was at Glasgow University in 1925. There he told the students,

> England had taken refuge in Utopia after Utopia of ever-mounting insanity, believing a world in which all labor and sorrow had vanished, with reforms by which every man could live to be three hundred years old. ... And now, after a century of such nonsense, we stand where we did. ... Whatever may have happened to the Liberal idea, what ... happened to the Liberal Party was that it ... failed to be itself.[10]

The Glasgow students, however, defeated Chesterton and elected Sir Austen Chamberlain, despite the fact that both Bentley and Ada Chesterton came to campaign for Chesterton; Ada said he lost because the women students resented his attitude about women's right to vote. In 1928 he lost to Winston Churchill at Edinburgh University, and he lost a third time at Aberdeen, though in that three-way race he still beat out Aldous Huxley.[11]

About the only recourse that Chesterton had was to "refound" his own paper as a place where he and like-minded friends could comment on the contemporary scene. *G.K.'s Weekly* finally did appear officially on March 21, 1925. It certainly was his weekly: he wrote a large part of it, signed and unsigned, and supported it the rest of his life. The paper sold for sixpence, and for the first few issues had Chesterton's picture on it, but he then quietly insisted that it be dropped.[12] Although a fairly large number of people have felt that *G.K.'s Weekly* contained pieces inferior to Chesterton's early writing and also kept him from writing more books of monumental stature, others, like Bentley, realized that to be editor was Chesterton's choice, and that the job kept him from being accused of "stagnating in a backwater."[13]

For the first issue of *G.K.'s Weekly* Chesterton wrote the lead article on the front page. Called "The First Principle," the article began with this explanation:

> This single adventure in weekly journalism cannot compete with our wealthy and world-wide press in resources and reports. [But] it exists to demand that we fight Bolshevism with something better than plutocracy. . . . The thing behind Bolshevism . . . is a new doubt . . . not merely a doubt about God, it is rather specially a doubt about man. The old morality, the Christian religion . . . really believed in the rights of man. . . . These [new] sages cannot trust the normal man to rule in the home; and most certainly do not want him to rule in the State. . . . They are not willing to give him a house, or a wife or a child or a dog, or a cow or a piece of land; because these things really do give him power. . . . We are far from denying . . . that there is much to be said on the other side. . . . Nearly everything that is said is said on the other side. We alone have the right to call ourselves democratic. That is what we think; and Bolshevism and Capitalism are absolutely at one in thinking the opposite. . . . We at least have seen sanity, if only in a vision, while they go forward chained eternally to enlargement without liberty and progress without hope.[14]

The remainder of that first issue had "Notes of the Week" (by Chesterton); "Why Wembly was Wobbly, Answers to the Poets" (by Chesterton); some poems, including one by Belloc; a "Report on Parliament from Within"; a story by Walter de la Mare; a column called "The Drama" by J.K. Prothero (Ada Chesterton); and reviews of current books. This issue was very much like all the others that appeared over the next eleven years, except for the fact that, by about 1926, there began to be more articles on "distributism" by people involved with it — G.C. Heseltine, Gregory Macdonald, and Maurice Reckitt.

Ada Chesterton was one of her brother-in-law's greatest problems. At this time she was neither a Roman Catholic (as many of his contributors tended to be), nor, by her definition, a Distributist; if anything, she seems to have been somewhat "Left." As a working companion she was, unfortunately, a born troublemaker. Since Chesterton planned to run the paper from Beaconsfield because he couldn't be in London on a regular basis, he could not have her fluttering the dovecote. It must have taken incredible courage for him to summon Ada to Beaconsfield and tell her gently that "one Chesterton was enough"; inevitably she took it badly, assuming that Chesterton was jealous of the memory of Cecil, of whose viewpoint she was sole high priestess. She did continue to write for the paper, largely about drama, maintaining to her dying day that Cecil had been the "greater brother" and never realizing that Chesterton completely agreed with her.

Fortunately, not too long after *G.K.'s Weekly* began, Ada started on a new project that was perfectly suited to her dramatic temperament. She made a bet with an editor that she could spend two weeks in London with no money and no place to live, and offered to write articles about her experience. She won the bet. Her articles were very effective (and later published in a book called *In Darkest London*). Bishops preached sermons about the problem of homeless women, and Queen Mary sent a check that helped to start an organization which set up hostels called "Cecil Houses," where any woman could have free room and board, no questions asked. Oddly enough, she was very surprised that Chesterton was sympathetic and ready to make large contributions to her project, and that Frances wrote a laudatory review of her book for *G.K.'s Weekly.* [15]

Chesterton, meanwhile, was faced with difficulties at his paper. Shaw claimed that Chesterton had "sold himself into slavery" because he drew a salary of only five hundred pounds a year, and did most of the writing and worked to get his other friends to contribute. Others shared his opinion, from Baring—who finally refused to be on the board, having neither the money nor the time for it—to H. G. Wells, Walter de la Mare, and many others. The only substantial donors to the paper were Lord Howard de Walden and Chesterton himself.

They started off with a staff of three: Chesterton; Bunny, Ada's protégée; and poor Gander, the business manager, whose job was hopeless. Chesterton soon called for Titterton, telling him he thought "there was a screw missing somewhere . . . probably in my own head. . . . A sub-editor might tighten it." Titterton, aware of all the work Chesterton was doing single-handedly, and fascinated by the "new" causes of distributism and Roman Catholicism, agreed to return for a tiny salary, much to Chesterton's joy. [16] Actually, neither Titterton nor Bunny proved to be much good at running the paper economically, but they had a good time together, and they provided a contrast to the more fanatical types who also wrote for the paper. One of these was the art editor, Eric Gill, a Roman Catholic convert cum radical, who insisted Chesterton must "accept my doctrine as the doctrine of *G.K.'s Weekly* — in matters of art as I do yours in other matters. . . . Have I not put almost my last quid into your blooming Company?" [17] (Gill soon moved near Beaconsfield. He was famous for his Giotto-like sculpture, and later created the Chestertons' monument, with its look of a medieval wayside shrine. He had been greatly intrigued by cooperative living communities specializing in small crafts, and was also an ardent student of Saint Thomas Aquinas.) This was the motley troop that Chesterton, who "didn't give a button for fame . . . regarded as a . . . very small army . . . fighting in a very big cause,"[18]

The arguments for and against the literary merit of *G.K.'s Weekly* usually end in agreement or refusal to appreciate Chesterton's sanity, his instinctive desire for mental balance that led him to counter the most heated and popular arguments. He chose the comic role of the clown rather than the superior stance of clerk; it was the best way he knew of to communicate, which was his primary function as journalist.[19]

What is truly amazing is that the paper survived both its publication and the weekly board meetings held to maintain it. When everyone had arrived, the office seemed too small for the meeting. Chesterton chewed on a cheroot and doodled on a pad of blotting paper, while everyone else attacked each other. Bunny took notes, Titterton sat ready to do battle, and the mayor of Bath and old Gander, both deaf as posts, sat silently. Lord Howard's solicitor was businesslike, and young Maurice Reckitt played at being a young man about town. Occasionally, Frances came to these odd affairs, and once she asked if the paper must be kept going at any cost, whereupon Chesterton told her that it must. Usually, however, various people said things could not go on like this, with Mr. Chesterton doing all the work, and Chesterton would stop doodling to reply in all honesty, "God knows, I'm the worst editor in the world," clearly meaning it. Then the paper would be "buried in state" by the Board — but would survive until the next time.[20]

Meanwhile, during June 1925, Chesterton also published an amusing collection of short stories, loosely connected by theme and characters, called *Tales of the Long Bow.* (The long bow is traditionally the weapon of the sturdy English yeoman, fighting for his home.) The book is another of Chesterton's so-called "distributist" novels, the first being *The Man Who Knew Too Much.* These tales are a story about a Distributist agrarian revolution, published just when Lloyd George was trying to revitalize the Liberal Party with a new scheme for land distribution that was really land nationalization.[21]

Chesterton himself is once again present as the genial narrator-author, a role in which he tightens the structure of the book while he makes friends with his reader. Given to self-mockery, he says things like, "The foolish scribe of the Long Bow will not commit the last folly of defending his dreams."[22] He even mocks his own allegorical style, gleefully pointing out to the reader a place where "a symbolic cloud ought to have come across the sun." The adventures which unite the leaders all represent trite old

English sayings, such as "Eat your hat," "Set the Thames on fire," and "When pigs have wings," and therefore, says the narrator, these stories have a strictly English application.[23]

The agrarian revolution is carried out by a "new" peasantry who "carried their medieval symbolism so far as to wear Lincoln green." They defeat the enemy by a kind of Gilbert-and-Sullivan version of Macbeth's Birnam Woods, a forest that springs up like a catapult (the long bows). The dénouement is not described directly, but told to the reader and the other characters by the protagonist, who is the group historian, Robin Hood. The real charm of these stories is not so much political as domestic. Each hero is an English gentleman and eccentric who unselfconsciously embarks on a quest and in the process finds and wins his lady love. The book ends with a house party reminiscent of those given at Top Meadow, where the hostess tells her husband, the historian, " 'Do come out of that book. . . . One of our visitors has just arrived.' "[24]

This middle-class atmosphere has upset those who think it indicates that Chesterton has become typically class-conscious. Except for a brash American millionaire (modeled after Henry Ford, whom Chesterton never met), all of his heroes are gentlemen: an ex-army officer, a don, a Church-of-England clergyman. The women, too, come from traditional backgrounds, and include an emancipated young Fabian, a lady, and an innkeeper's daughter. The opponents of the league are the English Establishment crossed with the plutocracy: Lord Northtowers (Northcliffe); Lord Eden, the prime minister (who will reappear in the industrial book); and a rich Jew interested in politics.[25] They are supported by a Chestertonian army of imported Chinese coolies, reminiscent of Lord Ivywood's Eastern mercenaries in *The Flying Inn.*

If this is a "class-conscious" novel, the reason is probably found in Chesterton's origins in the Liberal Party, with its ideal of an England in which everyone is his own master in a strictly middle-class sense. Its ideal had always been to "raise" everybody to the same level, not to create a classless society, or to perpetuate a society of "haves" and "have-nots" with the gulf between them that so upset the true Liberals — even Lloyd George. As the novel suggests, "These new peasant farmers must be treated like small squires and not like tenants or serfs."[26]

Ultimately, Chesterton's concern with practical politics and with Christianity meant that he stood for a Christian society in which the split between "town and gown" (clerks and the people), which had been growing greater since the Reformation, met in what has been called "the centre of hilarity" — that is, the "real" world. To him the Liberal creed did not favor pitting one class against another in practical, intellectual, or religious terms.[27] His ideal society in this novel is similar to the "co-inherence" of a Charles Williams, except that Williams had a greater love for a rigorously articulated hierarchy than Chesterton did, and Chesterton, as artist, had specifically defined his own task as that of communicating to and about the vulgar culture.[28]

At the same time, however, Chesterton's philosophical concerns are rooted in contemporary reality. Lloyd George's "Liberal" scheme for nationalizing the land, making the government the national "renter" and arbiter of agriculture, was real, as was the fact that by the end of the twenties the Conservative government had begun direct agricultural subsidies and quota systems that again made farming an attractive occupation.[29] It was therefore perfectly natural for Chesterton to feel that an eccentric American millionaire, "converted" to private property, might bankroll such a transformation with less arrogance than a government of Big Brothers.

Considering the fact that he was also continuing his day-to-day struggle to keep *G.K.'s Weekly* alive and well, Chesterton was "amazingly productive" during this period, belying the often repeated judgment that his creative life was best during the pre-Marconi times, and that he had already produced his best work by 1913. The basic disagreement on this point lies beneath the surface: on the one hand, it is related to the easy dismissal of him as an artist after he had joined the Roman Catholic Church; on the other, it reflects his loss of popularity among the postwar intelligentsia who were leaning toward the left.[30]

His next major work, *The Everlasting Man*, is both an explanation and an answer to these accusations. Unlike *Orthodoxy*, an earlier piece of "apologetics," it did poorly both in reviews and in sales.[31] Some critics insist that Chesterton's discussion is not scientific enough, an accusation that he would have taken as a compliment, judging from his introduction: there he reiterates his great admiration for Wells' monumental *Outline of History*, and claims Wells' privilege for himself—that of depending on those who are more learned, as well as the "reasonable right of the amateur to do what he can with the facts which the specialists provide."[32] But, in the ongoing paradox of Chesterton's fame and career, criticism of the book has been balanced by praise: it has also been hailed as one of his masterpieces.[33]

The Everlasting Man was published on September 30, 1925. Like most of Chesterton's "sociological" books, this was written as part of a public debate that had originally begun between Wells and Belloc over Wells' *Outline of History*. Belloc had attacked Wells' concept of man's history as a progress from slime to a world state, as well as his curious organization of historical periods, which made both Greece and Rome—because they were early civilizations—unimportant.[34] Not surprisingly, Wells had reserved his nastiest verbal attacks for the Roman Catholic Church. He had always hated Catholicism, but in the postwar world he was especially irritated because the Church had publicly scolded him for practicing "free love." Wells, of course, was once again writing his "secular" story of salvation by history, in which man evolved from the single cell to the moderns, who were to produce the millennium he was still searching for. He was also trying to win himself a "professorship" among the intellectuals, but his book was primarily a popular success.[35]

Chesterton, in turn, chose to write a "sacred" version of the odyssey, not his own (which he wrote about in *Orthodoxy*), but that of the human race. *The Everlasting Man* is divided into two parts. The story of mankind comes first; then, instead of following a course of "steady evolution," history divides in two at Christ's coming: "Right in the middle of all these things stands up an enormous exception ... nothing less than the loud assertion that this mysterious maker of the world has visited his world in person."[36] The second half of the book, therefore, is another of Chesterton's "biographical studies" which concentrate on the philosophical issues of a particular man's life. The scope and range of his criticism are balanced here, as always; his debater's shots, exchanged with Wells, are offset by his "comic" style. But essentially the second half is Chesterton's *Life of Christ and His Church*.

In *The Everlasting Man*, Chesterton's style comes into its own, with masterful analogies, ingenious paradoxes, and epigrams beyond the wildest dreams of his adolescent bête noir, Oscar Wilde. He cheerily explains the world to the world, talking about myth, religion, rite, story, and salvation, and discusses the differences between human affection, the love of the giraffes, and the river romances of the hippopotami. Although he adopted this jesting tone, Chesterton, like Wells, was making a huge effort to catch the attention not only of his beloved ordinary reader but also of the intellectuals, for his book appeared at the historical moment when the American terms "high-brow" and "low-brow" had been imported to explain the gap perceived between the two. The latest intellectual heroes were Albert Einstein, who had eliminated absolute space; Sir James Frazer, a Scottish anthropologist who had published *The Golden Bough*, which the literary world assumed had eliminated mystery and authority from religion and social customs; and Sigmund Freud, who offered new mysteries about man's subconscious and unconscious. At the same time official Christianity was being defended by the "gloomy" Dean Inge of St. Paul's, who despised Roman Catholicism for its "gorgeous promises and lurid threats" and wanted the "true" Church to steadily hold before their pure "Saxon" nation a "heroic ideal of belief and conduct." Dean Inge was a pure Chestertonian heretic, emotional rather than rational, elitist to his fingertips, and so inevitably, a natural "enemy" of Chesterton.

Chesterton, therefore, was fighting on several fronts simultaneously, as he usually did. On the one hand he was facing his old foe, humanism, which he divided into "Paganism" and "Puritanism," both forms of elitist despair dependent upon evolutionary "beliefs." He fought their habit of "disenfranchising their ancestors," or ignoring the influence of the past on the present, as well as the new "satirical" approach to biography used by Bloomsbury "lion" Lytton Strachey, because he saw this "debunking" as a kind of mirror image of making idols out of mankind. Strachey was his own subject, since he was the omnipresent god of his creation.

Chesterton made plain his own convictions about the universality of all human experience in his opening, which recapitulated the opening of his earlier "slovenly autobiography":

> There are two ways of getting home; and one of them is to stay there. The other is to walk round the whole world til we come back to the same place; and I tried to trace such a journey in a story I once wrote. . . . [This] is another story that I never wrote. Like every book I never wrote, it is by far the best book I have ever written. . . . I will use it symbolically here . . . a romance of those vast valleys with sloping sides, like those along which the ancient White Horses of Wessex are scrawled. . . . It concerned some boy whose farm stood on such a slope, and who went on his travels to find something, such as the effigy . . . of some giant; and when he was far enough from home he looked back and saw that his own farm . . . shining flat on the hill-side like the . . . quarterings of a shield, were but parts of some such gigantic figure, on which he had always lived, but which was too large and too close to be seen. . . . The point of this book, in other words, is that the next best thing to being really inside Christendom is to be really outside it. And . . . the popular critics of Christianity are not really outside it. . . .[37]

He goes on to explain how receptive the skeptical moderns would be to the Christian story if they perceived it as a Chinese myth:

> In other words I recommend these critics to try to do as much justice to Christian saints as if they were pagan sages . . . [for] it is stark hypocrisy to pretend that nine-tenths of the higher critics and scientific evolutionists and professors of comparative religion are . . . impartial. . . . I do not pretend to be impartial in the sense that the final act of faith fixes a man's mind because it satisfies his mind . . . but I can tell the story fairly . . . with . . . imaginative justice to all sides. . . . I should be ashamed to talk such nonsense about the Lama of Tibet as they do about the Pope. . . .[38]

In the first half of the book Chesterton traces humanity from its origins to the Incarnation, using the thesis that mankind is an animal like other animals, but unlike them because he has two special gifts: he is an artist (a creator), and he laughs. (These are the characteristics he had used to describe God.[39]) During his recounting of human history, Chesterton enjoys explaining that evolutionists suffer from the conviction that if an event happens slowly, it is less uncanny; he also reduces to absurdity the idea that a "cave man" would paint pictures of other animals like himself. When discussing mankind he touches on another familiar Chestertonian social theme: "the fact is the family," and one of the most recent books on human origins agrees with him.[40]

But he is not really basing his arguments upon the most recent scientific or psychological "truths," even when his statements are borne out by the specialists and scholars. He is determinedly using common sense and ordinary human experience as his justification, as he does when he says, "We cannot conclude with any certainty about these things . . . but we can say in what style . . . the best of it is built. . . . Round the family do gather the sanctities that separate men from ants and bees. . . . If we are not of those who . . . invoke a divine Trinity, we must nonetheless invoke a human Trinity. . . ."[41] He also insists that barbarism does not automatically precede civilization, but rather that the two can exist side by side, and that modern scientists tend to be talking about modern savages when describing ancient civilizations.

Chesterton attacks Wells' preference for Carthage over Rome, while refusing to agree that modern scholars have "proved" that Christianity is one of a multitude of Mediterranean sects. He insists that "Paganism" fell because of the same kind of dislocation between the philosophers and the common man that he is fighting now. Then the world grew dark with despair much as it had when he was a boy — not because it was tired of evil but because it was tired of good: "Despair does not lie in being weary of suffering, but being weary of joy. . . . When the good things in a society no longer work . . . the society begins to decline. . . ."[42] This was the time, Chesterton said, when if there was a God, He would have moved and saved the world, and he adds that, oddly enough, just then some members of an Eastern sect began to make a scene, saying God was dead and they had seen him die, but they seemed "quite unnaturally joyful about it."[43] This event brings Chesterton to Christ, *the* break in history. His Part Two begins with a chapter on the God in the cave, paralleling Part One, which began with the man in the cave.

It has been said that the second half of *The Everlasting Man* is an admirable exposition of the meaning of Christ-for-believing-Christians, but debatable by unbelievers. Even more startling is the accusation that Chesterton wrote about a "Unitarian" Christ because he described Christ's story as a human drama involving humans with a social and political problem.[44] This is a paradoxical twisting of Chesterton's real concern: to show the Incarnation was a real event in human history. To do so, he chose to treat Christ as "merely a man," but not the modern "merciful and humane lover of humanity . . . whose ideas were suitable to his time, but are no longer suitable to our time." As he pointed out, Christ was a radical and a revolutionary, and the "suitability" of His ideas to His own time is suggested by the end of His story.[45]

He also reminded his reader of the mysterious double nature of the Christ of the Gospels, whose recorded statements do not "tie him to his own time," and he insisted that a man reading the New Testament does not get the impression of a "made-up figure, a piece of artificial selection. . . ." In fact, Chesterton concluded, Christ must have been "many-sided" (i.e.,

God and Man) if so many Christs could be carved out of His portrait.[46] He then attacked the modern theory that all religions and all founders of religion are roughly the same, also insisting that if Christ were simply human, "he had the delusion he was God *and* he was wise and sane . . . two things that lie at the . . . extremes of human variation."[47]

Chesterton then talked about the Roman world of "Good Friday," describing it as a real event understandable to his audience: "Some brigand . . . was artifically turned into a . . . popular figure and run as a kind of candidate against Christ. In all this we recognize the urban population that we know, with its newspaper scares and scoops. . . . [Also] present in this ancient population [there was] an evil . . . the neglect of the individual. . . ."[48] Good Friday itself is "the end of human history which we call antiquity . . . buried [in the cave]. . . . They were looking at . . . the first day of a new creation . . . and in the semblance of a gardener God walked again in the garden, in the cool not of the evening but the dawn."[49]

Autobiographical echoes resound from that last statement, reminding one of the final sunrise in *The Man Who Was Thursday*, and making it clear that the Christ portrayed by Chesterton is a Chestertonian hero. Christ goes forth upon a quest, which is also a return: he is concerned with the immediate political and social world but in terms of individuals and eternal truths. He is someone with a strong, Dickensian love for ordinary people, and a great sense of humor. He is the everlastingly sane person in a mad world whom the powers that be cannot defeat, and so they try to get rid of him in the name of mankind. But Chesterton did not give the gospel his shape; he saw its shape as the only important story ever told, a story which was true. For Chesterton there could be no division between social and political and spiritual concerns, in Christ or in Christianity — to him they were the key to reading the events of 1925, to naming the pharisees like Lloyd George and the pagans like Wells, Shaw, Woolf, and Huxley.

Most disagreement with *The Everlasting Man* boils up over the chapters in which Chesterton talks about the history of the Church. His discussion is perfectly good-humored and not nearly as partisan as Wells' attack; in tone it is very similar to *Orthodoxy*. But to non-Catholic readers there is a subtle difference between a "slovenly spiritual biography" and a defense of Roman Catholicism, even though Chesterton is defending a Church that is more his name for "Christendom" than for papal religion. Because the history of Western Christianity is completely interrelated with Roman Catholicism, he tends to irritate any reader who is one of his "Protestants," "Pagans," or "Puritans" — all those with their own preconceptions — with his opening gambit:

> Christ founded the Church with two great figures of speech. . . . The first was the phrase about founding it on Peter as a rock; the second was the symbol of the keys. . . . The early Christian was very precisely a person

carrying about a key . . . that could unlock the prison of the whole world; and let in the white daylight of liberty. . . .[50]

The pity is that what Chesterton has to say is valuable to anyone thinking about the history of Western civilization, because what he was trying to explain was the spiritual motivation of Christendom's history — to put religion back in history — while fighting the modern outlook that "the Christian faith appeared in a simple age . . . and was a simple thing."[51] For him, the Church's justification is still her "flying balance." He claims that "the Faith is not a survival. . . . It was a surprise . . . unnatural, incongruous . . . comic upheaval, as if the Great Sea Serpent had suddenly risen out of the Round Pond," and in conclusion he restates his main argument:

> I do believe that the things on which I have insisted are more essential to an outline of history than the things I have subordinated or dismissed. I do not believe the past is most truly pictured as a thing in which humanity merely fades away into nature, or civilization . . . into barbarism . . . or religion . . . into mythology, or our own religion fades away into the religions of the world. In short I do not believe that the best way to produce an outline is to rub out the lines.[52]

Finally, he argues that "the religion of the world . . . is not divided into fine shades of mysticism or more or less rational forms of mythology. It is divided by the line between the men who are bringing that message and the men who have not yet heard it, or cannot yet believe it." The symbol he uses is the cross itself, which cut across the horizontal line of evolution.[53]

The world of 1925, which Chesterton himself recognized was "breaking up" (an occurrence that might let in some "fresh air"), was not the dogmatic place of his youth, when even "pessimism was orthodox." Although he had found in the Roman Catholic Church the solution to his own problems, as well as an even deeper understanding of others who differed from him, his message for the most part went unheard. But he himself would have seen it as good that in addition to acting as a founding father for a Roman Catholic literary revival, he also influenced two other non-Roman Christians who were to carry on his mission of relating our present to its Christian past: Dorothy L. Sayers and C. S. Lewis. (He also influenced Charles Williams, who said at Chesterton's death, "The last of my Lords is dead."[54])

Sayers had been a hopeful young contributor to the New Witness; she was an admirer of Chesterton's and got to know him personally.[55] Her series of radio plays about the life of Christ, The Man Born to Be King, is built upon Chesterton's method of describing him. Anyone reading her notes or the plays cannot escape the conclusion that her essential dramatic decision — to make Him a man of His own time and show these times in terms of our own — came to her by way of Chesterton and The Everlasting Man.[56] Since her plays gained the large general audience that Chesterton's book never had, she has, in a sense, completed his purpose.

Lewis got his first exposure to Chesterton as a young World War I veteran. Confined to a hospital bed, he began to read Chesterton's books; later he remarked, "A young man who wishes to remain a strong atheist cannot be too careful of his reading."[57] When *The Everlasting Man* was published, Lewis, then teaching at Oxford, found that he "for the first time saw the whole Christian outline of history set out in a form that seemed to me to make sense." His feelings were reinforced shortly afterward by a skeptical friend who told him that it looked as if "all that stuff of Frazer's about the Dying God . . . really happened once," completing the alteration of Lewis's perspective of historic Christianity.[58]

That October of 1925, meanwhile, Austen Chamberlain had just signed the Locarno pacts, in which England, France, Germany, Belgium, and Italy promised to maintain the boundaries of the Treaty of Versailles, and Germany was allowed into the League of Nations in return for her promise never to repossess the Rhineland or the Saar. All these countries were reviving economically, so it looked as if peace and prosperity were guaranteed forever, but Chesterton and Belloc continued to mistrust the rapidly prospering "Prussia." Belloc, however, wrote comparatively little for *G.K.'s Weekly*, and his only public role was as a foil to Chesterton's personality.[59]

That November Chesterton published a biography of Cecil Chesterton's favorite eighteenth-century Englishman, William Cobbett, who was to become the "patron saint" of distributism. Cobbett had been a fiery pamphleteer who labeled the English Reformation a "land grab." Politically he at first called himself a Tory, and later a Radical, being happy in neither camp.[60] With Chesterton, Cobbett shared the ideal of a nation of small farmers secure on their own land, but he also hated aristocratic government and industrial society, whose dark, Satanic mills "ruined the landscape." Unlike Cobbett, Chesterton was more the "reformed intellectual," more a "born again" man in his political and social outlook than a man of the people, with a simple, direct response to life, and his book about Cobbett revealed the unity of his own politics, philosophy of life, and style, all of which aimed at piercing the clichés that cloud experience.[61] Chesterton said that Cobbett was a man "without magical spectacles . . . which make most men see what they expect to see," and he inevitably read into Cobbett's work his own concern to see through the power structure as well as the courage to call out what he saw, so that Cobbett came to personify the perfect "journalist," more Cecil than Gilbert.[62]

Beginning in December, Chesterton's novel *The Return of Don Quixote* was serialized in *G. K.'s Weekly*. (It stopped appearing in November 1926 and was not actually published as a book until 1927, because it proved difficult to publish an elaborately planned novel in the very brief episodes needed by a weekly paper.) The book was dedicated to Titterton, "who knew this parable for social reformers was planned and partly written long ago before the War. . . . It was your too generous confidence that dragged it from its dusty drawer."[63] Passionately concerned with keeping *G. K.'s Weekly* afloat, Titterton had seen that this tale, begun in pre-Marconi days, would fit the present because the times were similar: another general strike was imminent. In fact, as the novel was being published in May of 1926, the general strike occurred. Titterton, who was in charge while Chesterton was abroad, supported the strikers, much to the anger of many readers, but on his return Chesterton agreed with him, because "trade-unionism was the only actual defense of the classes without property."[64]

The Return of Don Quixote is the classic example of a work that triggered misconceptions about Chesterton's wish to be medieval. On the one hand, he is accused of making heroes out of dilettantish aristocrats, fascinated by things medieval, who plot to overthrow the industrial state and return to Arcady; on the other hand, the plot has been said to exhibit the typical Chestertonian polarity between Catholicism and socialism, saturated with a specifically "Catholic," apolitical program for the future — a utopia presented by a man who did not believe in them.[65] In technical terms, however, *The Return of Don Quixote* can be shown to be the best and most interesting of all his novels. It is tightly constructed and well written; Chesterton in the role of narrator holds the story together. It is also the novel which best illustrates the position Chesterton now held, in contrast to the one he revealed in an early novel like *The Man Who Was Thursday*.

His position is defined by the book's real hero, the sympathetic but detached observer, Douglas Murrell. Murrell understands ordinary people but acts only in a private way, undertaking only "personal quests." The novel's basic tone is pessimistic, because the idea for it originated in an earlier period of Chesterton's life, but it also reflects his postwar sense of social confrontation between red (Bolshevist) and black (Fascist) revolutions. In no sense, however, does it preach a future in which England will again be Roman Catholic and happy ever after.[66]

This story is concerned with industry, not agriculture, but it is a "distributist" sequel to *Tales of the Long Bow*, with a returning character, Lord Eden. Much of the action takes place in a small mining town and at nearby Seawood Abbey (once a real monastery), the home of Lord Seawood, who has gotten rich from his coal mines. Lord Seawood tries to defeat the trade union of the Syndicalist Braintree by making use of a romantic, medieval League of the Lion, invented for a house party but made "real" by his scholarly librarian Michael Herne. When the League is taken over by a real Fascist named Julian Archer, the librarian, who has become the League's ruler, holds a trial in which Lord Eden and his confederates are convicted of subverting the League for their own ends. At the same time, the trade unionist is being shown up because he is more successful in society drawing rooms than at relating to real coal miners in pubs.

The novel's meaning is conveyed through its intricate personal relationships. There are three men — Braintree, Herne, and Murrell — and three

255

women they love who inspire their political action. Their romances all lead to marriage, not only invoking a conventional happy ending but illustrating a typically Chestertonian balance.[67] Olive Ashley wrote the play that inspires the League of the Lion, and sends Murrell on his quest for the special red paint that is no longer manufactured in this age of mass production; her romantic bias against progress balances the pragmatic nature of her Socialist lover, Braintree. Lord Seawood's daughter Rosamund has a dangerously romantic fondness for action and politics, which is balanced by her lover, the scholarly librarian Herne; the uncommitted Murrell marries a social activist, the daughter of Dr. Henry, an artist ruined by industrial society whom Murrell rescues from an insane asylum. In all three cases, however, the conclusion drawn is that these "romantic" politics will have little effect in "realistic" England.[68] Murrell makes the definitive summing up when he says of Herne's putting down the general strike, " 'Everything is too simple to him. . . . He will succeed . . . [and] a new sort of history will have begun . . . [with] a sword that divides. . . . It is not England. . . .' "[69] In *G. K.'s Weekly* Chesterton used almost the identical words to criticize the Conservative prime minister Baldwin and his actions that precipitated the real general strike.

Chesterton makes use of color to illustrate opposing views of life, but especially the difference between opaque color and transparent color — medieval manuscripts versus stained-glass windows. Opaqueness is secular and negative, whereas transparency is both religious and positive: when Seawood Abbey's library windows turn out to be the original stained glass of the old abbey, the light of heaven shines through them. When the abbey itself is returned to religious use by Rosamund, it is said to return to "the Thing" itself, Chesterton's term for Christianity or Roman Catholicism. In this novel, however, the general public is said to be color-blind, and the Syndicalist who wears the Socialist's red tie, though he does the most to bring color back to modern life, shows no sign of converting when he marries Olive, who is Catholic.[70]

The immediate relevancy of the novel lay in the fact that in December 1925 there were still 1,500,000 unemployed in England, and conditions in the coal mines were particularly bad, so that militancy among unions was building again, and the old Triple Alliance was resurrected.[71] Then the Royal Commission headed by the Liberal Sir Herbert Samuel recommended nationalizing the mines, to make them competitive with German and Polish coal mines, but also to stop the government subsidy, which meant, in the short run, that hours would be longer or pay would drop. As a consequence, on May Day 1926, the Trades Union Congress voted to strike the railways, mines, print shops, and the industries of building, iron, and steel. Although Parliament debated for two days, and negotiations were taking place, Baldwin broke them off, so that at midnight on May 3, 1925, the general strike began; it took out about three million workers.[72]

256

The strike was quickly declared illegal and only lasted until May 12. No one was killed, but there was some violence; the king helped Baldwin avoid the extreme measures urged by Churchill, Birkenhead, and Neville Chamberlain. Young Oxford undergraduates like W. H. Auden amused themselves by running the trains, but at *G.K.'s Weekly* Titterton went to great lengths not to cross the printers' picket lines.[73] At this point it was Chesterton and his paper which were unmistakably "revolutionary," although afterward the bright young things felt that 1926 had been their watershed, the real beginning of the postwar world of the thirties in which they became activists.[74]

Lloyd George roundly abused the Conservatives for not negotiating and then, upon missing a Liberal Party meeting, found that he and Asquith were waging their last, unexpected battle for party control. Lloyd George was basically pro-worker, Asquith pro-law and order, but the underlying row was also over Liberal suspicions that Lloyd George wanted to combine with Labour, as well as the result of an ongoing fight to get him to contribute "his" war chest to the party. It ended only with Asquith's death in 1928.[75] As usual, Chesterton clearly understood the spirit of the age, but his own position — offering a return to the spirit of liberalism — was clearly unacceptable to nearly everyone.

It was now that the U.S.S.R. began its very clever initiative to subvert young middle-class intellectuals, who were ashamed and pessimistic because of England's loss of stature; it made use of the "tightly meshed web of trusting relationships which were at once the strength and weakness of the class structure. . . ." Meanwhile, their elders looked back and blamed their troubles on the fight to defeat Germany, ignoring the fact that English industrial and commercial superiority had declined long before the war.[76]

That same June of 1926, Frances and Gilbert had celebrated their silver wedding anniversary in a festive manner, making accusations that they were not well-suited to each other seem beside the point. Frances was deeply and seriously considering joining the Roman Catholic Church as an outward and visible sign of the sacramental nature of their relationship. She wrote a great deal about it to Father O'Connor, who was more her confessor than Gilbert's. At almost the same time the Chestertons hired a new and "final" secretary who changed their daily lives for the better in hundreds of ways. This was Dorothy Collins, now Chesterton's literary executor, whom they had met because she was visiting friends next door. Not only was she a capable person who managed the incredible feat of "organizing" Chesterton's work, but she also knew how to type and drive a car, and took care of their business affairs, sparing Frances much anxiety. She started a filing system, answered letters, got the articles to town on time, and saw to it that Chesterton got to his speaking engagements as well. She claimed she could work with him because she, too, was untidy, but she helped him establish work habits that were more consistent than his old ways, allowing him to accomplish a great deal in the remaining years of his life.

When home Chesterton still rose late, unless it was a religious day of obligation, in which case he went to early mass, groaning and moaning, "What but religion would bring us to such a pass." Then he would be at work at his desk by 10:30 and work until dinner, with short pauses for lunch and tea. After dinner he sat with a cigar and read a detective story or made notes for the next day's work. If Dorothy Collins saw that their bank balance had gotten perilously low, she would tell him and he would wander off to think about an hour or so, then return with a few scribbled notes and begin slowly to dictate another Father Brown mystery.[77]

Chesterton wrote out his notes in a private shorthand no one else could read, and while he often talked about a piece before he wrote it, he never did so as he actually worked. He now dictated directly to Dorothy, who typed as he spoke; then he read the material fresh from her machine. He typically made very few changes, and, as always, he relied on his memory for quotations. He usually mapped out a book with chapter headings, then dictated it chapter by chapter, although not always in sequence. There is evidence in his writing that when a group of essays was made into a book, such as *The Outline of Sanity*, he did tighten and edit the writing, but it seems obvious that he did most of his editing mentally, before anything was written down.[78]

Best of all, Dorothy Collins became a daughter to both Frances and Gilbert. She was very fond of both of them, and so did not take sides, as some of their other acquaintances did; presumably, living with them, she could enjoy Chesterton as well as understand and appreciate the problems of being his wife. That kind of understanding takes daily experience to develop. When the legends began to grow that on trips Frances would not let her husband do what he wanted to do, Collins never added to them, though she did apparently share Frances' conviction that he should spend less time being an editor and more time writing great books.[79] She adjusted well to the Top Meadow household — filled with cats and dogs and visited frequently by nieces, nephews, and neighbor's children. After spending a few years in their company, she joined the Roman Catholic Church.

She became Chesterton's chief and valued researcher, going through books he was to review and marking certain passages, a daily exercise of the kind made famous by his request that she get him "some books on Saint Thomas Aquinas," which she painstakingly did — only to have him glance at one or two, and then quickly begin to dictate one of his best and most famous biographies. In appreciation of her help, Chesterton dedicated several books to her; one dedication read, "To Dorothy Collins, without whom this book would have been published upside down." She even won over Ada Chesterton because she persuaded Chesterton to charge more for his work and got him to build a large study at Top Meadow with room for them both to work. Still, he clung to his liking for small corners; he could work anywhere that Dorothy could prop a typewriter.[80]

The first collection of Father Brown stories published since the war came out in June 1926. Called *The Incredulity of Father Brown*, it included a number of stories with an American flavor, like "The Arrow of Heaven" and "The Miracle of Moon Crescent," which feature rich American pluto- crats as the villains and victims. As the narrator, Chesterton is often in the stories, and provides the structural continuity; the plots are often based upon the premise of Poe's "The Purloined Letter," known to the enthusiasts of "the golden age of the detective story" as the "locked room" plot. (Chesterton's disciple John Dickson Carr used it repeatedly himself.[81]) De- spite his claiming to be the guardian of reason, Father Brown (like Ches- terton) has been accused of solving crimes using his "intuition." But to Chesterton's "ordinary reader" the stories are effective because they combine his favorite ingredients of magic and common sense. The Father Brown stories are still the most widely read of all Chesterton's writings, and the art form in which he was most successful; in fact, these stories may be his "masterpiece."[82]

There is a change of emphasis in the postwar Father Brown stories which correlates with Chesterton's own religious experience, and with his own descriptions of public versus private "morality" as shown in *The Return of Don Quixote*. The earlier Father Brown stories tend to use Christian reason in solving the crime (public), whereas his postwar stories emphasize reason's use in saving a soul (private). While all the stories deal with "mental and moral morbidity," or what Chesterton saw to be the spirit of the age, the detective stories in *The Incredulity of Father Brown* focus on the idea of a protagonist's self-centeredness, which is a result of either crime or insanity. Father Brown exposes his guilt by identifying with the criminal's act, which makes the criminal confess. A criminal, however, would only confess in this way if he felt there was a God; thus Father Brown demonstrates to him that he is not truly self-centered.[83]

In this Father Brown collection the stories are usually about "men in high places," like the great novelist in "The Dagger with Wings," who is perceived as a kind of "artist" but is unable to accept or even recognize external authority — that is, to accept God. He has no sense of social re- sponsibility; in Chestertonian terms, he is a monomaniac — "insane." When Father Brown gets such men to confess, it not only saves them but keeps their egocentric perspective from affecting others. In a way, then, all Ches- terton's criminals are playing God, and Father Brown is different from Horne Fisher or other heroes of Chesterton's later tales because he does assume the role of priest to the world, making it his business not only to solve the crime but to save the souls of the criminals.[84] Although Father Brown has no visible parish and no ordinary duties, he is out in the streets dealing with day-to-day life, precisely the way Chesterton thought he should be as a journalist. Ches- terton expresses his identification with Father Brown in his *Autobiography*, when he calls his own life "very much a mystery story."

About 1922, Chesterton had resumed what became another ongoing job: he illustrated books for Belloc. He illustrated nine books between 1925 and 1931, which became known as the "Chesterbelloc" books, and firmly convinced the public that the two men were one entity. According to Dorothy Collins, the creation of these books usually followed a pattern. Belloc would appear one day at Beaconsfield with a few ideas for a plot. He and Chesterton would hole up in the study until teatime, talking and laughing, and then emerge with twenty-five or more drawings, for which Belloc would then write the text.[85] These books were a part of Belloc's never-ending fight to stay solvent, as well as a great expression of kindliness and friendship on Chesterton's part. In this way Chesterton assumed responsibility for someone whom he called "the man of letters I happen to know best, who had the same motives for producing journalism [I did] and yet has produced nothing but literature."

In addition to periodically rescuing Belloc, between 1926 and 1936 Chesterton took part in innumerable benefits. The one he enjoyed the most was the mock trial held every year at the London School of Economics for the benefit of King Edward VII Hospital. He played the judge, trying actors and actresses, politicians, lawyers, and headmasters of famous schools, using his favorite recipe for changing the modern world by attacking it rationally with great good humor. But in the meantime, *G. K.'s Weekly* was failing.

To save the paper, Titterton, Chesterton's faithful squire, got the bright idea of founding what was called the Distributist League. The idea of creating a league, in a period when there had been many other similar action-and-propaganda associations, was publicly attributed to a Captain Went, but it was actually Titterton's brainstorm. League members would be recruited both as salesmen for "distributism" and its principles and as subscribers to *G. K.'s Weekly*, which would be their "official organ."[86] Circulation of the paper did improve, but no one is certain whether this was because of the league or the drop in the price from sixpence to twopence a copy.

Although some of Chesterton's novels had already been labeled as distributist, the league only came into being at this time, and it was never a political party aimed at holding office.[87] It grew out of several earlier "leagues" established by Cecil and Ada Chesterton, the idea being to prevent the establishment of Belloc's servile state (although Belloc himself never pretended to have much interest in the organization). It was not so much a program for anything as it was a protest against things that were being done.[88] Its tone was often negative, as when Chesterton said, "To say we must have Socialism or Capitalism is like saying we must choose between all men going into monasteries and a few men having harems. . . . If I deny [this] I should not need to call myself a monogamist; I should call myself a man."[89] To Chesterton it was a question of letting the ordinary man control his own life by spreading property about like muck or giving each person "three acres and a cow."[90]

Chesterton had supported the basic ideas of distributism for some time, but the league helped to give his own convictions a bad name as well as to embarrass him. Its official beginning was at Essex Hall on September 17, 1926, where Chesterton was elected president; Captain Went, secretary; and young Maurice Reckitt, treasurer. Some branches did spring up in other industrial cities, and the circulation of *G.K.'s Weekly* went up to 8,000 copies, but the league soon became a cross between a late-night Fleet Street party and the kind of eccentric Bedford Park "club" in which middle-class intellectual "heretics" argued with one another.[91] Various members like Father McNabb were accused of being too socialist or too syndicalist; others felt there was too much Roman Catholic influence. The league tried to apply its teaching by sending Londoners (like the Frank Sheeds) back to the farm to create cooperative communities, but most of these efforts were slight and ineffectual, eventually turning into what Reckitt called escapism.[92] Poor Chesterton, always the peacemaker, found himself smoothing over more rows, although he personally was always very popular with the younger members who stirred up the fights. As time went on he came to as few meetings as possible, often only the annual one, although he continued to help by being the chief speaker at public debates explaining distributist positions on issues like "Poland" or "Coal."[93] One of these, held in 1928, was to be the last public debate he had with Shaw.

On All Saints' Day that fall, Frances Chesterton formally joined the Roman Catholic Church. She intensely disliked the international fuss about it (the Catholic Press hawked handbills in the London streets), and she hated the fact that it was said she had done it because of her husband. In spite of her understandable reactions, there is considerable reason to assume that it was largely because of Gilbert that she converted, having seen her own refusal to do so as the sin of "wanting her own way." A lifelong Anglican, she found it especially hard to leave the English *Book of Common Prayer* and familiar habits of worship, but she adjusted faster than he had, since it was the exchange of one set of devotional habits and discipline for another. Neither she nor Gilbert liked the hierarchy's habit of "lionizing" them for promotional purposes, and they both preferred to attend their own small parish church.[94]

The Outline of Sanity, made up of Chesterton's articles on distributism collected from *G. K.'s Weekly*, was published on December 2, 1926. Most of the material came from his lead editorials called "Straws in the Wind." In the book's conclusion, Chesterton summed up the connection between his work as editor, his beliefs, and his support of the league's "propaganda purposes":

> We are concerned to produce a particular sort of men ... who will not worship machines, even if they use machines. ... I do not think State action is immoral ... in itself. ... It is impossible to deny that there is a doctrine behind ... our political position ... [with] reference to an ultimate view of the universe and ... the nature of man. ... The old morality, the Christian

religion, the Catholic Church . . . believed in the rights of man. . . . The new philosophy utterly distrusts a man . . . while I sit amidst droves of overdriven clerks . . . in a tube. . . . I read of . . . Men Like Gods and I wonder when Men will be like men.[95]

Chesterton's taking this position publicly had the effect that T. S. Eliot summarized in his obituary of Chesterton: "Even if Chesterton's social and political ideas appear totally without effect . . . are demonstrated wrong . . . they were the ideas for his time that were fundamentally Christian. . . . He did more than any man of his time . . . to maintain the existence of the important minority in the modern world."[96]

That same December a collection of his poems called *The Queen of Seven Swords* was published by the new house of Sheed and Ward, which had just been established by his biographer Maisie Ward and her husband, Frank Sheed. (From then on Chesterton tried to help them by giving them his books, but as Dorothy Collins discovered, he was hopelessly involved with many different publishers, and had an incredible number of books promised, most of which he never had time to write.[97]) The poems in this collection are more explicitly Roman Catholic, since their central theme is the idea of the Virgin Mary as the great "white" witch who saved mankind from the ancient pagan curse of the wicked witch of fairy tale, myth, and legend.[98] Chesterton had always been fascinated by the Virgin Mary, whether always in strictly Catholic terms or as the ideal of womanhood celebrated in chivalry, it is hard to say.

During 1927 *The Return of Don Quixote* was published, as well as several books and pamphlets that Chesterton wrote especially for the Catholic public on topics like birth control and conversion. That same year, during a short vacation trip to Lyme Regis, the Chestertons met a delightful Roman Catholic family named Nichols, who soon moved to Christmas Cottage near Top Meadow. They became a much-loved part of the Chestertons' daily lives, a new reason for games, parties, secret jokes, and poems.[99]

That May, Poland invited Chesterton to come and see for himself the result of ten years of freedom. Chesterton had always had a special love for Poland, which he saw as a small peasant country "resurrected" from the dead, and a bastion of Christendom, so he, Frances, and Dorothy Collins accepted the official invitation and spent five weeks being feted like royalty. Chesterton adored Poland's romantic manners, as well as its religious outlook, summed up for him by an officer's welcome: "I will not say you are the chief friend of Poland, for God is our chief friend."[100]

Chesterton's *Collected Poems* appeared next. The collection included not only *The Wild Knight* but also *The Ballad of the White Horse, Wine, Water and Song,* and *The Ballad of Saint Barbara*, as well as an opening section called *New Poems*. A number of these were satiric, like "Commercial Candour":

Our fathers to creed and tradition were tied,
They opened a book to see what was inside,
And of various methods they deemed not the worst
Was to find the first chapter and look at it first.
But a literate age, unbenighted by creed,
Can find on two boards all it wishes to read;
For the front of the cover shows somebody shot,
And the back of the cover will tell you the plot.[101]

In September 1927 the next collection of Father Brown stories appeared: *The Secret of Father Brown*. The last story, "The Chief Mourner of Marne," which had been published several years earlier in *Cassells* magazine, is often anthologized; it is the probable source of the idea that all these tales are very "Catholic." Far more interesting is the fact that the book has a prologue and an epilogue in which Chesterton, as author, spells out Father Brown's methods: he tells an American journalist that his secret simply is that "it was I who killed all those people, so of course I knew how it was done." When the journalist wants to take that as a figure of speech, Father Brown becomes angry because he does not mean "the science of deduction . . . studying a man as if he were a gigantic insect . . . [but] getting inside a man . . . until I am thinking his thoughts." The journalist in the epilogue comes back at Father Brown — as narrator — by saying, " 'I don't know if you would make a really good criminal. But you ought to make a rattling good novelist.' "[102] Father Brown has become Chesterton.

Next Chesterton unexpectedly wrote another play, perhaps at the urging of Shaw, who had found a rich new backer and was now enjoying renewed success as a playwright. Called *The Judgment of Dr. Johnson*, the play was published in October by Sheed and Ward, although it was not performed until the Arts Theatre Club produced it in 1932, and Chesterton may not have seen it. Not only had Chesterton played "Dr. Johnson" in numerous amateur theatricals, but he clearly identified with him, both as a man of letters and as a Fleet Street reporter whose outlook matched his own. He said that "Dr. Johnson is immortal . . . because he . . . judged all things with a gigantic and detached common sense."[103] But although Chesterton had been practicing for some time by producing plays for his toy theatre "in the family," *The Judgment* is no *Magic*. It has many amusing lines, but the audience is reminded of the problem of *The Merry Wives of Windsor*: just as that play is missing the "real" Falstaff of *Henry IV*, who charges about his native heath, so *The Judgment* is missing the real Dr. Johnson of Fleet Street.

While he was traveling and carrying out all his other projects, Chesterton had also been at work on two of his best books, which resemble one another. It is clear that, as he wrote them, he was sitting back and reflecting upon his own life, subjecting it to a kind of reappraisal, and seeing it as a reaffirmation of the values he had always held. The two books are so close in mood and subject matter that they are often paired together as different parts of his own story. The first book is a biographical study, *Robert Louis Stevenson*, published in November 1927, and the other is his *Autobiography*, which was not published until after his death in 1936.

Virtually everyone agrees that *Robert Louis Stevenson* is Chesterton at his best, showing someone he admired against the backdrop of his age. This gave him a chance to reassess the fin de siécle atmosphere of the Slade, an attitude he saw resurrecting itself in the postwar world. Stevenson had refused to join the art-for-art's sake movement a generation earlier; in his crisp style and use of story he had also refused to join the movement toward a formlessness which "will be very much of a novelty but not much of a novel. . . . Nameless universal forces streaming through the subconsciousness, run very truly like that dark and sacred river that wound its caverns measureless to man . . . where . . . men may come upon a shape with something of a sharp surprise . . . a novel [or] a story, the first of childish and the last of human pleasures."[104] The book abounds with typically fascinating comments on the current scene like this one:

> Fashions change. . . . Let us leave Stevenson behind in the dead past, along with such lumber as Cervantes and Balzac and Dickens . . . [even if] the best poetry of Miss [Edith] Sitwell is after all a sort of parody of *A Child's Garden of Verses* . . . groping after her own lost shadow . . . decked with adjectives that would mildly surprise the child.[105]

Like Stevenson, Chesterton had always seen the world in romantic color, and they both loved the strict limits of a toy theatre as a definition of art. But the tendency to identify Chesterton's childhood with Stevenson's should be watched: Chesterton was not a sickly invalid who lay in bed without the company of family or peers. Similarly, Chesterton's statement that Stevenson represented "the sharp turn to simplicity" as an expression of the "fiery thirst for happiness" does not function as a good summary of his own more complicated public persona.

During the past year, the British Broadcasting Corporation had been chartered as a state-run monopoly, maintained by the sale of receiving licenses instead of private advertising. By 1930 there were three million license holders in the country, and the BBC was on its way to becoming a very important source of news, as well as the governmental agency which provided entertainment and made culture available to a wide public. It also became a kind of "public dictator," satirically represented as Big Brother in George Orwell's *1984.* Chesterton first became aware of its potential for propagandizing when Titterton pulled off a coup while again hunting for resources for *G. K.'s Weekly*.

Titterton had asked Shaw to write some articles for the paper (wanting to use the magic of his public name), but Shaw, with his usual common sense, told Titterton that the writing would take more time than he wanted to devote to the cause. Shaw rashly added that he hoped *G.K.'s Weekly* would die, because Chesterton was spending too much time "trying to establish a false anti-thesis between Distributism and Socialism, whereas Distributism is plumb-centre Socialism." Titterton rushed to tell Chesterton, "We've got him," and when Chesterton said splendid, but what are we going to do with him, Titterton answered that they were going to ask Shaw to debate that statement under the catchy title "Do We Agree?" To Titterton's joy and relief, both men agreed to do it, although Shaw said to Chesterton, "Look here. ... Is there really a Distributist League, or is it merely Titterton running in and out with a flag?"[106]

Once the idea was settled, everyone felt someone besides Titterton should handle the details, and Shaw typically took charge as young Gregory Macdonald, who worked for the Distributist League, was hiring Kingsway Hall. When Macdonald came up with the brilliant idea of negotiating with the BBC to broadcast the debate, Shaw told him to get a stiff fee because it would be worth "one hundred pounds to them to have Chesterton and me as a double turn." Shaw took over ticket printing and sales, and after noticing that the tickets were not numbered, made the group hire stewards to guard the doors, while fussing that all the money should be going to pay off Belloc's debts. Despite his sarcastic remarks, he acted like Santa Claus, making the thing work.[107]

The debate finally took place in December 1927. All of Shaw's worst prophecies did in fact come true: the doors were opened too soon, ticket holders were locked out, and a minor riot started. But Belloc — back in the position of chairman that he had held during their Fabian days — got the doors opened and began the meeting with his special brand of humor:

> I am here to take the chair in the debate between two men whom you desire to hear more than you could possibly desire to hear me. They will debate whether they agree or do not agree. ... There is a prospect of a very pretty fight. ... You are about to listen, I am about to sneer.[108]

Shaw urbanely tried to pre-empt the debate by announcing that "I suspect you do not care much about what we debate provided we entertain you by talking in our characteristic manners. ... Chesterton and I are two madmen [who] go about the world possessed by a strange gift of tongues ... uttering all sorts of extraordinary opinions for no reason whatever." He then declared that the question was one of the distribution of wealth: "If you take two shillings as your share and another man wants two shillings and sixpence, kill him. ... If a man accepts two shillings when you have two shillings and sixpence, kill him. Do you agree?"[109]

Chesterton instantly said, "The answer is in the negative," and added that Shaw really did not think that all the people in the hall should increase the confusion by killing each other and searching each other's pockets to see whether there was a half-crown or two shillings in them. Then he kidded Shaw about staying young while he grew old and experienced with the elementary facts of life, such as the fact that the state is not "identical with the Commons." He said he began at the other end, determining who or what is going to distribute the goods and asking if the distributor will "be permanently just, wise, sane, and representative of the conscience of the community which has created it. That is what we doubt. We say there ought to be ... scattered powers, privileges, limits, points of resistance...." When Shaw stated that in fact the government would own men and women, Chesterton agreed that "they would be slaves."[110] Chesterton's summarizing remark was that "Shaw proposes to distribute wealth. We propose to distribute power."[111]

As usual, the matter of who won the debate depended upon the point of view of the listener, but there were those who felt that Belloc's Orwellian summation was most interesting of all. He claimed he would not sum up, because in a very few years the whole debate would be antiquated. Instead, he would read them a poem that he had just written, which included the line, "Our civilization is built upon coal. ... In a very few years it will float upon oil." He felt that industrial civilization would break down and do one of three things — restore ordinary human affairs, lead to a desert, or make the mass of men slaves of a few. "Take your choice," he said.[112]

The Distributist League published the debate later, in July 1928, under the title *Do We Agree?* Although it was the last in a long series, this debate alone probably gave the public its conception of a Shaw-Chesterton debate. Younger people, however, had a reaction different from the popular one: to many of them the distinctions Chesterton tried to make between his position and socialism came out sounding "poetic."[113] In a sense, it was true that Shaw and Chesterton had reached the point where they had nothing more to debate, and socially — because of the physical distance between them, their different tastes, their ages, and Chesterton's poor health — they rarely met. Ironically, however, Shaw's last play, *The Apple Cart*, was called very "Chestertonian"; it exhibited a preference for the old established idea of a monarchy that represents the people better than do more "advanced" forms of government. It also showed Shaw's real disillusionment with Parliamentary government and his fear for the future.

In an updated final chapter for his book about Shaw, Chesterton pointed out that Shaw's last political phase seemed to be a "... general loathing for anarchy; and a disposition to accept whatever can reduce it to ... order ... be it Fascism or Bolshevism" — a fascinating commentary, since that is exactly the accusation often leveled at Chesterton himself. Like many of the Fabian intellectuals in the thirties, Shaw did flirt with Soviet Russia: he was impressed with its seeming efficiency, and by the forceful personalities of both Stalin and Hitler, whom he took to be examples of his long-sought supermen. Considering these opinions, it seems a bit hard that popular wisdom considers Chesterton to be the reactionary, sectarian saint but lets Shaw go on being a Grand Old Man of the modern "liberal" world.

By mid-1928 poor Chesterton was mediating another nasty row, brought about because some of the younger Distributists felt that *G. K.'s Weekly*, again in financial trouble, needed to be run in a more businesslike way. They brought the matter up at an open board meeting where Titterton, who took the whole charge personally, created a terrible scene about this lack of confidence in the staff. However, after telling Frances that the paper must continue, Chesterton chose to side with the "Palace revolution" and let the younger men take over, separating the paper from the Distributist League; Titterton resigned. After putting his beloved Chesterton in this appalling position, Titterton, who had lost his temper and called his opponents a bunch of Judases, felt terrible. The net result was that Chesterton had a new, young assistant editor called Edward Macdonald, whose brother Gregory had been one of the "regicides."

Still another collection of essays was culled from the *Illustrated London News*; this one, called *Generally Speaking*, came out in October 1928. Some claim that this writing is less wise and less clever, showing Chesterton's age. But several of these essays were chosen over many others to be included in the collections made by Bentley and Wyndham Lewis. The essay "On Funeral Customs" perfectly illustrates why, being full of incisive witticisms. The essay is actually a review of a learned new book on that subject. In assessing it, Chesterton comments that he wishes the most intelligent people would not insist on saying that "every obvious human custom is a relic of some base and barbaric custom." The writer had suggested that leading a riderless horse behind the hearse of a general is a "survival" of killing the horse as a sacrifice on the grave. This, comments Chesterton, "seems to me exactly like saying that taking off our hats to a lady is a survival of having our heads cut off when we were suitors for a fairy princess. . . . Those who write about primitive man's feelings always seem to start with the assumption that he had no feelings. . . ."[114]

Another essay in *Generally Speaking* is written with equal flair and insight. Called "On Leisure," it is a pleasant, low-key discussion of the confusion this term creates among modern social philosophers, who worry — statistically — about labor and leisure and the common man. In his usual deft way, Chesterton clears up a principal confusion that clouds the issue:

> A great part of the modern muddle arises from confusion and contradiction about the word "leisure." To begin with, of course, it should never be confused for a moment with the word "liberty." An artist has liberty, if he is free to create any image in any material that he chooses. But anyone who will try to create anything out of anything will soon discover that it is not a leisurely occupation.[115]

As it turned out, this distinction summed up both Chesterton's view of life and his circumstances in late 1928.

Chapter Fifteen

THE SPICE OF LIFE
1928-1936

We need not deny that modern doubt, like ancient doubt, does ask deep questions; we only deny that, as compared with our own philosophy, it gives any deeper answers. And it is a general rule, touching what is called modern thought, that while the questions are often really deep, the answers are often decidedly shallow. And it is even perhaps more important to remark that, while the questions are in a sense eternal, the answers are in every sense ephemeral. . . . Those who leave the tradition of truth do not escape into something which we call Freedom. They only escape into something else, which we call Fashion.

G.K. Chesterton, *The Well and the Shallows*[1]

Our generation does not have to be told that the world is changing: you have happened to hit an irritating angle of the Church; but you know the worst: you do not yet know the worst of the changing world. . . . If you . . . surmounted your natural anger at signing forms . . . I do not believe for a moment you would find any practical evil in having children trained in an old Christian tradition, admittedly suited to children. . . . You will find no dreadful secrets in the Faith, because there are none to find. [But] if you find . . . that in the chaos before us all the things you do believe in, justice and human dignity and the normal social and domestic ideals, have collapsed of themselves everywhere else and the Church is their last fortress . . . you will suffer . . . a horrible irony.

G.K. Chesterton in a letter to a young friend, quoted by Maisie Ward in
Return to Chesterton[2]

Some sneer; some snigger, some simper;
In the youth where we laughed, and sang.
And they may end with a whimper
But we will end with a bang.

G.K. Chesterton, *The Listener*, March 18, 1936[3]

268

B Y any standard, these were not the "best of times" in England. The Conservative government under Baldwin had been in office as long as it legally could be, so another General Election was scheduled for May 1929. The Conservatives stalled until that date because then a new law went into effect: finally, all women over twenty-one had the right to vote. There were more women than men in most constituencies, and each party hoped these women would give them the edge. Baldwin ran his campaign on his legend of being the plain man who stood for "safety first," not a Chestertonian principle, while the Liberal Party under Lloyd George and Sir Herbert Samuel made its last great, unified effort to regain a place in English politics. Lloyd George energetically produced studies on the current problems of rising unemployment, land, and agriculture, promising the voters a vast public works program, efforts designed to show that while Labour and Conservatives alike had no solutions, Liberals did.[4]

Although Lloyd George insisted that the Liberals were anti-Socialist, and, if elected, would not vote to support another Labour government, voters still mistrusted him because of his failures in the early postwar world. The Liberal program also seemed to be just another version of the Labourites program. In the election the Labour Party won 287 seats, the Conservatives went down to 260, but the Liberals won only 59, barely more than in the disastrous election of 1924. Among the chief deserters of their cause were the younger Nonconformists, most of whom voted Labour.[5] The few Liberal candidates elected to be M.P.'s also began to ally themselves with Labour, so that as a visible political party, liberalism was finished.

Chesterton, too, mistrusted Lloyd George and his associates — probably more than the typical Englishman did — and was bitter that his leadership had doomed the party. Philosophically he could never accept the rationality of a political climate which deliberately destroyed the middle ground in favor of such ideological polarization. Nor fundamentally, despite some comments he made about the state helping to redistribute land, would he consider the policy of "state nationalization" a better solution than what existed now. As he clearly saw, England was on her way, not quite knowing it, to the welfare state.[6]

Labour was called to form its second government, this time as the party with the most seats in the House of Commons. Ramsay MacDonald was still their leader, a man whom Fabian Beatrice Webb disliked for being nothing but a fine facade, mistrusting as much as Chesterton did his fondness for being an "aristocrat."[7] He appointed the first woman Cabinet minister, and also appointed to this Cabinet Chesterton's Socialist friend and editor,

George Lansbury. But his government was not able to function smoothly as a team — they were in fact far better at playing the role of the opposition, except in foreign affairs. In this area they successfully fought to get England's fair share of German reparations, worked for arms control, and again recognized Soviet Russia. All in all, Labour was helped less by its own programs than by problems plaguing the Conservative Party and the break-up of the Liberals. None of the parties was ready for the Great Depression, which was just around the corner.[8]

In July 1929 Chesterton published another book called *The Poet and the Lunatics*. Like the Father Brown books, it was a collection of short stories which had already been published. Many of his later works were this kind of "semi-novel" because he could quickly write a short story and send it off to make money for the insatiable *G. K.'s Weekly*, and because a long, carefully organized novel was impossible to serialize in the small space available in his own paper. This particular book, subtitled "Episodes in the Life of Gabriel Gale," works because it has a single hero and a single theme.[9]

Gabriel Gale is a poet, an older version of his namesake Gabriel Syme in *The Man Who Was Thursday*. His character is also remarkably similar to the "late" Father Brown, whose apparent simple-mindedness masks his mental alertness; he solves the puzzles presented to him by following moral clues and interpreting moral atmospheres. Like Chesterton himself, Gale — whose name echoes the great wind that drove Innocent Smith through the world on his mission — is still waging war against the "modern madness." He is considered mad but is shown to be the only sane person about.

Most of the stories have both personal and political meaning; they deal particularly with the definition of liberty. The story most interesting to Chesterton's biographers is the fourth one, "The Crime of Gabriel Gale," in which Gale befriends a young curate, who is convinced he controls the universe, and helps him to see that he "is a creature; [and] all his happiness consists in . . . becoming a child." Gale proves this by tying the curate to a tree and pinning him there with a pitchfork.[10] The cure comes from his realizing *physically* that try as he will, he cannot free himself. When an effort is made to certify that Gale is mad because he tied up the curate, his "victim" sends a telegram saying, "Can never be sufficiently grateful to Gale for his great kindness which more than saved my life."[11]

The book is given a "curious philosophical unity" through Gale and his ongoing role in the stories as the sane man who stands in opposition to the elitists: their egotism makes them the center of their world, whereas he understands the problems of ordinary people.[12] As in *The Man Who Was Thursday*, the heroine, who is more intelligent and understanding than the other characters, also unites the beginning and end by her acceptance of the poet. He promptly celebrates by standing on his head because "the world is upside down. . . . We're all flies crawling on a ceiling, and its an everlasting mercy that we don't drop off. . . ." He also notes that "it's a very good thing for a landscape-painter to see the landscape upside down. He sees things then as they really are." The artist's true role, in fact, is to be "centric. [Genius] . . . ought to be in the core of the cosmos, not on the revolving edges."[13]

This book has been accused of failing to produce a unified effect that has real social significance. Even more damning is the charge that it is a kind of retreat into "Tory" nostalgia that sees happiness as staying in the social class in which one was born, as well as a refusal to accept the nihilism of extreme, anarchical freedom. In addition, some readers use the fact that Gale sends for the police to prove that Chesterton has become a reactionary.[14]

The real answer to these charges of social irresponsibility on Chesterton's part comes from the first and last parts of the novel, in which the poet's life experience is described in terms that make him a stand-in for Chesterton. At a crucial point Gale identifies his artistic and religious understanding with what is clearly social prophecy, saying to his attackers, " 'Nothing for you has a central stalk of sanity. There is no core to your cosmos. . . .' " He then goes on to warn that " 'I can only exaggerate things the way they are going. But I am not often wrong about the way things are going. You may be sleek as a cat but I knew you were evolving into a tiger" — saying, in other words, that the way these people think will destroy them.[15] Then he rescues the heroine from "Wimbleton," which is another name for modern England, with its "skies of a strange and unique character. . . . [It] is not a lunatic asylum; it is a den of very accomplished professional criminals." Like England in the late twenties, the world is now ruled not just by "lunatics" but by "crooks."[16]

As the hero suggested in the beginning, at times like that, "one's life would be well spent in waking up the dead inns of England and making them English and Christian again" — and that is where he ends up, keeping traditional values alive at home once he has done his public duty. In this light it does not seem significant that Gale allows a plainclothesman to arrest a high-ranking criminal, nor that he meets the first of several "sympathetic" kings who are wise and moderate men and represent all the people. After all, in 1929 King George V was considerably more appealing than Baldwin, Ramsay MacDonald, or Lloyd George, who was close to being a crook.[17]

Nineteen twenty-nine was also the year that Anthony Berkeley, the mystery writer, started a group which met to eat and talk shop. He soon wrote Chesterton to say that any such gathering would be incomplete without the creator of Father Brown, and Chesterton promptly became a member. The original group was very select, even in this golden age of the detective story. Among them were Dorothy L. Sayers, Freeman Wills Crofts, Austen Freeman, Father Ronald Knox, E.C. Bentley, and Agatha Christie; eventually other writers were invited to join, including Margery Allingham,

Gladys Mitchell, Ngaio Marsh, and John Dickson Carr, creator of the Chestertonian detective Dr. Gideon Fell.

By 1932 it had officially become the Detection Club, formal and secret, with a Constitution and Rules and a very whimsical Initiation Ceremony written by Dorothy Sayers in the style of the Book of Common Prayer.[18] It was not only a mutual aid society; it also set out to establish standards for detective-story writing, particularly emphasizing "fair play" for the reader. In 1933 Chesterton wrote an article in which he described the Club as "a small and quiet conspiracy to which he was proud to belong," but he had every reason to believe its members had not "experimented in the coarser and more carnal manifestations of homicide, but confined themselves strictly to killing people on paper."[19]

Chesterton was elected as its first president, or Ruler, so that he had the fun of officiating at the club's initiation ceremony for new members. To qualify, they had to have written two mysteries, and to have been sponsored by two members — almost as if they were being baptized. At this yearly rite, first held at the Northumberland Hotel in a large basement party room, Chesterton sat waiting in total darkness, enthroned on a dais, ceremonially robed in a scarlet-and-black Mandarin coat, and wearing a tiny pillbox hat (much like Fu Manchu). The doors were flung open and the members entered in a procession, the first carrying Eric the skull on a black cushion, flanked by torch bearers; then came the other wardens with the implements of their trade — daggers, guns, vials of poison, and blunt instruments.[20] The Ruler (Chesterton) called out in a great voice, "What mean these lights, these ceremonies, and this reminder of our mortality?" At this point the real initiation began, carried out by candlelight, with the proper decorum of a religious service. Although many of the questions asked were most amusing, there was always a note of seriousness about the performance that reflected the craftsmanlike concerns of the members themselves.[21]

As Ruler, Chesterton asked the Candidate if it was his firm desire to become a Member, and the Candidate was expected to respond loudly, "That is my desire," whereupon the Ruler asked if he would promise that his "detectives would well and truly detect the crimes presented to them, using those wits which it may please you to bestow upon them and not placing reliance on nor making use of Divine Revelation, Feminine Intuition, Mumbo-jumbo, Jiggery-pokery, Coincidence or Act of God. . . ." The Candidate had to further swear never to conceal a vital clue and to observe a "seemly moderation" in the use of "Gangs, Conspiracies, Death-Rays, Ghosts, Hypnotism, Trap-Doors, Chinamen," and promise to honor the King's English. The Ruler then solemnly pronounced that if the member did not fulfill these vows, "May other writers anticipate your plots, may your publishers do you down in your contracts, may strangers sue you for libel, may your pages swarm with misprints and may your sales continually diminish. Amen!"[22]

To finance some club rooms on Gerrard Street in Soho, the Detection Club contributed their own writing in a collaboration that must have been a lot of fun. They not only wrote "joint" detective stories but also collaborated on radio scripts. In the introduction to their first published mystery, *The Floating Admiral*, Dorothy Sayers explained that except for Mr. Chesterton's picturesque prologue (which takes place in a very seamy Hong Kong), "each contributor tackled the mystery presented to him in the preceding chapters without having the slightest idea what solution . . . the previous authors had in mind . . . [but] ready to explain his own clues . . . and to deliver . . . his own proposed solution."[23] The result, which Chesterton described as a version of "paper games," was published in 1931; their first radio script, "Behind the Screen," was broadcast by the BBC in 1933.

It has been pointed out that Chesterton is most at home with the genre of the detective story, a form in which his interests and his talents are both at their best. For him, then, the Detection Club not only provided good fellowship and fun of a kind he loved, but stood for a standard he himself subscribed to: the seriousness of the artist's approach to his craft. Even when he insisted that if a thing was worth doing, it was worth doing badly, he knew that popular literature, like the mystery, was one of the most potent means of addressing the public. It is, in fact, the genre in which he has made his lasting impression.[24]

One of Chesterton's next books, which is clearly Roman Catholic apologetics, is the collection of articles published in October 1929 called *The Thing: Why I Am a Catholic*. In the introduction he complains convincingly about people like H. G. Wells and Dean Inge who are publicly rude to Roman Catholics, and he repeats his own belief that he must therefore stand beside his co-religionists to "be pelted with insults." At the same time, these essays sound more Chestertonian than Roman, because he is talking about "Catholicism" and "Protestantism" in much the same way he had in *Heretics* and *Orthodoxy*. His comment, however, is that the whole secret of the controversy about "Catholicism" is that the writer wants to say, "Even poor old Chesterton must think; he can't have actually left off thinking altogether . . . [but] it is obvious that [these writers feel] if a man begins to *think* he can only think more or less in the direction of Modernism. . . . That is the joke."

To that arrogance, Chesterton simply replies that it is clear to him that "the modern world is living on its Catholic capital. It is using . . . up the truths that remain to it out of the old treasury of Christendom."[25] Dorothy Sayers paraphrased this statement in a book she wrote at the beginning of World War II; in fact, the idea constituted her reason for devoting her final years as a writer to translating Dante's *Divine Comedy*.[26] This particular point of view is also shared by other Christians; it is really a definition of "post-Christianity," which assumes Chesterton's corollary that he who is not for the Church is against it.

In describing the conversion process, Chesterton uses his own life and experience. He defines "Protestantism" as "barbarism," as well as a kind of secular cult which claims the allegiance of agnostics, atheists, mystics, psychic investigators — in fact, most of mankind, while the real Protestantism of the Reformation is believed by almost nobody. Growing up in a nominally Protestant home, he discovered he was being asked to cling not "to the Protestant faith . . . but the Protestant feud," and the longer he lived the more he came to see that "in nine cases out of ten the Church simply stood for sanity and social balance against heretics who were very like . . . lunatics. . . . At every separate moment the pressure of the prevalent error was very strong. . . . The spirit of the ages [usually was] going wrong, and the Catholics at least relatively going right. . . . It is a mind surviving a hundred moods."[27] This clearly echoes *Orthodoxy* as well as *The Everlasting Man*.

Chesterton continues by calmly pointing out that the majority of moderns love to talk about Catholicism, but hate to be told about it; they are not only very ignorant about its beliefs but upset that a religion they had "left for dead" has come to life. In several essays he talks about the scientists who claim an impartiality they do not have, and refuse to allow any intellectual quality to Catholic doctrine.

In one of the last chapters he provides an interesting defense of the Papacy itself, discussing it in terms of the social value of a "general idea of an office or obligation" to erect

> . . . in some central city . . . the seat of a permanent official to represent peace and the basis for agreement among all the surrounding nations. . . . [Let] him be protected by a special sentiment from the pressures of kings and princes, let him be sworn in a special manner to the consideration of men as men. . . . If our civilization does not rediscover the need of a Papacy, . . . sooner or later it will try to supply the need. . . . The ideal has been abused like any other . . . but even those who most denounce the reality will probably begin again to search for . . . something that can unite us not . . . by being entirely international but by being universally human.[28]

In none of these essays does Chesterton sound strident or particularly partisan in an unpleasant way; he is a friend reasoning with another whom he loves, speaking in a conversational tone. At the same time, his Catholicism is, as usual, very Chestertonian.[29]

A collection of his prefaces for other books was published in late October under the catchy title *G.K.C. as M.C.* It reflected his love of literature, especially English literature, as well as his talents as a master of ceremonies and an after-dinner speaker. Some of the prefaces date back as far as 1903, and they deal with people as varied as Job, Cecil Chesterton, and George MacDonald.

That same fall Gilbert, Frances, and Dorothy Collins spent three months in Rome. They lived in the Hotel Hassler, which looked down over the

Spanish Steps, so that Chesterton was able to "look down at Rome." This view made him feel as if he understood her eternally rejuvenated, or resurrected, spirit. He had the "sensation of looking down into the chasms into which the seven hills are cloven," beneath which he sensed "a buried river or shifting and vanishing fountain . . . [where] secret things thrust upward from below . . . a place where the past can actually return to the present."[30]

Chesterton had a private interveiw with Pope Pius XI, who had just concluded a Concordat with the Italian state, ostensibly a monarchy, but in fact ruled by its Fascist dictator, Mussolini. (This trip took place before Mussolini began to attack Church organizations.) Chesterton never wrote up what he and the Pope talked about, but Dorothy Collins noticed that for several days before and after the visit he was too preoccupied to write; he apparently did mention that they had discussed his book *St. Francis of Assisi*.

His impressions of the Rome trip appeared the next year in a book called *The Resurrection of Rome*. He first discussed the causes of World War I, his last suggestion being that war had begun because Europe had been "standing on its head instead of its heels" — that is, it had been led by the Teutonic north when for "fully a thousand years . . . all the nations of the North lived cheerfully by a culture that had come from the South . . . the old international realm of Rome." Then he reported on his interview with Mussolini.

The interview was conducted in bad French, he explained, and Mussolini at once began to ask him about England, and Chesterton never had the nerve — so he said — to act the "properly pushy journalist" who would demand, "And what, Signore, was the proudest moment of your life?" He was too busy, he said, trying to help Mussolini understand distributism and the 1928 fight over revising the *Book of Common Prayer*. Mussolini had great charm, and Chesterton came away more impressed than he had expected to be.[31]

Because Chesterton was a celebrated "convert," his effort to explain Fascism intelligently simply made people assume that he was acting as apologist for a totalitarian state.[32] But with the unsettled political situation in England in 1929, he might well have thought a capable dictator who was popular with the ordinary people was better than the elected members of an oligarchy. He had "recognized" Adam Wayne in the Swiss Guards at the Vatican, the gaudy guardians of a small nation, and saw Italy herself as "reborn again" by the war.[33] At the same time, there is a feeling in his discussion of Italian politics that he is there as an Englishman who was raised a Protestant, and not too happy about many aspects of either Baroque or Fascist "culture." He ends by exclaiming sadly, "I wish there were in the world a real white flag of freedom . . . [not] the red flag of Communism or the black flag of Fascism . . . [for] by every instinct of my blood, I . . . prefer English liberty to Latin discipline."[34]

His position and reputation were further confused by the fact that other writers for *G.K.'s Weekly* took a far more Rightist position, even putting Chesterton in the embarrassing position of having his paper endorse the invasion of Ethiopia while he was away on a short trip. Chesterton never admired these European strong men the way his Leftist friends like Shaw or Wells did, or the way Belloc did from his Rightest position. Belloc wanted to establish the monarchy as a replacement for Parliamentary government and liked Mussolini because he "represented" the force that united Europe — Roman Catholicism. As usual, Chesterton was supporting the middle against *all* his friends at once.[35]

His old friend Hilaire Belloc turned sixty on July 27, 1930, and his friends threw a gargantuan party to celebrate. Chesterton, of course, served as master of ceremonies for the more than forty guests. He happily described the event in his *Autobiography* as "something between a Day of Judgment and a dream, in which men of many groups known to me . . . all appeared together as a sort of resurrection."[36] An ode by Father Ronald Knox, which appeared on the back of the menu, was recited by Maurice Baring, who simultaneously balanced a wine glass on his head. Having been told there were to be no speeches, Chesterton merely recited a poem when he presented their gift to Belloc, a wine-filled golden loving cup, which was then passed from guest to guest. When accepting it, Belloc said he understood that it was at seventy that a writer began to care frightfully if his writing lived forever, so he hoped to die at sixty-nine.[37]

After they had eaten, someone whispered in Chesterton's ear that it would be nice to say a word of thanks to the person who had arranged the affair. Chesterton rose and did so, only to have the praised individual rise solemnly and say that all the work had really been done by the person sitting next to him. Then that individual rose in turn and repeated this remark, until they had gone all the way around the table, each taking a bow, and everyone making more and more amusing comments. One pretended to be Lloyd George, another gave a trade unions pep talk, a third mentioned how happy they all were to have "ex-Druid Chesterton among them," until it became, as Chesterton said, "The only dinner I have ever attended at which it was literally true that every diner made an after-dinner speech."[38]

That August 1930 another loosely linked collection of Chesterton's stories was published: *Four Faultless Felons*. Ostensibly, the tales were told to an American journalist by the felons, who appeared to be crooks but were in fact heroes of modern life, dealing with forces that continued to concern Chesterton, including industrialism, science, imperialism, and the Jewish question.

Like its predecessor, *The Poet and the Lunatics*, this "novel" is reminiscent of both *The Club of Queer Trades* and *The Man Who Was Thursday*. It, too, reflects the fact that Chesterton was "reliving" his adolescent anxieties about society, and working his way through them for a second time. In spite of the fact that the book had been published piecemeal, the final product is very well-constructed, which shows that Chesterton had taken pains with its structure, especially with the framing story which begins and ends it, the "Prologue of the Pressman" and "Epilogue of the Pressman."[39] The felons recite their adventures to this pressman in the club to which they all belong. Though each of them represents a Chestertonian social concern, none of them makes large-scale suggestions for improvement or propagandizes for either Roman Catholicism or distributism. The book is also a satiric portrait of modern journalism, a highly relevant topic at a time when the Conservatives were being bullied by the press lords Beaverbrook and Rothermere, Northcliffe's brother and heir on Fleet Street.[40]

The first story is a parable about the dangers of political extremism, described in terms of a political naivete that resulted from "the folly of educating the comfortable classes in a false optimism about the record and security of the Empire . . . never [hearing] a word about the other side of the story . . . [so that] they often pass abruptly from a stupid Britishism to an equally stupid Bolshevism."[41] A young Englishwoman is told about her "innocence" by an Egyptian who, when she says England has a glorious Empire, replies, "So had Egypt"; then he points with his green umbrella to the distant pyramid and adds, "A glorious Empire . . . on which the sun never sets. Look — the sun is setting in blood."[42] This is one of several Chestertonian prophecies about the end of empire which are interesting to read, for they were written at a period when the big political issues involved the abandonment of British free trade for imperial preference as well as the Constitutional struggles, especially over India, that were to lead to the Statute of Westminster in 1931, which granted the colonies Dominion status. (One difficulty with reading Chesterton now is that such allusions, though they would have been clear to his contemporary readers, are no longer obvious to contemporary critics without a detailed knowledge of English political life in the twenties and thirties.)

One charming detail about the first part is that it centers on a heroine, Barbara Traill, "who was a girl with a good deal of the boy about her":

> This is very commonly said about modern heroines. . . . [But she] would be a very disappointing modern heroine. . . . The novelists who call their heroines boyish . . . know nothing whatever about boys. The girl they depict . . . [is] a bright young thing or a brazen little idiot . . . sublimely candid . . . slightly shallow . . . uniformly cheerful . . . entirely unembarrassed . . . everything a boy is not. But Barbara really was . . . like a boy . . . rather shy, obscurely imaginative, capable of intellectual friendships and . . . of emotional brooding over them . . . capable of being morbid . . . by no means incapable of being secretive. She had that sense of misfit which embarrasses so many boys; the sense of the soul being too big to be seen or confessed. . . .[43]

Clearly, Barbara is Chesterton in female form. She is reassured by the hero that she is not going mad just because she "had bad dreams and brooded over things of [her] imagination. It is not the imaginative people who go mad even when they are morbid, for they can always be woken up from bad dreams by broader prospects and brighter visions. . . . The men who go mad are . . . the stubborn, stoical men who have only room for one idea and take it literally . . ." — the Chestertonian "heretics," in fact.[44]

In the second section, called "The Honest Quack," the "religion of science" is attacked in a story about an artist who is saving a tree from the city; it is a modern-day parable about preserving both rural England and the forbidden tree in the Garden of Eden. The opposing attitudes of poetry (the poet) and common sense (represented by a doctor) are shown to be compatible, or the different sides of a single reality, in much the same way that Quin and Wayne were really comrades in *The Napoleon of Notting Hill*. With the characters' recognition that both poetry and ordinary life are important to mankind, there appears a kind of new creation in which the tree and the Garden it stands for are redeemed.[45]

Chesterton stresses similar social and theological truths in the third story. It is a curious tale about three brothers' different attitudes toward their family business (England). The first brother is a kind of Christian Socialist minister who wants to reform it as if it were his parish; the second is basically his father's business-oriented heir; and the third insists on a kind of repentance *before* any reforms can be implemented. Through this character Chesterton is suggesting that programs for social reform must involve sacrifice and repentance before they can work. As one character says, " 'The whole universe was wrong, while the lie of my father [his prosperity] flourished like the green bay-tree. It was not *respectability* that could redeem it. . . . [Instead] somebody must be . . . *needlessly* good, to weight down the scales of that judgment' " (italics mine).[46]

The fourth story is a political parable. "The Loyal Traitor" is about modern journalism and its effect on a small Ruritanian state, Pavonia, which is on the verge of a "real, international universal social revolution." This revolution is foiled by the report of a revolution, in a kind of dramatized version of Daniel Boorstin's pseudo "media event." But as a result of the journalists' invention of a revolution, Pavonia's leaders actually reform and allow the king to become a real ruler without any Bolshevist bloodbath. The story suggests that Chesterton now felt that avoiding violent revolution was desirable, as well as that older, established hierarchies could be more egalitarian than the modern bureaucracies.[47]

More essays from Chesterton's old standby column in the *Illustrated London News* came out that October of 1930 under the title *Come to Think of It*. In this book, as in most of his essays, Chesterton is chatting with his reader in a friendly fashion about things like the classics. He says that he still feels the classics are more desirable for educating the young than "facts":

Facts do not always create a spirit of reality, because reality is a spirit. Facts by themselves can often feed the flame of madness, because sanity is a spirit. . . . They lack proportion. . . . What culture ought to do is give a health of mind that is parallel to the health of the body. . . . The true teaching, which strengthens and steadies the mind so it knows and rejects madness at sight, has, in fact, come down to us very largely from the culture of those great languages in which were written . . . the Greek Testament and the Roman law.[48]

As always, Chesterton writes with both humor and common sense, a combination evident in his essay on the Bolshevist idea of "abolishing" Sunday. In it he suggests that their idea implies no "understanding of the fact that one thing essential to man is rhythm. . . . Man has always known this by instinct . . . and when all humanity has agreed on the necessity for something, we may be perfectly certain that some sort of humanitarian will want to destroy it."[49]

That same October *The Resurrection of Rome* came out; at that time Gilbert, Frances, and Dorothy Collins set sail again for the United States. On shipboard Chesterton spent a day with his beloved brown paper and chalks, drawing and inventing clues for a highly successful treasure hunt for the other passengers. But when Dorothy Collins went looking for the clues later, she found the other passengers had taken them all as collector's items. The three stayed in America for nearly seven months, despite the fact that Frances collapsed from exhaustion about midway through the trip and had to be left behind to recuperate while Dorothy Collins and Chesterton kept those engagements that could not be canceled. Most of the money made on the trip was already earmarked to help keep *G.K.'s Weekly* afloat.

Chesterton was scheduled to give two series of lectures that would run concurrently at the University of Notre Dame in South Bend, Indiana, as well as travel through the United States giving talks and visiting several Canadian cities. At the same time he had to keep up his regular articles and columns for his English audience. It was this trip, rather than his earlier one, which gave rise to most of the stories and legends about Chesterton in America; the fact that he had come as a Roman Catholic convert subtly affected how he was perceived. On the one hand, the Roman Catholic community treated him like family, showing him a loving kindness that he greatly appreciated; on the other hand, although the press and the general public liked him and treated him like a celebrity, they clearly typecast him as a kind of romantic reactionary belonging to a somewhat "unacceptable" sect.

As a formal lecturer, Chesterton as usual was disorganized and not too effective a speaker, holding his scraps of paper and quoting long passages from literature in a high-pitched voice that was not always audible. Visually, however, he was always an impressive sight: people noted his sheer bulk, his shaggy, tousled mane of streaky hair, his ruddy face, his full evening dress, the cape slung over his shoulders. But it was his spontaneous wit that usually put his audience in the palm of his hand. He won over his audience in Pittsburgh, for example, when he told them, "I want to reassure you I am not this size, really, dear no, I'm being amplified by the [mike]." In Chicago, someone yelled out that he could not hear, and Chesterton glanced up and said, "Good brother, don't worry, you're not missing a thing."[50]

At Notre Dame the Chestertons stayed with a faculty family named Bixler who had two small daughters with whom they soon were great friends. Chesterton worked during the day, dictating to Dorothy Collins, and then after dinner went to the university to give his lecture. One night he talked about Victorian literature; the next, about a great Victorian like Gladstone. There were thirty-six lectures in all, given to a crowd of over five hundred.[51] One student commented afterward that he was puzzled at first because Chesterton had the habit of chuckling aloud as he said something serious, but then the student realized that his thoughts were so far ahead of what he was actually saying that he was laughing at a joke he was about to make.

Chesterton clearly enjoyed the "family" atmosphere of a Catholic university, and stories are still told about him around South Bend, where his very presence helped to put the university "on the map." He endeared himself to the students by attending the football game against Navy in a year when their great coach, Knute Rockne, led them to an undefeated season. He did not understand football well, but, typically, he developed an analogy from it that he found appealing and wrote a poem about it. He compared the golden dome of the main campus building to Nero's Golden House in Rome, next to which stood the Colosseum, where the early Christians were forced to fight wild beasts. In the poem, called "The Arena," dedicated to Notre Dame, he describes the American version of the Golden House and the Colosseum:

> I have seen where a strange country
> Opened its secret plains about me
> One great golden dome stands lonely with its golden images . . .
> Through the sun-lit Indian summer
> That Apocalyptic potent that has clothed her with the Sun. . . .
> She, too, looks upon the Arena
> Sees the gladiators in grapple . . .
> On our Lady of the Victories
> The Mother of the Master of the Masters of the World. . . .[52]

On November 5, 1930, Chesterton was made an honorary doctor of laws in the first special convocation of the faculty of Notre Dame. The citation called him a "man of letters . . . defender of the Christian tradition, whose keen mind, right heart, and versatile literary genius have been valiantly devoted to eternal truth, goodness, and beauty, in literature and in life. . . ."[53]

During this trip Chesterton held a big public debate with Clarence Darrow at the Mecca in New York City. (Darrow was the Chicago lawyer who had recently defended the "scientific" theory of evolution against William Jennings Bryan in the Scopes "monkey trial."[54]) Darrow and Chesterton also debated the story of creation in Genesis, then discussed the history of religion, but as Chesterton commented, "When I tried to talk about Greek cults or Asiatic ascetism [he] appeared to be unable to think about anything except Jonah and the Whale."[55]

Two curious facts remain about the debate. On the one hand, people who admired Chesterton (and that included most of the audience who voted him the winner) felt that he made a monkey out of Darrow. The famous trial lawyer not only did not stick to the point, but was unable to keep up with Chesterton, who used his debater's wit and speed. At one point, for example, when their microphone failed, Chesterton happily shouted out, "Science, you see, is not infallible!"[56]

On the other hand, one recent biography of Darrow ignores this debate completely, largely, it would seem, because there is nothing "important" about reactionary Chesterton that would add to the story of the great "Liberal lawyer" who defended two rich boys — Loeb and Leopold — whom Chesterton would have seen as the epitome of the elite.[57] Another, more objective biography points out that Darrow was "as old-fashioned as William Jennings Bryan"; it says that Darrow lacked an appreciation of religious subtleties, and was not so much against religion as he was opposed to the Bible-Belt version of it, sharing H.L. Mencken's attitude.[58]

Chesterton returned home to England in the spring of 1931, still convinced that America and England are two separate countries and should think of themselves that way. He liked Americans but disliked "Americanization" for its materialism, although he admired some of the results of mass production, like Ford cars. He felt the one great American virtue was that "America really does remain democratic. . . . The citizens feel equal. . . . There may not be government of the people, by the people, and for the people, but there is not government of the people, *by* the governing class . . . *for* the governing class. . . . For anyone who knows anything about history . . . this really is and remains a remarkable achievement."[59]

The year of the Chestertons' return was described by the historian Arnold Toynbee as the "Annus Terribilis," the year when the Wall Street crash of late 1929 spread and involved the whole world in the Great Depression. He wrote that "men and women all over . . . were seriously contemplating and frankly discussing the possibility that the Western System of Society might break down and cease to work."[60] Since Chesterton was in favor of the "Western system" but also had said for some time that it had broken down, his general outlook in the next few years has been described as "approaching religious ecstasy" — that is, he is accused of being gleeful when in truth he only sounded the note of a prophet whose prophecy has come true.[61]

At the same time, Lloyd George, as titular leader of the demoralized Liberal Party, was spending these years as a kind of "Supporter-in-Chief" to the Labour prime minister, although he hammered hard at the fact that Labour could not seem to control unemployment.[62] But by mid-1930 Lloyd George had been a party to another "inter-party" conference aimed at coping with unemployment (over two million were unemployed in July 1930), and he was toying again with the idea of forming his own "Centre Party," made up of a few Liberal and Conservative and Labour members who were unhappy with their own parties.[63] His plan did not work out partly because Lloyd George got sick. Meanwhile, on December 1, 1930, the charismatic Sir Oswald Mosley published a manifesto, calling for a crash program of public works, protection of the home market, and "imperial" free trade — all to some extent Lloyd George's ideas. But by the mid-thirties Mosley's Black Shirts were clearly Fascists. In the spring of 1931 Beatrice Webb was writing in her diary that it looked as if Lloyd George and the Liberals were about to join the Labour Party's Front Bench.[64] None of these developments would fill Chesterton with ecstasy, but they made it painfully obvious that Lloyd George himself was again using the Liberals rather than helping them.

The summer and fall of 1931 England's intellectual mood was depressed; people were nostalgic for the good old days (that rosy pre-Marconi period before the war). The attitude was perfectly summed up in Noel Coward's play Cavalcade, a panorama of recent history which ends with a toast that "this country of ours will find dignity and greatness and peace again."[65] The most pressing problem was England's dire financial situation, which meant she could not finance the social programs needed, and by August the Labour government had resigned.

King George, who had been warned that the Labour Cabinet was deadlocked over the budget, which had to be balanced if American bankers were to guarantee another loan, talked to Liberal Herbert Samuel, deputizing for Lloyd George, who was ill, and the Conservative Baldwin. The result was a "National Government" with Labourite MacDonald staying on as prime minister.[66] Once again, Belloc's oligarchical "party system" was in charge, while the monarch, like those in Chesterton's recent novels, was forced by the political vacuum to "rule." By September, England had gone off the gold standard, and in October this government held a General Election without presenting a program at all. But it won an overwhelming victory, which showed the voters had lost confidence in party government, and that personalities now counted for more than principles.[67]

These events turned the younger generation political and doctrinaire, although many remained outspokenly pacifist. In G. K.'s Weekly Chesterton spoke out strongly against their isolationist attitude, which he said echoed the opinion of press lord Beaverbrook (a Canadian), who thought England was really just a part of Canada.[68] The League of Nations was ineffective and ignored by those offenders of world peace like Italy, Japan, and Germany, and Chesterton called it "a Tower of Babel" based on the old hope for the superman, which is "another name for despair of man."

The younger intellectuals, however, who saw the National Government as one lumpish, conservative "Establishment" (an attitude Chesterton shared), for the most part turned Left, seeing 1931 as the pivotal year in their own lives and development.[69] In this curious way they were Chesterton's heirs, for they felt one must take sides against one's own class. Those most disenchanted by the state of the world, or their own role in it, were now recruited by the Communist Party for future dirty work in the fifties and sixties. All of them exhibited both cynicism and sentimentality, which, as is pointed out by a historian of the period, "Chesterton said . . . are not far apart, for both lack vitality, resilience, and depth."[70]

Most of the bright, upper middle-class university students now began to see their role in literature as having social meaning; in this important — if unacknowledged — sense, they were also Chesterton's heirs, because they reacted as he did to a time demanding "public" art and propaganda. But unlike Chesterton, who generously acknowledged his intellectual ancestry, they never saw how much they resembled those young Edwardian Liberals who also ended at war. Their great spokesman became Auden, who had helped strike-break in the mid-twenties as a lark; he and his friends Isherwood, Day Lewis, MacNiece, and Spender became "the thirties generation." Paradoxically, they saw their literary ancestry as deriving from Henry James and the Bloomsbury group, partly because Hogarth Press (established by Leonard and Virginia Woolf) was often their first publisher. But they were not prepared to follow T. S. Eliot from *The Waste Land* to *Burnt Norton*. As the Bloomsbury grand dame, Virginia Woolf acted the part of Gertrude Stein and publicly called them to task for their attitude, so that they had to define themselves symbolically as the thirties' poets; it was her own nephews Julian and Quentin Bell at Cambridge "who took to politics with the exhilarated sense of shaking off the aestheticism of literary Cambridge and Bloomsbury."[71] The whole literary development of the thirties, therefore, is simply another round in the game known as "Cheat the Prophet."[72] But since the young did not read Chesterton, they did not know the name of the game.

Another living fossil, H. G. Wells, not only could not win the academic recognition he wanted, but also was increasingly unread by intellectuals, with the result that he became more and more prone to nasty personal attacks. After changing his mistress and his address, he, like Chesterton, began working on his autobiography. His readership was also like Chesterton's: he had a large popular audience that kept on growing.[73] But the Left saw Wells as a petty bourgeois humbug, and even his literary heirs like

Orwell thought Wells was naive — he regarded the Labour Party as silly and the Communists as impossible. In October 1930, at his seventieth birthday party at the Savoy, Wells echoed the mood of despair, but still hoped for a "freemasonry of science" that would establish a world republic.[74]

By the mid-thirties, he had been converted to the idea that F.D.R.'s New Deal would produce revolution by means of a Brains Trust, but he had also recognized that capitalism and communism were becoming more similar in their large-scale planning and production. Ideologically Orwell was much closer to Chesterton's position, but he resolutely refused to accept Chesterton's use of analogy, and like all his generation, he assumed Chesterton was Old King Cole.[75]

During the last decade of his life, then, Chesterton was still writing his own kind of revolutionary tracts and remaining a crusader against the fin de siècle. But his real position was radical, something unsuspected by the young intellectuals, who took Wells' scientific vocabulary and Shaw's Ibsenesque psychology to be modern, when they were actually using well-worn nineteenth-century terms.

All Is Grist, more essays from the *Illustrated London News*, came out in October of 1931. While it is undoubtedly true that all the essays Chesterton ever wrote are not equally entertaining or though-provoking, every collection has a surprising number of essays that are both. One in this group, "On Sightseeing," humorously contrasts "the age of monuments with the age of museums," and suggests that the problem with modern sightseeing is that it is "not meant either for the wanderer to see by accident or for the pilgrim to see with awe. It is meant for the mere slave of a routine of self-education to stuff himself with every incongruous intellectual food in one indigestible meal."[76]

Chesterton also touches a responsive chord in every reader of literary criticism when he says,

> Looking back over a wild and wasted life, I realized that I have especially sinned in neglecting to read novels. . . . If instead of trifling away my time over pamphlets about Collectivism or Co-operation, plunging for mere pleasure into the unhealthy excitement of theological debates . . . I had sat quietly at home doing my duty and reading every novel as it came out, I might be a more serious and earnest man than I am today.

He admits he had dodged these kinds of books because they lack the purpose still found in less intellectual stories which pointed toward a certain goal:

> The modern novel . . . is driven back . . . on the microscopic description of . . . aimless appetites . . . [and is] not very interesting to a middle-aged man with plenty of other things to think about. . . . The old literature, great and trivial, was built on the idea that there is a purpose in life [but] modern philosophy has taken the life out of modern fiction . . . [which] is . . .

dissolving into ... formlessness ... and deserves ... the modern reproach of being "sloppy."[77]

On Christmas Day, 1931, Chesterton began his newest career in earnest (although he did not begin a regular series for another year). The fledgling BBC had asked him to make a broadcast to the United States (like the king to the empire) about Christmas and Charles Dickens. Since it is hard to imagine a topic he would have liked better, it is not surprising that he was an instant success, coming across very naturally as the world's amusing, talkative friend. Fortunately, his high voice broadcast effectively, and his personality added something more — a touch of magic all his own.[78] In this first talk, Chesterton told his transatlantic audience:

> I have been asked to speak to you ... on Dickens and Christmas; or as I should prefer to say, on Christmas and Dickens. Why ... Christmas and Dickens? Perhaps the official organizers do not know me very well. Perhaps they have a grudge against you. Why, on this day of holiday, am I made to work. Why, on this day of rejoicing, are you made to suffer. Christmas and ... Dickens ... are both things that many people think very old-fashioned. But nobody, just yet, thinks the Wireless old-fashioned. ... We talk about Christmas because there is nothing else to talk about. We talk about Dickens because there is nobody else to talk about. ... First, there is no other festival to keep except Christmas. ... [The Modern Pagans] have failed to make a Feast. ... In the same way, [Dickens] is the only person who talked about Christmas as if it was Christmas; as if it was even more Christmas than it is. ... Dickens was separated by centuries of misunderstanding from that mysterious revelation that brought joy upon earth; but ... he was resolved to enjoy it. ... And now in the name of all such things, let us all go and do the same.[79]

Not too long afterward Chesterton also commented upon the dangers he saw in the BBC's state monopoly, saying,

> Suppose you had told some ... Liberals that there was an entirely new ... printing press eclipsing all others, and that as this was to be given to the King, all printing would henceforth be government printing. They would be roaring like rebels ... [but] that is exactly what we have done with the ... wireless. There is really no protection against propaganda. ... It is wicked to nationalize mines or railroads, but we lose no time in nationalizing tongues and talk.[80]

During the early part of 1932 the Chestertons had the unhappy experience of having both of their mothers ill. Frances commuted between Beaconsfield, where her mother lay dying in a nursing home, and London, where Mrs. Chesterton still lived at 11 Warwick Gardens. Ada Chesterton usually came by on Sunday evenings to see her, and occasionally took her to the seashore at Brighton, where Chesterton would try to join them for a few days. Ada began to notice that Mrs. Chesterton was eating less and not getting up easily. One Sunday night Ada stayed with her until Frances and Gilbert could get there from Beaconsfield, and shortly afterward Mrs. Chesterton died.[81]

The Chesterton family treasures were divided up among their relatives, but before anyone else had had a chance to sort through Mr. Ed's study, which was still piled high with family papers and memorabilia, Chesterton wandered in and told the servants to cart everything off to make a bonfire. Dorothy Collins, already dedicated to a lifework of collecting Chestertonia, arrived in time to save only a few things, which Chesterton let her take, but he muttered in the car all the way home about women's hoarding habits.[82] Later, Ada Chesterton was terribly angry with him because when she sat down to write her biography of the brothers, she found that the only material of Cecil's that had been saved was a small book full of his drawings and rhymes about "Bloppa," one of his childhood inventions. These items undoubtedly reminded Gilbert of his happy childhood associations with Cecil, but Ada always felt she alone had a right to Cecil and his memory, and never seems to have realized how much Cecil meant to Gilbert.[83]

The death of Chesterton's mother meant that Chesterton inherited some family money. This made it possible for him to make legacies to family and friends, to contribute to building a Beaconsfield parish church, and to start on the project dear to Dorothy Collins' heart — a larger study at Top Meadow.

That April Chesterton's biographical study of Chaucer came out, a book for which he received the largest advance he ever got — one thousand pounds. This book has not helped his reputation: it is used to label him as a writer lost in the past, caught up in mindless medievalism. Chesterton's thesis was that he liked and admired Chaucer immensely because he was "closer [than Shakespeare] to the meaning of Merrie England . . . festive and full of fun . . . the last full and free manifestation [of the spirit] which is *Pickwick*"; he called Chaucer "a novelist when there were no novels."[84]

Chesterton's basic approach to Chaucer was to recognize that his world was not like the modern one; it was a world in which the intellectuals and the ordinary people still related to one another. Therefore, Chaucer's profoundly comic irony had not only a popular simplicity, but also a depth of "clerkly" sophistication.[85] In other words, Chaucer wrote to be read by everybody, which was alse Chesterton's goal. This was the medieval, Christian world, which had its own version of "spiritual democracy," even though it also had a very structured society. It was this facet of Chaucer's time that had led Chesterton to feel that democracy — his own brand of Liberal democracy — had arisen from the world of medieval Christianity, and, in the end, from Christianity itself.[86]

Chesterton, however, recognized that his time and Chaucer's were not the same for he faced "pagan" humanism without the kind of world view and Roman Catholic underpinnings that kept Chaucer safe from humanisms' "colorful" dangers. Shakespeare, on the other hand, already exhibits a kind of sixteenth-century "nonsense" related to his "mad" characters, a wild fantasy that breaks the bonds of reason. Chaucer is too full of common sense, too much aware of the order of the world to do the same. He is, in fact, the most English of poets, because he represents a turning point in literature, religion, and history; he is a man who can live in and use the best of "both worlds." The common framework of a shared religion meant that Chaucer's own brand of humor and wisdom, supported by this social equilibrium between town and gown, could work.[87]

As in all of his "literary" criticism, Chesterton was also writing social commentary about his own time. As he tells his reader in the introduction,

> I fear the reader will . . . pause to wonder, with not unjust irritation, why I sometimes seem to be writing about modern politics instead of about medieval history. I can only say that the actual experience of trying to tell such truths as I know about the matter, left me with an overwhelming conviction that it is because we miss the point of the medieval history that we make a mess of the modern politics. I felt suddenly the fierce and glaring relevancy of all the walking social symbols of the Chaucerian scene to the dissolving views of our own social doubts and speculation today.[88]

In *Chaucer*, Chesterton once again was facing battle on several fronts. On the one hand, he was appealing to the young, cutting across the old visions of utopia and superman (or the Renaissance man) that were the fundamental beliefs of heretics like Wells and the Fabians.[89] On the other hand, he (and his friend Belloc) had recently begun a public battle with Dr. G.G. Coulton, a self-taught medieval scholar whose writings were devoted to describing medieval England as eclipsed by a ghastly Dark Age in which a Puritanical gloom hung over the brutish, Hobbesian landscape.[90] While Belloc routinely identified European culture with the old Holy Roman Empire, Chesterton wanted England to recognize that she, too, was part of the Continent and of a stable spiritual tradition, especially at this time, when pacifism and isolationism were rampant, as was the new growth of "heretical" creeds.

As Chesterton saw it, the idea of Europe for which Sir Thomas More had died was not entirely a religious idea, any more than Dante's *Comedia* is only a personal, spiritual quest. Chesterton distinguished sharply between the culture itself and its underlying theology: "the one was not limited, but its opportunities were limited; the other gave him . . . in a decaying civilization . . . the breadth and depth of a complicated creed," a distinction Chesterton made because, to him, the simplification of life or ideas was always the ultimate heresy.[91] In a revolutionary epoch when civilization is dissolving, such a faith provides equilibrium, as it did for More and Cervantes and Chaucer himself, because "Catholicism is not medievalism":

> It is only something that could make medievalism tolerable to a man like Chaucer ... [going] back to ... Boethius ... a Christian and a Stoic. .... That is the heritage that had been handed down to Christian men; and it was not lopsided or bigoted ... [but] a balance ... like the two eyes of a man. ... It is a dying civilization that never dies. .... The moral is that no man should desert that civilization. It can cure itself, but those who leave it cannot cure it ... not Mahomet, nor Calvin nor Lenin ... have cured or will cure the real evils of Christendom; for the severed hand does not heal the whole body.[92]

Chesterton's second book on his impressions of America, called *Sidelights on New London and Newer York*, was published in May 1932, and that October the BBC finally arranged to have him do a regular radio series reviewing books. Ada Chesterton commented that considering how Chesterton hated mechanical devices, it was amazing that he could use a microphone so easily, but she agreed that his voice came across beautifully modulated and that he seemed perfectly at ease. The result, according to her, was that Chesterton now gained a "new and idolatrous following"; the BBC wrote him that the "building rings with your praises."[93]

Dorothy Collins noted in her diary that Chesterton was not only giving innumerable talks and lectures, going to dinners like those of the Detection Club and the Distributist League, and attending mock trials and the king's garden party; he was also making these fortnightly radio appearances, which required a considerable amount of preparation. First Chesterton gave Dorothy Collins a list of topics, and she looked through books on that subject; next he dictated a kind of talk which discussed a few books at greater length. This script was then published two weeks later in the BBC's magazine, *The Listener*. (She was impressed by the fact that no author — even though many were Chesterton's friends — ever approached Chesterton asking to be reviewed.) Chesterton actually was very nervous before a show. He had agreed to do the series only on the condition that Frances and Dorothy come and sit in the studio so that he could speak to them, which is what gave his talks the personal, intimate tone his wide audience loved.[94] They also adored his charm and his chuckle, and his delightful way of ad-libbing, which once prompted him to turn a common phrase: "We talk about life as being dull as ditchwater, but is ditchwater dull? Naturalists with microscopes have told me that it teems with quiet fun." People who had never read his books nor cared about either his politics or his religion became his fans. The result was that, by being himself and using this newest and best of all the media, he became a missionary. He clearly knew it, because he kept to his schedule despite the time the broadcasts took, and despite his frequent attacks of bronchitis.[95]

In 1932 the world was not getting better from anyone's standpoint. The National Government under MacDonald passed Joe Chamberlain's tariff and imperial protection system under the leadership of his son Neville, allowing those government Liberals who disagreed to "differ" or resign. The Japanese had successfully invaded Manchuria without action from the Great Powers or the League of Nations; the Weimar Republic in Germany was being ruined by the Depression, and by January 1933 Adolph Hitler had become its chancellor, and within a few months had destroyed the republic and begun to re-arm. Lloyd George spoke out about their persecution of the Jews, but in general took the attitude that it was everyone else's fault for insisting on German reparations. Basically, he rather admired a "strong" Germany, and a little later he visited Hitler, becoming one of his "fans."[96] In *G.K.'s Weekly* Chesterton had more sensibly called Hindenburg "the man who keeps the seat warm for a Dictator."

By 1934, when German Nazis staged a coup in Austria, Chesterton felt the Turks were already at the heart of European civilization in a resurgence of the old "Paganism" and "Prussianism."[97] Nazism itself was the old elitism under a new shirt; it was undemocratic, aping "Nietzsche's . . . pretentious claim of the fastidious . . . the disgust and disdain which consume him at the sight of the common people. . . ."[98] At the same time, Chesterton's very moderate admiration for Mussolini (which would not have survived the Axis Pact) was tempered by his feeling that the man and his fascism were "un-English," or, as Murrell (his spokesman) said in *The Return of Don Quixote*, "Our people like to be ruled by gentlemen, in a general sort of way. But nobody could stand being ruled by one gentleman. The idea is too horrible."[99]

Echoes of these worrisome current events are heard in his next book of essays collected from the *Illustrated London Times*, which came out on March 23, 1933, with the title *All I Survey*. In one essay, "On Saint George Revisited," he points out that "the disadvantage of men not knowing the past is that they do not know the present. History is a hill or a high point of vantage, from which alone men see the . . . age in which they are living. . . . Yet this sense of the past is curiously patchy among the most intelligent and instructed people. . . ." He goes on to say that everybody thinks the joke is in "showing how unlike Saint George's time ours is," but this is not so:

> A man in the later Roman Empire . . . would have seen all around him an ancient world that was astonishingly like the modern world. . . . He would think he had got back into the old bewildered and decaying world of the last phase of Paganism, loud with denials of religion and louder with the howlings of superstition. . . . He would be quite at home . . . and he would prepare for death [as a martyr under Diocletian].[100]

Meanwhile, Chesterton had been asked to write a companion study to his highly successful *St. Francis of Assisi*. It was to be a brief review of the life of the great Roman Catholic theologian Saint Thomas Aquinas, whose writings were gaining a new hearing from the growing group of neo-Thomist scholars. The book was published that fall on September 21, 1933.

Chesterton had read *Summa Theologica* at some point much earlier, and because of the Thomist revival in Roman Catholic circles, he had heard a great deal about the saint at Distributist meetings, too. But no one could claim that in any strict sense Chesterton was a systematic philosopher or a Thomist, although much critical work on Chesterton tries to prove just that.[101] The basis for such an assertion, however, usually ends up being that Chesterton was an "intuitive" Thomist, which is certainly true if one accepts his characterization of the angelic doctor, with whom he clearly did identify, both physically and rationally. Chesterton supplied the connecting link in *Chaucer*; there he said that "the meaning of Aquinas is that medievalism was always seeking a center of gravity. The meaning of Chaucer is that, when found, it was always a center of gaiety."[102]

Dorothy Collins' account reveals that for *St. Thomas Aquinas: The Dumb Ox*, Chesterton followed his normal pattern of research and writing. As he wrote or dictated other things, he thought about Saint Thomas; then saying, "Shall we do a bit of Tommy?" he would dictate to her. About half the book was done when he told her to get him some books on Aquinas, and when she asked him what books he replied, "I don't know." First his efficient secretary wrote to Father O'Connor, who sent her a list of the classic and recent studies, and then she went to London and bought them. When she got them back to Beaconsfield, Chesterton casually flipped through them, reading here and there in his typically "aimless" fashion, then dumped the books down in a pile somewhere and finished dictating his book without referring to them again. The only mark Dorothy Collins found in any of them was a tiny drawing of Saint Thomas.[103]

Sheed and Ward had been granted the American rights to the book, and Mrs. Ward admits that had they known how he worked, they would have been appalled. But *St. Thomas Aquinas: The Dumb Ox* was not only a popular success, but a critical success as well. In a Parisian bookstore the great Thomist theologian Etienne Gilson told Frank Sheed that Chesterton's book was so good that it made him despair: "I have been studying Saint Thomas all my life, and I could never have written such a book."[104] But, of course, Chesterton did not write the book for the Gilsons of the world, but for his favorite reader. According to him, it was no more than a "popular sketch of a great historical character. . . . Its aim will be achieved if it leads those who have hardly heard of [him] to read about him in better books. . . ." He added that it was written largely for those who are not Roman Catholics because "the biography is an introduction to the philosophy and . . . the philosophy . . . to the theology," and he was chiefly explaining Aquinas' life and times.[105]

In the book Chesterton insisted that Saint Thomas, like Saint Francis, had "reaffirmed the Incarnation, by bringing God back to earth." Aristotle had provided him with the materials he needed to build a philosophic structure "to defend creation" against the age-old heresy of Manicheism, a revulsion against matter and the world. Like his biographer, Saint Thomas was fighting against annihilating mystics and minimizing rationalists, insisting that "man is not a balloon going up into the sky, nor a mole burrowing . . . in the earth; but rather a thing like a tree, whose roots are fed from the earth, while its highest branches . . . rise almost to the stars."[106]

Chesterton's loving portrait of the "Dumb Ox" shows that he identified with Aquinas' life story: he sympathetically describes the "huge, heavy bull of a man, fat and slow and quiet . . . the big boy left behind in the lowest form . . . called the Dunce . . . a thinker who loved books." To Chesterton, Saint Thomas was Chaucer's clerk, who lived on books and occasionally wrote a hymn the way other men took a holiday. Saint Thomas had reconciled Aristotle to Christ, not the other way around; Chesterton now baptized him as a Distributist saint of common sense, a guardian against the tendencies of intellectuals to be heretics — that is, unbalanced people guilty of oversimplifying. Chesterton insisted that the Thomist tradition was the guardian of sanity and then declared it was the only possible basis for radical political reform.[107]

In this way he was using Aquinas to win debating points for down-to-earth, Aristotelian common sense, as opposed to the abstract and patterned Platonic world view of Saint Augustine; he was also trying to make a real human being of the angelic doctor. But those who want to make Chesterton an intellectual Roman Catholic saint use this book to prove that Chesterton is relevant because he was a Thomist by "connaturality." This approach curiously divorces Chesterton the man from his own "historical figure in history."

Whichever of his books are chosen for the category of apologetics, Chesterton is fairly called one of a long line of Christian "humanists" who since 1200 A.D. have been at work defining the central tradition of Western thought, which "combines the often conflicting elements of classical thought and culture and the accepted truths of Christian revelation."[108] Chesterton was torn between feeling and reason, because reason, too, is fallacious and must be completed by faith. The result is a central tension between order and emotion that can be seen in all his writing. To Chesterton it appeared that this kind of restriction, or tension, was what is meant by the Prayer Book phrase about God — "Whose Service is Perfect Freedom."

He does seem to be summing up his own artistic vision when he makes this statement:

> That *strangeness* of things, which is the light in all poetry, and indeed in all art, is really connected with their otherness; or what is called their objectivity.
> . . . In this the great contemplative is the complete contrary of that false

contemplative, the mystic, who looks only into his own soul, the selfish artist who shrinks from the world and lives only in his own mind. According to St. Thomas, the mind acts freely of itself, but its freedom exactly consists in finding a way out to liberty and the light of day; to reality and the land of the living.[109]

During 1934 the world had begun to work its way out of the Depression, but foreign affairs seemed only to get worse. The Conservative leader Baldwin had begun to "fill in" for the Labour prime minister, whom he shortly succeeded in office; the Liberals still squabbled and split. Meanwhile, Chesterton continued editing and writing for *G.K.'s Weekly*, making his BBC broadcasts, and maintaining his schedule for columns and lectures; another essay collection, *Avowals and Denials*, appeared that November. That year he was also elected an honorary member of the prestigious Athenaeum Club, and the Pope made both him and Belloc Knight Commanders of Saint Gregory. At home in Beaconsfield the Chestertons continued to enjoy the company of the Nichols family, now living nearby. In retrospect the family realized that Chesterton was spending more time listening, less time talking, and moving slower and slower.

By January 1935 the Saar had been returned to Germany, and Hitler re-occupied the Rhine. Despite peace rallies, England began to re-arm. The last collection of Chesterton's Father Brown stories, *The Scandal of Father Brown*, was put out that March, the same month that Dorothy Collins acted as chauffeur for Frances and Gilbert on a pleasant holiday trip. They drove across France, through Spain, and on to Italy, where Chesterton lectured on English literature; then they drove back through Switzerland and Belgium. Dorothy Collins remembered the day that she struggled in a Spanish town to get them room and board while Chesterton sat in the back of their car, reading a detective story. When she accused him of not being much help, he calmly replied that he was more help than if he had shouted directions at her from the back seat.

That May, King George V had his Silver Jubilee, and the entire British empire took the occasion to demonstrate how very much they appreciated his public service, as well as the quality about him that Chesterton labeled his "genuineness." Given his feelings, it is highly unlikely that Chesterton would have been very sympathetic to Edward VIII's abdication over marrying Mrs. Simpson; unlike Lloyd George and Churchill, who took a very pragmatic view of royal matrimony, Chesterton would have understood the symbolism of its mystique.[110]

Another collection of Chesterton's essays, *The Well and The Shallows*, was published by Sheed and Ward in September 1935. These essays, collected from a number of sources, had been written as Catholic apologetics. In many Chesterton used a debating style, as he did in the essay in which he discusses the loud controversy stirred up by the effort to revise the *Book of*

Common Prayer. Often he is defending his own conversion by demonstrating the topsy-turvyness of its opponents; he also "wanders" into discussions about currently prominent issues and people, such as free trade and Adolph Hitler. All the essays are written in his characteristically genial tone, and his typical approach to a topic is illustrated in "The Religion of Fossils," in which he says,

> At least six times . . . I have found myself in a situation in which I should certainly have become a Catholic, if I had not been restrained from that rash step by the fortunate accident that I was one already. . . . [This point] has representative interest because our critics constantly expect the convert to suffer some . . . reaction . . . perhaps desertion. As a rule, the most that they will concede to us is that we have found peace by the surrender of reason.[111]

The book does not explain Chesterton's conversion, nor is it an *apologia pro vita sua*. He is defending the Roman Catholic Church (the well) against the modern world (the shallows), and in that spirit he is himself: loyal, glad he made the decision he did, optimistic, but looking ahead to an "Armageddon." This is what he is talking about in "Frozen Free Will," in which he says he had discovered that the "tone of the old Fleet Street atheism, which I knew and loved of old, has entirely altered. It has come to resemble . . . the tone of the Seventh Day Adventists . . . all those queerly prosaic and even prim fanatics who wander about handing out pamphlets. . . . The new Freethinker does not *read* a book. He looks through it feverishly for texts to be twisted in favor of a prejudice."[112]

In the very last essay, "Where Is the Paradox?" Chesterton is characteristically concerned with the present day. An Anglo-Catholic paper for which he had written had accused Chesterton of "being a prolix papist professor of paradox on a matter that concerned all Christendom . . . especially this country"; he shows the separate accusations actually cancel one another out. First they claimed that he had said England and Germany (Prussia) are alike because they are both Protestant countries, so that the blame for the Nazi is clearly Protestant; then they insisted that Adolph Hitler, being Austrian, is clearly Roman Catholic, so his excesses may be blamed on the Pope. As Chesterton says in answer to these charges and countercharges: "[It] would be much truer to call Hitler a Catholic than to call Bertrand Russell an Anglo-Catholic. . . . The whole historic . . . origin . . . of the heathenish Hitlerism . . . began . . . in Prussia. . . . The racial pride of Hitler . . . is of the Reformation. . . . It divides. . . . It is fatalistic. . . . It makes superiority depend not upon choice but only on being of the chosen."[113]

This book makes it plain that Chesterton's faith was not in eschatology but in history, where the Roman Catholic Church had managed to survive for two thousand years. He ends by detecting a faint hint of paradox in the fact that a "few fanatics tell me they are devoted to liberty of thought and in the next moment that I have disgraced myself by saying what I thought so plainly. . . . But they are only a few [compared] to the vast number of messages I received from Protestants, or even from Pagans, recognizing or discussing what I had really said."[114]

By November 1935 the Conservative Party under Baldwin had won a General Election, standing by a pledge to support the League of Nations against Italy, while Labour now was getting a younger generation of leaders like Clement Attlee, Herbert Morrison, and Sir Stafford Cripps, Beatrice Webb's nephew (later kicked out for support of the Communist Party). The Liberals in Parliament were reduced to Lloyd George's immediate family.

Once back in power, Baldwin actually agreed to let Italy take over a part of invaded Ethiopia. This action caused a public uproar, and by May 1936 Italy had swallowed the entire country, making English prestige suffer a bitter blow. Baldwin made Neville Chamberlain his Foreign Secretary at about the time that the Spanish Civil War was to break out, the war that the young English Leftists took to be *their* crusade, a war of light against dark.[115] None of them ever comprehended that their sense of "class" guilt was one Chesterton understood and shared, although he would have felt the worker would prefer running his own life to being told how to do it by a young Oxford graduate.

At this point Chesterton was chronically worn out. Early in 1936 he had finished his *Autobiography*, and a friend had remarked, "Nunc dimittis." But he was alive to the dangers of the Ethiopian adventure and the coming Spanish war, and also arbitrating the increasing rows among the doctrinaire staff of *G.K.'s Weekly*. In February the study at Top Meadow was finally completed, and he and Dorothy Collins moved in. But his bronchitis kept coming back, and he suffered frequent bouts of fever. The doctors diagnosed his essential problem as heart trouble. To see if a change of scene would help him relax, Dorothy Collins took him and Frances on a car trip to France that spring, where they visited the shrines at both Lourdes and Lisieux. Chesterton commented that Lourdes did not seem commercial, just a good place for ordinary people like himself, and coming home he tunelessly regaled his ladies with snatches of Gilbert and Sullivan.

Maurice Baring, stricken with incurable paralysis, looked forward to hearing from his old friend Chesterton through his radio talks — he was an avid listener, like many of his countrymen. On March 18, 1936, Chesterton gave his last talk, fittingly called "We Will End With a Bang." Echoing T.S. Eliot's lines from "The Hollow Men" ("This is the way the world ends/Not with a bang but a whimper"), his parody read, "And they may end with a whimper/But we will end with a bang."[116] He had had his disagreements, both public and private, with Eliot, who has been characterized as a kind of "Christian clerk" trying to re-animate English culture, but Eliot was to write a moving obituary for him, recognizing (more than others Chesterton influenced) his own "debt" to Chesterton.

During the summer of 1936 Chesterton began to fall asleep at his desk, and finally the doctors put him to bed. With Dorothy Collins' help, Frances began her own campaign to keep the media away and the world from knowing about Chesterton's condition, so that they might have privacy. Ada Chesterton was very critical of her attitude, apparently feeling that the "great man" ought to have the kind of hourly BBC bulletins put out when King George was ill; and Bentley, who had come down to Beaconsfield was amazed when Dorothy Collins asked an editor not to tell anyone that Chesterton was sick, because it must be quiet for him, but the editor did as she asked. Since the press kept his illness quiet, however, Chesterton's death on June 14, 1936, came not only as a surprise to the world but as a terrible shock to his friends.

That Sunday evening Bentley broadcast a tribute to Chesterton, and people all over the world began to call and send messages to Frances. Shaw wrote the next day, bitterly complaining that he who was eighteen years the elder should be heartlessly surviving his friend, and making sure that Frances had enough money to live on.[117] (Dorothy Collins was made Chesterton's literary executor, a job she is still handling in her small cottage in the Top Meadow gardens.) The Pope proclaimed him a "Defender of the Faith," a very awkward title for an Englishman, because it had been one of the British royal titles since the time of Henry VIII and appeared on British coins; consequently, the English newspapers could not print it. Chesterton would have enjoyed the paradox of that.

Ada Chesterton left her own grumbling account of getting the coffin down the tiny winding stairs of Top Meadow, and of the funeral with its long, slowly moving cortege that went the long way through both the New Town and the Old Town at the wish of the local people, to the little railway church. The route was lined with people from all over the world. She was appalled by the fact that, upon returning from the funeral mass, Frances simply took to her room and would talk to no one; Ada, pragmatic as ever, thought there was not enough food for the funeral guests. But Ada was not the only one with complaints: another eye witness said that he was told by Max Beerbohm that as he was kneeling in church, trying to concentrate, all he kept seeing was the back of Ada's head and the line where her hair turned orange.

On Saturday, June 27, a solemn requiem was held at Westminster Cathedral near Kensington, where Chesterton had been born. Father O'Connor sang the mass, with the help of Father Ignatius Rice and Father Vincent McNabb; the eulogy was given by Father Ronald Knox, "the Public Orator of English Catholicism." Poor Belloc was heard to say that "Chesterton will never occur again," and H. G. Wells reportedly said that if he ever got to Heaven "it would be by the intervention of Gilbert Chesterton."[118]

After Chesterton's death, *G.K.'s Weekly* was first taken over by Belloc, then by his son-in-law Reginald Jebb, under whom it became far more

Rightist and doctrinaire. Within a few years, Frances, greatly at a loss without Gilbert to "need her," died of cancer. Top Meadow was then given to the Roman Catholic Church, which uses it as a hostel for Anglican priests who have converted to Rome. It is run by Warden Henry Reed, secretary of the Chesterton Society.

Chesterton's *Autobiography* appeared posthumously in November 1936; his last collection of short stories, *The Paradoxes of Mr. Pond*, came out in March 1937. (Since that time Dorothy Collins, living and working at Top Meadow among Chesterton's things, has put out a number of collections of his unpublished essays.) *The Paradoxes of Mr. Pond* deals with characteristic Chestertonian themes, like a good king (called the Unmentionable Man), and says positive things about the Jews and varieties of imperialism. This last novel turned out to be very timely: within the year George V died, and the English public was far more deeply moved by his death than that of either Queen Victoria or Edward VII.

Chesterton would not have cared particularly that this last book is considered inferior as literature; he had always been more interested in playing the journalist, sharing his ideas, shaped by his experiences, with people of his own time. That is why there seems to be a childish, heretical simplicity about Walter de la Mare's description of him in his famous "Epitaph":

> Knight of the Holy Ghost, he goes his way
> Wisdom his motley, Truth his loving jest;
> The mills of Satan keep his lance in play,
> Pity and Innocence his heart at rest.[119]

It would be nearer the truth to quote Chesterton on Chesterton in a letter he wrote to a friend:

> I believe the biographers ... of the future, if they find any trace of me at all, will say ... Chesterton, Gilbert Keith. From the fragments left by this now forgotten writer it is difficult to understand the cause of even such publicity as he obtained in his own day; nevertheless, there is reason to believe that he was not without certain fugitive mental gifts.[120]

Epilogue
THE EVERLASTING MAN
1937-1984

It was G.K. Chesterton's life-long fate to be taken seriously when he was being flippant and flippantly when he was being serious. . . . He fell between dozens of stools. His friends rushed to the rescue, to plant him firmly on the stool nearest themselves. But he did not seem to appreciate their help; he only fell over again on the other side, like the White Knight. . . .

F.A. Lea, *The Wild Knight of Battersea*, 1945

In any final assessment of Chesterton . . . it is likely to be not the writer, nor even the brilliant controversialist in print, or in public debate, that will ultimately be memorable, but rather the man who was the focus of so many friendships . . . whose laugh could be heard many doors away and could direct its ridicule most successfully on itself. . . . Encyclopaedia Britannica, 1969

Chesterton's joy in life [was] . . . too extravert to be acceptable.
Anthony Burgess in the introduction to *The Autobiography of G.K. Chesterton*, 1969

The sense of the world as a moral battlefield is at the centre of Chesterton's thought; it underlies his allegorical fiction, and it informs his criticism. It made it possible for him to live in a world of anarchies and negations and yet preserve that moral energy that he called optimism.

Samuel Hynes, *Edwardian Occasions*, 1972

. . . what . . . is the measure of a "revival"? . . . In Books in Print I found nine volumes of H.G. Wells and eleven volumes of G.B. Shaw . . . for Chesterton . . . eighteen [adding] the special library editions. . . . The list goes up to more than thirty. With thirty volumes listed . . . who needs a "revival"?
Andrew Greeley in the introduction to *The Napoleon of Notting Hill*, 1978

The Everlasting Man

*All the old genial days, all the beer-drinking and fiery moods
and table-pounding conversations beamed . . . in the person of
Dr. Fell. . . . There was the doctor, bigger and stouter than ever.
He wheezed. His red face shone, and his small eyes twinkled over
eyeglasses on a broad black ribbon. There was a grin under his
bandit's moustache, and chuckling upheavals animated his several
chins. On his head was the inevitable black shovel-hat; his paunch
projected from a voluminous cloak. . . . it was like meeting Father
Christmas or Old King Cole. Indeed, Dr. Fell had frequently
impersonated Old King Cole . . . and enjoyed the role immensely.*
John Dickson Carr, *The Mad Hatter Mystery* [1]

THE final verdict on Gilbert Keith Chesterton is not yet in, but he is
being paid the compliment of being listened to again. Slowly but surely,
he is being seen as one of those who "ask the right questions," and occasionally he is even given credit for knowing the right answers. At the time
of his death, the common portrait of him was Old King Cole who called
for his bowl, and very few people bothered to remember what Chesterton
knew: that according to folklore, Old King Cole was the grandfather of
Constantine the Great. [2]

Chesterton was a lovable buffoon, so the fact that he was also a Christian
soldier who had enlisted under the banner of the Lord of Hosts for the
duration of the war was treated as a lovable foible, giving focus to his use
of paradox. He had called Shaw a "capering humorist" who was "holding
his fortress night and day," a man thoroughly consistent and deadly serious,
but no one took Chesterton's own ideas seriously. [3] Few believed that he
meant it when he proclaimed the good news that "the men signed of the
cross of Christ/ Go gaily in the dark." [4]

Some who owed him a debt acknowledged it, as Anglican Dorothy L.
Sayers did when she wrote in 1952,

> To the young people of my generation, G.K.C. was a kind of Christian
> liberator. Like a beneficent bomb, he blew out of the Church a quantity of
> stained glass of a very poor period, and let in gusts of fresh air, in which the
> dead leaves of doctrine danced with all the energy and indecorum of Our
> Lady's Tumbler. [5]

Although his fellow Roman Catholics, beginning with Hilaire Belloc, admitted a similar debt, they were wary of suggesting that Chesterton spoke to all Christians, and they tended to patronize him by suggesting that he was not publicly partisan enough.[6] Later the Schoolmen tried to make Chesterton intellectually respectable, as literary scholars are starting to do today, by removing any trace of the "buffoon" whom Cecil had so deplored. Yet then and now the very idea of Chesterton as a portly theologian makes him sound totally irrelevant to most intellectuals. Meanwhile, the ordinary readers who share Chesterton's instinct for conserving what is good from the past and who prefer to be allowed to run their own lives — "the secret people" — continue to read the "essential" Chesterton incarnated in his Father Brown mysteries.

Histories of his period routinely ignore him, but many of his literary judgments, like his praise of Dickens, are coming home to roost, and his social and economic concerns are once again topical. Whatever label he is given, Chesterton was always a Liberal convinced of the ultimate importance of the individual. He speaks to our contemporary condition; no other "unknown" writer is so often quoted to a world that does not recognize his name, a simple paradox that would greatly amuse him.[7]

It is impossible to follow the popular media without confronting subjects to which he brought his curiosity and concern. Within this year a Liberal Party has been resurrected in a former empire, whose royal wedding brought public talk of a "little England" worthy of patriotism. Weighty volumes on the Boer War now side with the Boers. Nobel Prizes are given to economists who teach the Third World to better use its agricultural methods, while ecologists who believe that "small is beautiful" picket in an attempt to save the world from rampant industrialism. The twin issues of abortion and the treatment of mental patients grab headlines, while the foremost feminist, Betty Friedan, suddenly starts to talk about the *family* as the building block of society. France goes Socialist, and the present Baron Rothschild sputters about his family's inalienable right to run their banking business for themselves. On Fleet Street an upstart press lord from the Antipodes buys the august *Times* to turn it into a tabloid. No wonder Chesterton's prediction in *The Napoleon of Notting Hill*, published in 1904, sounds startlingly relevant today:

> ... the wise men grew like wild things ... crying ... What will London be like a century hence? Is there anything we have not thought of? Houses upside down. Men walking ... on the Moon. ... So they wondered until they died. ... Then the people went and did what they liked. Let me no longer conceal the painful truth. ... When the curtain goes up on this story, eighty years after the present date, London is almost exactly like what it is now. ...[8]

Chesterton's world is still our modern age of anxiety, with seekers after esoteric truths and warring heresies. It is just, therefore, that as we approach 1984, Chesterton should be heard again. This is also a moment in history when telling our story from the giant's point of view is clearly wrong, for we can see that "the old and correct story of Jack [the Giant-Killer] . . . is simply the whole story of man, where only the weak can be brave and only those who can be brave can be trusted to be strong. . . . If we are not tall enough to reach the giant's knee, that is no reason why we should become shorter by falling on our own."[9]

This is why one reads Chesterton. Both in public and in private he maintained his rational balance, refusing to be pushed into extremism, which is the spiritual illness of our age. Instead he loudly and cheerfully called upon his fellowmen to step back or stand on their heads or sail around the world to see the other side. He would have been enchanted by our spacemen's discovery that the Earth, seen from a distance, is really a jewel. No one knew better than Chesterton how easy and intellectual it is to become a cultured despiser of the world, but when he became a man, he put away such childish things. If he were alive today, Chesterton obviously would be a Russell Baker or an Andy Rooney, live on *Sixty Minutes* with cape and sword, delighting a worldwide audience with his amusing observations. But his underlying message would always be there, too: that one must learn how to love the world without trusting it, and that the historic Christian Church was founded on a real man, and for that reason it is indestructible.

Certainly Chesterton would burst out of the ark in which his co-religionists have locked him, which kept him in his place as the saint who won them a measure of acceptance in the intellectual Establishment. Just as clearly, he would be placed beside Pope John Paul II and pitted against the superman Hans Küng. But the person with whom Chesterton could have the best debates today is the latter-day saint and sometime journalist Malcolm Muggeridge. Back in 1963, Muggeridge, by then a cultured despiser of Fabianism, Freudianism, Marxism, and other heresies of the Left, the editor of *Punch*, and a pundit whose attitude toward his journalistic trade was cynical and self-serving, had lost his childhood admiration of Chesterton. Reviewing a posthumously published collection of Chesterton's essays, he characteristically proclaimed the not-too-startling truth that Chesterton was "a superb melancholy . . . [who] underneath the happy Christian and happy husband, lover of peasants, Fleet Street roistering and country inns, had a brooding, anguished, frightened spirit. . . . [He] was a . . . frustrated romantic, a displaced person, a letter delivered to the wrong address."[10]

In the kind of true-to-life paradox which Chesterton celebrated, this comment, which states the truth — as much as Muggeridge was able to see it — is today appropriate for Muggeridge himself. Heartily disliking the world to which he feels overwhelmingly superior, Muggeridge now writes about the "end of Christendom," by which he means, like Chesterton, the end of

Western civilization. Having wittily denied Chesterton the right to the "complexity of a complete character"—that is, the possibility that Chesterton was both a fool for Christ and a man of sorrows, acquainted with grief—Muggeridge, who was raised an Evangelical Fabian, has never lost the old Puritanical Socialist belief in Progress with a capital "P." He sees himself today as a Saint Augustine, drawing the next blueprint for the post-Christian world, completely missing Chesterton's point.

To Chesterton, man is a unique creation, and so, therefore, is Christendom—"the Thing." It is a "half-built villa never finished," not a Wellsian stage in mindless development from a single cell to superman. Both Muggeridge and Chesterton are melancholy, both understand the Christian duty to be cheerful, but Chesterton alone is unwilling to forget this world while he basks in the promise of life everlasting, for to do so is to deny the Incarnation. On the secular front, Chesterton remains the pleasant, ordinary neighbor of the family of Jones, while Muggeridge is another of Chesterton's famous heretics, someone "whose philosophy is quite solid, quite coherent, and quite wrong," because it is too simple for real life.[11]

Chesterton understood that two passages in Saint Paul belong together—and not only because one follows the other. The first is Romans 13:8-9, which tells us that "he that loveth another hath fulfilled the law . . . thou shalt love thy neighbor as thyself. . . ." The second is Romans 13:11-12, the summation of what Chesterton believed and struggled to convey:

> Now it is high time to awake out of sleep; for now is our salvation nearer than we believed. The night is far spent, and the day is at hand: let us therefore cast off the works of darkness and let us put on the armor of light. . . .

Like King Alfred, Chesterton calls us to be ready to seize the high tide.

Notes

PROLOGUE

1. E.C. Bentley, *Biography for Beginners*, "Being A Collection of Miscellaneous Examples for the Use of the Upper Forms. Edited by E. Clerihew, B.A., with 40 Diagrams by G.K. Chesterton" (London: T. Werner Laurie, 1905), title page.

2. Cecil Chesterton, *G.K. Chesterton: A Criticism* (London: Alston Rivers, 1908), p. 248

3. *Ibid.*, pp. xii-xiii.

4. *Ibid.*, pp. xiv-v.

5. *Ibid.*, p. xii.

6. See John Sullivan, *G.K. Chesterton: A Bibliography* (London: University of London Press, 1958), whose meticulous efforts demonstrate that Chesterton was not an overnight success on Fleet Street by 1901, but began to be well known later in 1902; or compare the actual school date of Chesterton's friends and the account of the J.D.C. in Leonard Woolf, *Sowing* (New York: Harcourt Brace, 1960), with the version first given by Cecil Chesterton and then adopted by Chesterton himself in his *Autobiography*, and by Maisie Ward, *Gilbert Keith Chesterton* (New York: Sheed & Ward, 1944); E.C. Bentley, *Those Days* (London: Constable, 1940); and Dudley Barker, *G.K. Chesterton* (New York: Stein & Day, 1973).

7. See Barker, *G.K. Chesterton*, on Chesterton's facts in *Charles Dickens*, his lack of dates in *Robert Browning*, etc.

8. G.K. Chesterton, *Robert Louis Stevenson* (New York: Dodd, Mead, 1928), p. 92.

9. Rewey Belle Inglis, Alice Cecilia Cooper, Celia Oppenheimer, and William Rose Benét, *Adventures in English Literature* (New York: Harcourt Brace, 1947; rev. ed., 1967).

10. See Samuel Hynes, *Edwardian Occasions* (London: Routledge & Kegan Paul, 1972).

11. See Frank Swinnerton, *The Georgian Scene: A Literary Panorama* (New York: Farrar, Straus & Rinehart, 1934); Garry Wills, *Chesterton: Man and Mask* (New York: Sheed & Ward, 1961); Margaret Canovan, *G.K. Chesterton: Radical Populist* (New York: Harcourt Brace Jovanovich, 1977), and Ian Boyd, *The Novels of G.K. Chesterton* (London: Paul Elek, 1975).

12. G.K. Chesterton, *Robert Browning* (London: Macmillan, 1903), pp. 1-3.

13. G.K. Chesterton, *The Victorian Age in Literature* (London: Williams & Norgate, Home University Library, 1913), pp. 9-10.

14. G.K. Chesterton, *The Napoleon of Notting Hill* (New York: John Lane, 1904; rpt. New York: Paulist Press, 1978), p. 1.

CHAPTER ONE

1. G.K. Chesterton, *Orthodoxy* (New York: Dodd, Mead, 1908), pp. 98-100.

2. G.K. Chesterton, *St. Francis of Assisi* (New York: Doubleday, 1923; rpt. New York: Image Books, 1957), p. 153.

3. See Laurence Lafore, *The Long Fuse* (Philadelphia: J.B. Lippincott, 1965).

4. G.K. Chesterton, *Autobiography* (London: Hutchinson, 1936), p. 26.

5. *Ibid.*, p. 15.

6. *Ibid.*, p. 20; Ada Chesterton, *The Chestertons* (London: Chapman & Hall, 1941), pp. 34-37.

7. G.K. Chesterton in the introduction to Cecil Chesterton's *A History of the United States* (New York: George Doran, 1919), pp. vii-viii.

8. Cecil Chesterton, *G.K. Chesterton: A Criticism* (London: Alston Rivers, 1908), pp. 8-9.

9. Chesterton, *Autobiography*, pp. 26-27.

10. Hilaire Belloc, *On the Place of Gilbert Chesterton in English Letters* (New York: Sheed & Ward, 1940), p. 5.

11. Chesterton, *Autobiography*, pp. 9-10.

12. *Ibid.*, pp. 54-55.

13. *Ibid.*, pp. 35-36.

14. *Ibid.*, p. 197.

15. G.K. Chesterton, "Cecil Chesterton" in *G.K.C. as M.C.* (London: Methuen, 1929; rpt. Freeport, New York: Books for Libraries Press, 1967), p. 122.

16. G.K. Chesterton, *The Napoleon of Notting Hill* (New York: Paulist Press, 1978), pp. 196-197.

CHAPTER TWO

1. E.C. Bentley, *Those Days* (London: Constable, 1940), p. 1.

2. Ada Chesterton, *The Chestertons* (London: Chapman & Hall, 1941), pp. 19-20.

3. E.C. Bentley in the introduction to *The Selected Essays of G.K. Chesterton* (London: Methuen, 1949), pp. v-vi.

4. Bentley, *Those Days*, pp. 48-49.

5. Dudley Barker, *G.K. Chesterton* (New York: Stein & Day, 1973), p. 21.

6. G.K. Chesterton, *Autobiography* (London: Hutchinson, 1936), p. 31.

7. G.K. Chesterton, "The Toy Theatre" in *Tremendous Trifles* (London: Methuen, 1909; rpt. Beaconsfield, England: Darwen Finlayson, 1968), p. 110.

8. G.K. Chesterton, "Louisa May Alcott" in *A Handful of Authors*, ed. Dorothy Collins (New York: Sheed & Ward, 1953), pp. 166-167.

9. See the picture facing page 76 in John Sullivan, ed., *G.K. Chesterton: A Centenary Appraisal* (London: Paul Elek, 1974).

10. G.K. Chesterton, "Review of Andrew Lang's Violet Fairy Book" in the *Speaker* (1907), in A.L. Maycock, ed., *The Man Who Was Orthodox* (London: Dobson, 1963), p. 111.

11. Bruno Bettelheim, *The Uses of Enchantment* (New York: Alfred Knopf, 1976), p. 59.

12. G.K. Chesterton, *St. Francis of Assisi* (New York: Image Books, 1957), p. 17.

13. G.K. Chesterton, "Christmas" in *All Things Considered* (London: Methuen, 1908), p. 285.

14. G.K. Chesterton, *Orthodoxy* (New York: Dodd, Mead, 1908), p. 89.

15. G.K. Chesterton, "The Case for Macaulay" in *A Handful of Authors*, p. 111.

16. See Norman and Jeanne MacKenzie, *The Time Traveller: The Life of H.G. Wells* (London: Weidenfeld & Nicolson, 1973).

17. G.K. Chesterton, "The Invisible Man" in *The Innocence of Father Brown* (London: Cassell, 1911; rpt. New York: Penguin Books, 1975), p. 92.

18. G.K. Chesterton, *The Napoleon of Notting Hill* (New York: Paulist Press, 1978), p. 87.

19. Cecil Chesterton, *G.K. Chesterton: A Criticism* (London: Alston Rivers, 1908), pp. 3-4.

20. G.K. Chesterton, speech made as candidate for Rector of Glasgow University, 1925, copyright 1981 by Dorothy Collins; part of the Marion E. Wade Collection, Wheaton College, Wheaton, Illinois.
21. Chesterton, *Orthodoxy*, pp. 83-84.
22. Chesterton, *Autobiography*, p. 29.

CHAPTER THREE
1. G.K. Chesterton, *Autobiography* (London: Hutchinson, 1936), pp. 59-60.
2. See Michael F. McDonnell, *The History of St. Paul's School* (London: Chapman & Hall, 1909).
3. Maisie Ward, *Gilbert Keith Chesterton* (London: Sheed & Ward, 1944), p. 91.
4. Chesterton, *Autobiography* pp. 57-58.
5. Horton Davies, *Worship and Theology in England*, Vol. V: *The Ecumenical Century, 1900-1965* (Princeton, N.J.: Princeton University Press, 1965), p. 133.
6. Maurice Reckitt, *G.K. Chesterton: A Christian Prophet for England Today* (London: S.P.E.C.K., 1950), p. 14.
7. John P. McCarthy, *Hilaire Belloc: Edwardian Radical* (Indianapolis: Liberty Press, 1978), p. 21.
8. Chesterton, *Autobiography*, p. 70.
9. Leonard Woolf, *Sowing* (New York: Harcourt Brace, 1960), pp. 96-97.
10. Chesterton, *Autobiography*, p. 61.
11. *Ibid*.
12. E.C. Bentley, *Trent's Last Case* (orig. pub. 1912, rpt. New York: Harper & Row, 1978), dedication page.
13. Garry Wills, *Chesterton: Man and Mask* (New York: Sheed & Ward, 1961), p. 14.
14. Woolf, *Sowing*, pp. 100-101.
15. Cecil Chesterton, *G.K. Chesterton: A Criticism* (London: Alston Rivers, 1908), p. 13.
16. G.K. Chesterton, *The Coloured Lands* (New York: Sheed & Ward, 1938), p. 59.
17. E.C. Bentley, *Those Days* (London: Constable, 1940), p. 46.
18. Cyril Clemens, *Chesterton as Seen by His Contemporaries* (Webster Groves, Mo.: Mark Twain Society, 1939), p. 7.
19. John Sullivan, *G.K. Chesterton: A Bibliography* (London: University of London Press, 1958), p. 128.
20. Woolf, *Sowing*, pp. 80-81. See also Bentley, *Those Days*, pp. 57-58.
21. Ward, *Gilbert Keith Chesterton*, Appendix B., pp. 557-558.
22. Sullivan, *G.K. Chesterton: A Bibliography*, p. 129.

CHAPTER FOUR
1. G.K. Chesterton, *The Man Who Was Thursday* (New York: Boni & Liveright, 1908, rpt. New York: Capricorn Books, 1960), dedication page.
2. Oscar Wilde in the preface to *The Picture of Dorian Gray* (New York: Oxford University Press, 1974), p. xxxiii.
3. G.K. Chesterton, "A Defence of Nonsense" in *The Defendant* (London: Brimley Johnson, 1901), p. 47.
4. Dudley Barker, *G.K. Chesterton* (New York: Stein & Day, 1974), p. 45.
5. E.C. Bentley, *Those Days* (London: Constable, 1940), p. 67.

6. G.K. Chesterton, *Autobiography* (London: Hutchinson, 1936), p. 90.

7. G.K. Chesterton, *St. Francis of Assisi* (New York: Image Books, 1957), p. 71.

8. Barker, *G.K. Chesterton*, pp. 50-52.

9. Chesterton, *Autobiography*, p. 79.

10. See E.C. Bentley, *Those Days*. In one passage Bentley says that they went to the university when Gilbert went to the Slade; in another he discusses taking an examination for a scholarship with Hilaire Belloc in January 1894. Under the circumstances he could not have matriculated before fall 1894.

11. Leonard Woolf, *Sowing* (New York: Harcourt Brace, 1960), p. 100. Woolf discusses meeting Bentley at Saturday meetings of the J.D.C. when Bentley was a student at Oxford, and Woolf was still at St. Paul's with Cecil Chesterton. Woolf was sixteen the year he was asked to join the J.D.C. — that is, in 1895, the year Gilbert finished at the Slade.

12. Barker, *G.K. Chesterton*, pp. 48-51.

13. G.K. Chesterton, "Slade School Notebook," copyright Dorothy Collins, micro-film reel #8, the Wade Collection, Wheaton College, Wheaton, Illinois. See also Maisie Ward, *Gilbert Keith Chesterton* (London: Sheed & Ward, 1944), p. 56; and Garry Wills, *Chesterton: Man and Mask* (New York: Sheed & Ward, 1961), p. 219.

14. G.K. Chesterton, *The Poet and the Lunatics* (New York: Dodd, Mead, 1929), pp. 116-117.

15. G.K. Chesterton, *The Collected Poems of G.K. Chesterton* (London: Cecil Palmer, 1927), p. 301.

16. Chesterton, *Autobiography*, p. 81.

17. Chesterton, *The Collected Poems of G.K. Chesterton*, p. 175.

18. G.K. Chesterton, *Orthodoxy* (New York: Dodd, Mead, 1908), pp. 153-157.

19. See Norman and Jeanne MacKenzie, *The Fabians* (New York: Simon & Schuster, 1977); and G.K. Chesterton, *Heretics* (New York: Dodd, Mead, 1905; rpt. 1923).

20. Samuel Hynes, *The Edwardian Turn of Mind* (Princeton, N.J.: Princeton University Press, 1968), pp. 138-140.

21. John O'Connor, *Father Brown on Chesterton* (London: Oates & Washbourne, 1938), p. 74.

22. G.K. Chesterton, *The Thing: Why I Am a Catholic* (New York: Dodd, Mead, 1930), pp. 15-17.

23. G.K. Chesterton, "In Defence of Detective Stories" in *The Defendant*, pp. 119-120.

24. G.K. Chesterton, *The Coloured Lands* (New York: Sheed & Ward, 1980), p. 25.

25. Chesterton, *Autobiography*, p. 91.

26. G.K. Chesterton, *The Victorian Age in Literature* (London: Williams & Norgate, Home University Library, 1913), pp. 217-218.

27. *Ibid.*, pp. 219-222.

28. P. N. Furbank, "Chesterton the Edwardian" in John Sullivan, ed., *G.K. Chesterton: A Centenary Appraisal* (London: Paul Elek, 1974), p. 18.

29. Oscar Wilde, "The Fisherman and His Soul" in *The Poems and Fairy Tales of Oscar Wilde* (New York: Random House, Modern Library, 1932), p. 105.

30. Chesterton, *The Coloured Lands*, p. 104.

31. Chesterton, "Slade School Notebook," the Wade Collection.

32. Chesterton, *Autobiography*, pp. 99-100.

33. Chesterton, *The Victorian Age in Literature*, pp. 195-197.

34. Chesterton, *Autobiography*, pp. 94-95.

35. Chesterton, "Slade School Notebook," the Wade Collection.

36. G.K. Chesterton, "The Diabolist" in *Tremendous Trifles* (Beaconsfield, England: Darwen Finlayson, 1968), pp. 158-162.

Notes

CHAPTER FIVE

1. G.K. Chesterton, "The Taming of the Nightmare" in *The Coloured Lands* (New York: Sheed & Ward, 1938), pp. 175-176.

2. Leonard Woolf, *Sowing* (New York: Harcourt Brace, 1960), pp. 115-116 and p. 141; and Andrew Boyle, *The Climate of Treason: Five Who Spied for Russia* (London: Hutchinson, 1979), p. 70.

3. G.K. Chesterton, *All Things Considered* (London: Methuen, 1908), pp. 96-97.

4. Alfred Havighurst, *Britain in Transition* (Chicago: University of Chicago Press, 1962; new ed., 1979), p. 4; and Brocard Sewell, *Cecil Chesterton* (Faversham, Kent: St. Albert's Press, 1975), p. 4.

5. Maisie Ward, *Gilbert Keith Chesterton* (London: Sheed & Ward, 1944), p. 73. The term "the Notebooks" represents the material Mrs. Ward used, but it also includes any and all Chesterton material that dates from this period and was never published. Among his biographers the term is used confusingly.

6. E.C. Bentley, *Those Days* (London: Constable, 1940), pp. 85-86.

7. John P. McCarthy, *Hilaire Belloc: Edwardian Radical* (Indianapolis: Liberty Press, 1978), p. 16.

8. Ward, *Gilbert Keith Chesterton*, p. 65.

9. *Ibid.*, p. 67.

10. *Ibid.*, p. 68.

11. G.K. Chesterton, *Charles Dickens* (London: Methuen, 1906), p. 284.

12. G.K. Chesterton, *The Victorian Age in Literature* (London: Williams & Norgate, Home University Library, 1913), p. 11.

13. See both Thomas Pakenham, *The Boer War* (New York: Random House, 1979); and Byron Farwell, *The Great Anglo-Boer War* (New York: Harper & Row, 1976).

14. Norman and Jeanne MacKenzie, *The Fabians* (New York: Simon & Schuster, 1977), pp. 214-215.

15. McCarthy, *Hilaire Belloc: Edwardian Radical*, pp. 20-22.

16. *Ibid.*, pp. 39-40.

17. Ada Chesterton, *The Chestertons* (London: Chapman & Hall, 1941), pp. 2-3.

18. G.K. Chesterton, *Autobiography* (London: Hutchinson, 1936), p. 139.

19. G.K. Chesterton, *The Man Who Was Thursday* (New York: Capricorn Books, 1960), p. 5.

20. *Ibid.*, p. 6.

21. Ward, *Gilbert Keith Chesterton*, pp. 93-94.

22. Ada Chesterton, *The Chestertons*, p. 1.

23. Cecil Chesterton, *G.K. Chesterton: A Criticism* (London: Alston Rivers, 1908), p. 98.

24. G.K. Chesterton, *The Ballad of the White Horse* in *The Collected Poems of G.K. Chesterton* (London: Cecil Palmer, 1927), p. 202.

25. Garry Wills, *Chesterton: Man and Mask* (New York: Sheed & Ward, 1961), p. 229.

26. See Jeanne MacKenzie, *A Victorian Courtship* (New York: Oxford Press, 1979); as well as E.C. Bentley, *Trent's Last Case* (New York: Harper & Row, 1978).

27. Chesterton, *Autobiography*, p. 154.

28. G.K. Chesterton, "Louisa May Alcott" in *A Handful of Authors*, ed. Dorothy Collins (New York: Sheed & Ward, 1953), p. 165.

29. D.B. Wyndham Lewis, ed., *G.K. Chesterton: An Anthology* (London: Oxford University Press, 1957), p. 5.

30. Dudley Barker, *G.K. Chesterton* (New York: Stein & Day, 1974), p. 99.

31. Ward, *Gilbert Keith Chesterton*, pp. 81-83.

32. Cecil Chesterton, *G.K. Chesterton: A Criticism*, p. 29.

33. See particularly Peter Rowland, *The Last Liberal Governments: The Promised Land, 1905-1910* (London: Barrie & Rockliff, Cresset Press, 1968), p. xvii; and Stephen Koss,

The Pro-Boers: The Anatomy of an Antiwar Movement (Chicago: University of Chicago Press, 1973), p. xxxvii.

CHAPTER SIX

1. G.K. Chesterton, *Autobiography* (London: Hutchinson, 1936), p. 289.
2. E.C. Bentley, ed., *The Selected Essays of G.K. Chesterton* (London: Methuen, 1949), p. vii.
3. Cecil Chesterton, *G.K. Chesterton: A Criticism* (London: Alston Rivers, 1908), p. 30.
4. Maisie Ward, *Gilbert Keith Chesterton* (London: Sheed & Ward, 1944), pp. 103-104.
5. Brocard Sewell, *Cecil Chesterton* (Faversham, Kent: St. Albert's Press, 1975), pp. 17-18.
6. Chesterton, *Autobiography*, p. 159.
7. Stephen Koss, *The Pro-Boers: The Anatomy of an Antiwar Movement* (Chicago: University of Chicago Press, 1973), p. xxvii.
8. Thomas Pakenham, *The Boer War* (New York: Random House, 1979), p. 409.
9. E.C. Bentley, *Those Days* (London: Constable, 1940), p. 15.
10. See both Dudley Barker, *G.K. Chesterton* (New York: Stein & Day, 1973), p. 107; and Garry Wills, *Chesterton: Man and Mask* (New York: Sheed & Ward, 1961), pp. 26-39.
11. G.K. Chesterton, *The Collected Poems of G.K. Chesterton* (London: Cecil Palmer, 1927), p. 291.
12. Ward, *Gilbert Keith Chesterton*, p. 126. Brimley Johnson was the fiance of Frances' sister, Gertrude, who was struck and killed by a bus. She had been Kipling's secretary.
13. See Ian Boyd, "The Essential Chesterton," *Seven*, 1 (1980), 44; and Wills, *Chesterton: Man and Mask*, pp. 36-37.
14. W. R. Titterton, *G.K. Chesterton: A Portrait* (London: Douglas Organ, 1936), p. 7.
15. See William B. Furlong, *Shaw and Chesterton: The Metaphysical Jesters* (University Park, Pa.: Pennsylvania State University Press, 1970).
16. G.K. Chesterton, *Twelve Types* (London: Arthur Humphreys, 1910), pp. 67-68.
17. Chesterton, *Twelve Types*, pp. 29-30.
18. G.K. Chesterton in the introduction to *The Defendant* (London: Brimley Johnson, 1901), pp. 6-7.
19. Ward, *Gilbert Keith Chesterton*, p. 113.
20. Koss, *The Pro-Boers*, p. xxix.
21. For a typical "lumping together," see Alfred Havighurst, *Britain in Transition* (Chicago: University of Chicago Press, 1979), p. 40.
22. See Cecil Chesterton, *G.K. Chesterton: A Criticism*; Maisie Ward, *Gilbert Keith Chesterton*; Robert Speaight, *The Life of Hilaire Belloc* (New York; Farrar, Straus & Cudahy, 1957); and John P. McCarthy, *Hilaire Belloc: Edwardian Radical* (Indianapolis: Liberty Press, 1978).
23. See Richard Ingram, Introduction in Aidan Mackey's *Mr. Chesterton Comes to Tea, or How the King of England Captured Redskin Island* (Bedford, England: Vintage Publications, 1978), p. 10; and Samuel Hynes, *Edwardian Occasions* (London: Routledge & Kegan Paul, 1972), pp. 80-90.
24. To demonstrate that their relationship was not monolithic, this book will follow their actual association chronologically.
25. Hynes, *Edwardian Occasions*, p. 2. For an opposite point of view, see Leon Edel, *Bloomsbury: A House of Lions* (New York: J.B. Lippincott, 1979), pp. 189-191.
26. Norman and Jeanne MacKenzie, *The Fabians* (New York: Simon & Schuster, 1977), p. 17ff.
27. Havighurst, *Britain in Transition*, p. 41.

28. Stephen Koss, *Fleet Street Radical* (London: Allen Lane, 1973), pp. 7-8.
29. *Ibid.*, pp. 26-41.
30. G.K. Chesterton, "A Denunciation of Patriotism" in *The Defendant*, pp. 125-131.
31. Koss, *Fleet Street Radical*, p. 54.
32. See Barker, *G.K. Chesterton*, p. 111.
33. Ada Chesterton, *The Chestertons* (London: Chapman & Hall, 1941), pp. 170-172.
34. See Ward, *Gilbert Keith Chesterton*, pp. 559-564.
35. Chesterton, *Autobiography*, pp. 36-37.
36. Ward, *Gilbert Keith Chesterton*, p. 562.
37. Mary Soames, *Clementine Churchill: The Biography of a Marriage* (Boston: Houghton Mifflin, 1979).
38. Edel, *Bloomsbury: A House of Lions*, pp. 174-186.
39. Bentley, *Those Days*, pp. 221-222.
40. Barker, *G.K. Chesterton*, p. 99 and pp. 111-114; and Hynes, *Edwardian Occasions*, p. 149.
41. Bentley, ed., *The Selected Essays of G.K. Chesterton*, pp. iv-vii.
42. Margaret Canovan, *G.K. Chesterton: Radical Populist* (New York: Harcourt Brace Jovanovich, 1977), p. 158.
43. See Furlong, *Shaw and Chesterton: The Metaphysical Jesters*, pp. 3-4. In typical fashion, Cecil suggested that it was like a bolt from the blue.
44. Furlong, *Shaw and Chesterton: The Metaphysical Jesters*, pp. 3-4
45. Norman and Jeanne MacKenzie, *The Fabians*, pp. 277-278.
46. Furlong, *Shaw and Chesterton: The Metaphysical Jesters*, pp. 180-181; end notes, #4 (7).
47. G.K. Chesterton, "In Defence of Rash Vows" in *The Defendant*, p. 23.
48. Barker, *G.K. Chesterton*, pp. 120-124.
49. *Ibid.*, pp. 14-15.
50. G.K. Chesterton, "The Position of Sir Walter Scott" in *Twelve Types*, pp. 179-180.
51. *Ibid.*, p. 180.
52. Koss, *Fleet Street Radical*, p. 44.
53. *Ibid.*, p. 53.
54. *Ibid.*, p. 55.
55. Cecil Chesterton, *G.K. Chesterton: A Criticism*, pp. 60-61.

CHAPTER SEVEN

1. John Sullivan, *G.K. Chesterton: A Bibliography* (London: University of London Press, 1958), p. 17.
2. G.K. Chesterton, *Autobiography* (London: Hutchinson, 1936), p. 110.
3. Garry Wills, *Chesterton: Man and Mask* (New York: Sheed & Ward, 1961), p.48.
4. G.K. Chesterton, *A Miscellany of Men* (New York: Dodd Mead, 1912), p. 122.
5. Cecil Chesterton, *G.K. Chesterton: A Criticism* (London: Alston Rivers, 1908), p. 224. See also Leo Hetzler's "Chesterton's Political Views" in *The Chesterton Review*, VII, No. 2 (Spring 1981), 119-120.
6. Margaret Canovan, *G.K. Chesterton: Radical Populist* (New York: Harcourt Brace Jovanovich, 1977), p. 41.
7. R.C.K. Ensor, *England: 1870-1914* (London: Oxford University Press, 1936), p. 355.
8. Anne Fremantle, *This Little Band of Prophets* (New York: Macmillan, 1960), p. 136.
9. Stephen Koss, *Nonconformity in Modern British Politics* (Hamden, Conn.: Archon Books, Shoe String Press, 1975), pp. 38-39.

10. Maisie Ward, *Gilbert Keith Chesterton* (London: Sheed & Ward, 1944), p. 250.

11. W.R. Titterton, *G.K. Chesterton: A Portrait* (London: Douglas Organ, 1936), pp. 75-76.

12. Robert Speaight, *The Life of Hilaire Belloc* (New York: Farrar, Straus & Cudahy, 1957), pp. :64-167; and John P. McCarthy, *Hilaire Belloc: Edwardian Radical* (Indianapolis: Liberty Press, 1978), p. 76.

13. Stephen Koss, *Fleet Street Radical* (London: Allen Lane, 1973), pp. 66-73.

14. Alfred Havighurst, *Radical Journalist: H. W. Massingham* (London: Cambridge University Press, 1974), p. 26.

15. Koss, *Fleet Street Radical*, pp. 74-75.

16. Norman and Jeanne MacKenzie, *The Fabians* (New York: Simon & Schuster, 1977), p. 187.

17. Wills, *Chesterton: Man and Mask*, p. 85.

18. Chesterton, *Autobiography*, p. 180.

19. Dudley Barker, *G.K. Chesterton* (New York: Stein & Day, 1973), p. 169.

20. *Ibid.*, p. 158.

21. Cecil Chesterton, *G.K. Chesterton: A Criticism*, p. 71.

22. Wills, *Chesterton: Man and Mask*, p. 63.

23. G.K. Chesterton, *Robert Browning* (London: Macmillan, 1903), p. 50.

24. G.B. Shaw in the introduction to *Man and Superman* (New York: Simon & Schuster, Pocket Books, 1972); and Norman and Jeanne MacKenzie, *The Fabians*, pp. 294-295.

25. W.W. Robson, "Father Brown and Others" in *G.K. Chesterton: A Centenary Appraisal*, ed. John Sullivan (London: Paul Elek, 1974), p. 69.

26. Lawrence J. Clipper, *G.K. Chesterton* (New York: Twayne Publishers, 1974), p. 37.

27. Wills, *Chesterton: Man and Mask*, p. 105.

28. Titterton, *G.K. Chesterton*, pp. 44-45.

29. Wills, *Chesterton: Man and Mask*, pp. 49-50. See reference to C.S. Lewis article.

30. G.K. Chesterton, *The Napoleon of Notting Hill* (New York: Paulist Press, 1978), pp. 196-197.

31. Norman and Jeanne MacKenzie, *The Fabians*, pp. 321-322.

32. At Notre Dame University there is a series of notes that Cecil sent Mrs. Bland. In them he included his poems, told her his hopes, and begged for her concern.

33. Fremantle, *This Little Band of Prophets*, p. 54.

34. John O'Connor, *Father Brown on Chesterton* (London: Oates & Washbourne, 1938), p. 61.

35. Robson, "Father Brown and Others," pp. 58-72.

36. Brocard Sewell, *Cecil Chesterton* (Faversham, Kent: St. Albert's Press, 1975), p. 20.

37. Peter Fraser, *Joseph Chamberlain, Radicalism and Empire* (London: Cassell, 1966), p. 208.

38. G.K. Chesterton, "A Defence of Detective Stories" in *The Defendant* (London: Brimley Johnson, 1901), p. 123.

39. Ward, *Gilbert Keith Chesterton*, p. 140.

40. Sewell, *Cecil Chesterton*, pp. 22-23.

41. *Episcopal Church Hymnal* (Church Pension Fund), p. 521.

42. E.C. Bentley, *Those Days* (London: Constable, 1940), p. 150.

43. Barker, *G.K. Chesterton*, p. 15.

44. G.E. Brown, *George Bernard Shaw* (New York: Arco, 1971), pp. 9-24.

45. Norman and Jeanne MacKenzie, *The Fabians*, p. 309.

46. Samuel Hynes, *Edwardian Occasions* (London: Routledge & Kegan Paul, 1972), p. 19.

47. G.K. Chesterton, *Heretics* (New York: Dodd Mead, 1923), pp. 12-15.

48. *Ibid.*, p. 20.

49. *Ibid.*, p. 159.

50. *Ibid.*, p. 303.
51. *Ibid.*, pp. 23-24.
52. G.K. Chesterton, *All Things Considered* (London: Methuen, 1908), p. 1.
53. Koss, *Fleet Street Radical*, p. 84.

CHAPTER EIGHT
1. G.K. Chesterton, the *Daily News*, October 28, 1911.
2. G.K. Chesterton, *Orthodoxy* (New York: Dodd, Mead, 1908), p. 82.
3. G.K. Chesterton, *All Things Considered* (London: Methuen, 1908), p. 46.
4. John P. McCarthy, *Hilaire Belloc: Edwardian Radical* (Indianapolis: Liberty Press, 1978), p. 81.
5. Robert Speaight, *The Life of Hilaire Belloc* (New York: Farrar, Strauss & Cudahy, 1956), p. 207.
6. Samuel Hynes, *The Edwardian Turn of Mind* (Princeton, New Jersey: Princeton University Press, 1968), p. 389 (Appendix B). See also Quentin Bell, *Virginia Woolf: A Biography* (New York: Harcourt Brace Jovanovich, A Harvest Book, 1972), the family tree, p. xviii.
7. Stephen Koss, *Nonconformity in Modern British Politics* (Hamden, Conn.: Archon Books, Shoe String Press, 1975), p. 73.
8. Anne Fremantle, *This Little Band of Prophets* (New York: Macmillan, 1960), p. 166.
9. Leo Hetzler, "Chesterton's Political Views" in *The Chesterton Review*, VII, No. 2 (Spring 1981), 122-140.
10. Chesterton, *Orthodoxy*, pp. 18-19.
11. Jackson Holbrook, *The Eighteen Nineties* (Middlesex, England: Penguin Books, 1939), p. 111.
12. Alfred Havighurst, *Britain in Transition* (Chicago: University of Chicago Press, 1979), pp. 33-49; 78-79.
13. Hynes, *The Edwardian Turn of Mind*, p. 390.
14. Norman and Jeanne MacKenzie, *The Fabians*, (New York: Simon & Schuster, 1977), p. 329.
15. See especially William B. Furlong, *Shaw and Chesterton: The Metaphysical Jesters* (University Park, Pa.: Pennsylvania State University Press, 1970), pp. 3-4. I am indebted to Mr. Furlong for sorting out the real course of events. Maisie Ward, for example, took as her guides Shaw and Lucian Oldershaw, as well as Cecil Chesterton; following her lead, Dudley Barker telescopes the events of ten years into a single incident. See Dudley Barker, *G.K. Chesterton* (New York: Stein & Day, 1974), pp. 181-182.
16. Furlong, *Shaw and Chesterton: The Metaphysical Jesters*, pp. 4-9; and Norman and Jeanne MacKenzie, *The Fabians*, pp. 331-343.
17. Lawrence J. Clipper, *G.K. Chesterton* (New York: Twayne Publishers, 1974), p. 21; and G.K. Chesterton, *Charles Dickens* (London: Methuen, 1906).
18. "Books," *Time* Magazine, October 27, 1980, p. 100.
19. John Cawalti, *Adventure, Mystery, and Romance* (Chicago: University of Chicago Press, 1976), pp. 268-269.
20. Lawrence J. Clipper, "G.K. Chesterton and Charles Dickens," lecture given at "A Chesterton Celebration: 1930-1980," Notre Dame University, South Bend, Indiana, 15 Nov. 1980. Copyright Notre Dame University.
21. Chesterton, *Charles Dickens*, p. xv.
22. *Ibid.*, pp. 17-19.

23. Margaret Canovan, *G.K. Chesterton: Radical Populist* (New York: Harcourt Brace Jovanovich, 1977), p. 33.

24. Chesterton, *Charles Dickens*, pp. 296-297.

25. Charles Masterman, *The Condition of England* (London: Methuen, 1909), pp. 72-73.

26. McCarthy, *Hilaire Belloc: Edwardian Radical*, p. 113.

27. Chesterton, *Orthodoxy*, p. 82.

28. Ian Boyd, *The Novels of G.K. Chesterton* (London: Paul Elek, 1975), p. 11.

29. Boyd, *The Novels of G.K. Chesterton*, p. 22.

30. G.K. Chesterton, *The Ball and the Cross* (New York: John Lane, 1909), p. 19.

31. G.K. Chesterton, *The Ballad of the White Horse* in *The Collected Poems of G.K. Chesterton* (London: Cecil Palmer, 1927), p. 212.

32. Norman and Jeanne MacKenzie, *The Fabians*, pp. 342-344; Fremantle, *This Little Band of Prophets*, pp. 156-170.

33. Samuel Hynes, *Edwardian Occasions* (London: Routledge & Kegan Paul, 1972), pp. 39-45.

34. See Brocard Sewell, *Cecil Chesterton* (Faversham, Kent: St. Albert's Press, 1975), p. 26 — versus Fremantle, *This Little Band of Prophets*, p. 160; and Norman and Jeanne MacKenzie, *The Fabians*, p. 343.

35. Fremantle, *This Little Band of Prophets*, p. 161.

36. See John Sullivan, *G.K. Chesterton: A Bibliography* (London: University of London Press, 1958), pp. 146, 161. See also Furlong, *Shaw and Chesterton: The Metaphysical Jesters*, p. 65.

37. Fremantle, *This Little Band of Prophets*, pp. 170-171.

38. Furlong, *Shaw and Chesterton: The Metaphysical Jesters*, pp. 10-11; Hynes, *Edwardian Occasions*, p. 88; and Garry Wills, *Chesterton: Man and Mask* (New York: Sheed & Ward, 1961), pp. 113-115.

39. G.K. Chesterton, *Autobiography* (London: Hutchinson, 1936), pp. 226-227.

40. Hynes, *Edwardian Occasions*, p. 72; and Clipper, *G.K. Chesterton*, p. 120.

41. G.K. Chesterton, *The Man Who Was Thursday* (New York: Capricorn Books, 1960), dedication page.

42. Clipper, *G.K. Chesterton*, p. 121.

43. John F. Maguire, letter in *The Chesterton Review*, III, No. 1 (1976), 161.

44. Wills, *Chesterton: Man and Mask*, p. 49.

45. G.K. Chesterton, *The Man Who Was Thursday*, p. 192.

46. Barbara Tuchman, *The Proud Tower: A Portrait of the World Before the War, 1890-1914* (New York: Bantam Books, 1967), p. 2.

47. G.K. Chesterton, *Heretics* (New York: Dodd, Mead, 1923), p. 58.

48. Norman and Jeanne MacKenzie, *Dickens: A Life* (New York: Oxford University Press, 1979), p. 58.

49. Chesterton, *Autobiography*, p. 218.

50. G.K. Chesterton, *The Victorian Age in Literature* (London: Williams & Norgate, Home University Library, 1913), p. 229.

51. Norman and Jeanne MacKenzie, *The Time Traveller: The Life of H.G. Wells* (London: Weidenfeld & Nicolson, 1973), p. 341. The MacKenzies' thesis — that Wells and the others of the Fabian Old Gang were seeking to establish utopias based upon their nostalgia for certain aspects of the Victorian past — is one which is remarkably well suited to Chesterton as well. His "past" was a Dickensian era of Gladstonian liberalism.

52. Chesterton, *All Things Considered*, p. 1.

53. Wills, *Chesterton: Man and Mask*, pp. 86-87.

54. Canovan, *G.K. Chesterton: Radical Populist*, p. 26.

55. Chesterton, *Orthodoxy*, p. 14.

56. *Ibid.*, p. 15.

57. *Ibid.*, pp. 18-19.
58. *Ibid.*, p. 58.
59. *Ibid.*, p. 146.
60. *Ibid.*, pp. 144-145. This is an early example of his use of the term "the Thing" to mean Christianity, Christendom, or the Church.

CHAPTER NINE
1. G.K. Chesterton, *Autobiography* (London: Hutchinson, 1936), p. 215.
2. Ada Chesterton, *The Chestertons* (London: Chapman & Hall, 1941), p. 82.
3. E.C. Bentley in the introduction to *The Selected Essays of G.K. Chesterton* (London: Methuen, 1949), p. vii.
4. A.L. Maycock, ed., *The Man Who Was Orthodox* (London: Dobson, 1963), p. 23.
5. Alfred Havighurst, *Radical Journalist: H.W. Massingham* (London: Cambridge University Press, 1974), p. 6.
6. Elie Halevy, *A History of the English People, Epilogue*, Vol. II: *The Rule of Democracy, 1905-1914* (London: Ernest Benn, 1934), pp. 302-308.
7. Stephen Koss, *Fleet Street Radical* (London: Allen Lane, 1973), pp. 114-115.
8. *Ibid.*, pp. 115-116.
9. See Dudley Barker, *G.K. Chesterton* (New York: Stein & Day, 1973), p. 190. He tries to insist, in defiance of the actual poem, that Chesterton is homesick for Fleet Street.
10. G.K. Chesterton, *The Collected Poems of G.K. Chesterton* (London: Cecil Palmer, 1927), pp. 167-168.
11. Stephen Koss, *Asquith* (New York: St. Martin's Press, 1976), p. 8.
12. Norman and Jeanne MacKenzie, *The Fabians* (New York: Simon & Schuster, 1977), p. 358.
13. *Ibid.*, p. 367.
14. William B. Furlong, *Shaw and Chesterton: The Metaphysical Jesters* (University Park, Pa.: Pennsylvania State University Press, 1970), pp. 37-39; and Lawrence J. Clipper, *G.K. Chesterton* (New York: Twayne Publishers, 1974), pp. 25-27.
15. Garry Wills, *Chesterton: Man and Mask* (New York: Sheed & Ward, 1961), pp. 116-117; and Furlong, *Shaw and Chesterton: The Metaphysical Jesters*, p. 42.
16. Margaret Canovan, *G.K. Chesterton: Radical Populist* (New York: Harcourt Brace Jovanovich, 1977), pp. 64-65.
17. G.K. Chesterton, *George Bernard Shaw* (orig. pub. 1909; rpt. New York: Hill & Wang, 1956), pp. 14-15.
18. Furlong, *Shaw and Chesterton: The Metaphysical Jesters*, pp. 43-50.
19. See Samuel Hynes, *Edwardian Occasions* (London: Routledge & Kegan Paul, 1972), p. 82.
20. Wills, *Chesterton: Man and Mask*, p. 48. See also Hugh Kenner, *Paradox in Chesterton* (New York: Sheed & Ward, 1947), for the most explicit statement of this thesis, which insists that Chesterton essentially was a serious philosopher — a view not unlike that of Cecil Chesterton.
21. Wills, *Chesterton: Man and Mask*, pp. 50-51.
22. G.K. Chesterton, "A Piece of Chalk" in *Tremendous Trifles* (Beaconsfield, England: Darwen Finlayson, 1968), pp. 14-15.
23. G.K. Chesterton, *Orthodoxy* (New York: Dodd, Mead, 1908), p. 48.
24. G.K. Chesterton, "The Riddle of the Ivy" in *Tremendous Trifles*, p. 147.
25. G.K. Chesterton, *What's Wrong With the World* (Leipzig: Bernhard Tauchnitz, 1910), pp. 79-80.

26. Chesterton, *Autobiography*, p. 237.

27. *Ibid*.

28. Aidan Mackey, *Mr. Chesterton Comes to Tea* (Bedford, England: Vintage Publications, 1978).

29. Dorothy Collins, "Recollections" in *G.K. Chesterton: A Centenary Appraisal*, ed. John Sullivan (London: Paul Elek, 1974), p. 157.

30. Frank Sheed, remarks at a meeting of the Chesterton Society, Chicago, December 1979.

31. G.K. Chesterton, *Lunacy and Letters*, ed. Dorothy Collins (New York: Sheed & Ward, 1958), pp. 147-150.

32. G.K. Chesterton, *A Handful of Authors*, ed. Dorothy Collins (New York: Sheed & Ward, 1953), pp. 139-140.

33. George Dangerfield, *The Strange Death of Liberal England: 1910-1914* (New York: Capricorn Books, 1961), p. 45; and Samuel Hynes, *The Edwardian Turn of Mind* (Princeton, New Jersey: Princeton University Press, 1968), p. 172.

34. Brocard Sewell, *Cecil Chesterton* (Faversham, Kent: St. Albert's Press, 1975), p. 32; and John P. McCarthy, *Hilaire Belloc: Edwardian Radical* (Indianapolis: Liberty Press, 1978), pp. 156-161.

35. Lucy Masterman, *G.F.G. Masterman* (London: Nicholson & Watson, 1939), p. 384, Appendix 2.

36. Chesterton, *What's Wrong With the World*, pp. 125-128.

37. See Dorothy L. Sayers, "Are Women Human?" in *Unpopular Opinions* (London: Gollancz, 1946); Humphrey Carpenter, *Tolkien: A Biography* (Boston: Houghton Mifflin, 1977); Humphrey Carpenter, *The Inklings* (London: Allen & Unwin, 1978); and C.S. Lewis, *The Four Loves* (New York: Harcourt Brace Jovanovich, 1960).

38. Canovan, *G.K. Chesterton: Radical Populist*, p. 107.

39. P. N. Furbank, "Chesterton the Edwardian" in *G.K. Chesterton: A Centenary Appraisal*, p. 21.

40. Alfred Havighurst, *Britain in Transition* (Chicago: University of Chicago Press, 1979), p. 97.

41. Peter Rowland, *The Last Liberal Governments: The Promised Land, 1905-1910* (London: Barrie & Rockliff, Cresset Press, 1968), pp. 237-239.

42. John P. McCarthy, *Hilaire Belloc: Edwardian Radical* (Indianapolis: Liberty Press, 1978), p. 137; see also Leo Hetzler, "Chesterton's Political Views" in *The Chesterton Review* VII, No. 2 (Spring 1981), 128-129. Hetzler suggests too much sympathy between Belloc and Chesterton and ignores other Liberal influences on Chesterton, like Gardiner and Masterman. Like many others, he is reading back into 1910 attitudes more appropriate to the time between 1925-1930 — certainly more appropriate to 1914. For proof, see the quotation referred to in the following footnote.

43. Neal Blewett, *The Peers, the Parties, and the People: The British General Elections of 1910* (London: Macmillan, 1972), pp. 53-54.

44. Rowland, *The Last Liberal Governments,*, pp. 248-249.

45. Blewett, *The Peers, the Parties, and the People*, pp. 141-143.

46. McCarthy, *Hilaire Belloc: Edwardian Radical*, pp. 163-165.

47. Sewell, *Cecil Chesterton*, pp. 32-33; and Halevy, *A History of the English People*, p. 306.

48. Chesterton, *Autobiography*, pp. 123-124.

49. Hynes, *The Edwardian Turn of Mind*, p. 58.

50. Charles Masterman, *The Condition of England* (London: Methuen, 1909), p. 80.

51. Chesterton, *What's Wrong With the World*, pp. 5-6.

52. Canovan, *C.K. Chesterton: Radical Populist*, pp. 39-41.

53. Chesterton, *What's Wrong With the World*, pp. 9-10.

54. *Ibid.*, pp. 16-17.
55. Canovan, *G.K. Chesterton: Radical Populist*, pp. 45-48.
56. Chesterton, *What's Wrong With the World*, pp. 36-37.
57. *Ibid.*, pp. 32-36.
58. *Ibid.*, p. 203.
59. Canovan, *G.K. Chesterton: Radical Populist*, pp. 47-48.
60. McCarthy, *Hilaire Belloc: Edwardian Radical*, p. 296.
61. Chesterton, *What's Wrong With the World*, p. 47.
62. See Hynes, *The Edwardian Turn of Mind*, chapters five, six, and seven.
63. Chesterton, *What's Wrong With the World*, p. 266.
64. Havighurst, *Britain in Transition*, p. 102.
65. Hynes, *The Edwardian Turn of Mind*, p. 326. See also Appendix D.
66. Virginia Woolf, "Mr. Bennet and Mrs. Brown" in *The Captain's Death Bed* (New York: Harcourt Brace, 1950), p. 104.
67. See especially Leon Edel, *Bloomsbury: A House of Lions* (Philadelphia: J.B. Lippincott, 1979), pp. 189-191.
68. Chesterton, "The Surrender of a Cockney" in *The Selected Essays of G.K. Chesterton*, p. 251.
69. Rowland, *The Last Liberal Governments*, pp. ix-x.

CHAPTER TEN
1. G.K. Chesterton, "The Secret People" in *The Collected Poems of G.K. Chesterton* (London: Cecil Palmer, 1927), pp. 157-160. (As recently as the last General Election, the Labour prime minister quoted this poem during his campaign.)
2. Peter Rowland, *The Last Liberal Governments: The Promised Land, 1905-1910* (London: Barrie & Rockliff, Cresset Press, 1968), p. 332.
3. E.C. Bentley, *Those Days* (London: Constable, 1940), pp. 204-208.
4. G.K. Chesterton, "The Revolutionist, or Lines to a Statesman" in *The Collected Poems of G.K. Chesterton*, p. 140.
5. Neal Blewett, *The Peers, the Parties, and the People: The British General Elections of 1910* (London: Macmillan, 1972), p. 414.
6. *Ibid.*, p. 45; and Rowland, *The Last Liberal Governments*, p. 344.
7. Norman and Jeanne MacKenzie, *The Fabians* (New York: Simon & Schuster, 1977), pp. 373-380.
8. *Ibid.*, p. 380.
9. Anne Fremantle, *This Little Band of Prophets* (New York: Macmillan, 1960), pp. 196-198.
10. Christopher Armstrong, *Evelyn Underhill* (Grand Rapids, Mich.: Eerdmans, 1976), p. 66. See also Horton Davies, *Worship and Theology in England, Vol. V: The Ecumenical Century, 1900-1965* (Princeton, N.J.: Princeton University Press, 1965), pp. 138-144.
11. Armstrong, *Evelyn Underhill*, pp. 114-116.
12. G.K. Chesterton, *Orthodoxy* (New York: Dodd, Mead, 1908), p. 244; and Margaret Canovan, *G.K. Chesterton: Radical Populist* (New York: Harcourt Brace Jovanovich, 1977), p. 122.
13. Davies, *Worship and Theology in England*, pp. 130-139.
14. *Ibid.*, p. 153; and Armstrong, *Evelyn Underhill*, pp. 118-119.
15. John P. McCarthy, *Hilaire Belloc: Edwardian Radical* (Indianapolis: Liberty Press, 1978), p. 165; and Canovan, *G.K. Chesterton: Radical Populist*, p. 16.
16. Andrew Boyle, *The Climate of Treason: Five Who Spied for Russia* (London: Hutchinson, 1979), p. 14.

17. This thesis owes much to Ian Boyd's lecture on Father Brown given at the meeting of the Chesterton Society at the MLA Convention, Chicago, in 1979.

18. Elie Halevy, *A History of the English People, Epilogue,* Vol. II: *The Rule of Democracy, 1905-1914* (London: Ernest Benn, 1934), pp. 305-308.

19. Samuel Hynes, *The Edwardian Turn of Mind* (Princeton, N.J.: Princeton University Press, 1968), pp. 34-35.

20. Alfred Havighurst, *Britain in Transition* (Chicago: University of Chicago Press, 1979), p. 102.

21. Canovan, *G.K. Chesterton: Radical Populist*, pp. 117-118. See also the discussion about Jews in Leon Hetzler's "Chesterton's Political Views" in *The Chesterton Review*, VII, No. 2 (Spring 1981), 129-137.

22. John Sullivan, *G.K. Chesterton: A Bibliography* (London: University of London Press, 1958), p. 40.

23. William B. Furlong, *Shaw and Chesterton: The Metaphysical Jesters* (University Park, Pa.: Pennsylvania State University Press, 1970), pp. 84-85.

24. *Ibid.*, p. 87.

25. Frank Swinnerton, "A Beautiful Character" in *The Mark Twain Quarterly*, I (1979), 9.

26. Furlong, *Shaw and Chesterton: The Metaphysical Jesters*, p. 100.

27. Norman and Jeanne MacKenzie, *The Fabians*, p. 386. The Fabians had given up the idea of using Wells as a sparring partner for Shaw, while Chesterton, according to Shaw's biographer, "was sent into the world by an all-just God, for the exclusive purpose of saying the opposite to Mr. Shaw. He has to restore the balance which Mr. Shaw very vigorously disturbs."

28. Furlong, *Shaw and Chesterton: The Metaphysical Jesters*, p. 108.

29. *Ibid.*, p. 115.

30. Robert Speaight, *The Life of Hilaire Belloc* (New York: Farrar, Straus & Cudahy, 1957), p. 245.

31. See Cecil Chesterton's letter to Mrs. Hubert Bland (E. Nesbit), written on *Eye-Witness* stationery, in which he writes, "I'm so glad you like [it]. I enjoy it myself — it's fun throwing brick-bats about." (The letter is part of the John Bennett Shaw Collection, University of Notre Dame, South Bend, Indiana.)

32. G.K. Chesterton, *Autobiography* (London: Hutchinson, 1936), p. 201.

33. McCarthy, *Hilaire Belloc: Edwardian Radical*, p. 230.

34. Some examples in the Liberal Party's leadership included Herbert Samuel, the Postmaster General and later leader of the party, as well as Rufus Isaacs, Solicitor General and later Lord Chancellor, Viceroy of India, and Marquis of Reading. Both men were also implicated in the Marconi Scandal (see Chapter Eleven).

35. See Frances Donaldson, *The Marconi Affair* (New York: Harcourt, Brace & World, 1962). Donaldson assumes that Cecil Chesterton was totally anti-Semitic, and that Gilbert Chesterton was virtually the same, but gives Belloc the benefit of the doubt. She does not really understand the underlying political concerns of any of them, while she insists that English society was not anti-Semitic. By contrast, Margaret Canovan in *G.K. Chesterton: Radical Populist* gives a far more understanding analysis of this situation (pp. 136-140). It is also useful to see Leon Edel, *Bloomsbury: A House of Lions* (New York: J.B. Lippincott, 1979), pp. 174-181, for a frank discussion of the uneasy social acceptance granted someone like Leonard Woolf — even by his future wife, Virginia Stephen.

36. G.K. Chesterton, "The Ballad of the Anti-Puritan" in *The Collected Poems of G.K. Chesterton*, p. 172.

37. Garry Wills, *Chesterton: Man and Mask* (New York: Sheed & Ward, 1961), p. 174.

38. Canovan, *G.K. Chesterton: Radical Populist*, p. 59.

39. Brocard Sewell, *Cecil Chesterton* (Faversham, Kent: St. Albert's Press, 1975), pp. 38-39; see also Speaight, *The Life of Hilaire Belloc*, pp. 299-300.

40. George Dangerfield, *The Damnable Question* (Boston: Little, Brown, 1976), p. 26.

41. Chesterton, *Autobiography*, pp. 273-274.

42. McCarthy, *Hilaire Belloc: Edwardian Radical*, pp. 233-234.

43. *Ibid.*, p. 243; and Norman and Jeanne MacKenzie, *The Fabians*, p. 356.

44. Stephen Koss, *Nonconformity in Modern British Politics* (Hamden, Conn.: Archon Books, Shoe String Press, 1975), pp. 100-125.

45. Alfred Havighurst, *Radical Journalist: H.W. Massingham* (London: Cambridge University Press, 1974), pp. 222-225.

46. W.W. Robson, "Father Brown and Others" in *G.K. Chesterton: A Centenary Appraisal*, ed. John Sullivan (London: Paul Elek, 1974), pp. 68-69; and Newgate Callendar, "Crime" in the *New York Times Book Review*, p. 35.

47. Ian Boyd, "Philosophy in Fiction" in *G.K. Chesterton: A Centenary Appraisal*, pp. 44-45.

48. Canovan, *G.K. Chesterton: Radical Populist*, p. 7.

49. Wills, *Chesterton: Man and Mask*, p. 124.

50. Robson, "Father Brown and Others," pp. 67-68.

51. Chesterton, *Autobiography* p. 322.

52. See Julian Symons, *Mortal Consequences: A History from the Detective Story to the Crime Novel* (New York: Harper & Row, 1972), p. 105; John Cawalti, *Adventure, Mystery, and Romance* (Chicago: University of Chicago Press, 1976), pp. 140-141; and Lynette Hunter, *G.K. Chesterton: Explorations in Allegory* (New York: St. Martin's Press, 1979), p. 134. Dr. Hunter is particularly interested in showing that Chesterton's most characteristic writing is his detective stories.

53. See John Dickson Carr's Chestertonian detective Dr. Gideon Fell in his mysteries like *Hag's Nook*, *It Walks by Night*, and *Death Turns the Tables*.

54. G.K. Chesterton, "A Defence of Detective Stories" in *The Defendant* (London: Brimley Johnson, 1901), pp. 122-123.

55. Ian Boyd, "Father Brown," The Chesterton Society, MLA Convention, Chicago, 1977.

56. G.K. Chesterton, "The Queer Feet" in *The Innocence of Father Brown* (New York: Curtis Publishing, 1910: rpt. New York: Penguin Books, 1975), p. 64.

57. Symons, *Mortal Consequences*, p. 81.

58. Cawalti, *Adventure, Mystery, and Romance*, pp. 103-105.

59. Chesterton, "The Queer Feet," p. 53.

60. L. Garnett Thomas, "Mysticism in *The Ballad of the White Horse*" in *The Chesterton Review*, VI, No. 2 (Spring-Summer 1980), 205.

61. W.H. Auden, "The Gift of Wonder" in *G.K. Chesterton: A Centenary Appraisal*, p. 74.

62. G.K. Chesterton, *A Short History of England* (London: Chatto & Windus, 1917), pp. 40-42. A recent public television documentary on the Vikings offered the same point as the vital fact for civilization.

63. G.K. Chesterton, *The Ballad of the White Horse* in *The Collected Poems of G.K. Chesterton*, p. 206.

64. Canovan, *G.K. Chesterton: Radical Populist*, pp. 112-113.

65. G.K. Chesterton, *The Ballad of the White Horse*, pp. 284-286.

66. Wills, *Chesterton: Man and Mask*, p. 229, footnote 11.

67. Maurice Baring, "Punch and Judy" in the *Eye-Witness*, September 7, 1911.

68. Dangerfield, *The Damnable Question*, pp. 73-74.

69. Havighurst, *Britain in Transition*, p. 109.

70. Stephen Koss, *Asquith* (New York: St. Martin's Press, 1976), pp. 135-138.

71. Norman and Jeanne MacKenzie, *The Fabians*, p. 394.

72. Havighurst, *Radical Journalist: H.W. Massingham*, p. 177.
73. G.K. Chesterton, "The Song of Wheels" in *The Collected Poems of G.K. Chesterton*, p. 157.
74. Wills, *Chesterton: Man and Mask*, p. 123.
75. Ian Boyd, *The Novels of G.K. Chesterton* (London: Paul Elek, 1975), pp. 51-52.

CHAPTER ELEVEN

1. G.K. Chesterton, *Autobiography* (London: Hutchinson, 1936), p. 202.
2. Garry Wills, *Chesterton: Man and Mask* (New York: Sheed & Ward, 1961), p. 77.
3. G.K. Chesterton, *The Victorian Age in Literature* (London: Williams & Norgate, Home University Library, 1913), pp. 39-40.
4. *Ibid.*, p. 251.
5. Stephen Koss, *Asquith* (New York: St. Martin's Press, 1970), p. 143.
6. Samuel Hynes, *The Edwardian Turn of Mind* (Princeton, New Jersey: Princeton University Press, 1968), pp. 47-48.
7. Stephen Koss, *Haldane: Scapegoat for Liberalism* (New York: Columbia University Press, 1969), p. 138.
8. Chesterton, *Autobiography*, p. 262.
9. Margaret Canovan, *G.K. Chesterton: Radical Populist* (New York: Harcourt Brace Jovanovich, 1977), p. 59.
10. Frances Donaldson, *The Marconi Affair* (New York: Harcourt, Brace & World, 1962), book jacket blurb: "This is the dramatic account of one of the great scandals in English history. . . . For fifteen months the Marconi Scandal held the headlines. . . . [As a result of the scandal] . . . in 1914, although Germany had a complete wireless chain connecting her colonies, England had only two half-finished stations." See also Stephen Koss, *Fleet Street Radical* (London: Allen Lane, 1973), p. 132; and Lord Birkenhead (F.E. Smith), *Famous Trials of History* (New York: Garden City, 1926). As part of the prosecution, he says that everything about the libel trial of Cecil Chesterton was handled perfectly, both in the Cabinet and in court.
11. Maisie Ward, *Gilbert Keith Chesterton* (London: Sheed & Ward, 1944), pp. 285-287.
12. Brocard Sewell, *Cecil Chesterton* (Haversham, Kent: St. Albert's Press, 1975), p. 43; and Robert Speaight, *The Life of Hilaire Belloc* (New York: Farrar, Straus & Cudahy, 1957), p. 297.
13. Dudley Barker, *G.K. Chesterton* (New York: Stein & Day, 1973), pp. 174, 251.
14. See Hilaire Belloc, *On the Place of Gilbert Chesterton in English Letters* (New York: Sheed & Ward, 1940).
15. Leonard Woolf, *Sowing* (New York: Harcourt Brace, 1960), pp. 100-101.
16. John P. McCarthy, *Hilaire Belloc: Edwardian Radical* (Indianapolis: Liberty Press, 1978), p. 287. There is a tendency to assume that only Belloc spoke for this point of view, as well as to assume that Chesterton was his only echo. Neither assumption is accurate.
17. Hilaire Belloc, *The Servile State* (orig. pub. 1913; rpt. Indianapolis; Liberty Press, 1979), p. 138.
18. Canovan, *G.K. Chesterton: Radical Populist*, pp. 14-15.
19. *Ibid.*, pp. 72-73; McCarthy, *Hilaire Belloc: Edwardian Radical*, p. 287; and the "World" column, "Reassessing the Welfare State: A Humanitarian Dream Becomes an Economic Nightmare," *Time* Magazine, January 12, 1981.
20. Belloc, *The Servile State*, p. 80.
21. Anne Fremantle, *This Little Band of Prophets* (New York: Macmillan, 1960), p. 84.
22. Speaight, *The Life of Hilaire Belloc*, p. 308.

23. G.K. Chesterton, "The Horrible Story of Jones" in *The Collected Poems of G.K. Chesterton* (London: Cecil Palmer, 1927), p. 142.

24. Donaldson, *The Marconi Affair*, pp. 21-22.

25. *Ibid.*, p. 44.

26. *Ibid.*, pp. 58-71.

27. Julian Symons, *Mortal Consequences: A History from the Detective Story to the Crime Novel* (New York: Harper & Row, 1972), pp. 93-94.

28. E.C. Bentley, *Trent's Last Case* (New York: Harper & Row, 1978), dedication page.

29. Dorothy L. Sayers in her introduction to *Trent's Last Case*. pp. x-xii. Sayers used Bentley's plot for her first novel, *Whose Body?*

30. Bentley, *Trent's Last Case*, p. 123.

31. See Canovan, *G.K. Chesterton: Radical Populist*, pp. 74-75, for the typical reaction to Chesterton's women, as well as Malcolm Muggeridge, *Chronicles of Wasted Time*, Vol. I: *The Green Stick* (London: Collins, 1972), p. 38; and Hynes, *The Edwardian Turn of Mind*, Chapter VI.

32. G.K. Chesterton, *A Miscellany of Men* (New York: Dodd, Mead, 1912), p. 171. See also Lawrence J. Clipper, *G.K. Chesterton* (New York: Twayne Publishers, 1974), p. 47.

33. Bentley, *Trent's Last Case*, p. 6.

34. Chesterton, *A Miscellany of Men*, pp. 89-96.

35. Nicholas Bentley, *Edwardian Album: A Photographic Excursion into a Lost Age of Innocence* (London : Sphere Books, 1974), pp. 60-61.

36. Lucy Masterman, *C.F.G. Masterman* (London: Nicholson & Watson, 1939), p. 255; and Donaldson, *The Marconi Affair*, p. 17.

37. Ward, *Gilbert Keith Chesterton*, pp. 289-290.

38. Alfred Havighurst, *Radical Journalist: H.W. Massingham* (London: Cambridge University Press, 1974), p. 210.

39. Mary Soames, *Clementine Churchill: The Biography of a Marriage* (Boston: Houghton Mifflin, 1979), p. 199.

40. Donaldson, *The Marconi Affair*, pp. 96-124.

41. Ada Chesterton, *The Chestertons* (London: Chapman & Hall, 1941), pp. 85-86.

42. Ward, *Gilbert Keith Chesterton*, p. 282.

43. Speaight, *The Life of Hilaire Belloc*, p. 308.

44. Donaldson, *The Marconi Affair*, p. 72.

45. Barker, *G.K. Chesterton*, p. 212.

46. Donaldson, *The Marconi Affair*, p. 119.

47. G.K. Chesterton, "Wine and Water" in *The Collected Poems of G.K. Chesterton*, p. 180.

48. G.K. Chesterton, "The Rolling English Road" in *The Collected Poems of G.K. Chesterton*, p. 183.

49. G.K. Chesterton, "The Song of Quoodle" in *The Collected Poems of G.K. Chesterton*, p. 185.

50. G.K. Chesterton, *The Flying Inn* (London: Methuen, 1914), p. 39.

51. Donaldson, *The Marconi Affair*, p. 80; and Ada Chesterton, *The Chestertons*, p. 94.

52. Donaldson, *The Marconi Affair*, pp. 80-96; and Chesterton, *Autobiography*, p. 204.

53. McCarthy, *Hilaire Belloc: Edwardian Radical*, pp. 259-261.

54. Ward, *Gilbert Keith Chesterton*, pp. 298-299.

55. Sewell, *Cecil Chesterton*, p. 45.

56. Donaldson, *The Marconi Affair*, pp. 171-173.

57. Quoted in Koss, *Fleet Street Radical*, p. 116.

58. Koss, *Fleet Street Radical*, p. 116.

59. Barker, *G.K. Chesterton*, p. 220.

60. Norman and Jeanne MacKenzie, *The Fabians* (New York: Simon & Schuster, 1977), pp. 351-357.

61. See Ward, *Gilbert Keith Chesterton*, p. 255; Barker, *G.K. Chesterton*, p. 220; Canovan, *G.K. Chesterton: Radical Populist*, p. 82; and Leo Hetzler, "Chesterton's Political Views" in *The Chesterton Review*, VII, No. 2 (Spring 1981), 245-246.

62. Paul Ferris, *The House of Northcliffe* (London: Weidenfeld & Nicolson, 1971), p. 4.

63. Barker, *G.K. Chesterton*, p. 215.

64. Ada Chesterton, *The Chestertons*, p. 101.

65. Sewell, *Cecil Chesterton*, pp. 50-52.

66. *Ibid.*, p. 65.

67. Ward, *Gilbert Keith Chesterton*, p. 300.

68. Donaldson, *The Marconi Affair*, pp. 186-188.

69. Sewell, *Cecil Chesterton*, p. 69.

70. Donaldson, *The Marconi Affair*, p. 189.

71. Quoted in *The Man Who Was Orthodox*, ed. A.L. Maycock (London: Dobson, 1963), p. 28.

72. Ward, *Gilbert Keith Chesterton*, pp. 306-309.

73. Chesterton, *Autobiography*, pp. 210-211.

CHAPTER TWELVE

1. G.K. Chesterton, "On War Memorials" in *The Selected Essays of G.K. Chesterton*, ed. E.C. Bentley (London: Methuen, 1949), p. 42.

2. Lawrence J. Clipper, *G.K. Chesterton* (New York: Twayne Publishers, 1974), p. 94.

3. William B. Furlong, *Shaw and Chesterton: The Metaphysical Jesters* (University Park, Pa.: Pennsylvania State University Press, 1970), pp. 12-14.

4. *Ibid.*, p. 16. (*Androcles* is a play in which Shaw talks about his own view of Christianity.)

5. *Ibid.*, p. 20; and Maisie Ward, *Gilbert Keith Chesterton* (London: Sheed & Ward, 1944), p. 315.

6. Garry Wills, *Chesterton: Man and Mask* (New York: Sheed & Ward, 1961), pp. 125-126; and G.K. Chesterton, *Magic: A Fantastic Comedy* (New York: G.P. Putnam's Sons, 1913), p. 80.

7. Chesterton, *Magic*, pp. 87-88.

8. Ward, *Gilbert Keith Chesterton*, p. 208.

9. Furlong, *Shaw and Chesterton: The Metaphysical Jesters*, pp. 17-18.

10. G.K. Chesterton, "Magic" in the *Dublin Review*, January 1914, reprinted in *Chesterton Continued: A Bibliographical Supplement*, ed. John Sullivan (London: University of London Press, 1968), pp. 90-91.

11. Furlong, *Shaw and Chesterton: The Metaphysical Jesters*, p. 31; Ada Chesterton, *The Chestertons* (London: Chapman & Hall, 1941), pp. 144-148; and Brocard Sewell, *Cecil Chesterton* (Faversham, Kent: St. Albert's Press, 1975), pp. 74-79.

12. Cyril Clemens, *Chesterton as Seen by His Contemporaries* (Webster Groves, Mo.: Mark Twain Society, 1939), p. 27; pp. 85-87.

13. Samuel Hynes, *The Edwardian Turn of Mind* (Princeton, N.J.: Princeton Universtiy Press, 1968), p. 34.

14. Alfred Havighurst, *Radical Journalist: H.W. Massingham* (London: Cambridge University Press, 1968), p. 171; Margaret Canovan, *G.K. Chesterton: Radical Populist* (New York: Harcourt Brace Jovanovich, 1977), p. 61; and Garry Wills, *Chesterton: Man and Mask*, p. 152.

15. G.K. Chesterton, *The Flying Inn* (London: Methuen, 1914), p. 268.

16. *Ibid*, pp. 30-45.

17. Ian Boyd, *The Novels of G.K. Chesterton* (London: Paul Elek, 1975), p. 66.

18. Chesterton, *The Flying Inn*, p. 253.

19. *Ibid*., p. 280.

20. Boyd, *The Novels of G.K. Chesterton*, pp. 71-73. See Boyd's reference to C.S. Lewis's comment on this particular novel.

21. See Julius West, *G.K. Chesterton* (New York: Dodd, Mead, 1916), for a scathing Fabian account of Chesterton when he began to work as an editor, which suggests that he was completely unrelated to "reality." But in a letter to E.C. Bentley during the war, Chesterton commented, "I see the Germans have actually done what I described as a wild fancy in *The Flying Inn*, combined the Cross and the Crescent in one ornamental symbol." (This letter is part of the John Bennett Shaw Collection at the University of Notre Dame. It is also quoted in Ward, *Gilbert Keith Chesterton*, p. 340.)

22. Norman and Jeanne MacKenzie, *The Fabians* (New York: Simon & Schuster, 1977), p. 394.

23. Peter Rowland, *The Last Liberal Governments: The Promised Land, 1905-1910* (London: Barrie & Rockliff, Cresset Press, 1968), pp. 276-277.

24. Stephen Koss, *Haldane: Scapegoat for Liberalism* (New York: Columbia University Press, 1969), pp. 106-107; and George Dangerfield, *The Damnable Question* (Boston: Little, Brown, 1976), p. 83.

25. Koss, *Haldane: Scapegoat for Liberalism*, pp. 112-114. Masterman lost his first bid for re-election by only twenty-six votes. Thereafter, Belloc and Cecil Chesterton began to appear to heckle him, Lord Northcliffe's papers went after him, and, finally, when he took control of the government, Lloyd George refused to let him run for a "safe" seat. In spite of this treatment, Masterman continued to be fascinated by Lloyd George. (See also Lucy Masterman, *C.F.G. Masterman* [London: Nicholson & Watson, 1939].) While Asquith was still prime minister, Masterman was given the job of running a propaganda office for which Chesterton also worked.

26. Norman and Jeanne MacKenzie, *The Time Traveller: The Life of H.G. Wells* (London: Weidenfeld & Nicolson. 1973), p. 287.

27. G.K. Chesterton, *Autobiography* (London: Hutchinson, 1936), pp. 232-234.

28. *Ibid*., p. 234.

29. *Ibid*., p. 235.

30. Malcolm Muggeridge, *Chronicles of Wasted Time*, Vol. I: *The Green Stick* (London: Collins, 1972), pp. 12-13.

31. Barbara Tuchman, *The Proud Tower: A Portrait of the World Before the War, 1890-1914* (New York: Bantam Books, 1967), pp. 53-56.

32. See Laurence Lafore, *The Long Fuse* (Philadelphia: J.B. Lippincott, 1965); and Leonard Woolf, *Beginning Again* (New York: Harcourt Brace, 1964).

33. Chesterton, *Autobiography*, p. 246.

34. Stephen Koss, *Fleet Street Radical* (Hamden, Conn.: Archon Books, Shoe String Press, 1973), p. 143.

35. Koss, *Haldane: Scapegoat for Liberalism*, pp. 114-118.

36. Lucy Masterman, *C.F.G. Masterman*, p. 266.

37. Cecil Chesterton, *The Prussian Hath Said in His Heart* (New York: Lawrence Gonne, 1915), p. 1. See also Robert Speaight, *The Life of Hilaire Belloc* (New York: Farrar, Straus & Cudahy, 1957), p. 368.

38. Havighurst, *Radical Journalist: H.W. Massingham*, pp. 228-229.

39. Alfred Havighurst, *Britain in Transition* (Chicago: University of Chicago Press, 1979), p. 126.

40. Anne Fremantle, *This Little Band of Prophets* (New York: Macmillan, 1960), p. 205.

41. Canovan, *G.K. Chesterton: Radical Populist*, pp. 108-109.

42. Chesterton, *Autobiography*, pp. 245-247.

43. Norman and Jeanne MacKenzie, *The Time Traveller: The Life of H.G. Wells*, pp. 297-310.

44. George Dangerfield, *The Strange Death of Liberal England* (New York: Capricorn Books, 1961), p. 439.

45. G.K. Chesterton, "The Purple Wig" in *The Wisdom of Father Brown* (orig. pub. 1914; rpt. New York: Penguin Books, 1975), p. 108.

46. Chesterton, "The Purple Wig." pp. 119-120. See also Leo Hetzler, "Chesterton's Political Views" in *The Chesterton Review*, VII, No. 2 (Spring 1981), 229-230.

47. G.K. Chesterton, "The Fairy Tale of Father Brown" in *The Wisdom of Father Brown*, p. 187.

48. Dudley Barker, *G.K. Chesterton* (New York: Stein & Day, 1974), pp. 223-224.

49. Lucy Masterman, *C.F.G. Masterman*, p. 372.

50. Canovan, *G.K. Chesterton: Radical Populist*, p. 109; and Barker, *G.K. Chesterton*, p. 223. Also see Stephen Spender, *The Thirties and After: Poetry, Politics, People, 1930's-1970's* (New York: Random House, Vintage Books, 1979).

51. W.R. Titterton, *G.K. Chesterton: A Portrait* (London: Douglas Organ, 1936), p. 111.

52. Barker, *G.K. Chesterton*, pp. 228-229.

53. Barker, *G.K. Chesterton*, pp. 227-229; and Ward, *Gilbert Keith Chesterton*, p. 329.

54. Hilaire Belloc, *On the Place of Gilbert Chesterton in English Letters* (New York: Sheed & Ward, 1940); and John O'Connor, *Father Brown on Chesterton* (London: Oates & Washbourne, 1938), p. 98. See also Chapter V, "The Notebook," pp. 56-64, in Ward's *Gilbert Keith Chesterton*; and Titterton, *G.K. Chesterton*, p. 83.

55. Ada Chesterton, *The Chestertons*, p. 174.

56. Sewell, *Cecil Chesterton*, pp. 85-90.

57. *Ibid.*, pp. 88-90.

58. Speaight, *The Life of Hilaire Belloc*, p. 364.

59. Koss, *Fleet Street Radical*, pp. 158-196.

60. G.K. Chesterton in a letter to E.C. Bentley, copyright Dorothy Collins; part of the John Bennett Shaw Collection, the University of Notre Dame, South Bend, Indiana.

61. Havighurst, *Radical Journalist: H.W. Massingham*, p. 264.

62. Lucy Masterman, *C.F.G. Masterman*, p. 290.

63. Cecil Chesterton in a letter to a potential donor to the *New Witness*, copyright O. Chesterton; part of the John Bennett Shaw Collection at the University of Notre Dame, South Bend, Indiana.

64. Chesterton, *Autobiography*, p. 256.

65. Koss, *Fleet Street Radical*, p. 158.

66. Chesterton, *Autobiography*, p. 256.

67. Canovan, *G.K. Chesterton: Radical Populist*, p. 84.

68. *Ibid.*, pp. 84-85.

69. Leo Hetzler, "Chesterton's Political Views" in *The Chesterton Review*, VII, No. 2 (August 1981), 246-247.

70. Ada Chesterton, *The Chestertons*, pp. 201-206; and Sewell, *Cecil Chesterton*, p. 92.

71. G.K. Chesterton, *A Short History of England* (London: Chatto & Windus, 1917), p. 1.

72. John R. Green, *A Short History of the English People*, Vol. 1 (New York: The Nottingham Society, 1960), p. 30.

73. Chesterton, *A Short History of England*, p. 18.

74. William Stubbs, *The Constitutional History of England*, Vol. 1 (London: Oxford at the Clarendon Press, 1874), pp. 2-3.

75. Chesterton, *A Short History of England*, p. 241.

76. Havighurst, *Britain in Transition*, p. 130.

77. Norman and Jeanne MacKenzie, *The Time Traveller: The Life of H.G. Wells*, pp. 310-312.

78. *Ibid.*, pp. 316-317.
79. *Ibid.*, p. 318; and Wills, *Chesterton: Man and Mask*, pp. 153-154.
80. Chesterton, *Autobiography*, p. 258.
81. Barker, *G.K. Chesterton*, p. 237.
82. Sewell, *Cecil Chesterton*, pp. 95-96.
83. Ward, *Gilbert Keith Chesterton*, pp. 360-361.

CHAPTER THIRTEEN
1. G.K. Chesterton in the introduction to Cecil Chesterton's *A History of the United States* (New York: George Doran, 1919), p. xiv.
2. Maisie Ward, *Gilbert Keith Chesterton* (London: Sheed & Ward, 1944), pp. 358-382.
3. Alfred Havighurst, *Britain in Transition* (Chicago: University of Chicago Press, 1979), p. 136.
4. Neal Blewett, *The Peers, the Parties, and the People: The British General Elections of 1910* (London: Macmillan, 1972), p. 415.
5. Alfred Havighurst, *Radical Journalist: H.W. Massingham* (London: Cambridge University Press, 1974), pp. 263-273.
6. Lucy Masterman, *C.F.G. Masterman* (London: Nicholson & Watson, 1939), p. 310.
7. A. Herbold, "Chesterton and *G.K.'s Weekly*," Diss. University of Michigan 1963, p. 323.
8. Frank Swinnerton, *The Georgian Scene: A Literary Panorama* (New York: Farrar, Straus & Rinehart, 1934), p. 96.
9. G.K. Chesterton, *St. Francis of Assisi* (New York: Image Books, 1957), pp. 19-20.
10. W.R. Titterton, *G.K. Chesterton: A Portrait* (London: Douglas Organ, 1936), p. 119.
11. Peter Rowland, *David Lloyd George: A Biography* (New York: Macmillan, 1975), pp. 464-465; Havighurst, *Radical Journalist: H.W. Massingham*, pp. 266-269; and Havighurst, *Britain in Transition*, p. 148.
12. Stephen Koss, *Nonconformity in Modern British Politics* (Hamden, Conn.: Archon Books, Shoe String Press, 1975), p. 235; and Rowland, *David Lloyd George*, p. 474.
13. Havighurst, *Britain in Transition*, p. 164.
14. G. K. Chesterton, *The New Jerusalem* (New York: George Doran, 1921), p. 18.
15. G.K. Chesterton in his speech for Rector of Glasgow University, 1925, copyright Dorothy Collins; the Wade Collection, Wheaton College, Wheaton, Illinois.
16. G.K. Chesterton, *Autobiography* (London: Hutchinson, 1936), pp. 241-242.
17. Rowland, *David Lloyd George*, pp. 548-549; and Havighurst, *Britain in Transition*, pp. 170-176.
18. Ward, *Gilbert Keith Chesterton*, p. 377.
19. *Ibid.*, p. 391.
20. Chesterton, *The New Jerusalem*, pp. 13-52.
21. *Ibid.*, pp. 88-89.
22. *Ibid.*, pp. 54-57.
23. *Ibid.*, pp. 69-70.
24. *Ibid.*, pp. 245-247.
25. *Ibid.*, p. 268.
26. Goldwin Smith, *A History of England* (New York: Charles Scribner's Sons, 1944), p. 810.
27. Rowland, *David Lloyd George*, p. 424.
28. Garry Wills, *Chesterton: Man and Mask* (New York: Sheed & Ward, 1961), p. 154;

and Margaret Canovan, *G.K. Chesterton: Radical Populist* (New York; Harcourt Brace Jovanovich, 1977), p. 136.

29. Chesterton, *The New Jerusalem*, p. 221.

30. *Ibid.*, p. 276.

31. Canovan, *G.K. Chesterton: Radical Populist*, pp. 136-138. Her discussion of Chesterton's "anti-Semitism" is the best and fairest to date. See also Leo Hetzler, "Chesterton's Political Views" in *The Chesterton Review*, VII, No. 2 (Spring 1981), pp. 131-137.

32. Chesterton, *The New Jerusalem*, pp. 287-288.

33. *Ibid.*, p. 306.

34. Quoted in Wills, *Chesterton: Man and Mask*, p. 161.

35. See Barker, *G.K. Chesterton* (New York: Stein & Day, 1973), p. 242; and Ward, *Gilbert Keith Chesterton*, p. 378.

36. Barker, *G.K. Chesterton*, pp. 242-243.

37. Ronald Knox, *A Spiritual Aeneid* (London: Longmans, Green, 1918), p. 179. See also references to Knox's "scholarship" in Dorothy L. Sayers, "Aristotle on Detection Fiction" in *Unpopular Opinions* (London: Gollancz, 1946), pp. 7-8.

38. G.K. Chesterton, "The Irish Language" in *G.K. Chesterton: An Anthology*, ed. D.B. Wyndham Lewis (London: Oxford University Press, 1957), pp. 124-125.

39. Norman and Jeanne MacKenzie, *The Time Traveller: The Life of H.G. Wells* (London: Weidenfeld & Nicolson, 1973), pp. 319-323.

40. John Sullivan, "The Everlasting Man" in *Seven*, 2 (March 1981), 58-59.

41. H.G. Wells, *The Outline of History* (New York: Doubleday, 1920), p. 4.

42. Norman and Jeanne MacKenzie, *The Time Traveller: The Life of H.G. Wells*, p. 334.

43. G.K. Chesterton, *The Superstition of Divorce* (London: Chatto & Windus, 1920), p. 12, pp. 58-59.

44. G.K. Chesterton, *The Collected Poems of G.K. Chesterton* (London: Cecil Palmer, 1927), pp. 38-40.

45. Barker, *G.K. Chesterton*, p. 248.

46. G.K. Chesterton, "The Irishman" in *The Selected Essays of G.K. Chesterton*, ed. E.C. Bentley (London: Methuen, 1949), pp. 182-183.

47. Cecil Chesterton, *The Prussian Hath Said in His Heart* (New York: Lawrence Gonne, 1915), p. xv; and Canovan, *G.K. Chesterton: Radical Populist*, p. 104.

48. Cecil Chesterton, *A History of the United States*, p. 299. See also Woodrow Wilson, *History of the American People* (New York: Harper Brothers, 1906).

49. G.K. Chesterton, *The Incredulity of Father Brown* (New York: Dodd, Mead, 1926; rpt. New York: Penguin Books, 1975), p. 25.

50. *Ibid.*, pp. 25-26.

51. Canovan, *G.K. Chesterton: Radical Populist*, p. 132.

52. John Drinkwater, "The Bookman," 58, No. 5 (January 1924), 538-540.

53. Ward, *Gilbert Keith Chesterton*, pp. 479-480.

54. William B. Furlong, *Shaw and Chesterton: The Metaphysical Jesters* (University Park, Pa.: Pennsylvania State University Press, 1970), p. 156.

55. G.B. Shaw, *Short Stories, Scraps, and Shavings* (London: Constable, 1934), p. 143.

56. *Ibid.*, p. 144.

57. *Ibid.*, p. 159.

58. *Ibid.*, pp. 161-162.

59. Furlong, *Shaw and Chesterton: The Metaphysical Jesters*, p. 169.

60. Rowland, *David Lloyd George*, p. 482.

61. Ada Chesterton, *The Chestertons* (London: Chapman & Hall, 1941), pp. 241-252; Ward, *Gilbert Keith Chesterton*, pp. 363-373; and Ian Boyd, "Chesterton and Poland: The Myth and the Reality" in *The Chesterton Review*, V, No. 1 (Fall-Winter 1978-1979), 22-42.

62. Rowland, *David Lloyd George*, pp. 505-506.

63. *Ibid.*, pp. 513-520.

64. *Ibid.*, pp. 555-561; and Havighurst, *Britain in Transition*, p. 175. What will happen by 1984 remains to be seen.

65. Stephen Koss, *Fleet Street Radical* (London: Allen Lane, 1973), p. 276; Koss, *Nonconformity in Modern British Politics*, p. 166; and Malcolm Muggeridge, *Chronicles of a Wasted Life*, Vol. I: *The Green Stick* (London: Collins, 1968), p. 134.

66. Lucy Masterman, *C.F.G. Masterman,* p. 328; and Rowland, *David Lloyd George.* p. 604.

67. Stephen Koss, *Haldane: Scapegoat for Liberalism* (New York: Columbia University Press, 1969), pp. 236-246; Rowland, *David Lloyd George*, pp. 608-614.

68. G.K. Chesterton, *Eugenics and Other Evils* (London: Cassell, 1922), pp. v-vi.

69. Canovan, *G.K. Chesterton: Radical Populist*, pp. 67-71.

70. Chesterton, *Eugenics and Other Evils*, p. 164.

71. *Ibid.*, pp. 170-188.

72. See Ward, *Gilbert Keith Chesterton*, pp. 394-398; Lawrence J. Clipper, *G.K. Chesterton* (New York: Twayne Publishers, 1974), p. 8 (preface); footnote 3, p. 161; G.K. Chesterton, *The Thing: Why I Am a Catholic* (New York: Dodd, Mead, 1930), pp. v-vi; and Barker, *G.K. Chesterton*, p. 251.

73. Chesterton, *The New Jerusalem*, pp. 275-276.

74. Barker, *G.K. Chesterton*, p. 247; and Robert Speaight, *The Life of Hilaire Belloc* (New York: Farrar, Straus & Cudahy, 1957), p. 373.

75. Ward, *Gilbert Keith Chesterton*, pp. 396-397.

76. Chesterton, *The Thing*, pp. vii-viii.

77. Lynette Hunter, *G.K. Chesterton: Explorations in Allegory* (New York: St. Martin's Press, 1979), pp. 159-160. See her description of G.K.C. as a "mystic artist," whom she defines as one who must relate the divine to the human — a man with a message.

78. *Ibid.*, pp. 127-129.

79. Horton Davies, *Worship and Theology in England* Vol. V: *The Ecumenical Century, 1900-1965* (Princeton, N.J.: Princeton University Press, 1965), pp. 258-290.

80. Canovan, *G.K. Chesterton: Radical Populist*, pp. 117-119. This is precisely the message that Dorothy Sayers was to give her public on the eve of World War II in her book *Begin Here: A Statement of Faith*.

81. Ward, *Gilbert Keith Chesterton*, pp. 395-397; and John O'Connor, *Father Brown on Chesterton* (London: Oates & Washbourne, 1938), pp. 127-129; pp. 131-132.

82. Chesterton, *Autobiography*, p. 329.

83. *Ibid.*, p. 343.

84. Speaight, *The Life of Hilaire Belloc*, pp. 373-374; Ward, *Gilbert Keith Chesterton*, pp. 403-404; and Barker, *G.K. Chesterton*, pp. 249-251. See also Belloc, *On the Place of Gilbert Chesterton in English Letters* (New York: Sheed & Ward, 1940).

85. Furlong, *Shaw and Chesterton: The Metaphysical Jesters*, p. 129.

86. *Ibid.*, pp. 123-133.

87. G.K. Chesterton, *What I Saw in America* (New York: Dodd, Mead, 1922), p. 2.

88. G.K. Chesterton, "Empire Day" in *The Collected Poems of G.K. Chesterton*, p. 86.

89. G.K. Chesterton, "The Old Song" in *The Collected Poems of G.K. Chesterton*, pp. 59-61.

90. G.K. Chesterton, "Elegy in a Country Churchyard" in *The Collected Poems of G.K. Chesterton*, p. 55.

91. Havighurst, *Britain in Transition*, pp. 176-177. As Lord Reading, however, Isaacs continued to be a kind of "eminence grise" mediating inter-party rows, while Samuel became titular head of the Liberal Party during the thirties.

92. Ian Boyd, *The Novels of G.K. Chesterton* (London: Paul Elek, 1975), p. 80.

93. *Ibid.*, pp. 80-84; pp. 92-98.

94. G.K. Chesterton, *The Man Who Knew Too Much* (New York: Harper Brothers, 1922), pp. 364-365.

95. W.W. Robson, "Father Brown and Others" in *G.K. Chesterton: A Centenary Appraisal*, ed. John Sullivan (London: Paul Elek, 1974), p. 72.

96. G.K. Chesterton, "Milton and Merrie England" in *G.K. Chesterton: An Anthology*, ed. D.B. Wyndham Lewis (London: Oxford University Press, 1957), p. 147.

97. *Ibid.*, pp. 148-158.

98. Michael Mason, *The Centre of Hilarity: A Play upon Ideas about Laughter and the Absurd* (London: Sheed & Ward, 1959), pp. 178-179. For a fascinating discussion of literary and historical analysis that parallels Chesterton's, see pages 127-130.

99. Chesterton, *St. Francis of Assisi*, pp. 9-10.

100. *Ibid.*, pp. 11-12.

101. *Ibid.*, pp. 73-74.

102. *Ibid.*, pp. 156-157.

103. Mason, *The Centre of Hilarity*, pp. 183-185.

104. Chesterton, *St. Francis of Assisi*, p. 152.

105. *Ibid.*, p. 153.

106. G.K. Chesterton in a letter to E.C. Bentley, written at Overroads, 1920, copyright Dorothy Collins; part of the John Bennett Shaw Collection, the University of Notre Dame, South Bend, Indiana.

107. Rowland, *David Lloyd George*, pp. 593-598.

108. *Ibid.*, pp. 603-610; and Havighurst, *Britain in Transition*, p. 182.

CHAPTER FOURTEEN

1. G.K. Chesterton, *The Outline of Sanity* (London: Methuen, 1926), pp. 229-230.

2. G.K. Chesterton, "Apologia" in *G.K.'s Weekly*, reprinted in *G.K.C. as M.C.* (Freeport, New York: Books for Libraries, 1967), p. 265.

3. G.K. Chesterton, *Autobiography* (London: Hutchinson, 1936), p. 244.

4. Alfred Havighurst, *Britain in Transition* (Chicago: University of Chicago Press, 1979), p. 188; and Peter Rowland, *David Lloyd George: A Biography* (New York: Macmillan, 1975), p. 614. The turncoats were Austen Chamberlain, Winston Churchill, F.E. Smith (Lord Birkenhead), and Herbert Samuel, who together represented most of the younger leadership of the Liberal Party.

5. Samuel Hynes, *The Auden Generation: Literature and Politics in England in the 1930's* (New York: Viking Press, 1977), pp. 19-25.

6. Michael Mason, *The Centre of Hilarity: A Play upon Ideas about Laughter and the Absurd* (London: Sheed & Ward, 1959), pp. 150-167.

7. Stephen Spender, *The Thirties and After: Poetry, Politics, People, 1930's-1970's* (New York: Random House, Vintage Books, 1979), p. 3.

8. Graham Greene, *Collected Essays* (London: The Bodley Head, 1969), p. 2. Greene recently edited a new collection of Chesterton's works.

9. *Ibid.*, pp. 136-137; Mason, *The Centre of Hilarity*, p. 188.

10. G.K. Chesterton, in his speech for Rector of Glasgow University, 1925, copyright Dorothy Collins; part of the Wade Collection, Wheaton College, Wheaton, Illinois.

11. Compare these candidacies with two more recent, celebrated cases: that of Lord Snow (C.P. Snow), the writer and labor baron who sent his son to Eton, who declared that winning a rectorship was worth more than the sight in one eye; and that of Malcolm Muggeridge, TV personality and editor of *Punch*, who, elected rector, resigned rather than provide students with free pills and pot.

12. Maisie Ward, *Gilbert Keith Chesterton* (London: Sheed & Ward, 1944), p. 415.

13. See Ward, *Gilbert Keith Chesterton*, pp. 420-422; E.C. Bentley, ed., in the introduction to *The Selected Essays of G.K. Chesterton* (London: Methuen, 1949), pp. v-x; Frank Swinnerton, *The Georgian Scene: A Literary Panorama* (New York: Farrar, Straus & Rinehart, 1934), p. 103; Margaret Canovan, *G.K. Chesterton: Radical Populist* (New York: Harcourt Brace Jovanovich, 1977), p. 19; and A. Herbold, "Chesterton and *G.K.'s Weekly*," Diss. University of Michigan 1963, pp. 313-343.

14. G.K. Chesterton, "The First Principle" in *G.K.'s Weekly*, March 21, 1925, pp. 3-4.

15. Ada Chesterton, *The Chestertons* (London: Chapman & Hall, 1941), pp. 271-273.

16. W.R. Titterton, *G.K. Chesterton: A Portrait* (London: Douglas Organ, 1936), p. 139.

17. Ward, *Gilbert Keith Chesterton*, p. 422; and Horton Davies, *Worship and Theology in England*, Vol. V: *The Ecumenical Century, 1900-1965* (Princeton, N.J.: Princeton University Press, 1965), pp. 92-93.

18. Titterton, *G.K. Chesterton*, p. 145.

19. Herbold, "Chesterton and *G.K.'s Weekly*," pp. 320-321.

20. Titterton, *G.K. Chesterton*, pp. 155-156.

21. Rowland, *David Lloyd George*, p. 618.

22. G.K. Chesterton, *Tales of the Long Bow* (New York: Sheed & Ward, 1925), p. 219.

23. *Ibid.*, p. 214.

24. *Ibid.*, p. 197.

25. Ian Boyd, *The Novels of G.K. Chesterton* (London: Paul Elek, 1975), pp. 106-107; and Canovan, *G.K. Chesterton: Radical Populist*, pp. 92-93.

26. Chesterton, *Tales of the Long Bow*, p. 143. See also John P. McCarthy, *Hilaire Belloc: Edwardian Radical* (Indianapolis: Liberty Press, 1978), pp. 24-25.

27. Mason, *The Centre of Hilarity*, pp. 179-180.

28. *Ibid.*, pp. 187-189. See also Charles Williams, *The Descent of the Dove* (London: Faber & Faber, 1939), p. 46; and Lynette Hunter, *G.K. Chesterton: Explorations in Allegory* (New York: St. Martin's Press, 1979), p. 160.

29. Havighurst, *Britain in Transition*, pp. 209-238.

30. See Hunter, *G.K. Chesterton: Explorations in Allegory*, p. 163; and Dudley Barker, *G.K. Chesterton* (New York: Stein & Day, 1973), p. 222.

31. John Sullivan, "The Everlasting Man" in *Seven*, 2 (March 1981), 62-63.

32. G.K. Chesterton, *The Everlasting Man* (New York: Dodd, Mead, 1925; rpt. New York: Image Books, 1955), p. 7.

33. See Hugh Kenner, *Paradox in Chesterton* (New York: Sheed & Ward, 1947); and W.H. Auden, *G.K. Chesterton: A Selection from His Non-Fictional Prose* (London: Faber & Faber, 1970). See also Ward, Barker, Hunter, and Mason, as well as Garry Wills, *Chesterton: Man and Mask* (New York: Sheed & Ward, 1961); and C.S. Lewis, *Surprised by Joy* (New York: Harcourt Brace, 1955). A parenthetical note: it is possible that the reason why Belloc does not mention *The Everlasting Man* as one of Chesterton's greatest books is that he never read it.

34. Wills, *Chesterton: Man and Mask*, p. 180; and Robert Speaight, *The Life of Hilaire Belloc* (New York: Farrar, Straus & Cudahy, 1957), p. 490.

35. Sullivan, "The Everlasting Man," pp. 58-59.

36. Chesterton, *The Everlasting Man*, pp. 265-266.

37. *Ibid.*, p. 9.

38. *Ibid.*, p. 13.

39. See Chesterton's *Orthodoxy* (New York: Dodd, Mead, 1908).

40. Peter Gorner, "An Old Fossil Named Lucy," review of *Lucy: Beginnings of Human Kind* by D. Johanson in the *Chicago Tribune*, April 2, 1981, section 2, p. 1.

41. Chesterton, *The Everlasting Man*, p. 54.

42. *Ibid.*, p. 154.

43. *Ibid.*, p. 165.

44. See Lawrence J. Clipper, *G.K. Chesterton* (New York: Twayne Publishers, 1974), pp. 108-110.

45. Chesterton, *The Everlasting Man*, pp. 189-199.

46. *Ibid.*, p. 198.

47. *Ibid.*, p. 203.

48. *Ibid.*, pp. 209-211.

49. *Ibid.*, p. 212.

50. *Ibid.*, p. 213.

51. *Ibid.*, p. 218.

52. *Ibid.*, p. 262.

53. *Ibid.*, p. 267. See also Canovan, *G.K. Chesterton: Radical Populist*, pp. 122-123.

54. Hunter, *G.K. Chesterton: Explorations in Allegory*, pp. 159-165, especially the quotation from the 1925 dramatization of *The Man Who Was Thursday*; Charles Williams in *G.K.'s Weekly*, June 18, 1936, p. 230; and Sullivan, "The Everlasting Man," pp. 62-63.

55. James Brabazon, *Dorothy L. Sayers: A Biography* (New York: Charles Scribner's Sons, 1981), pp. 68-69.

56. Alzina Stone Dale, "The Man Born to be King" in *As Her Whimsey Took Her*, ed. Margaret Hannay (Kent, Ohio: Kent University Press, 1979), pp. 78-90.

57. Sullivan, "The Everlasting Man," pp. 63-64.

58. C.S. Lewis, *Surprised by Joy*, pp. 223-224. The recent claim in Ann Boaden's "Falcons and Falconers: Vision in the Novels of George MacDonald" in *Christianity and Literature*, XXXI, L (Fall 1981), 9, that C.S. Lewis credited *MacDonald* with his conversion to Christianity is an interesting example of the tendency to "eliminate" Chesterton's influence. Chesterton, of course, admired MacDonald, although he felt there was something a trifle Puritanical about his views. See Chesterton's *Autobiography*, pp. 171-172.

59. Wills, *Chesterton: Man and Mask*, p. 179. See also Herbold, "Chesterton and *G.K.'s Weekly*," p. 334; Ward, *Gilbert Keith Chesterton*, p. 431; and G.C. Heseltine, "G.K. Chesterton — Journalist" in *G.K. Chesterton: A Centenary Appraisal*, pp. 135-136.

60. Canovan, *G.K. Chesterton: Radical Populist*, p. 34.

61. *Ibid.*, p. 36.

62. *Ibid.*, p. 37.

63. G.K. Chesterton, *The Return of Don Quixote* (London: Chatto & Windus, 1927), dedication page.

64. Boyd, *The Novels of G.K. Chesterton*, p. 215; see footnote 136.

65. See Wills, *Chesterton: Man and Mask*, p. 179; Clipper, *G.K. Chesterton*, pp. 138-139; Ward, *Gilbert Keith Chesterton*, p. 465; and Boyd, *The Novels of G.K. Chesterton*, pp. 115-116. The author is particularly indebted to Boyd's careful literary analysis of the novel, as well as his conclusions about its message.

66. Boyd, *The Novels of G.K. Chesterton*, pp. 116-117. See also Ward, *Gilbert Keith Chesterton*, p. 465.

67. Boyd, *The Novels of G.K. Chesterton*, p. 119.

68. *Ibid.*, p. 120.

69. Chesterton, *The Return of Don Quixote*, p. 263.

70. Hunter, *G.K. Chesterton: Explorations in Allegory*, pp. 162-164; and Boyd, *The Novels of G.K. Chesterton*, pp. 134-135.

71. Rowland, *David Lloyd George*, pp. 620-621.

72. Havighurst, *Britain in Transition*, pp. 191-196.

73. Rowland, *David Lloyd George*, p. 621; Havighurst, *Britain in Transition*, p. 197; Spender, *The Thirties and After*, p. 612; and Titterton, *G.K. Chesterton*, pp. 150-154.

74. Hynes, *The Auden Generation*, pp. 33-35.

75. Rowland, *David Lloyd George*, pp. 625-633.

76. Andrew Boyle, *The Climate of Treason: Five Who Spied for Russia* (London: Hutchinson, 1979), pp. 14-16.

77. Dorothy Collins, "Recollections" in *G.K. Chesterton: A Centenary Appraisal*, pp. 157-158.

78. See Herbold, "Chesterton and *G.K.'s Weekly*," pp. 315-317. The author has also seen manuscript pages in the Wade Collection at Wheaton College, Wheaton, Illinois, in which there are revisions made by Chesterton in a typed script; this tends to show that he did do some work on items after dictating them. The idea that he never revised is a part of his myth—one that he himself deliberately fostered.

79. Gossip at Notre Dame University still tells the visitor that Frances tried to keep Chesterton from "having a good time" or "going out with the boys." But her concern is made more understandable by the facts that Chesterton was in poor health and was both carrying on with his usual work and lecturing. In any case, he *was* feted: the written account in *Notre Dame Magazine* (December 1976) reminisces about a faculty bootleg party held for him in the bell tower until the wee hours of the morning.

80. Collins, "Recollections," p. 157.

81. Julian Symons, *Mortal Consequences: A History from the Detective Story to the Crime Novel* (New York: Harper & Row, 1972), pp. 119-120.

82. Hunter, *G.K. Chesterton: Explorations in Allegory*, p. 134. See also Canovan, *G.K. Chesterton: Radical Populist*, pp. 123-124.

83. Hunter, *G.K. Chesterton: Explorations in Allegory*, pp. 135-136.

84. *Ibid.*, pp. 148-152. "The Dagger With Wings" contains the most overt statement supporting Hunter's basic thesis.

85. Collins, "Recollections," p. 161; Ward, *Gilbert Keith Chesterton*, p. 466.

86. Titterton, *G.K. Chesterton*, pp. 160-163.

87. Canovan, *G.K. Chesterton: Radical Populist*, pp. 18-19.

88. Ward, *Gilbert Keith Chesterton*, pp. 433-435; G.K. Chesterton, *The Outline of Sanity* (London: Methuen, 1926), pp. 85-86.

89. Chesterton, *G.K.'s Weekly*, Nov. 1924.

90. Canovan, *G.K. Chesterton: Radical Populist*, p. 89; and John P. McCarthy, *Hilaire Belloc: Edwardian Radical* (Indianapolis: Liberty Press, 1978), p. 310.

91. Canovan, *G.K. Chesterton: Radical Populist*, pp. 89-90; Titterton, *G.K. Chesterton*, pp. 176-177.

92. Canovan, *G.K. Chesterton: Radical Populist*, pp. 89-90; Frank Sheed, remarks at the meeting of the Chesterton Society, Chicago, 1979; and Maurice Reckitt, "G.K. Chesterton: A Christian Prophet for Today" in *The World and the Faith: Essays of a Christian Sociologist* (London: Faith Press, 1954), p.33.

93. Maisie Ward, *Return to Chesterton* (New York: Sheed & Ward, 1952), pp. 150-151; and Brocard Sewell, "Devereux Nights" in *G.K. Chesterton: A Centenary Appraisal*, pp. 146-152.

94. Ward, *Gilbert Keith Chesterton*, p. 460; and Barker, *G.K. Chesterton*, pp. 268-269. Items in the John Bennett Shaw Collection at the University of Notre Dame (South Bend, Indiana) show that the Chestertons were asked to assist many Roman Catholic causes.

95. Chesterton, *The Outline of Sanity*, pp. 224-230.

96. Quoted in Patrick Cahill, "Chesterton and the Future of Democracy" in *G.K. Chesterton: A Centenary Appraisal*, pp. 182-183.

97. Ward, *Gilbert Keith Chesterton*, p. 384.

98. Wills, *Chesterton: Man and Mask*, p. 164. It is interesting that this theme is also reflected in C.S. Lewis's Narnia tales, beginning with *The Lion, the Witch and the Wardrobe*.

99. Ward, *Return to Chesterton*, p. 192.

100. Ian Boyd, "Chesterton and Poland: The Myth and the Reality" in *The Chesterton Review*, V, No. 1 (Fall-Winter 1978-79), 22-42.

101. G.K. Chesterton, *The Collected Poems of G.K. Chesterton* (London: Cecil Palmer, 1927), p. 26.

102. Hunter, *G.K. Chesterton: Explorations in Allegory*, p. 152; and G.K. Chesterton, *The Secret of Father Brown* (New York: Dodd, Mead, 1927; rpt. New York: Penguin Books, 1975), pp. 11, 172.

103. G.K. Chesterton, *G.K.C. as M.C.*, p. 68.

104. Quoted in Barker, *G.K. Chesterton*, p. 273.

105. G.K. Chesterton, *Robert Louis Stevenson* (New York: Dodd, Mead, 1928), pp. 208-209.

106. William B. Furlong, *Shaw and Chesterton: The Metaphysical Jesters* (University Park, Pa.: Pennsylvania State University Press, 1970), p. 136; and Titterton, *G.K. Chesterton*, p. 183.

107. Barker, *G.K. Chesterton*, p. 276; and Ward, *Return to Chesterton*, p. 272.

108. G.K. Chesterton and G.B. Shaw, *Do We Agree?* (London: Cecil Palmer, 1928), pp. 7-8.

109. *Ibid.*, p. 17.

110. *Ibid.*, pp. 17-45.

111. *Ibid.*, p. 26.

112. *Ibid.*, pp. 44-47; and Furlong, *Shaw and Chesterton: The Metaphysical Jesters*, pp. 149-150.

113. Frank Swinnerton, *Background with Chorus* (London: Hutchinson, 1956), p. 157.

114. G.K. Chesterton, "On Funeral Customs" in *The Selected Essays of G.K. Chesterton*, ed. E.C. Bentley (London: Methuen, 1949), p. 268.

115. *Ibid.*

CHAPTER FIFTEEN

1. G.K. Chesterton, *The Well and the Shallows* (New York: Sheed & Ward, 1935), pp. 66-67.

2. Maisie Ward, *Return to Chesterton* (New York: Sheed & Ward, 1952), p. 247.

3. G.K. Chesterton, "The Spice of Life" in *The Spice of Life* (Beaconsfield, England: Darwen Finlayson, 1964), pp. 166-167.

4. Stephen Koss, *Nonconformity in Modern British Politics* (Hamden, Conn.: Archon Books, Shoe String Press, 1975), pp. 181-183; Alfred Havighurst, *Britain in Transition* (Chicago: University of Chicago Press, 1979), pp. 208-209; and Peter Rowland, *David Lloyd George: A Biography* (New York: Macmillan, 1975), pp. 652-656.

5. Koss, *Nonconformity in Modern British Politics*, p. 182.

6. Margaret Canovan, *G.K. Chesterton: Radical Populist* (New York: Harcourt Brace Jovanovich, 1977), pp. 146-153.

7. G.K. Chesterton, *Autobiography* (London: Hutchinson, 1936), pp. 268-269.

8. Laurence Lafore, Author's Seminar Notes (1-18-51) in Modern British History, 1950-1951; and Havighurst, *Britain in Transition*, pp. 217-218.

9. Ian Boyd, *The Novels of G.K. Chesterton* (London: Paul Elek, 1975), pp. 139-140.

10. G.K. Chesterton, *The Poet and the Lunatics* (New York: Dodd, Mead, 1929), p. 110.

11. *Ibid.*, p. 113.

12. Boyd, *The Novels of G.K. Chesterton*, p. 142.

13. Chesterton, *The Poet and the Lunatics*, p. 9; pp. 24-25.

14. Boyd, *The Novels of G.K. Chesterton*, pp. 145-155.

15. Chesterton, *The Poet and the Lunatics*, pp. 240-249.

16. *Ibid.*, p. 266.

17. See Canovan, *G.K. Chesterton: Radical Populist*, p. 136.

18. James Brabazon, *Dorothy L. Sayers: A Biography* (New York: Charles Scribner's Sons, 1981), p. 144.

19. G.K. Chesterton, "The Detection Club" in *The Strand* Magazine, May 1933, pp. 462-463.

20. Gwen Robyns, *The Mystery of Agatha Christie* (New York: Doubleday, 1978), pp. 103-105; and Ngaio Marsh, letter to the author, July 9, 1979, copyright N. Marsh.

21. Gladys Mitchell, letters to the author, October 16, 1979, and November 6, 1979, copyright G. Mitchell.

22. Chesterton, "The Detection Club," pp. 463-465.

23. Dorothy L. Sayers in the introduction to *The Floating Admiral* (London: Hodder & Stoughton, 19 ; rpt. New York: Charter, 1980), pp. 3-4.

24. Lynette Hunter, *G.K. Chesterton: Explorations in Allegory* (New York: St. Martin's Press, 1979), p. 134.

25. G.K. Chesterton, *The Thing: Why I Am a Catholic* (New York: Dodd, Mead, 1930), pp. 209-210.

26. See Dorothy L. Sayers, *Begin Here: A Statement of Faith* (New York: Harcourt Brace, 1941). It seems very likely that in reading *The Thing* or other of Chesterton's writings, Sayers had been introduced to this idea, and its vital importance for Western-Mediterranean Christendom was brought home to her by World War II. As a result, of course, she in turn was treated to Roderick Jellema's description of her outlook in *Christian Letters to a Post-Christian World*: he says she is writing from somewhere between the Middle Ages and the Sun.

27. Chesterton, *The Thing*, pp. 64-65; pp. 70-71.

28. Chesterton, *The Thing*, pp. 246-248. Comparing Pope John Paul II's public image with that of someone like the recent U.N. secretary General Kurt Waldheim, one has to feel that Chesterton is making sense. This statement is also an excellent rationale for the continuation of the British Monarchy.

29. See Canovan, "The Ball and the Cross" in *G.K. Chesterton: Radical Populist*, pp. 112-146.

30. G.K. Chesterton, *The Resurrection of Rome* (New York: Dodd, Mead, 1930), p. 183.

31. Dorothy Collins, "Recollections" in *G.K. Chesterton: A Centenary Appraisal*, ed. John Sullivan (London: Paul Elek, 1974), p. 163.

32. See Dudley Barker, *G.K. Chesterton* (London: Constable, 1973), p. 275.

33. Garry Wills, *Chesterton: Man and Mask* (New York: Sheed & Ward, 1961), pp. 206-207.

34. Canovan, *G.K. Chesterton: Radical Populist*, pp. 126-129; and Chesterton, *The Resurrection of Rome*, p. 283.

35. John P. McCarthy, *Hilaire Belloc: Edwardian Radical* (Indianapolis: Liberty Press, 1978), pp. 336-338.

36. Chesterton, *Autobiography*, p. 303.

37. Robert Speaight, *The Life of Hilaire Belloc* (New York: Farrar, Straus & Cudahy, 1957), p. 480.

38. Chesterton, *Autobiography*, p. 306.

39. Boyd, *The Novels of G.K. Chesterton*, pp. 155-157.

40. Havighurst, *Britain in Transition*, pp. 218-219.

41. G.K. Chesterton, *Four Faultless Felons* (New York: Dodd, Mead, 1930), p. 23.

42. *Ibid.*, p. 25.

43. *Ibid.*, p. 27.

44. *Ibid.*, p. 83.

45. Boyd, *The Novels of G.K. Chesterton*, pp. 162-163.

46. Chesterton, *Four Faultless Felons*, pp. 219-221.

47. Boyd, *The Novels of G.K. Chesterton*, pp. 175-176.

48. G.K. Chesterton, "On the Classics" in *The Selected Essays of G.K. Chesterton*, ed. E.C. Bentley (London: Methuen, 1949), pp. 22-25.

49. G.K. Chesterton, "On Abolishing Sunday" in *The Selected Essays of G.K. Chesterton*, p. 292.

50. Cyril Clemens, *Chesterton as Seen by His Contemporaries* (Webster Groves, Mo.: Mark Twain Society, 1939), p. 71.

51. Student notes on Chesterton's two lecture series were published in *The Chesterton Review* in three issues: Vol. III, No. 2 (Spring-Summer 1977), 165-195; Vol. IV, No. 1 (Fall-Winter 1977-78), 115-143; and Vol. IV, No. 2 (Spring-Summer 1978), 285-302.

52. G.K. Chesterton, "The Arena," published in *The Chesterton Review*, VI, No. 1 (Fall-Winter 1979-80), 144-145; copyright Dorothy Collins. The poem was publicly recited in Chesterton's honor at Notre Dame University's Fiftieth Anniversary Celebration, November 1980.

53. Clemens, *Chesterton as Seen by His Contemporaries*, p. 106.

54. Ward, *Gilbert Keith Chesterton*, p. 496.

55. Chesterton, *Autobiography*, p. 310.

56. Ward, *Gilbert Keith Chesterton*, pp. 496-497; Clemens, *Chesterton as Seen by His Contemporaries*, pp. 66-67; and John Martin, "Chesterton and Lewis: The Necessary Angels," *Bulletin of the New York C.S. Lewis Society*, January 1978, pp. 6-7.

57. See Arthur and Lila Weinberg, *Clarence Darrow: A Sentimental Rebel* (New York: G.P. Putnam's Sons, 1980). The index makes no reference to the debate under the headings "Scopes," "Creation," "Monkey," "Evolution," or "Chesterton," and the sympathetic treatment of the Loeb-Leopold case is elitist; see pp. 13-26 and pp. 297-317. The irony is that much of the authors' preoccupation with trade unionism, civil rights, etc., would have been very appealing to Chesterton.

58. Kevin Tierney, *Darrow: A Biography* (New York: Crowell, 1979), pp. 352-361.

59. Quoted by Robert Knille in "Chesterton Today," an unpublished article.

60. Havighurst, *Britain in Transition*, p. 229.

61. Lawrence J. Clipper, *G.K. Chesterton* (New York: Twayne Publishers, 1974), p. 56.

62. Rowland, *David Lloyd George*, pp. 656-665.

63. *Ibid.*, pp. 671-673.

64. *Ibid.*, pp. 676-681.

65. Havighurst, *Britain in Transition*, p. 230. See also David Thompson, "The Optical Illusion" in *England in the Twentieth Century* (Middlesex, England: Penguin Books, The Pelican History of England, 1965), pp. 16-18.

66. Rowland, *David Lloyd George*, p. 687.

67. Havighurst, *Britain in Transition*, pp. 230-231.

68. Ward, *Gilbert Keith Chesterton*, p. 538. In February 1933 the Oxford Union passed a motion that "this House will in no circumstances fight for its King and Country." See Havighurst, *Britain in Transition*, p. 234; and Samuel Hynes, *The Auden Generation: Literature and Politics in England in the 1930's* (New York: Viking Press, 1977), p. 65.

69. Stephen Spender, *The Thirties and After: Poetry, Politics, People, 1930's-1970's* (New York: Random House, Vintage Books, 1979), p. 3.

70. Havighurst, *Britain in Transition*, p. 234. Havighurst barely mentions Chesterton and puts him in the backward group, but he also uses G.K.C. to sum up a generation.

71. Hynes, *The Auden Generation*, p. 86; and Spender, *The Thirties and After*, pp. 5-8.

72. See Chesterton, *The Napoleon of Notting Hill* (New York: Paulist Press, 1978), p. 1.

73. Norman and Jeanne MacKenzie, *The Time Traveller: The Life of H.G. Wells* (London: Weidenfeld & Nicolson, 1973), pp. 347-370.

74. *Ibid.*, pp. 395-396.

75. G.K. Chesterton, *Chaucer* (London: Faber & Faber, 1932), pp. 8-9.

76. G.K. Chesterton, "On Sightseeing" in *The Selected Essays of G.K. Chesterton*, ed. E.C. Bentley (London: Methuen, 1949), p. 108.

77. *Ibid.*, pp. 134-135.

78. Barker, *G.K. Chesterton*, pp. 278-279.

79. Quoted in John Sullivan's *Chesterton Continued: A Bibliographical Supplement* (London: University of London Press, 1968), pp. 98-104.

80. Ward, *Gilbert Keith Chesterton*, p. 534. See also Anthony Burgess, *1985* (Boston: Little, Brown, 1978), for its discussion of Orwell's sources and et cetera for *1984* — among others, the fact that Big Brother represents the hierarchy of the BBC.

81. Ward, *Gilbert Keith Chesterton*, pp. 535-536; and Ada Chesterton, *The Chestertons* (London: Chapman & Hall, 1941), pp. 285-291.

82. Ward, *Gilbert Keith Chesterton*, p. 536.

83. Ada Chesterton, *The Chestertons*, p. 293.

84. G.K. Chesterton, *A Handful of Authors*, ed. Dorothy Collins (New York: Sheed & Ward, 1953), p. 214.

85. Michael Mason, *The Centre of Hilarity: A Play upon Ideas about Laughter and the Absurd* (London: Sheed & Ward, 1959), p. 124.

86. *Ibid.*, pp. 120-121. See also Lynette Hunter, *G.K. Chesterton: Explorations in Allegory* (New York: St. Martins Press, 1979), pp. 160-161.

87. Wills, *Chesterton: Man and Mask*, pp. 207-208.

88. Chesterton, *Chaucer*, pp. 8-9.

89. Mason, *The Centre of Hilarity*, pp. 85-95.

90. Ward, *Gilbert Keith Chesterton*, p. 513. See also George Coulton, *The Medieval Panorama* (New York: Cambridge University Press, 1945).

91. Chesterton, *Chaucer*, pp. 270-272.

92. *Ibid.*, pp. 274-277.

93. Ada Chesterton, *The Chestertons*, p. 278; and Ward, *Gilbert Keith Chesterton*, pp. 534-542.

94. Collins, "Recollections," pp. 158-159.

95. Ward, *Gilbert Keith Chesterton*, p. 546.

96. Rowland, *David Lloyd George*, pp. 702-706; and Havighurst, *Britain in Transition*, pp. 232-234.

97. Ward, *Gilbert Keith Chesterton*, pp. 537-538.

98. Canovan, *G.K. Chesterton: Radical Populist*, p. 142.

99. *Ibid.*, p. 145.

100. G.K. Chesterton, "On St. George Revisited" in *The Selected Essays of G.K. Chesterton*, pp. 42-45.

101. See particularly Ward, *Gilbert Keith Chesterton*; Wills, *Chesterton: Man and Mask*; and Hugh Kenner, *Paradox in Chesterton* (New York: Sheed & Ward, 1941). They all tend toward this thesis.

102. Chesterton, *Chaucer*, p. 273.

103. Collins, "Recollections," pp. 158-159.

104. Frank Sheed, Address of the Chesterton Society, Chicago, December 1979.

105. G.K. Chesterton, *St. Thomas Aquinas: The Dumb Ox* (London: Sheed & Ward, 1933; rpt. New York: Image Books, 1956), pp. 11-13.

106. *Ibid.*, pp. 164-165.

107. Canovan, *G.K. Chesterton: Radical Populist*, pp. 124-125.

108. Clipper, *G.K. Chesterton*, pp. 80-83.

109. Chesterton, *St. Thomas Aquinas: The Dumb Ox*, pp. 182-183.

110. See Jay Cocks, "Royal Wedding" in *Time* Magazine, August 10, 1981, pp. 22-31.

111. Chesterton, *The Well and the Shallows*, pp. 45-52.

112. *Ibid.*, pp. 201-202.

113. *Ibid.*, pp. 273-275.
114. *Ibid.*, pp. 276-277.
115. Havighurst, *Britain in Transition*, pp. 246-250.
116. Ward, *Gilbert Keith Chesterton*, p. 546.
117. William B. Furlong, *Shaw and Chesterton: The Metaphysical Jesters* (University Park, Pa.: Pennsylvania State University Press, 1970), p. 184.
118. John O'Connor, *Father Brown on Chesterton* (London: Oates & Washbourne, 1938), p. 152.
119. Quoted in John Sullivan's *G.K. Chesterton: A Bibliography* (London: University of London Press, 1958), p. 195.
120. Randolph Hogan, "Chesterton: A Presence on 60th Street," *The New York Times*, April 24, 1981, p. C-32.

EPILOGUE
1. John Dickson Carr, *The Mad Hatter Mystery* (New York: Macmillan, 1933; rpt. New York; Colliers, 1975), p. 13.
2. See Dorothy L. Sayers, *The Emperor Constantine* (London: Gollancz, 1951).
3. G.K. Chesterton, *Heretics* (New York: Dodd, Mead, 1923), pp. 56-57.
4. G.K. Chesterton, *The Ballad of the White Horse* in *The Collected Poems of G.K. Chesterton* (London: Cecil Palmer, 1927), p. 211.
5. Dorothy L. Sayers in the preface to *The Surprise* (London: Sheed & Ward, 1952), p. 5.
6. Hilaire Belloc, *On the Place of Gilbert Chesterton in English Letters* (New York: Sheed & Ward, 1940), p.30. See also Christopher Hollis, *Gilbert Keith Chesterton* (London: Longmans, Green, 1954); and Graham Greene, *Collected Essays* (London: The Bodley Head, 1969).
7. John Sullivan, *Chesterton Continued: A Bibliographical Supplement* (London: University of London Press, 1968), p. xi. (See, for example, David Thompson, *England in the Twentieth Century* [Middlesex, England: Penguin Books, The Pelican History of England, 1965]; or Wayne Booth, *The Rhetoric of Fiction* [Chicago: University of Chicago Press, 1961], as examples of places where he is left out.)
8. G.K. Chesterton, *The Napoleon of Notting Hill* (New York: Paulist Press, 1978), p. 6.
9. Chesterton, *Heretics*, pp. 87-89.
10. Malcolm Muggeridge, "GKC" in the *New Statesman*, August 23, 1963, p. 226.
11. See Malcolm Muggeridge, *The End of Christendom* (Grand Rapids, Mich.: Eerdmans, 1980), pp. 22-23.

Bibliography of Primary Sources

Below is a chronological listing of Chesterton's works. (In those instances in which later editions of his works were used, the publication date given differs from that of the first edition, by which it is grouped.) Because there is no uniform edition of Chesterton's work, anyone writing about him must depend upon John Sullivan's *G.K. Chesterton: A Bibliography* (London: University of London Press, 1958), and its sequels, published in 1968 and 1980.

1900:   *Greybeards at Play*. London: Sheed & Ward, 1930.
        The Wild Knight. London: Grant Richards.

1901:   *The Defendant*. London: Brimley Johnson.

1902:   *Twelve Types*. London: Arthur Humphreys, 1910.

1903:   *Robert Browning*. London: Macmillan.

1904:   *G.F. Watts*. London: Duckworth.
        The Napoleon of Notting Hill. New York: Paulist Press, 1978.

1905:   *The Club of Queer Trades*. New York: Harper Brothers.
        Heretics. New York: Dodd, Mead, 1923.

1906:   *Charles Dickens*. London: Methuen.

1908:   *The Man Who Was Thursday*. New York: Capricorn Books, 1960.
        All Things Considered. London: Methuen.
        Orthodoxy. New York: Dodd, Mead.

1909:   *George Bernard Shaw*. New York: Hill & Wang, 1956.
        Tremendous Trifles. Beaconsfield, England: Darwen Finlayson, 1968.
        The Ball and the Cross. New York: John Lane.

1910:   *What's Wrong With the World*. Leipzig: Bernhard Tauchnitz.
        Alarms and Discursions. New York: Dodd, Mead, 1911.
        William Blake. New York: Dutton.

1911:   *The Innocence of Father Brown*. New York: Penguin Books, by arrangement
            with Dodd, Mead, 1975.
        The Ballad of the White Horse. Kirkwood, Mo.: Catholic Authors Press, 1950.

1912:   *Manalive*. London: John Lane, 1913.
        A Miscellany of Men. New York: Dodd, Mead.

1913:   *The Victorian Age in Literature*. London: Williams & Norgate, Home University Library.
        Magic: A Fantastic Comedy. New York: G.P. Putnam's Sons.

1914:   *The Flying Inn*. London: Methuen.
        The Wisdom of Father Brown. New York: Penguin Books, by arrangement with Dodd, Mead, 1975.
        The Barbarism of Berlin. London: Cassell.

1915:   *Poems*, published in *The Collected Poems of G.K. Chesterton*. London: Cecil Palmer, 1927.
        The Crimes of England. London: Cecil Palmer and Hayward.

1917:   *A Short History of England*. London: Chatto & Windus.
        Utopia of Usurers. New York: Boni & Liveright.

1919:   *Irish Impressions*. New York: John Lane, 1920.

1920:   *The Superstition of Divorce*. London: Chatto & Windus.
        The Uses of Diversity. London: Methuen.
        The New Jerusalem. New York: George Doran, 1921.

1922:   *Eugenics and Other Evils*.London: Cassell.
        What I Saw in America. New York: Dodd, Mead.
        The Ballad of St. Barbara, published in *The Collected Poems of G.K. Chesterton*. London: Cecil Palmer, 1927.
        The Man Who Knew Too Much. New York: Harper Brothers.

1923:   *Fancies Versus Fads*. London: Methuen.
        St. Francis of Assisi. New York: Image Books, 1957.

1925:   *Tales of the Long Bow*. New York: Sheed & Ward.
        The Everlasting Man. New York: Image Books, 1955.
        William Cobbett. New York: Dodd, Mead.

1926:   *The Incredulity of Father Brown*. New York: Penguin Books, 1975.
        The Outline of Sanity. London: Methuen.
        The Queen of Seven Swords. London: Sheed & Ward.

1927:   *The Return of Don Quixote*. London: Chatto & Windus.
        The Collected Poems of G.K. Chesterton. London: Cecil Palmer.
        The Secret of Father Brown. New York: Penguin, 1975.
        The Judgment of Dr. Johnson. London: Sheed & Ward.
        Robert Louis Stevenson. New York: Dodd, Mead, 1928.

1928:   *Generally Speaking*. London: Methuen.

1929:   *The Poet and the Lunatics*. New York: Dodd, Mead.
        The Thing: Why I Am a Catholic. New York: Dodd, Mead, 1930.
        G.K.C. as M.C. London: Methuen.

1930: *Four Faultless Felons*. New York: Dodd, Mead.
       The Resurrection of Rome. New York: Dodd, Mead.
       Come to Think of It. London: Methuen.

1931: *All Is Grist*. London: Methuen.

1932: *Chaucer*. London: Faber & Faber.
       Sidelights on New London and Newer York. London: Sheed & Ward.

1933: *All I Survey*. New York: Dodd, Mead.
       St. Thomas Aquinas: The Dumb Ox. New York: Image Books, 1956.

1934: *Avowals and Denials*. London: Methuen.

1935: *The Scandal of Father Brown*. New York: Penguin Books, 1975.
       The Well and the Shallows. New York: Sheed & Ward.

1936: *As I Was Saying*. London: Methuen.

Posthumously Published Works

1936: *Autobiography*. London: Hutchinson.

1937: *The Paradoxes of Mr. Pond*. London: Cassell.

1938: *The Coloured Lands*. New York: Sheed & Ward.

1940: *The End of the Armistice*. New York: Sheed & Ward.

1950: *The Common Man*. New York: Sheed & Ward.

1952: *The Surprise*. New York: Sheed & Ward.

1953: *A Handful of Authors*. New York: Sheed & Ward.

1955: *The Glass Walking-Stick*. New York: Sheed & Ward.

1958: *Lunacy and Letters*. New York: Sheed & Ward.

Selected Bibliography of Secondary Sources

This listing includes works about G.K. Chesterton and his period which were particularly useful to the author and may be of interest to the general reader. For more information about critical commentary, the reader is once again referred to the superb bibliographies by John Sullivan, as well as to *G.K. Chesterton* by Lawrence J. Clipper.

Armstrong, Christopher. *Evelyn Underhill*. Grand Rapids, Mich.: Eerdmans, 1976.

Auden, W.H. *G.K. Chesterton: A Selection from His Non-Fictional Prose*. London: Faber & Faber, 1970.

Barker, Dudley. *G.K. Chesterton*. New York: Stein & Day, 1973.

Baring, Maurice. *Puppet Show of Memory*. Boston: Little, Brown, 1923.

Bell, Quentin. *Virginia Woolf: A Biography*. New York: Harcourt Brace Jovanovich, 1972.

Belloc, Hilaire. *On the Place of Gilbert Chesterton in English Letters*. New York: Sheed & Ward, 1940.

―――――. *The Servile State*. Originally pub. 1913; rpt. Indianapolis: Liberty Press, 1979.

Bentley, E.C. *Biography for Beginners*, "Being a Collection of Miscellaneous Examples for the Use of the Upper Forms. Edited by E. Clerihew, B.A., with 40 Diagrams by G.K. Chesterton." London: T. Werner Laurie, 1905.

―――――, ed. *The Selected Essays of G.K. Chesterton*. London: Methuen, 1949.

―――――. *Those Days*. London: Constable, 1940.

―――――. *Trent's Last Case*. Originally pub. 1912; rpt. New York: Harper & Row, Perennial Library, 1978. Introduction by Dorothy L. Sayers.

Blewett, Neal. *The Peers, the Parties, and the People: The British General Elections of 1910*. London: Macmillan, 1972.

Boyd, Ian. *The Novels of G.K. Chesterton*. London: Paul Elek, 1975.

Boyle, Andrew. *The Climate of Treason: Five Who Spied for Russia*. London: Hutchinson, 1979.

Burgess, Anthony. *1985*. Boston: Little, Brown, 1978.

Canovan, Margaret. *G.K. Chesterton: Radical Populist*. New York: Harcourt Brace Jovanovich, 1977.

Cawalti, John. *Adventure, Mystery, and Romance*. Chicago: University of Chicago Press, 1976.

Chesterton, Ada (Mrs. Cecil). *The Chestertons*. London: Chapman & Hall, 1941.

Chesterton, Cecil. *G.K. Chesterton: A Criticism*. London: Alston Rivers, 1908.

————. *A History of the United States*. New York: George Doran, 1919. Introduction by G.K. Chesterton.

Chesterton, G.K., and G.B. Shaw. *Do We Agree?* London: Cecil Palmer, 1928.

Clemens, Cyril. *Chesterton as Seen by His Contemporaries*. Webster Groves, Mo.: Mark Twain Society, 1939.

Clipper, Lawrence J. *G.K. Chesterton*. New York: Twayne Publishers, 1974.

Dangerfield, George. *The Damnable Question*. Boston: Little, Brown, 1976.

————. *The Strange Death of Liberal England: 1910-1914*. New York: Capricorn Books, 1961.

Davies, Horton. *Worship and Theology in England*, Vol. V: *The Ecumenical Century, 1900-1965*. Princeton, N.J.: Princeton University Press, 1965.

Donaldson, Frances. *The Marconi Affair*. New York: Harcourt, Brace & World, 1962.

Farwell, Byron. *The Great Anglo-Boer War*. New York: Harper & Row, 1976.

Ferris, Paul. *The House of Northcliffe*. London: Weidenfeld & Nicolson, 1971.

Fremantle, Anne. *This Little Band of Prophets*. New York: Macmillan, 1960.

Furlong, William B. *Shaw and Chesterton: The Metaphysical Jesters*. University Park, Pa.: Pennsylvania State University Press, 1970.

Graves, Robert, and Alan Hodge. *The Long Week-end: A Social History of Great Britain, 1918-1939*. London: Faber & Faber, 1940.

Halevy, Elie. *A History of the English People*. 6 vols. London: Ernest Benn, 1934.

Havighurst, Alfred. *Britain in Transition*. Chicago: University of Chicago Press, 1962; new ed., 1979.

————. *Radical Journalist: H.W. Massingham*. London: Cambridge University Press, 1974.

Haycraft, Howard. *The Art of the Mystery Story*. New York: Grosset & Dunlap, 1946.

Herbold, A. "Chesterton and *G.K.'s Weekly*." Diss. University of Michigan 1963.

Hunter, Lynette. *G.K. Chesterton: Explorations in Allegory*. New York: St. Martin's Press, 1979.

Hynes, Samuel. *The Auden Generation: Literature and Politics in England in the 1930's*. New York: Viking Press, 1977.

————. *Edwardian Occasions*. London: Routledge & Kegan Paul, 1972.

————. *The Edwardian Turn of Mind*. Princeton, N.J.: Princeton University Press, 1968.

Jackson, Holbrook. *The Eighteen Nineties*. Originally pub. 1913; rpt. Middlesex, England: Penguin Books, 1950.

Kenner, Hugh. *Paradox in Chesterton*. New York: Sheed & Ward, 1947.

Koss, Stephen. *Fleet Street Radical*. London: Allen Lane, 1973.

————. *Nonconformity in Modern British Politics*. Hamden, Conn.: Archon Books, Shoe String Press, 1975.

Lafore, Laurence. *The Long Fuse*. Philadelphia: J.B. Lippincott, 1965.

Lewis, C.S. *Surprised by Joy*. New York: Harcourt Brace, 1955.

————. *The Four Loves*. New York: Harcourt Brace Jovanovich, 1960.

McCarthy, John P. *Hilaire Belloc: Edwardian Radical*. Indianapolis: Liberty Press, 1978.

Mackey, Aidan. *Mr. Chesterton Comes to Tea, or How the King of England Captured Redskin Island*. Bedford, England: Vintage Publications, 1978.

MacKenzie, Norman and Jeanne. *The Fabians*. New York: Simon & Schuster, 1977.

_____. *The Time Traveller: The Life of H.G. Wells*. London: Weidenfeld & Nicolson, 1973.

Mason, Michael. *The Centre of Hilarity: A Play upon Ideas about Laughter and the Absurd*. London: Sheed & Ward, 1959.

Masterman, Charles. *The Condition of England*. London: Methuen, 1909.

Masterman, Lucy. *C.F.G. Masterman*. London: Nicholson & Watson, 1939.

Muggeridge, Malcolm. *Chronicles of Wasted Time*. 2 vols. London: Collins, 1972.

_____. *The End of Christendom*. Grand Rapids, Mich.: Eerdmans, 1980.

O'Connor, John. *Father Brown on Chesterton*. London: Oates & Washbourne, 1938.

Pakenham, Thomas. *The Boer War*. New York: Random House, 1979.

Rowland, Peter. *David Lloyd George: A Biography*. New York: Macmillan, 1975.

_____. *The Last Liberal Governments: The Promised Land, 1905-1910*. London: Barrie & Rockliff, Cresset Press, 1968.

Sayers, Dorothy L. *Unpopular Opinions*. London: Gollancz, 1946.

_____. *Begin Here: A Statement of Faith*. New York: Harcourt Brace, 1941.

Sewell, Brocard. *Cecil Chesterton*. Faversham, Kent: St. Albert's Press, 1975.

Shaw, G.B. *Back to Methuselah: A Metabiological Pentateuch*. New York: Oxford University Press, 1921.

_____. *Short Stories, Scraps, and Shavings*. London: Constable, 1934.

Soames, Mary. *Clementine Churchill: The Biography of a Marriage*. Boston: Houghton Mifflin, 1979.

Speaight, Robert. *The Life of Hilaire Belloc*. New York: Farrar, Straus & Cudahy, 1957.

Spender, Stephen. *The Thirties and After: Poetry, Politics, People, 1930's-1970's*. New York: Random House, Vintage Books, 1979.

Sullivan, John. *Chesterton Continued: A Bibliographical Supplement*. London: University of London Press, 1968.

_____. *G.K. Chesterton: A Bibliography*. London: University of London Press, 1958.

_____, ed. *G.K. Chesterton: A Centenary Appraisal*. London: Paul Elek, 1974.

Swinnerton, Frank. *Background with Chorus*. London: Hutchinson, 1956.

Symons, Julian. *Mortal Consequences: A History from the Detective Story to the Crime Novel*. New York: Harper & Row, 1972.

_____. *The Georgian Scene: A Literary Panorama*. New York: Farrar, Straus & Rinehart, 1934.

Tierney, Kevin. *Darrow: A Biography*. New York: Crowell, 1979.

Titterton, W.R. *G.K. Chesterton: A Portrait*. London: Douglas Organ, 1936.

Tuchman, Barbara. *The Proud Tower: A Portrait of the World Before the War, 1890-1914*. New York: Bantam Books, 1967.

Ward, Maisie. *Gilbert Keith Chesterton*. London: Sheed & Ward, 1944.

_____. *Return to Chesterton*. New York: Sheed & Ward, 1952.

Weinberg, Arthur and Lila. *Clarence Darrow: A Sentimental Rebel*. New York: G.P. Putnam's Sons, 1980.

Wells, H.G. *The Outline of History*. New York: Doubleday, 1920.

Wills, Garry. *Chesterton: Man and Mask*. New York: Sheed & Ward, 1961.

Woolf, Leonard. *Sowing*. New York: Harcourt Brace, 1960.

Wyndham Lewis, D.B., ed. *G.K. Chesterton: An Anthology*. London: Oxford University Press, 1957.

INDEX

170, 203, 233-234; Oxford Movement of, 61

Churchill, Sir Winston, 48, 55, 72, 84, 97, 127, 137, 139, 148, 151, 157, 193, 196, 205, 229, 236, 243, 257, 292; Dardanelles expedition of, 199; joins Liberal government, 115; Marconi maneuvering of, 176; social legislation of, 128

civilization (Western), 45, 68, 163, 191, 198, 218, 253, 301; quest for the Grail as archetypal myth, 113, 118

The Club of Queer Trades, 8, 94, 108, 158, 276; "The Adventure of Major Brown," 95

clubs, social (see also Detection Club, the), 51; the I.D.K., 52-53; the Moderns, 51, 61; the Pharos Club, 61, 65

Cobbett, William, 254

Colet Court (Bewsher's), 19, 25

The Collected Poems of G. K. Chesterton, 262

Collins, Dorothy, 14, 257-258, 260, 262, 274-275, 279-280, 286, 288, 294; asks reporters to keep G.K.C.'s illness quiet, 295; conversion to Roman Catholicism, 258; helps G.K.C. with *St. Thomas Aquinas*, 290; living at Top Meadow, 295

Come to Think of It, 278

Conan Doyle, Sir Arthur, 36, 94-95

Conservative Party (see also Chamberlain, family of; Ireland; Liberal Party), 82, 85, 147, 160, 205, 229, 240, 248, 257 260, 270, 277, 283, 294; during World War I, 198; George Wyndham in, 156, 207, 267; in coalition with Lloyd George, 215; imperial preference of (tariffs), 277,289; in general strike, 257; Licensing Act of 1904, 83; programs of, 79, 81-82; Unionist (Ulster) part of, 193

Coward, Noel *(Cavalcade)*, 282

creeds (Christian and Liberal), 104, 113, 220

The Crimes of England, 201, 204

Cross, the, 187, 217, 219, 233, 253

culture, concepts of, 21, 66; elitists of, 270, 289; high-brow versus low-brow, 249; represented by Freud, Einstein, and Sir James Frazer, 249

Daily Herald, the (see also Lansbury, George), 180, 207

Daily Mail, the (see also Harmsworth, Alfred), 69, 206

Daily News, the (see also Fleet Street and Gardiner, A. G.), 60-61, 69, 73, 76, 78-79, 84, 86, 97, 99, 102, 107, 127, 130, 135,

138, 146, 149, 154, 157, 164, 172, 174, 179-180, 197, 199, 223; Cadbury's purchase of, 77; A. G. Gardiner editor of, 70; G.K.C. fired by, 177; R. C. Lehman editor of, 70

Daily Telegraph, the (see also Bentley, E. C.), 173, 205, 217, 224

Dante Alighieri, *Divine Comedy*, 96, 273, 287; Beatrice in, 53, 109, 114

Darrow, Clarence, 281

Daumier, Honoré, 31

de la Mare, Walter, "Epitaph," 296

Debater, the (see also J.D.C., the), 27-28, 37; G.K.C.'s contributions to: "Ave Maria," 34; "Dragons," 27; "Half Hour in Hades, An Elementary Handbook on Demonology," 26

The Defendant, 66, 70, 75; "A Defence of Detective Stories," 94; "A Defence of Patriotism," 70

"The Democrat, the Socialist and the Gentleman" (G.K.C. debate), 153

Detection Club, the, 271-273, 288; initiation rites of, 272; members of, 271-272; works: "Behind the Screen," 273; *The Floating Admiral*, 273

determinism (see "Puritanism")

Dickens, Charles, 5, 20, 24, 77, 82, 103, 106, 108, 113, 115, 128, 158, 223, 299; admired by G.K.C. and G. B. Shaw, 105; daughter admires G.K.C.'s biography of, 107; and the Dickens Fellowship, 190, 227; and Mr. Pickwick, 5, 12, 105, 107, 286; works: *A Child's History of England*, 162; *Household Words*, 239; *The Mystery of Edwin Drood*, 158, 190

disenfranchisement of ancestors (democracy and tradition), 77, 89, 119, 249

Disraeli, Benjamin (Lord Beaconsfield), 4

distributism (see also liberalism), 85, 111, 229, 245-246, 254, 260-261, 267, 277

Distributist League, the, 260, 265, 288; Captain Went, founder of, 260

Do We Agree? (Shaw-Chesterton debate), 265-266

DORA (Defense of the Realm Act), 197-198

Eccles, Francis, 58, 61, 66

education, 4, 83, 112, 143; Education Bill of 1902 (Conservative), 83, 101; Education Bill of 1909 (Liberal), 115

Edward VII (king of England), 55, 68, 139-140, 148, 162

0-595-34076-8

Printed in the United Kingdom by
Lightning Source UK Ltd., Milton Keynes
136843UK00001B/436/A